S0-CTT-547

CANADIAN POETRY

in English

CANADIAN POETRY *in English*

Chosen by Bliss Carman, Lorne Pierce & V. B. Rhodenizer

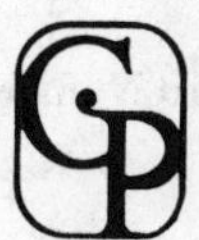

GREENWOOD PRESS, PUBLISHERS
WESTPORT, CONNECTICUT

Library of Congress Cataloging in Publication Data

Carman, Bliss, 1861-1929, comp.
Canadian poetry in English.

Reprint of the rev. and enl. ed. of the English part of the authors' Our Canadian literature, published by Ryerson Press, Toronto, in series: Canadian literature series.

1. Canadian poetry. I. Pierce, Lorne Albert, 1890- II. Rhodenizer, Vernon Blair, 1886- III. Title.
PR9190.25.C3 1976 811'.008 76-22428
ISBN 0-8371-9008-8

For

E.C.P.

Originally published in 1954 by The Ryerson Press, Toronto

Reprinted with the permission of McGraw-Hill Ryerson, Limited

Reprinted in 1976 by Greenwood Press,
a division of Williamhouse-Regency Inc.

Library of Congress Catalog Card Number 76-22428

ISBN 0-8371-9008-8

Printed in the United States of America

FOREWORD

Bliss Carman desired to compile a comprehensive anthology, covering the field of Canadian poetry from the earliest times to the present, and interpreting both east and west. Moreover, he aimed at a reasonably critical collection. While verses were included which time has endeared to a host of readers, he sifted from the body of Canadian poetry those poems which are significant, both for their content and their technical merit. He was friendly to poems reflecting the genius of the Dominion, as well as those cast in traditional moulds. Still, he was willing to welcome others representing days of change and experiment, provided there was substance in them, and music.

Much of his time, during the last three years of his life, was occupied with this anthology. While the selections reflected his personal tastes, Bliss Carman felt that they also represented the progress of poetry in Canada. It was my duty, as his literary executor, to put the manuscript in shape for the press. We had often discussed the anthology together, and I adhered as closely as possible to his known wishes. Some abridgment was necessary, chiefly owing to copyright restrictions. On the other hand I included poems which appeared after his death, feeling that they represented what he was pleased to call, "the valiant and joyous spirit which we find in the verse of our own times."

Within a few months of his death the world plunged into the abyss of the great depression, and then came another and more wicked World War. Suffering and despair overwhelmed us on a world scale. Bitterness, fear, and disillusionment profoundly affected the arts and letters for an entire generation. A new era had begun.

There have been numerous anthologies of Canadian verse published since 1935, the year in which the latest revision of this anthology appeared. With one or two exceptions they have been concerned with the work of our new poets, and have performed a useful service. There has been a remarkable flowering of Canadian verse during the past quarter of a century, and I am happy that the publishing House of which I have been editor has been an unfailing ally of these new voices. Certainly it seemed our duty to assist these young poets, full, though they were, of the attitudes and techniques o their mentors abroad, for we knew that time would ripen them, that personal experience of a more mature kind would refine away their second-hand notions and tricks of style. A birthright Canadian poetry was in the making.

In completing the anthologies, known as *Our Canadian Literature Series*, which contains the most representative of our short stories, humour, essays and speeches, we decided to revise Carman's anthology as a part of the series. We hoped to make the revision in the spirit of the first edition, believing that his point of view was sound. It would be historical and representative, and it would present no thesis nor favour any school. With that in mind, as well as a general intention to avoid duplicating the left-of-centre collections, we invited Professor V. B. Rhodenizer, Ph.D., Litt.D., Head of the Department of English at Acadia University, to assume the principal responsibility of revision. We are grateful to him for the care with which he has completed his task.

Bliss Carman was most anxious, when the first edition appeared, that both poets and publishers should be thanked. This I do gladly once again, both for him, and for Dr. Rhodenizer and myself.

LORNE PIERCE.

CONTENTS

INTRODUCTION

I

By Way of Background

The history of Canadian poetry is so short, compared with that of Old-World nations, that the general reader requires little in the way of historical background in order to enjoy it. He naturally expects to find that our earliest poetry in English was written by men and women who came to what is now Canada from England, Scotland, and Ireland (the absence of a Welsh strain is conspicuous), either directly or by way of what is now United States. Some poets of Irish extraction, unless they had come under the influence of the contemporaneous English tradition before coming to Canada, may show delightful traces of Irish folklore and, if they did not leave Ireland too early, of the romanticism of Tom Moore, who himself visited Canada in 1804, making the occasion memorable by giving us one of our two highly prized Canadian boat songs. Similarly, and more definitely, early poets from Scotland wrote in the manner of Burns. The early poets who came from England brought with them the classic tradition of the eighteenth century, and they and their successors were considerably slower than poets who remained in England in accepting, but ultimately did accept, the Romantic mode of writing poetry.

Two migrations from the United States, a minor and a major, affected the development of Canadian poetry. The minor, that of New Englanders to the lands from which the Acadians had been removed, could result, because of the predominance of Puritanism among the settlers, in religious literature only, which reached its lyric best in Henry Alline's *Hymns* (1786). The major migration, that of the Loyalists, not only contributed largely to the development of Canadian poetry but reinforced for a time the prevailing conservative adherence to the eighteenth-century classical tradition.

In the poetry of those who came to Canada after reaching maturity in the land of their birth, whether across the Atlantic or in what is now United States, there is bound to be some expression of homesickness. What is significant from the Canadian point of view is the change by which the country of their adoption comes to be loved as home.

Patriotism in any land rests on two fundamental bases, love of the country itself and admiration for the achievements of its great men. Canada is still a young country, and in the days of the early settlers and for a considerable period thereafter, its history was very much in the making, so that patriotism rested almost wholly on the first basis, and even that, up to the time of Confederation, was regional. Till then, patriotism in what is now Canada could not be based on a unit larger than a province, and sometimes the patriotic unit was even smaller than that.

This makes it easier to understand the tremendous impetus that Confederation gave to poetry by Canadian-born poets, especially those who were entering the most impressionable period of their lives in 1867. All of the major poets of the "Confederation School"—Roberts, Carman, Campbell, Pauline Johnson, Lampman, and the Scotts—were born in the short period 1860-1862. Even the youngest of them could probably remember the accomplished fact of Confederation, and all received the full impact of its early effect on the new nation. They established a poetic tradition that is still the true Canadian variant of the great poetic tradition of the English-speaking nations, itself only a variant of the fundamental and indispensable poetic tradition of all time.

Of this tradition, no requirement is more fundamental than one that poetry shares with all literature and all of the other arts; namely, that the art process is not complete until the experience of the artist is communicated, through the appropriate medium of the art, to those aesthetically capable of sharing the experience. Failure so to communicate can be due only to incompetence of the would-be artist in the use of his medium.

This and other basic aspects of poetic tradition Canadian poets on the whole, with characteristically sane conservatism, followed until after the First World War. Very few of them, major or minor, attempted even free verse, which, however it may have appealed to certain types of French and American temperaments and however much it may be justified *in theory* as an artistic rhythmic intermediary between the rhythm of prose and the meter of verse, seems to have had little appeal to Canadian poets and to have elicited little response from Canadian readers. Even MacInnes and Service, who stand strikingly apart from the main current of Canadian verse, do so almost wholly because of the content of their work, not because of their attitude to traditional poetic form. In general it may be said that the difference between major and minor poets is not in the kind of subject matter chosen or the artistic mould into which it is cast but in the degree of excellence attained in the use of similar subject matter expressed in traditional forms.

Also, the best Canadian poetry since the First World War has been written by poets who have remained true to the basic fundamentals of the authentic Canadian poetic tradition, modifying the merely conventional aspects, as is always permissible, to suit their individual artistic temperaments. Without in any way sacrificing the clarity and power of their work, they have expressed themselves, to a large extent in genuine free verse, by means of imagery as startlingly original as that of the neometaphysicals at their most obscure. In this worthy succession, outstanding new names are Kenneth Leslie, Arthur S. Bourinot, Robert Finch, Earle Birney, Audrey Alexandra Brown, Laurence Dakin, Charles Bruce, Anne Marriott, James Wreford (Watson), and Raymond Souster. Others who have made a commendable contribution will be noted at the appropriate places in the anthology.

In comparison with lyric poetry, narrative poetry, especially when based on actual occurrences, has little opportunity to depart from indispensable tradition, so that Pratt, because of his almost exclusive devotion to narrative poetry based on fact, stands apart in solitary grandeur, an isolated mountain peak on one of the tablelands of the Canadian Olympus. In his critical discussion of the attitude of the poet to the permanent core of tradition (University of Toronto *Quarterly*, October, 1938, pp. 1-10), he is solidly on the side of the angels.

Had all of Canada's potential poets who have begun to publish since the First World War adopted the same sane attitude toward what is unchangeable in poetic tradition, it would have been much better for Canadian poetry. And such would probably have been the case had Canadian poetry been left to continue its natural course of development without the introduction of new or revived poetic techniques from abroad. As the co-editor of this anthology has sagely remarked, "No nation can achieve its true destiny that adopts without profound and courageous reasoning and selection the thoughts and styles of another." Left to themselves or aided by sound constructive criticism, most or all of the younger Canadian poets interested in experimentation with new content and modification of established forms, as well as those who were unduly imitative of the work of the "Confederation Group," would probably have worked out their own salvation, as others before them had done, and as some of both groups did despite the fact that they were not left to themselves.

Three of our professorial critics were unduly impressed by the value of the poetry they studied while doing research abroad. In their criticism of Canadian poetry, though still talking about the old "colonial" criticism, which seemed to regard Canadian literature as necessarily inferior to English and American literature but which had disappeared evidently without their being aware of the fact, they introduced, ironically enough, a new and more harmful colonial attitude to Canadian poetry; namely, that its development would be faster and greater by grafting certain foreign techniques on the native tradition. Most of all they favoured the method of one poem, *The Waste Land* (1922), by T. S. Eliot, who himself had said, at least two years before that poem was published, that youth is everywhere prone "to form itself on one or two private admirations." (*The Sacred Wood: Essays on Poetry and Criticism* [1920].) Moreover, many of Eliot's admirers do not yet seem to realize that, soon after writing *The Waste Land*, Eliot himself turned wholeheartedly to the English classic tradition.

What is the method employed by Eliot, an American expatriate who became a resident of England in 1914 and a naturalized subject in 1927, in writing *The Waste Land?* In content it shows, as C. Day Lewis (*A Hope for Poetry*, Eighth Edition, p. 23) aptly phrases it, "symptoms of the psychic disease that ravaged Europe as mercilessly as the Spanish influenza." The method is a blend of that of the seventeenth-century English metaphysical poets with that of the French symbolists, by now influenced for the worse by inheritance or accretion of undesirable aspects of the practice of the French decadents and Parnassians, by dadaism, dating from 1916 and in purpose utterly destructive of all accepted values in art and elsewhere, and by a development within itself, surrealism, which by 1924 was strong enough to become a separate cult. Symbolism at its best, that is, when it has both clarity and imaginative power, is only one means of poetic expression; at its worst it results in obscurity, sometimes to the degree of incomprehensibility. The latter result is almost certain with the method of the metaphysical poets, for their imagery is characteristically far-fetched.

To give the ideas of his poem imaginative expression by this synthetic method Eliot turned for image and symbol to *From Ritual to Romance* (1920), by Jessie Laidlay Weston (? -1928), a book on the Grail legend that shows its relation to pre-Christian fertility cults and that gave Eliot his title, plan, and much of his symbolism, and to Frazer's *The Golden Bough*, in particular to the material on the Phrygian deity Attis, the Greek Adonis, and the Egyptian Osiris, all three associated in one way or another with death and revival. These main sources of image and symbol are supplemented by quotations from and allusions to various literary and religious works, with most of which the general reader would be as little acquainted as with the main sources.

With regard to the influence of *The Waste Land* on Canadian poetry, W. E. Collin, who studied at the University of Toulouse, tells us in *The White Savannahs* (1936) that one of its effects was "to convert *The Golden Bough* into a manual for young Canadian poets," giving them a body of "myth and ritual and symbolism" through which to express their emotions, thereby increasing "the interest and strength" of their poetry (p. 194). Few persons acquainted with Frazer's monumental achievement would question the judgment of a recent panel of competent critics placing the one-volume edition among the first five of the ten greatest books, but to attempt to make its content the basis of imaginative appeal in poetry before that content has become generally known is to take poetry away from the people, especially in a country like Canada, where the population as shown by the 1951 census is still only slightly less than half rural and where a large part of the statistically urban population was rurally reared.

By having access to the manuscripts of the "new poets" who were to appear in *New Provinces: Poems of Several Authors* (1936) Collin was able to write of their work and yet synchronize the publication of his book with that of theirs. Of the six poets in *New Provinces*, Pratt and Finch, as we have already seen, are in the great tradition. The other four are F. R. Scott, largely responsible for the publication of the volume, A. J. M. Smith, Leo Kennedy, and A. M. Klein. With the finest of scholarship but with amazing critical inconsistency, Collin proceeds to minimize the achievement of two of Canada's great poets, Marjorie Pickthall and Archibald Lampman, by showing the influences that had shaped their poetry, and then to magnify the achievement of the Waste-Landish poets by exactly the same method, showing what influences had shaped their poetry. The "new poets" discussed by Collin, as well as others that may be similarly classified, will receive individual consideration at the appropriate places in this volume.

The late E. K. Brown (1905-1951) studied at the Sorbonne. His criticism of Canadian poetry in the annual *Letters in Canada* from 1935 to 1949 and in the Governor-General's-Award-Winning *On Canadian Poetry* (1943, 1944) tends to underrate the work of conservative Canadian poets and to overrate that of those who follow the Waste-Land formula. Answering complaints of admirers of the poetry of Roberts to the effect that the critic had been "grudging" in his comments on the work of the poet, Brown says that if there is any ground for such complaint, "it lies in the fear I had lest his great age, the strong loyalties he evoked, and the immense influence he had come to wield should prejudice the reception throughout the country of some kinds of poetry that he did not fully appreciate." (*Letters in Canada*, 1943, p. 314.) In his book he says, "The poetry of the Montreal group and their disciples and associates is the core of Canadian verse during the past twenty years" (p. 70, 1944 ed.). He gives them space in proportion to this opinion.

The attitude of A. J. M. Smith to the established Canadian poetic tradition seems to be almost wholly the result of a bias in favour of the seventeenth-century English metaphysical poets acquired while doing graduate work at Edinburgh under Professor Grierson, authority on John Donne, although before he left McGill he had come into close contact with symbolism by way of study of the later and more obscure Yeats, who, like Eliot, was influenced by French symbolism. In any case, Smith, in his introductions to the different editions of *The Book of Canadian Poetry* (1943, 1948), is fair to the poets who established the Canadian tradition, though his criticism of the "new poets" of Canada is unduly slanted in their favour.

As might be expected, the new poets and their sponsoring critics tended to blame the difficulty that Canadian readers experienced with the new poetry because of its obscurity on the inability of those readers to appreciate ideas in poetry. This attitude is clearly implied as late as 1952, when the journalistic critic B. K. Sandwell, an ardent admirer of the new poets and critics, intimates in a review of Earle Birney's *Trial of a City and Other Verse* that Canadians are not so surprised as they used to be at finding ideas in poetry. Canadians have never been surprised at finding ideas in poetry. They have been surprised and mystified at finding ideas presented in the form of virtual cryptograms instead of in the form of genuine poems, but not in the works of Earle Birney.

This obscurity of much of the new poetry, the almost inevitable result of the methods of the new poets, whether the cocktail method of *The Waste Land* or the revived pure method of the seventeenth-century metaphysical poets of England, is particularly unfortunate, for it did its greatest harm in the field in which Canadian poetry most needed development, the field of the poetry of ideas, of reflective lyric.

New Provinces was followed by *Unit of Five* (1944), edited by Ronald Hambleton, who had visited England and there met some of the new poets. Besides examples of his own work, he included poems by James Wreford (Watson), who has so far rid himself of metaphysical tendencies as to win the Governor-General's Award, P. K. Page, Louis Dudek, and Raymond Souster, who does not belong here, still less among the unit of three—Irving Layton,

Louis Dudek, and himself—represented in *Cerberus* (1952), the title of which we hope is not indicative of future titles by the Contact Press, in which the same three are interested.

Poets of *Unit of Five*, along with Kay Smith, Irving Layton, and Patrick Anderson, appear in *Other Canadians, an Anthology of New Poetry in Canada, 1940-1946* (1947), edited by John Sutherland, of Montreal, Managing Editor of *Northern Review*, who has been associated with a number of new but sometimes shortlived magazines and who seems hospitable to poetry of social amelioration, but, whether or not in the pure metaphysical tradition, certainly not in the Eliotic manner.

To the inherent weakness of at least the pure metaphysical theory and practice was added the utterly mistaken idea, particularly emphasized by Smith, that poetry speaks the language of the intellect. Ideas, the legitimate basic content of reflective lyric, can never *in themselves* be poetry, for the simple reason that they *are* expressed in the language of the intellect. They become poetry only when expressed in language that *communicates* them to the reader with clarity approaching the best of which the language of the intellect is capable and also with the power that all readers have the right to expect from poetry; that is, in the language of the imagination, which always has been, still is, and always will be (unless the leftists should succeed in destroying poetry altogether) the language of poetry.

Even the language of imagination will not produce poetry of ideas (or any other kind) unless the imagery, symbolism, and other means of appeal to the imagination fall within the range of the reader's experience. He will not get the ideas because he cannot comprehend their intended expression. Hence the absurdity of trying to write Canadian poetry of ideas for the imaginative appeal of which *The Golden Bough* is a manual or the far-fetched imagery of the metaphysicals the only means. In the latter case, the "new poets" fail to realize that originality is not enough. The imagery of the lunatic is the most original possible to man but the least sharable. Some of the imagery of our neometaphysicals is dangerously near the "lunatic fringe." The newest idea cannot become poetry unless it is *communicated* with clarity and power through the language of the imagination. The oldest significant idea will make a good new poem whenever a good new poet expresses it in imaginative language that is startlingly fresh and yet so sharable that some readers may even wonder why they themselves had not thought of putting it that way.

Where were the supporters of our Canadian variant of world poetic tradition while leftist critics were encouraging "new poets" to write in the manner of foreign poets? By the time *New Provinces* was published, the older university professors interested in Canadian literature and the journalistic critics had for several years been working so harmoniously together that the former were no longer regarded as "academic" but rather were looked upon as guides, philosophers (in critical theory), and friends. Indeed, some of the professors had been conducting weekly book columns in the newspapers, notably A. M. MacMechan (1862-1933) as "The Dean" in the Montreal *Standard* and W. T. Allison as literary editor of the Winnipeg *Tribune*. The professorial critics who had a sound attitude to tradition either did not fully realize or did not take seriously what the leftists were trying to do or were so busy with their worthy intellectual pursuits that, except for the article by Pratt referred to earlier, virtually nothing was published to correct the errors in the theory of poetry advanced by their leftist fellow professors. This theory either bewildered the journalistic critics (who had come to trust professors) or gave them an inferiority complex as regards their ability as critics.

The harmful effect that this state of affairs has had on the Canadian reflective lyric may be partly indicated by a brief general consideration of the work of poets who consciously followed the "new" theory of poetry and of those who, without realizing the nature of the theory, simply wrote in the manner of the former. (To a leftist critic it is highly commendable for one leftist to write in the manner of another but reprehensible for one traditionalist to write like another.) If we symbolize by sunlight the clarity of expression that characterizes every good reflective lyric, then the various degrees of obscurity found in the works of the "new poets," whether from poet to poet or from poem to poem by the same poet, may be symbolized by haze, smoke, fog, mist, and "smog." At times, even the most obscure achieve clarity by letting genuine poetic gift triumph over mistaken theory, as shown by the poems by which they are represented in this volume. But a preponderance of obscure poems in an anthology or a book by an individual poet made it decidedly detrimental to the cause of true poetry, never more so than when it was a book that had been awarded a Governor-General's Medal by a panel of leftist judges. Such an award might ensure the sale of the book but would not ensure its being read. Readers confronted with such a book naturally said, if this be poetry, I'll none of it, which means that they turned away not only from the "new poetry" but also from that written in the authentic tradition. Canadian poetry was relatively the least read of literary types in Canada from 1936 to the end of the first half of Canada's century. The "new poets" took poetry away from the people, and, as one college president wittily remarked, they did not give it to anybody else. A good omen is that Charles Bruce and E. J. Pratt won the latest two Governor-General's Awards. It is the hope of the editors of this anthology to give poetry back to the people by presenting them with poetry they can understand and to heighten their enjoyment of it by giving them a few suggestions for its appreciation.

II

In Aid of Appreciation

The reader of Canadian poetry will enjoy its distinctive characteristics more intelligently if he appreciates them against the background of the characteristics common to all poetry. Like the other forms of literature and also like the fine arts other than literature, poetry depends for its effects on the communication, through an artistic medium, to persons of taste, of a sharable aesthetic experience. The medium of poetry, as of all literature, is language, and the poet's command of this medium depends on his imaginative ability to make his language as specific and concrete as possible, by the use of examples, illustrations, incidents, comparisons, figures of speech, symbols, and literal images, the last of which it is the primary function of imagination to create. Imagination in its basic aspect is the power of calling to mind absent objects that we have formerly experienced by one or more of the five senses. Since most people recall most readily objects experienced by the sense of sight, the word *image*, which originally meant a mental picture only, has been extended in meaning to include a mental impression of any kind of sense experience. Thus we have, according to the five senses, visual, auditory, gustatory (or palatal), olfactory, and tactile images. A special kind, the motor image, is experienced when the reader or hearer performs in imagination movements suggested by words or phrases.

The language of poetry is rhythmical as well as imaginative, and so we consider briefly the nature of rhythm as it occurs in the English language in general and in Canadian poetry in particular. The inadequate conventional explanation that it depends merely on a succession of accented and unaccented syllables and has nothing to do with time (as have the classical meters made up of a succession of long and short syllables) may cause most readers to miss the major part of its appeal. Rhythm depends not merely on accents but also on their recurrence at *approximately* equal time intervals. (Mechanical regularity is the negation of art.) When approximately the same time interval between accents is continuously maintained and the number of unaccented syllables to each accent kept down to one or two, the resulting rhythm is regular verse, or meter, which every normal person can appreciate, because, once the pattern is established in the mind, it is easy to follow. When approximately the same time interval between accents is maintained for only a few beats in succession and then changed and when more than two syllables occur between some of the accents, the result is the rhythm of prose or of free verse, as the case may be. Readers unable to appreciate these constantly changing rhythms need not be disturbed by the fact, for they are in a position analogous to that of a dancer who, accustomed to dancing to orchestras that play one kind of dance through to the end before beginning another kind, is suddenly confronted by an orchestra that plays three bars of a polka, five bars of a waltz, four bars of a foxtrot, similarly small portions of a rumba, a samba, a conga, and so on. Not many can make the constant readjustment essential to an appreciation of rhythms other than metrical.

The tendency to write in free verse instead of meter has decidedly increased among modern Canadian poets. Even those who have succeeded have handicapped their readers as indicated above, and those who do not know what free verse is have achieved nothing better than shredded prose, or, as Sydney J. Harris, of the Ottawa *Evening Citizen*, phrases it, "hysterical prose."

Canadian poetry employs all of the four primary modes of literary writing that communicate sharable aesthetic experience through the medium of imaginative and rhythmical language—the descriptive, the lyric, the narrative, and the dramatic. Of these, the simplest (not necessarily the easiest to appreciate) is the descriptive. Of literary description there are two pure types, the pictorial and the atmospheric. The poet writes pictorial description primarily or wholly to communicate to the reader a mental picture of some object, scene, or person, observed as he writes, or remembered, or imagined. He has in mind a definite physical point of view, which may be implied or definitely stated. The reader of a pictorial description may enjoy it to the maximum by noticing what visual images give the outline of the picture, fill in the colour, and suggest light and shade; what images of other kinds make the description more vivid; whether there is also a trace of atmospheric description; to what extent the total effect is heightened by appropriateness of form.

In atmospheric description the poet communicates to the reader the mood evoked by what is observed, remembered, or imagined. He never ceases to describe, but he chooses only or mainly such images and uses only or mainly only such other imaginative devices as will cumulatively suggest in the course of the description the mood to be communicated. The less trace there is of word picture, the more impressive the atmospheric effect will be. The appreciation of atmospheric description thus depends on perceiving the predominating mood, recognizing the skill with which it is more and more powerfully communicated, and noticing, even more than in pictorial description, the added effectiveness of harmonizing content and form.

The Canadian scene lends itself admirably to descriptive writing, and Canadian poetry is consequently rich in both pictorial and atmospheric description, not only as pure types, but also as incidental material in lyric, narrative, and dramatic poetry, in the last of which it is restricted to the description of characters and stage setting.

Next to the descriptive mode of writing in simplicity (though not necessarily the easiest or even second easiest to appreciate) is the lyric mode, of the production of which the most obvious example is of course the lyric, originally a poem suited to being sung to the accompaniment of a lyre and therefore naturally emotional in content and musical in expression. As a result of its origin, most conventional comment on the lyric has made and still makes it always emotional in content. This theory, if it ever did correspond wholly with the facts, does so no longer. Of the great body of modern lyrics, more are reflective in content than are emotional; that is, they are written primarily to express *thought* rather than emotion. Thus there are two simple or pure types of lyric, the emotional and the reflective, according to whether the purpose is to express the emotion or the thought of the poet.

In either kind, the stimulus may or may not be recorded. If the emotion or the thought cannot be effectively communicated to the reader without his sharing in imagination the experience that gave rise to it, the good poet records the stimulus. This is frequently the case when the contemplation of some aspect of nature gives rise to the emotion or thought, and then the stimulus is likely to be recorded by pictorial description or atmospheric description or both, kinds of writing that the reader has already learned how to appreciate. If the stimulus is not recorded, the reader immediately proceeds to determine the emotion or the thought that constitutes the basic subject matter of a lyric. After that comes the culminating phase of appreciation, the discovery of the ways in which the emotion or the thought is given concrete expression through appeal to the imagination. In the case of a reflective lyric, the imaginative expression of the thought creates a *by-product* of emotion, without which the finished poem would not be poetry at all, but merely expository verse. Failure of conventional criticism to realize that the emotional appeal of reflective lyric is in the *expression* and not in the *matter expressed* may be another reason why such criticism makes the lyric always emotional in content.

The progressive and desirable change to more reflective content in the lyric has during the second quarter of the twentieth century been accompanied by an undesirable and largely unnecessary departure from the other primal characteristic of the lyric, musical language. Even in Canada, where, as we have seen, the attitude to literary tradition has formerly tended to a sound conservatism, some of the "new poets" previously discussed have endeavoured to dissolve the felicitous union, mythologically approved of Apollo, of "music married to immortal verse." What Apollo has joined together let not the metaphysicals put asunder.

The more complex lyric types are simple or pure lyrics with modifications or additions in content or in form or in both. The content of the simple or pure lyric is always the poet's own emotion or thought. If he expresses instead the emotion or thought of another with whom he imaginatively identifies himself, the result is the dramatic lyric in its simplest form. If he expresses his own emotion or thought to an audience (of one or more) indicated but not identified, the result is a dramatic lyric of a slightly different but still simple kind. If he expresses the emotion or thought of another who speaks for himself to an audience as in the immediately preceding type, the result is a dramatic lyric of the subtlest kind. Again, pure lyric content may be expressed in one of the most exacting of forms, the sonnet. Even so elaborate a type as the formal elegy consists of an artistic sequence of three lyric responses to a stimulus (the death of an individual): the grief (emotional), the questioning (reflective), and the consolation (reflective).

As in the case of the simple or pure types of description, the Canadian scene lends itself admirably to the writing of nature lyrics of the two simple or pure types. In fact, the reader who knows how to appreciate simple or pure lyrics, emotional and reflective, written in ordinary metrical and stanzaic patterns, and lyrical content expressed in one or the other of the two types of sonnet, knows how to appreciate almost the entire body of Canadian lyric poetry.

The fundamental content of the third mode of writing, the narrative, is action. The nature of action may most easily be understood by considering it against the background of our discussion of the method of pictorial description, which depends very largely on visual imagery. Action may be regarded as a specialized form of visual imagery. To make this clear, let us use an ant hill as an example. We might come upon it when all of the ants were at rest. A word picture of it in that state would be a "still-life" description. We might then disturb the ants and cause a scene of disorderly movement. A word picture of this scene would still be description, but the movement depicted would cause it to differ from and become more interesting than the "still-life" description. After a few moments of disorder, we might discover on the part of one or more ants a purposive movement in the face of obstacles; for example, the struggle to carry a pupa to a place of safety. This purposive movement, communicated to the reader by a special use of visual imagery, becomes action. That is, we have passed from description to narration. In this case, as in many narratives, the struggle that gives rise to the outward and physical action is itself outward and physical. A more subtle kind of outward and physical action is that which proceeds from an inner conflict, mental, or moral, or both.

Whatever the origin of the struggle or conflict, the simplest kind of narrative requires purposive movement or action made by characters within appropriate limits of space and time. Hence the three essential elements of narration are action, character, and setting. To these may be added either or both of two other elements: atmosphere, to which all three of the essential elements may contribute and the nature of which is already clear from our discussion of atmosphere in description; and idea, which is expressed indirectly by means of the narrative, not directly as in the reflective lyric.

The simplest kind of narration follows the course of a single line of action resulting from a struggle or conflict between two opposing forces and ending, after a period of suspense during which it seems at times as if the character or characters are winning and at other times quite the reverse, in final success (happy ending) or final failure (unhappy ending, which if made to seem inevitable and to end in catastrophe, becomes tragic). The various turns in favour of or against the central character or characters in the course of the action that precedes the decisive turn (major crisis) may be called minor crises, and their artistic purpose is to hold and increase interest. Since even so simple a plot can have a high degree of interest, it is obvious that the interest intensifies as further conflicts are added.

Canadian narrative poetry has thus far been largely concerned with the heroic struggles of actual persons—discoverers, explorers, pioneer settlers, missionaries, and railroad builders—in actual settings, and so has a strong historical as well as literary appeal.

The preceding discussion of narrative technique leads easily and naturally to a consideration of the last of the four modes of writing, the dramatic. To make successful acted drama, in which the story is not narrated but presented in dialogue and action on the stage by actors who impersonate the characters, the plot must be such that it can be presented in no other way so well as on the stage, and it must fall within the time limits set by the stage. Drama is at once the most vivid and the most difficult of all forms of literary art. The one-act play makes even more exacting demands on the skill of the dramatist than does the full-length play, for the former, if true to type has perfect unity of time (unbroken action) and perfect unity of place (a single scene).

In addition to plays written primarily for the stage, there are also "closet dramas," which, though having every aspect of dramatic form, are better suited to reading than to stage representation. This is a fortunate state of affairs for the writers of poetic drama in Canada, for while some of the verse plays by Canadians may be "good theatre," most of them are intended to be read. Canadian readers may enjoy them in printed form as readily as they enjoy descriptive, lyric, and narrative poetry. Complete verse plays are beyond the scope of an anthology of poetry, but skilful choosing of extracts can suggest their poetic power.

V. B. RHODENIZER.

Acadia University,
Wolfville, Nova Scotia,

CANADIAN POETRY IN ENGLISH

INDIAN POETRY

There is a keen and steadily growing interest in all of the cultural achievements of the earliest known Canadians, the Indians and Eskimos who occupied this country for untold generations before the white man came. Fortunately for the student of Indian poetry in particular, especially that of the Haidas of the British Columbia coast, a considerable amount of what was passed on from generation to generation by oral tradition has been taken down and preserved in adaptation or translation through the medium of the printed page, notably by Constance Lindsay Skinner and Hermia (Harris) Fraser, in songs that represent various aspects of the life cycle of the Indian from birth to death. Interesting poems about the native races, the majority of them concerned with the relation of the aborigines to the white man, have been written by Bishop G. J. Mountain, Joseph Howe, Alexander McLachlan, Charles Sangster, W. D. Lighthall, Pauline Johnson, Duncan Campbell Scott, Annie Charlotte Dalton, J. E. Middleton, Frederick Niven, and Arthur S. Bourinot, and Indian life has been poetically treated in the dramatic tragedies *Ponteach, a Tragedy* (1776), by Robert Rogers, *De Roberval* (1888), by John Hunter-Duvar, and *Tecumseh, a Drama* (1886, 1901), by Charles Mair.

CONSTANCE LINDSAY SKINNER [1879-1939]

Constance Lindsay Skinner, daughter of Robert James and Anne (Lindsay) Skinner, both of literary ancestry, was born in northern British Columbia, where her father was a Hudson's Bay Company factor. She was educated by tutors at home and by attendance at private schools in Vancouver. At sixteen she was publishing short stories in newspapers. After eight years of journalism, first as a reporter on the Los Angeles *Times and Examiner* and then on the staff of the Chicago *American*, she became a full-time writer. Her prose works include regional histories of the old Southwest and of Oregon, a history of the fur trade, the Missouri volume in the Rivers of America series, which she edited, several novels, juvenile and adult, and a play entitled *David.* Her poetry volumes are *Song of David* (1920), *Song of the Long River* (1924), and *Songs of the Coast Dwellers* (1930), for some of the contents of which she began receiving prizes as early as 1913.

SONG OF CRADLE-MAKING

Thou hast stirred!
When I lifted thy little cradle,
The little cradle I am making for thee,
I felt thee!
The face of the beach smiled,
I heard the pine trees singing,
In the White Sea the Dawn-Eagle dipped his wing.
Oh, never have I seen so much light
Through thy father's doorway!

(Wast thou pleased with thy cradle?)

Last night I said: "When the child comes,
If it is a Son—
I will trim his cradle with shells;
And proudly I will bear him in his rich cradle
Past the doors of barren women.
All . all . shall see my Little Chief
In his rich cradle!

That was last night:—
Last night thou hadst not stirred!

Oh, I know not if thou be son—
Strong Chief, Great Fisher, Law-of-Woman,
As thy father *is;*
Or only Sorrow-Woman, Patient Serving Hands,
Like thy Mother.
I only know I love thee,—
Thou Little One under my heart!
For thou *didst* move; and every part of me trembled.
I will trim thy cradle with *many* shells,
And with cedar-fringes;
Thou shalt have goose-feathers on thy blanket!
I will bear thee in my hands along the beach,
Singing—as the sea sings,
Because the little mouths of sand
Are ever at her breast.
Oh, Mother-face of the Sea, how thou dost smile—
And I have wondered at thy smiling!

Aiihi! Thy little feet—
I felt them press me!
Lightly, lightly
I hear them coming:
Like little brown leaves running over the earth—
Little running leaves, wind-hastened,
On the sudden Autumn trails!
Earth loves the little running feet of leaves,

(Thy little feet!)

O K'antsamiqala'soe, our Praised One,
Let there be no more barren women!
May thou bring no tears, my child,
When I bear thee in thy rich cradle
By the chanting sea-paths where the women labour.

Thou hast stirred!

Oh, haste, haste, little feet—
Little brown feet lightly running
Down the trail of the hundred days!
The wind is white with the rocking bird-cradles;
Day is in the eyes of the Sea.
Ah! never have I seen so much light
Through thy father's doorway.

NOTE: 'K'antsamiqala'soe: God, literally "our Supreme or Highest Praised One." The language is that of a British Columbian coast tribe.

SONG OF THE FULL CATCH

Here's good wind, here's sweet wind,
Here's good wind and my woman calls me!
Straight she stands there by the pine-tree,
Faithful waits she by the cedar,
She will smile and reach her hands
When she sees my thousand salmon!
Here's good wind and my woman calls me.

Here's clear water, here's swift water,
Here's bright water and my woman waits me!
She will call me from the sea's mouth—
Sweet her pine-bed when the morning
Lights my canoe and the river ends!
Here's good wind, here's swift water,
Strong as love when my woman calls me!

HERMIA (HARRIS) FRASER [1902-]

Hermia (Harris) Fraser, Mrs. Wallace I. Fraser, was born as Buctouche, New Brunswick, the daughter of James Parkin and Sophia Margaret (MacManus) Fraser, and educated at Dawson, Yukon, and Victoria, British Columbia. In addition to writing poetry, she has contributed numerous short stories to many popular magazines. Of the ten poems in her *Songs of the Western Islands* (1945), five are on Haida Indian tribal themes, of which three are reprinted here.

SONG OF WELCOME

Ai, ai, my small red man,
Why do you weep on my bosom,
Here in the Hut of the Newborn,
Fresh from the beak of the Raven,
He who made earth from the rain clouds,
He who made Queen Charlotte Islands,
He who made men from the clam mounds?

Long did you lie in a hammock
Swung near the Hanging Horizons,
Trailing your feathers of swansdown
Blown through the masks of Divine Ones,
Hearing the Whistlers, the spirits,
Pierce the dense blueness of Starland;

Lost until my heart called to you,
Lost until my body bore you.
Wah, ah wah, my small red man,
Welcome, the journey is ended.

THE COPPER SONG

The Copper was a large shield on which the names of great chiefs were written. It was usually won in the many battles fought by the Haida.

Beaten, beaten, beaten, beaten,
Lies the oblong plaque of splendour,
Lies the massive great Bear Copper,
Beaten on the copper stand
By the copper men of old,
Till the air is trembling yellow
And the ground with dust agleam.

What great name carved on the Copper?
Proud the name, her name,
Great-grandmother of chieftains,
Even the Foam Woman whose first offspring
With a moist and foaming mouth
Almost caused the second flood.
Even the Foam Woman who was rolled
By the phosphorescent sea.

Tell then, how the Great Bear Copper
Came into our glad possession!
Each who held it doubled value
Till the wonderful Bear Copper
Taken in a bitter battle
From those born at Qu-gialis,
They, the Cockle-Shell descendants,
Came into our glad possession.

None shall take it,
While the lifeblood
Runs in Gao-haida-gai!

THE ROUSING CANOE SONG

Hide not, hide not,
Deer in lowlands,
Elk in meadows,
Goats on crag-lands.
Hide not brown bear,
Island black bear,
Lynx and cougar,
Mink and beaver.

Safe the martin,
Safe the racoon,
Now we hunt not
Wolf and cougar,
Brant nor swan
Nor wild geese soaring,
Porpoise, whale
Nor cod nor herring.
Nor bald eagles
From the snow peaks
Curving where the bay is misty.

Lo! we hunt the female otter!
With our spears
We shall surround her.
He who slays her triumphs doubly,
Double prize shall be his portion.

Lo! We hunt the red witch-woman,
Who with magic tricks has harmed us
Even seizing our Great Copper!

Hide not, hide not,
Game in caverns,
Only hide *thee*, Lost Enchantress!

JONATHAN ODELL [1737-1818]

Jonathan Odell, son of John and Temperance (Dickinson) Odell, was born at Newark, New Jersey. After graduating from the College of New Jersey, now Princeton University, he studied medicine and became a surgeon in the British army in the West Indies, but resigned to study in England for holy orders, and was later appointed rector of St. Mary's Parish, Burlington, New Jersey. Driven from there in 1777 because he opposed armed resistance by the colonies, he joined a Loyalist regiment. In 1784 he settled in New Brunswick, where he served as provincial secretary, registrar of records, and clerk of the council till 1812, and where his family became substantial citizens. He brought into Canada the eighteenth-century traditions of political satire and of the use of the heroic couplet. His poems are preserved in Winthrop Sargent's collection entitled *Loyal Verses of Stansbury and Odell* (1860). (Cf. Ray Palmer Baker (1883-), *A History of English-Canadian Literature to the Confederation* (1920), pp. 27-30.)

ON OUR THIRTY-NINTH WEDDING DAY

[6th Jan., 1810]

Twice nineteen years, dear Nancy, on this day
Complete their circle, since the smiling May
Beheld us at the altar kneel and join
In holy rites and vows, which made thee mine.
Then, like the reddening East without a cloud,
Bright was my dawn of joy. To Heaven I bowed
In thankful exultation, well assured
That all my heart could covet was secured.

But ah, how soon this dawn of Joy so bright
Was followed by a dark and stormy night!
The howling tempest, in a fatal hour,
Drove me, an exile from our nuptial bower,
To seek for refuge in the tented field,
Till democratic Tyranny should yield.
Thus torn asunder, we, from year to year,
Endured the alternate strife of Hope and Fear;
Till, from Suspense deliver'd by Defeat,
I hither came and found a safe retreat.

Here, join'd by thee and thy young playful train,
I was o'erpaid for years of toil and pain.
We had renounced our native hostile shore;
And met, I trust, till Death to part no more!
But fast approaching now the verge of life,
With what emotions do I see a Wife,
And Children, smiling with affection dear,
And think—how sure that parting, and how near!
The solemn thought I wish not to refrain:
Tho' painful, 'tis a salutary pain.
Then let this verse in your remembrance live,
That, when from life released, I still may give
A token of my love; may whisper still
Some fault to shun, some duty to fulfil;
May prompt your Sympathy, some pain to share;
Or warn you of some pleasures to beware;
Remind you that the Arrow's silent flight,
Unseen alike at noon or dead of night,
Should cause no perturbation or dismay,
But teach you to enjoy the passing day
With dutiful tranquility of mind;
Active and vigilant, but still resign'd.
For our Redeemer liveth, and we know,
How or whenever parted here below,
His faithful servants, in the Realm above,
Shall meet again as heirs of His eternal love.

JOSEPH STANSBURY [1740-1809]

Joseph Stansbury emigrated from England to Philadelphia, whence he was banished in 1776 for singing the British National Anthem in his own house and fled to New York. After peace was concluded, he settled in New Jersey but was imprisoned and then paroled on the condition of leaving the State within nine days. He came to Shelburne, Nova Scotia, one of the important Loyalist settlements, where he remained for two years. During that time he wrote "To Cordelia," among the best verse of its time and historically significant because it expresses characteristic early moods of the Loyalists in British North America. (Cf. ref. for Odell, and Baker, *op. cit.*, pp. 24-25.)

TO CORDELIA

Believe me, Love, this vagrant life
O'er Nova Scotia's wilds to roam,
While far from children, friends, or wife,
Or place that I can call a home
Delights not me;—another way
My treasures, pleasures, wishes lay.

In piercing, wet, and wintry skies,
Where man would seem in vain to toil
I see, where'er I turn my eyes,
Luxuriant pasture, trees and soil.
Uncharm'd I see:—another way
My fondest hopes and wishes lay.

Oh could I through the future see
Enough to form a settled plan,
To feed my infant train and thee
And fill the rank and style of man:
I'd cheerful be the livelong day;
Since all my wishes point that way.

But when I see a sordid shed
Of birchen bark, procured with care,
Designed to shield the aged head
Which British mercy placed there—
'Tis too, too much: I cannot stay,
But turn with streaming eyes away.

Oh! how your heart would bleed to view
Six pretty prattlers like your own,
Expos'd to every wind that blew;
Condemn'd in such a hut to moan.
Could this be borne, Cordelia, say?
Contented in your cottage stay.

'Tis true, that in this climate rude,
The mind resolv'd may happy be;
And may, with toil and solitude,
Live independent and be free.
So the lone hermit yields to slow decay:
Unfriended lives—unheeded glides away.

If so far humbled that no pride remains,
But moot indifference which way flows the stream;
Resign'd to penury, its cares and pains;
And hope has left you like a painted dream;
Then here, Cordelia, bend your pensive way,
And close the evening of Life's little day.

HENRY ALLINE [1748-1784]

Henry Alline was born at Newport, Rhode Island. In 1760 his parents and their seven children settled at Falmouth, Nova Scotia. As an ardent itinerant evangelist he led the revolt against the formality of Congregationalism and became "The Whitefield of the Province," the "Apostle of Nova Scotia," the founder of the sect designated "New Lights," some of whom became the Baptists who founded Acadia University. The poetry of this zealous Puritan is naturally confined to hymns, in which he expresses in the main spiritual agony or religious ecstasy with unusual lyric power. His *Hymns and Spiritual Songs* (1786, 1802) is divided into five Books and contains 488 religious lyrics. (Cf. Baker, *op. cit.*, pp. 11-15; G. E. Levy (1902-), *The Baptists of the Maritime Provinces 1753-1946* (1946); R. S. Longley (1896-), *Acadia University, 1838-1938* (1939).)

From CHRIST INVITING SINNERS TO HIS GRACE

[*Bk. II, hymn XXXVII*]

Amazing sight, the Saviour stands,
And knocks at ev'ry door;
Ten thousand blessings in his hands
For to supply the poor.

"Behold," saith he, "I bleed and die
To bring poor souls to rest;
Hear sinners while I'm passing by,
And be forever blest.

"Will you despise such bleeding love,
And choose the way to hell;
Or in the glorious realms above,
With me forever dwell?

"Not to condemn your sinking race,
Have I in judgment come;
But to display unbounded grace,
And bring lost sinners home.

"May I not save your wretched soul
From sin, from death and hell?
Wounded or sick, I'll make you whole,
And you with me shall dwell. . . ."

JOHN GALT [1779-1839]

John Galt, the Scottish novelist, was successively secretary of the board of directors, commissioner, and superintendent of the Canada Company. He visited Canada in the interests of that Company in 1825 and again in 1826 (remaining till 1829). His *Autobiography* (1833) tells of his life in Canada. He wrote on Canadian affairs, published a story about the Hurons, and has been credited with the authorship of "Canadian Boat Song, which appeared anonymously in *Blackwood's Magazine* in 1829. Even if the author was David Macbeth Moir instead of Galt, as Professor G. H. Needler (1886-   ) has put the case, Galt furnished the experience on which the poem is based. (Cf. R. K. Gordon (1887-   ), *John Galt* (1920), G. H. Needler, *The Lone Shieling* (1941).)

CANADIAN BOAT SONG

Listen to me, as when ye heard our father
Sing long ago the song of other shores—
Listen to me, and then in chorus gather
All your deep voices, as ye pull your oars:

Fair these broad meads—these hoary woods are grand;
But we are exiles from our fathers' land.

From the lone shieling of the misty island
Mountains divide us, and the waste of seas—
Yet still the blood is strong, the heart is Highland,
And we in dreams behold the Hebrides.

Fair these broad meads—these hoary woods are grand;
But we are exiles from our fathers' land.

We ne'er shall tread the fancy-haunted valley
Where 'tween the dark hills creeps the small clear stream,
In arms around the patriarch banner rally,
Nor see the moon on royal tombstones gleam.

Fair these broad meads—these hoary woods are grand;
But we are exiles from our fathers' land.

When the bold kindred, in the time long vanished,
Conquer'd the soil and fortified the keep,
No seer foretold the children would be banished,
That a degenerate lord might boast his sheep.

Fair these broad meads—these hoary woods are grand;
But we are exiles from our fathers' land.

Come foreign rage, let discord burst in slaughter!
O! then, for clansmen true, and stern claymore—
The hearts that would have given their blood like water
Beat heavily beyond the Atlantic roar.

Fair these broad meads—these hoary woods are grand;
But we are exiles from our fathers' land.

ANTOINE GERIN-LAJOIE [1824-1882]

Antoine Gerin-Lajoie was born at Yamachiche, Quebec, and educated at the College of Nicolet. He was called to the bar but chose journalism instead of law. From 1852 to 1880 he held government positions. He wrote history and drama in French. He is introduced here slightly out of chronological order for the double purpose of illustrating the French-Canadian song and the reversal of the situation in which, as in a number of previous poems, the immigrant to Canada regards himself as an exile. Here is Gerin-Lajoie's "Un Canadien errant," written while he was still a schoolboy, as translated by John Boyd (1864-1933), journalist, biographer, and author of occasional poems.

THE CANADIAN EXILE

Weeping sorely as he journeyed
Over many a foreign strand,
A Canadian exile wandered,
Banished from his native land.

Sad and pensive, sitting lonely
By a rushing river's shore,
To the flowing waters spake he
Words that fondest memories bore:

"If you see my own dear country—
Most unhappy is its lot—
Say to all my friends, O river,
That they never are forgot.

"Oh! those days so full of gladness,
Now forever are they o'er,
And alas! my own dear country,
I shall never see it more.

"No, dear Canada, O my homeland!
But upon my dying day,
Fondly shall my last look wander
To thee, beloved, far away."

BISHOP G. J. MOUNTAIN [1789-1863]

George Jehoshaphat Mountain, son of Rev. Jacob and Mrs. Mountain (born Kentish), was born in Norwich, England. The family came to Quebec in 1793, but the future bishop was educated at Trinity College, Cambridge. From 1814 on he had a distinguished record in the Anglican Church, at Fredericton, New Brunswick, in Quebec, and in Montreal. His book of poems is *Songs of the Wilderness* (1846). (Cf. *A Memoir of George Jehoshaphat Mountain* (1866), by his son, Armine Wale Mountain (1823-1885).)

THE INDIAN'S GRAVE

Bright are the heavens, the narrow bay serene;
No sound is heard within the shelter'd place,
Save some sweet whisper of the pines—nor seen
Of restless man nor of his works a trace;
I stray, through bushes low, a little space;
Unlook'd-for sight their parted leaves disclose:
Restless no more, lo! one of Indian race,
His bones beneath that roof of bark repose.
Poor savage! in such bark through deepening snows
Once didst thou dwell; in this through rivers move.
Frail house, frail skiff, frail man! Of him who knows
His master's will, not thine the doom shall prove.
What will be yours, ye powerful, wealthy, wise,
By whom the heathen unregarded dies?

STANDISH O'GRADY [fl. 1793-1841]

Standish O'Grady, who, according to his own statements, was a graduate of Trinity College, Dublin, a classmate of Robert Emmet (1778-1803), a Protestant clergyman in Ireland, and an immigrant who settled on a farm near Sorel, Quebec, in 1836, planned a poem to consist of four cantos, but *The Emigrant* (1841) contains only the first canto, with a Preface, a dedication to Nobody, copious notes, and some miscellaneous poems. The canto begins with his leaving Ireland, and there is much about the trip and the past and contemporaneous state of Ireland in addition to the material about his experiences in Canada. He favours Ontario rather than Quebec as the destination of new settlers.

From THE EMIGRANT

And first Morency, far famed water, you,
As if from heaven propell'd, astound my view,
Fantastic crash as if by chaos hurl'd,
To burst thy bounds and inundate a world;
Yet even thus, thy cataract in vain
Pours forth its torrent on the icebound plain,
Absorbing nature acts by strict control,
Arrests thy progress and ingulphs the whole . . .
Here rests the Rainbow in its magic sphere,
Reflection's pride conceived in circling air,
Beneath its ark thy deafening waters roll,
Impetuous urged and glide from pole to pole,
O'er thy rude base its vast extension lies,
As if to mark heaven's entrance to the skies.

. . .

The weighty pine now feels the well judged stroke,
And falls recumbent on the neighbouring oak;
The half cut oak imparts the dexterous blow,
And branch to branch fall prostrate in a row;
Thus forests fall, the weak, the mighty feel
The toilsome influence of Canadian steel;
Hard earned task, the meed of other days,
Though hard the task, yet ill the toil repays!

. . .

See now rude spring, his wished for visit pays,
And teeming earth an hideous form displays;
The ruptured rivers scarce their banks restrain,
And fractured ice rolls headlong to the main;
The swollen brooks extend their awful course,
Dissolving snow supplies each trackless source;
The chequered landscape varying as it goes,
Still adds to hope and promises repose.

OLIVER GOLDSMITH [1794-1861]

Oliver Goldsmith, Canada's first native-born poet in English, one of the fourteen children of Henry and Mary (Mason) Goldsmith, was born at St. Andrews, New Brunswick, to the neighbourhood of which the family had moved in 1785. In 1796 the father was made Assistant Engineer at Annapolis Royal, somewhat later, Assistant Commissary in Halifax, and in 1810, Commissary for New Brunswick. Oliver was early placed in the Dispensary and Surgery of the Naval Hospital, Halifax. After this and other temporary positions, he "entered the Commissariat at Halifax as a Volunteer." Except for some time spent in travel and on sick leave, the rest of his working life was spent in commissary service—in Halifax (1810-1833), New Brunswick (1833-1844), Hong Kong (1844-1848), Newfoundland 1848-1853), and Corfu (1854-1855). While in Halifax he wrote *The Rising Village* (1825). He published *The Rising Village with Other Poems* in 1834. (Cf. Rev. Wilfrid E. Myatt, *The Autobiography of Oliver Goldsmith* (1943), with a Foreword by Lorne Pierce.)

THE RISING VILLAGE

While now the Rising Village claims a name,
Its limits still increase and still its fame,
The wand'ring pedlar, who undaunted traced
His lonely footsteps o'er the silent waste;
Who traversed once the cold and snow-clad plain,
Reckless of danger, trouble or of pain,
To find a market for his little wares,
The source of all his hopes and all his cares,
Establish'd here, his settled home maintains,
And soon a merchant's higher title gains.

Around his store, on spacious shelves array'd,
Behold his great and various stock in trade.
Here nails and blankets, side by side, are seen,
There, horses' collars and a large tureen;
Buttons and tumblers, codhooks, spoons and knives,
Shawls for young damsels, flannels for old wives;
Woolcards and stockings, hats for men and boys,
Mill-saws and fenders, silks, and infants' toys;
All useful things and joined with many more,
Compose the well assorted country store . . .

The half-bred Doctor next here settles down,
And hopes the village soon will prove a town.
No rival here disputes his doubtful skill,
He cures, by chance, or ends each human ill:

By turns he physics, or his patient bleeds,
Uncertain in what case each best succeeds.
And if, from friends untimely snatch'd away,
Some beauty fall a victim to decay;
If some fine youth, his parents' fond delight,
Be early hurried to the shades of night;
Death bears the blame, 'tis his envenom'd dart
That strikes the suff'ring mortal to the heart . . .

Beneath the shelter of a log-built shed
The country school-house next erects its head.
No "man severe" with learning's bright display,
Here leads the op'ning blossoms into day;
No master here, in ev'ry art refin'd,
Through field of science guides th' aspiring mind;
But some poor wand'rer of the human race,
Unequal to the task, supplies his place,
Whose greatest source of knowledge or of skill
Consists in reading or in writing ill;
Whose efforts can no higher merit claim
Than spreading Dilworth's great scholastic fame.
No modest youths surround his awful chair,
His frowns to deprecate or smiles to share,
But all the terrors of his lawful sway,
The proud despise, the fearless disobey;
The rugged urchins spurn at all control,
Which cramps the movements of the free-born soul,
Till, in their own conceit so wise they've grown
They think their knowledge far exceeds his own.

SUSANNA MOODIE [1803-1885]

Mrs. Susanna (Strickland) Moodie, daughter of Thomas Strickland, of Reydon Hall, Bungay, England, and wife of Lieut. J. W. D. Moodie, came to Canada with her husband in 1832. After brief residences first at Cobourg and then north of Peterborough, they moved to Belleville in 1839. On the death of her husband in 1869, Mrs. Moodie moved to Toronto. Her interesting accounts of pioneer life reflect the change of attitude by which she came to regard Canada as her homeland. Her *Enthusiasm and Other Poems* (1830) contains poetry on native themes and shows the influence of Romanticism modifying the eighteenth-century classic manner.

INDIAN SUMMER

By the purple haze that lies
  On the distant rocky height,
By the deep blue of the skies,
  By the smoky amber light
Through the forest arches streaming,
Where Nature on her throne sits dreaming,
And the sun is scarcely gleaming
  Through the cloudlets, snowy white,
Winter's lovely herald greets us
Ere the ice-crowned tyrant meets us.

A mellow softness fills the air,
  No breeze on wanton wing steals by
To break the holy quiet there,
  Or make the waters fret and sigh,
Or the golden alders shiver
That bend to kiss the placid river,
Flowing on and on for ever.
But the little waves are sleeping,
O'er the pebbles slowly creeping,
That last night were flashing, leaping,
Driven by the restless breeze,
In lines of foam beneath yon trees.

Dressed in robes of gorgeous hue,
  Brown and gold with crimson blent;
The forest to the waters blue
  Its own enchanting tints has lent;
In their dark depths, life-like glowing,
We see a second forest growing,
Each pictured leaf and branch bestowing
A fairy grace to that twin wood,
Mirror'd within the crystal flood.

'Tis pleasant now in forest shades;
  The Indian hunter strings his bow
To track through dark, entangling glades
  The antler'd deer and bounding doe,
Or launch at night the birch canoe,
To spear the finny tribes that dwell
On sandy bank, in weedy cell,
Or pool the fisher knows right well—
Seen by the red and vivid glow
Of pine-torch at his vessel's bow.

This dreamy Indian-summer day
   Attunes the soul to tender sadness;
We love—but joy not in the ray:
   It is not summer's fervid gladness,
But a melancholy glory
   Hovering softly round decay,
Like swan that sings her own sad story
   Ere she floats in death away.

The day declines; what splendid dyes,
   In flickered waves of crimson driven,
Float o'er the saffron sea that lies
   Glowing within the western heaven!
   Oh, it is a peerless even!
See, the broad red sun is set,
But his rays are quivering yet
Through nature's veil of violet,
Streaming bright o'er lake and hill;
But earth and forest lie so still,
It sendeth to the heart a chill;
We start to check the rising tear—
'Tis Beauty sleeping on her bier.

JOSEPH HOWE [1804-1873]

Joseph Howe was born at Halifax, Nova Scotia, the son of John and Mary (Edes) Howe. His formal education was slight. At the age of thirteen he began work in his father's printing-shop. In 1825 he acquired the *Novascotian*, which he edited till 1841 and returned to in 1843. A powerful advocate of the freedom of the press and of responsible government, his political career began in 1836 and continued through the rest of his life, culminating in his being appointed lieutenant-governor of Nova Scotia. His great contribution to the literature of affairs is preserved in the two volumes of his *Speeches and Public Letters* (1858, ed. William Annand; 1909, ed. J. A. Chisholm). His poetry, with its Loyalist regard for eighteenth-century English models and its fresh and vigorous originality, is found in *Poems and Essays* (1874). (Cf. Baker, as above, pp. 57-67, and biographies by G. E. Fenety (1896), J. W. Longley (1904), W. L. Grant (1914), and J. A. Roy (1935).)

THE SONG OF THE MICMAC

Oh! who on the mountain, the plain, or the wave,
With the arm of the Micmac will dare to contend?
Who can hurl the keen spear with the sons of the brave
Or who can the bow with such energy bend?

Who can follow the Moose, or the wild Cariboo,
With a footstep as light and unwearied as he?
Who can bring down the Loon with an arrow so true,
Or paddle his bark o'er as stormy a sea?

Who can traverse the mountain or swim the broad lake?
Who can hunger and thirst with such fortitude bear?
Or who can the Beaver as skilfully take?
Or the Salmon so nimbly transfix with his spear?

And if the wild war whoop ascends on the gale,
Who can with the Micmac the tomahawk wield?
Oh! when was he known in the combat to quail?
Who e'er saw him fly from the red battle field?

Free sons of the forest, then peal forth the song,
Till each valley and rock shall of victory tell,
And the ghosts of our heroes, while flitting along
With triumph shall smile on the spots where they fell.

From ACADIA

In ev'ry thought, in ev'ry wish I own,
In ev'ry prayer I breathe to Heaven's high throne
My country's welfare blends—and could my hand
Bestow one flower't on my native land,
Could I but light one Beacon fire, to guide
The steps of those who yet may be her pride,
Could I but wake one never dying strain
Which Patriot hearts might echo back again,
I'd ask no meed—no wreath of glory crave
If her approving smile my own Acadia gave.

What though the Northern winds that o'er thee blow
Borrow fresh coolness from thy hills of snow,
And icy Winter, in his rudest form,
Breathes through thy valleys many a chilling storm
Still there is health and vigour in the breeze
Which bears upon its wing no fell disease
To taint the balmy freshness of the air
And steal the bloom thy hardy children wear . . .

And when mild Spring, with all her magic powers,
Spreads o'er the land her simple robe of flowers, . . .
And clad in green thy teeming vales appear,
Oh! then, Acadia, thou art doubly dear . . .

For, though Acadia's sons may stray at times
To lands more fruitful, and to milder climes, . . .
The exile pines to tread his native land;
Her fertile valleys and her lovely forms,
Crowd on the mind with dreams of mighty power,
And cheer his heart in many a lonely hour.

JAMES McCARROLL [1815-1896]

James McCarroll was born in Ireland. The family came to Canada in 1831. As a journalist he became proprietor of the Peterborough *Chronicle* in 1843 and of the *Newcastle Courier*, of Cobourg, Ontario, in 1847. He also founded a humorous weekly, the *Latchkey*, in which appeared the material of his *Letters of Terry Finnegan to the Hon. T. D. McGee* (1864). His poetry is preserved in *Madeline and Other Poems* (1889).

THE GREY LINNET

There's a little grey friar in yonder green bush,
 Clothed in sackcloth—a little grey friar,
Like a druid of old in his temple—but hush!
 He's at vespers; you must not go nigher.

Yet, the rogue! can those strains be addressed to the skies,
 And around us so wantonly float,
Till the glowing refrain like a shining thread flies,
 From the silvery reel of his throat?

When he roams, though he stains not his path through the air
 With the splendour of tropical wings,
All the lustre denied to his russet plumes there
 Flashes forth through his lay when he sings;

 For the little grey friar is so wondrous wise,
 Though in such a plain garb he appears,
That on finding he can't reach your soul through your eyes,
 He steals in through the gates of your ears.

But the cheat!—'tis not heaven he's warbling about—
 Other passions, less holy, betide—
For, behold, there's a little grey nun peeping out
 From a bunch of green leaves at his side.

CHARLES HEAVYSEGE [1816-1876]

Charles Heavysege was born of Yorkshire parentage near Liverpool, England, and left school at the age of nine to begin work. He settled in Montreal in 1853 as a worker in wood and also did some newspaper work. His prose publication is a melodramatic novel set in Montreal. He wrote lyric, narrative, and dramatic poems. Of his poetry written in England, all but *The Revolt of Tartarus* (1852), a drama in blank verse, was destroyed. Later he published *Sonnets* (1854); *Saul, A Drama in Three Parts* (three editions, 1857, 1859, 1869); *Count Fillipo; or, The Unequal Marriage* (1860), a drama in five acts; *Shakespearean Tercentenary Ode* (1864); *The Owl* (1864); *The Dark Huntsman; Jephthah's Daughter* (1865), containing also twenty fourteen-line poems (some of them sonnets) reprinted from the earlier sonnet volume; *Jezebel* (1867). (Cf. L. J. Burpee (1873-1946), *Charles Heavysege* (1901); *Canadian Who was Who*, vol. 2 (1938).)

From SAUL

[*Pt. III, Act II, Sc. v*]

To hunt and to be hunted make existence;
For we are all or chasers or the chased;
And some weak, luckless wretches ever seem
Flying before the hounds of circumstance,
Adown the windy gullies of this life;
Till, toppling over death's uncertain verge,
We see of them no more. Surely this day
Has been a wild epitome of life!
For life is merely a protracted chase;
Yea, life itself is only a long day,
And death arrives like sundown. Lo, the sun
Lies down i' the waters, and the murky moon
Out of the east sails sullen. 'T is the hour
Of fear and melancholy, when the soul
Hangs poised, with folded wings, 'tween day and night.

From JEPHTHAH'S DAUGHTER

Oh, think how hard it is to die when young!
To leave the light; to leave the sun and moon;
To leave the earth, and glory of the heavens;
To see no more your countenance, nor my mother's;
To lie enlocked within the stony ground,
Deaf, blind, to all forgetful . . .
But soothe, support me; with your words console;
So shall the memory of my latest hour
Prove grateful to you when I am no more.

"No more, no more." Still that recurring phrase
Tolls in my set discourse, a funeral knell.
Now is the burden of it all "No more."
No more shall, wandering, we go gather flowers,
Nor tune our voices by the river's brink,
Nor in the grotto fountain cool our limbs,
Nor, walking in the winter, woo the sun.

THE STARS ARE GLITTERING IN THE FROSTY SKY

The stars are glittering in the frosty sky,
Frequent as pebbles on a broad sea-coast;
And o'er the vault the cloud-like galaxy
Has marshalled its innumerable host.
Alive all heaven seems! with wondrous glow
Tenfold refulgent every star appears,
As if some wide, celestial gale did blow,
And thrice illume the ever-kindled spheres.
Orbs, with glad orbs rejoicing, burning, beam,
Ray-crowned, with lambent lustre in their zones,
Till o'er the blue, bespangled spaces seem
Angels and great archangels on their thrones;
A host divine, whose eyes are sparkling gems,
And forms more bright than diamond diadems.

HOW GREAT UNTO THE LIVING SEEM THE DEAD!

How great unto the living seem the dead!
How sacred, solemn; how heroic grown;
How vast and vague, as they obscurely tread
The shadowy confines of the dim unknown!—
For they have met the monster that we dread,
Have learned the secret not to mortal shown.
E'en as gigantic shadows on the wall
The spirit of the daunted child amaze,
So on us thoughts of the departed fall,
And with phantasma fill our gloomy gaze.
Awe and deep wonder lend the living lines,
And hope and ecstasy the borrowed beams;
While fitful fancy the full form divines,
And all is what imagination dreams.

SIR JOHN H. HAGARTY [1816-1900]

Sir John Hawkins Hagarty was a native of Dublin, the son of Matthew Hagarty. He came to Canada in 1835, before finishing his course at Trinity College, Dublin, and settled in Toronto. Called to the bar in 1840, he rose in the legal profession till he became chief justice of Ontario. He wrote occasional poems and one narrative poem, *A Legend of Marathon* (1888). (Cf. Nicholas Flood Davin (1843-1901), *The Irishman in Canada* (1877).)

FUNERAL OF NAPOLEON I

Cold and brilliant streams the sunlight on the wintry banks of
Seine;
Gloriously the imperial city rears her pride of tower and fane;
Solemnly with deep voice pealeth Notre Dame, thine ancient
chime;
Minute-guns the death-bell answer in the same deep, measured
time.

On the unwonted stillness gather sounds of an advancing host,
As the rising tempest chafeth on St. Helen's far-off coast;
Nearer rolls a mighty pageant, clearer swells the funeral strain;
From the barrier arch of Neuilly pours the giant burial train.

Dark with eagles is the sunlight, darkly on the golden air
Flap the folds of faded standards, eloquently mourning there;
O'er the pomp of glittering thousands, like a battle-phantom flits
Tatter'd flag of Jena, Friedland, Arcola, and Austerlitz.

Eagle-crown'd and garland-circled, slowly moves the stately car
'Mid a sea of plumes and horsemen, all the burial pomp of war.
Riderless, a war-worn charger follows his dead master's bier;
Long since battle-trumpet roused him, he but lived to follow here.

From his grave 'mid Ocean's dirges, moaning surge and sparkling
foam,
Lo, the Imperial Dead returneth! lo, the Hero dust comes home!
He hath left the Atlantic island, lonely vale and willow-tree,
'Neath the Invalides to slumber, 'mid the Gallic chivalry.

Glorious tomb o'er glorious sleepers! gallant fellowship to share—
Paladin and peer and marshal—France, thy noblest dust is there!
Names that light thy battle annals, names that shook the heart of
earth!
Stars in crimson War's horizon—synonyms for martial worth!

Room within that shrine of heroes! place, pale spectres of the past!
Homage yield, ye battle-phantoms. Lo, your mightiest comes at last!
Was his course the Woe out-thunder'd from prophetic trumpet's lips?
Was his type the ghostly horseman shadow'd in the Apocalypse?

Grey-hair'd soldiers gather round him, relics of an age of war,
Followers of the Victor-Eagle, when his flight was wild and far.
Men who panted in the death-strife on Rodrigo's bloody ridge,
Hearts that sicken'd at the death-shriek from the Russian's shatter'd bridge;

Men who heard the immortal war-cry of the wild Egyptian fight—
"Forty centuries o'erlook us from yon Pyramid's grey height!"
They who heard the moans of Jaffa, and the breach of Acre knew,
They who rushed their foaming war-steeds on the squares of Waterloo;

They who loved him, they who fear'd him, they who in his dark hour fled,
Round the mighty burial gather, spellbound by the awful Dead!
Churchmen, princes, statesmen, warriors, all a kingdom's chief array,
And the Fox stands, crownèd mourner, by the Eagle's hero clay!

But the last high rite is paid him, and the last deep knell is rung,
And the cannons' iron voices have their thunder-requiem sung;
And, 'mid banners idly drooping, silent gloom and mouldering state,
Shall the trampler of the world upon the Judgment-trumpet wait.

Yet his ancient foes had given him nobler monumental pile,
Where the everlasting dirges moan'd around the burial isle;
Pyramid upheaved by Ocean in his loneliest wilds afar,
For the War-King thunder-stricken from his fiery battle-car!

ALEXANDER McLACHLAN [1818-1896]

Alexander McLachlan, son of Charles and Jane (Sutherland) McLachlan, was born at Johnstone, Renfrewshire, Scotland. After a rather rudimentary education, he learned the tailor's trade in Glasgow. He came to Ontario in 1840 and made several unsuccessful attempts at farming before settling on a one-acre lot at Erin, where he lived for twenty-five years. He then lived on his farm at Amaranth until, shortly before his death, he went to live with a daughter at Orangeville. During his lifetime he published five volumes of poems, and after his death appeared *The Poetical Works of Alexander McLachlan* (1900), with a Biographical Sketch by Rev. Edward Hartley Dewart (1828-1903). (Cf. also *Canadian Who was Who*, vol. 2 (1938).)

From TO AN INDIAN SKULL

And art thou come to this at last,
Great Sachem of the forest vast!
E'en thou who wert so tall in stature,
And modelled in the pride of Nature;
High as the deer you bore your head;
Swift as the roebuck was thy tread;
Thine eye, bright as the orb of day—
In battle a consuming ray!
Tradition links thy name with fear,
And strong men hold their breath to hear
What mighty feats by thee were done—
The battles by thy strong arm won!
The glory of thy tribe wert thou—
But—where is all thy glory now?

. . .

What tho' a wild rude life was thine,
Thou still hadst gleams of the divine—
A sense of something undefined—
A Presence—an Almighty mind,
Which guides the planets, rocks the sea,
And through the desert guided thee.
The dark woods, all around thee spread;
The leafy curtain overhead;
The great old thunder-stricken pine,
And the cathedral elms divine;
The dismal swamp, the hemlock hoar;
Niagara's everlasting roar;
The viewless winds which rushed to wake
The spirit of Ontario's lake;
Did not its mighty anthems roll
Through all the caverns of thy soul,
And thrill thee with a sense sublime,
With gleams of that eternal clime
Which stretches over Death and Time?
And oft, like me, thou'dst ask to know,
"Whence came we, whither do we go?"
A marvel, ah, poor soul! to thee,
As it has ever been to me.

From the unknown, we issued out,
With mystery compassed round about;
Each with his burden on his back,
To follow in the destined track,
With weary feet, to toil and plod
Through nature, back to nature's God . . .

From A BACKWOODS HERO

Where yonder ancient willow weeps,
The father of the village sleeps;
Tho' but of humble birth,
As rare a specimen was he,
Of Nature's true nobility,
As ever trod the earth . . .
He sought not fame, nor did he e'er
Find fault with his too narrow sphere,
Tho' many a body said
"He was the man who should be sent
To rule our rabble Parliament,—
It wanted such a head."
And here he ruled, and here he reigned,
And no man lost by what he gained;
And here he lies at rest!
And may his mem'ry never fade,
And may the turf upon him laid,
Lie lightly on his breast!

From WOMAN

When my gloomy hour comes on me,
And I shun the face of man,
Finding bitterness in all things,
As vex'd spirits only can:

When of all the world I'm weary,
Then some gentle woman's face,
Coming like a blessed vision,
Reconciles me to our race.

All the children of affliction,
All the weary and oppress'd,
Flee to thee, beloved woman,
Finding shelter in thy breast.

While we follow mad ambition,
Thine is far the nobler part;
Nursing flowers of sweet affection
In the valleys of the heart . . .

From GOD

Hail, Thou great mysterious Being!
Thou the unseen, yet All-seeing,
  To Thee we call.
How can a mortal sing Thy praise,
Or speak of all Thy wondrous ways?
  God over all.

God of the great old solemn woods,
God of the desert solitudes
  And trackless sea;
God of the crowded city vast,
God of the present and the past,
  Can man know Thee?

God of the blue vault overhead,
Of the green earth on which we tread,
  Of time and space;
God of the worlds which Time conceals,
God of the worlds which Death reveals
  To all our race. . . .

CHARLES SANGSTER [1822-1893]

Charles Sangster, born at Kingston, Ontario, had only a common-school education. From 1838 to 1849 he worked in the ordnance office in his home city. He then joined the staff of the Kingston *Whig*, almost from the first as sub-editor, and remained till 1861. From 1867 on he was in the Civil Service. He published two volumes of poetry, largely on Canadian themes, *The St. Lawrence and the Saguenay and Other Poems* (1850) and *Hesperus and Other Poems and Lyrics* (1860). (Cf. *Canadian Who was Who*, vol. 2 (1938). *Leading Canadian Poets*, ed. by W. P. Percival (1948), and *Five Canadian Poets* (1954), by Arthur S. Bourinot.)

THE RAPID

All peacefully gliding,
The waters dividing,
The indolent batteau moved slowly along,
The rowers, light-hearted,
From sorrow long parted,
Beguiled the dull moments with laughter and song;
"Hurrah for the rapid! that merrily, merrily
Gambols and leaps on its tortuous way;
Soon we will enter it, cheerily, cheerily,
Pleased with its freshness, and wet with its spray."

More swiftly careering,
The wild rapid nearing,
They dash down the stream like a terrified steed;
The surges delight them,
No terrors affright them,
Their voices keep pace with the quickening speed;
"Hurrah for the rapid! that merrily, merrily
Shivers its arrows against us in play;
Now we have entered it, cheerily, cheerily,
Our spirits as light as its feathery spray."

Fast downward they're dashing,
Each fearless eye flashing,
Though danger awaits them on every side;
Yon rock—see it frowning!
They strike—they are drowning!
But downward they speed with the merciless tide;
No voice cheers the rapid, that angrily, angrily
Shivers their bark in its maddening play;
Gaily they entered it—heedlessly, recklessly,
Mingling their lives with its treacherous spray!

EVENING

One solitary bird melodiously
Trilled its sweet vesper from a grove of elm,
One solitary sail upon the sea
Rested, unmindful of its potent helm.

And down behind the forest trees the sun,
Arrayed in burning splendours, slowly rolled,
Like to some sacrificial urn, o'errun
With flaming hues of crimson, blue and gold.

The fisher ceased his song, hung on his oars,
Pausing to look, a pulse in every breath,
And, in imagination, saw the shores
Elysian, rising o'er the realms of Death.

And down on tiptoe came the gradual night,
A gentle twilight first, with silver wings,
And still from out the darkening infinite
Came shadowy forms, like day's imaginings.

There was no light in all the brooding air,
  There was no darkness yet to blind the eyes,
But through the space interminable, there
  Nature and Silence passed in solemn guise.

THE RED MEN

My footsteps press where, centuries ago,
  The Red Men fought and conquered; lost and won.
Whole tribes and races, gone like last year's snow,
  Have found the Eternal Hunting-Grounds, and run
The fiery gauntlet of their active days,
  Till few are left to tell the mournful tale!
And these inspire us with such wild amaze
  They seem like spectres passing down a vale
Steeped in uncertain moonlight, on their way
Towards some bourne where darkness blinds the day,
  And night is wrapped in mystery profound.
We cannot lift the mantle of the past:
  We seem to wander over hallowed ground:
We scan the trail of Thought, but all is overcast.

THOMAS D'ARCY McGEE [1825-1868]

Thomas D'Arcy McGee, son of James and Dorcas Catherine (Morgan) McGee, was born at Carlingford, Ireland. Before coming to Montreal, he had worked for, edited, and founded periodicals successively in Boston, Dublin, New York, Boston again, and Buffalo. He founded the *New Era* in Montreal in 1857, the year of his arrival there. He represented Montreal West in the Legislative Assembly of Canada from 1858 to Confederation (of which he was one of the Fathers), and was elected to represent that constituency in the first Canadian House of Commons. His prose works deal with Irish history and affairs, particularly in relation to the United States and Canada, and with Canadian affairs, especially Confederation. His poetry is found in two volumes, *Canadian Ballads and Occasional Verses* (1858) and *The Poems of Thomas D'Arcy McGee* (1869), the latter collected and edited, with a biographical introduction, by Mrs. Mary Anne (Madden) Sadlier (1820-1903), whose husband, James Sadlier, died in the year in which the poems were published. (Cf. John Fennings Taylor (1817-1882), *Thomas D'Arcy McGee, Sketch of his Life and Death* (1868); Isabel Skelton, *The Life of Thomas D'Arcy McGee* (1925); Alexander Brady (1896-), *Life of Thomas D'Arcy McGee* (1925); Josephine Phelan, *The Ardent Exile* (1951).)

JACQUES CARTIER

In the seaport of Saint Malo 'twas a smiling morn in May,
When the Commodore Jacques Cartier to the westward sailed away;
In the crowded old Cathedral all the town were on their knees
For the safe return of kinsmen from the undiscovered seas;
And every autumn blast that swept o'er pinnacle and pier
Filled manly hearts with sorrow, and gentle hearts with fear.

A year passed o'er Saint Malo—again came round the day,
When the Commodore Jacques Cartier to the westward sailed away;
But no tidings from the absent had come the way they went,
And tearful were the vigils that many a maiden spent;
And manly hearts were filled with gloom, and gentle hearts with fear,
When no tidings came from Cartier at the closing of the year.

But the earth is as the Future, it hath its hidden side,
And the Captain of Saint Malo was rejoicing in his pride
In the forests of the North—while his townsmen mourned his loss,
He was rearing on Mount-Royal the fleur-de-lis and cross;
And when two months were over and added to the year,
Saint Malo hailed him home again, cheer answering to cheer.

He told them of a region, hard, ironbound, and cold,
Where no seas of pearl abounded, nor mines of shining gold,
Where the wind from Thulé freezes the word upon the lip,
And the ice in spring comes sailing athwart the early ship;
He told them of the frozen scene until they thrill'd with fear,
And piled fresh fuel on the hearth to make them better cheer.

But when he changed the strain—he told how soon are cast
In early Spring the fetters that hold the waters fast;
How the Winter causeway broken is drifted out to sea,
And rills and rivers sing with pride the anthem of the free;
How the magic wand of Summer clad the landscape to his eyes,
Like the dry bones of the just when they wake in Paradise.

He told them of the Algonquin braves—the hunters of the wild;
Of how the Indian mother in the forest rocks her child;
Of how, poor souls, they fancy in every living thing
A spirit good or evil, that claims their worshipping;
Of how they brought their sick and maim'd for him to breathe upon,
And of the wonders wrought for them through the Gospel of
St. John.

He told them of the river, whose mighty current gave
Its freshness for a hundred leagues to ocean's briny wave;
He told them of the glorious scene presented to his sight,
What time he reared the cross and crown on Hochelaga's height,
And of the fortress cliff that keeps of Canada the key,
And they welcomed back Jacques Cartier from his perils o'er the sea.

JOHN HUNTER-DUVAR [1830-1899]

John Hunter-Duvar, known as "the Bard of Hernewood," from his estate at Fortune Cove, Alberton, Prince Edward Island, was born in Scotland and spent most of his life in the Maritime Provinces of Canada, in army service and, from 1879 to 1889, as federal inspector of fisheries for Prince Edward Island. He then retired to Hernewood. In prose he published *Stone, Bronze, and Iron Ages* (1892). In verse he wrote narrative poems and closet dramas: *The Enamorado: A Drama* (1879); *De Roberval: A Drama* (1888); with which were printed two mock-heroic narrative poems, *The Emigration of the Fairies* (who land on "Epaygooyat," that is, "Abegweit," Micmac name of Prince Edward Island) and *The Triumph of Constancy; Annals of the Court of Oberon* (1895). His also is *John a'Var: His Lais*, privately printed lyrics.

From DE ROBERVAL

ROBERVAL (*at Quebec*):

Here, then, we stand on the Canadian shore,
My foot the first; this steep-walled promontory—
The key by land and sea to Canada— . . .
And all the natural features of the scene
Excel description with reality. . . .

ROBERVAL (*at Niagara*):

This wall of falling waters to the eye
Itself a miracle, but when conjoined
With this incessant slumberous monotone
That causes heart and ear alike to throb,
Addressing ear and eye alike, it reads
The occult riddle, how, in former times,
The very God came down and talked with men.

What can the hearer do but reverent say
This is the voice of God. The resonant rocks
And caverns echo it. Above the flume
And all along the stately rocking shore
The aged forests that, like sentinels
With their gaunt shadows dim and tenebrous
Shut in the world's wonder, echo it,
While leagues away, through all the sylvan shades,
Outborne by the vibrating earth and air,
The cause unseen, the deep-toned murmur sounds
Like rolling of the Almighty's chariot wheels.
Nature's grand pæan to that Nature's God,
Throughout the ages an unresting hymn. . . .

OHNAWA ("Swift Brook"), *an Iroquois maiden:*

The Great Spirit,
Master of Life, is good; He sends the rain
And sun that makes the yellow corn to grow,
And, when the ice breaks up, makes fish to swim,
And game return at time of opening leaves.
We are the creatures of His unseen hand.
Our God has never died, but lives. We hear
His whispered orders speaking in our hearts,
And, though he knows, to show we reverence him
We cast shells in the streams and burn sweet weeds;
In war our warriors offer sacrifice.
He loves the Red Men. When the lamp goes out
From forth our bodies, if we do His will
He will relight the light of life again,
And lead us to the happier hunting woods.

ROBERVAL (*leaving Quebec*):

Fair scene! a lingering and a latest look,
Although it needs me not to count or scan
To stamp the features on my memory.
This is the land where I had hoped to live,
And where I would have no regret to die.
A touch of tenderness, a clasp of grief,
Fingers the inner tendrils of my heart . . .
France needs my aid as mother needs her child's,
Yet not the less it touches me. My foot,
As 'twas the first, shall be the last to press
This wild and noble shore. A fond farewell!

From THE EMIGRATION OF THE FAIRIES

First halt. They heard within a sugar patch
The rhyming tic-a-tac of axes chopping,
So scouts were sent ahead to try to catch
A glimpse of whom or what 'twas caused the lopping,
And bring back a description of the natives—
If they were cannibals, or friends, or caitiffs.

The scouts returned, and said where they had stole
They'd seen a score or so of stalwart creatures
In flannel shirts, not smock frocks; on the whole
They rather liked their friendly bearded features,
And that the first glance of these live Canadians
Impressed them favourably—(they were Acadians).

THEODORE HARDING RAND [1835-1900]

Theodore Harding Rand, the son of Thomas Woodworth and Eliza Irene (Barnaby) Rand, was born at Canard, Nova Scotia, and educated at Acadia University. He taught at the Normal School, Truro, from 1860 to 1864, was Superintendent of Education for Nova Scotia from 1864 to 1870 and for New Brunswick from 1871 to 1883, taught at Acadia University from 1883 to 1885 and at McMaster from 1885 to 1895, from 1891 as Chancellor. He edited *A Treasury of Canadian Verse* (1900), and published *At Minas Basin and Other Poems* (1897), and *Song Waves and Other Poems* (1900). (Cf. *Canadian Who was Who*, vol. 1 (1934).)

THE DRAGONFLY

I

Winged wonder of motion
In splendour of sheen,
Cruising the shining blue
Waters all day,
Smit with hunger of heart
And seized of a quest
Which nor beauty of flower
Nor promise of rest
Has charm to appease
Or slacken or stay,—
  What is it you seek,
  Unopen, unseen?

II

Are you blind to the sight
Of the heavens of blue,
Or the wing-fretted clouds
On their white, airy wings,
Or the emerald grass
That velvets the lawn,
Or glory of meadows
Aflame like the dawn?
  Are you deaf to the note
  In the woodland that rings
  With the song of the whitethroat,
  As crystal as dew?

III

Winged wonder of motion
In splendour of sheen,
Stay, stay a brief moment
Thy hither and thither
Quick-beating wings,
Thy flashes of flight;
And tell me thy heart;
Is it sad, is it light,
Is it pulsing with fears
Which scorch it and wither,
  Or joys that up-well
  In a girdle of green?

IV

"O breather of words
And poet of life,
I tremble with joy,
I flutter with fear!
Ages it seemeth,
Yet only today
Into this world of
Gold sunbeams at play,
I came from the deeps.
  O crystalline sphere!
  O beauteous light!
  O glory of life!

V

"On the watery floor
Of this sibilant lake,
I lived in the twilight dim.
'There's a world of Day,'
Some pled, 'a world
Of ether and wings athrob
Close over our head.'
'It's a dream, it's a whim,
A whisper of reeds,' they said,—
And anon the waters would sob.
And ever the going
Went on to the dead
Without the glint of a ray,
  And the watchers watched
  In their vanishing wake.

VI

"The passing
Passed for aye,
And the waiting
Waited in vain!
Some power seemed to enfold
The tremulous waters around,
Yet never in heat
Nor in shrivelling cold,
Nor darkness deep or grey,—
Came token of sound or touch,—
A clear unquestioned 'Yea!'
  And the scoffers scoffed,
  In swelling refrain,
  'Let us eat and drink,
  For tomorrow we die.'

VII

"But, O, in a trance of bliss,
With gauzy wings I awoke!
An ecstasy bore me away
O'er field and meadow and plain.
  I thought not of recent pain,
  But revelled, as splendours broke
  For sun and cloud and air,
  In the eye of golden Day.

VIII

"I'm yearning to break
To my fellows below
The secret of ages hoar;
In the quick-flashing light
I dart up and down,
Forth and back, everywhere;
But the waters are sealed
Like a pavement of glass,—
Sealed that I may not pass.
  O for waters of air!
  Or the wing of an eagle's might
  To cleave a pathway below!"

IX

And the Dragonfly in splendour
Cruises ever o'er the lake,
Holding in his heart a secret
Which in vain he seeks to break.

JUNE

Now weave the winds to music of June's lyre
Their bowers of cloud whence odorous blooms are flung
Far down the dells and cedarn vales among,—
See, lowly plains, sky-touched, to heaven aspire!
Now flash the golden robin's plumes with fire,
The bobolink is bubbling o'er with song,
And leafy trees, Aeolian harps new-strung,
Murmur far notes blown from some starry choir.

My heart thrills like the wilding sap to flowers,
And leaps as a swollen brook in summer rain
Past meadows green to the great sea untold.
O month divine, all fresh with falling showers,
Waft, waft from open heaven thy balm for pain,
Life and sweet earth are young, God grows not old!

THE LOON

'Neath northern skies thou hid'st thy punctual nest
By crystal waters in their lonely play,
Meeting the challenge with which instant day
And night thy chariness and courage test.

Half bird, half spirit!—O elusive quest
That thinks thy dappled mould but common clay!
Thou wak'st with demon laughter Ha Ha Bay,
Art soul of solitariness, unblest.

Flash of pure wildness on dusk Saguenay,
Awareness of wild nature's subtle breast,
Freight and athrill with weirdsome life, yet gay,
Thou cleav'st the deluge dense, a wingèd jest!—
That rallying mock and jeer's an impish mark—
The echo of thy flout of Noah's ark!

AGNES MAULE MACHAR [1837-1927]

Agnes Maule Machar, who sometimes used the pen name "Fidelis," was the daughter of Rev. John Machar, Principal of Queen's University from 1846 to 1854, and she was born, educated, and spent her life in Kingston. She did some work in collaboration, published historical material and several novels, and wrote a book of verse, *Lays of the True North* (1899, 1902). (Cf. *Canadian Who was Who*, vol. 1 (1934).)

UNTRODDEN WAYS

Where close the curving mountains drew,
To clasp the stream in their embrace,
With every outline, shade and hue
Reflected in its placid face,

The ploughman stops his team to watch
The train, as swift it thunders by;
Some distant glimpse of life to catch,
He strains his eager, wistful eye.

His waiting horses patient stand
With wonder in their gentle eyes,
As through the tranquil mountain land
The snorting engine onward flies.

The morning freshness is on him,
Just wakened from his balmy dreams;
The wayfarers, all soiled and dim,
Think longingly of mountain streams.

Oh, for the joyous mountain air,
The long, delightful autumn day
Among the hills!—the ploughman there
Must have perpetual holiday!

And he, as all day long he guides
His steady plough with patient hand,
Thinks of the train that onward glides
Into some new enchanted land,

Where, day by day, no plodding round
Wearies the frame and dulls the mind,
Where life thrills keen to sight and sound,
With ploughs and furrows left behind!

CHARLES MAIR [1838-1927]

Charles Mair, the son of James and Margaret (Holmes) Mair, was born at Lanark, Ontario. He attended Queen's University and then entered the field of journalism. He was one of the originators of the "Canada First" movement, experienced both Riel rebellions, spent most of his life, from 1870 on, in the prairie Provinces and British Columbia, part of the time in the Canadian civil service (in Winnipeg and Lethbridge). He wrote some prose, but will be remembered chiefly for his *Dreamland and Other Poems* (1868), and *Tecumseh, a Drama* (1886, 1901). (Cf. *Master Works of Canadian Authors*, vol. xiv (1926); *Canadian Who was Who*, vol. 1 (1934).)

From TECUMSEH

[*Act IV. Scene vi*]

SIR ISAAC BROCK:
Tell me more of those unrivalled wastes
You and Tecumseh visited.

LEFROY: We left
The silent forest, and, day after day,
Great prairies swept beyond our aching sight
Into the measureless West; uncharted realms,
Voiceless and calm, save when tempestuous wind
Rolled the rank herbage into billows vast,
And rushing tides which never found a shore.
And tender clouds, and veils of morning mist,
Cast flying shadows, chased by flying light,
Into interminable wildernesses,
Flushed with fresh blooms, deep perfumed by the rose,
And murmurous with flower-fed bird and bee.
The deep-grooved bison-paths like furrows lay,
Turned by the cloven hoofs of thundering herds
Primeval, and still travelled as of yore.

And gloomy valleys opened at our feet—
Shagged with dusk cypresses and hoary pine;
And sunless gorges, rummaged by the wolf,
Which through long reaches of the prairie wound,
Then melted slowly into upland vales,
Lingering far-stretched among the spreading hills.

BROCK:

What charming solitudes! And life was there!

LEFROY:

Yes, life was there! inexplicable life,
Still wasted by inexorable death.
There had the stately stag his battle-field—
Dying for mastery among his hinds.
There vainly sprung the affrighted antelope,
Beset by glittering eyes and hurrying feet.
The dancing grouse, at their insensate sport,
Heard not the footstep of the fox;
The gopher on his little earthwork stood,
With folded arms, unconscious of the fate
That wheeled in narrowing circles overhead;
And the poor mouse, on heedless nibbling bent,
Marked not the silent coiling of the snake.
At length we heard a deep and solemn sound—
Erupted moanings of the troubled earth
Trembling beneath innumerable feet.
A growing uproar blending in our ears,
With noise tumultuous as ocean's surge,
Of bellowings, fierce breath and battle shock,
And ardour of unconquerable herds.
A multitude whose trampling shook the plains
With discord of harsh sound and rumblings deep,
As if the swift-revolving earth had struck,
And from some adamantine peak recoiled,
Jarring. At length we topped a high-browed hill—
The last and loftiest of a file of such—
And lo! before us lay the tameless stock,
Slow wending to the northward like a cloud!
A multitude in motion, dark and dense—
Far as the eye could reach, and farther still,
In countless myriads stretched for many a league.

BROCK:

You fire me with the picture! What a scene!

LEFROY:

Nation on nation was envillaged there,
Skirting the banks of that imbanded host;
With chieftains of strange speech and port of war,
Who, battle-armed, in weather-brawny bulk,
Roamed fierce and free in huge and wild content.
These gave Tecumseh greetings fair and kind,
Knowing the purpose havened in his soul.
And he, too, joined the chase as few men dare;
For I have seen him leaping from his horse,
Mount a careering bull in foaming flight,
Urge it to fury o'er its burden strange,
Yet cling tenacious with a grip of steel,
Then by a knife-plunge, fetch it to its knees
In mid career, and pangs of speedy death.

BROCK:

You rave, Lefroy! or saw this in a dream.

LEFROY:

No, no; 'tis true—I saw him do it, Brock!
Then would he seek the old, and with his spoils
Restore them to the bounty of their youth,
Cheering the crippled lodge with plenteous feasts,
And warmth of glossy robes, as soft as down,
Till withered cheeks ran o'er with feeble smiles,
And tongues long silent babbled of their prime.

BROCK:

This warrior's fabric is of perfect parts!
A worthy champion of his race—he heaps
Such giant obligations on our heads
As shall outweigh repayment. It is late,
And rest must preface war's hot work tomorrow,
Else would I talk till morn. How still the night!
Here Peace has let her silvery tresses down,
And falls asleep beside the lapping wave.

From DREAMLAND

We are not wholly blest who use the earth,
Nor wholly wretched who inherit Sleep.
Behold, it is a palace of delight
Built beyond fear of storms by day or night;
And whoso enters doth his station keep
Unmindful of the stain upon his birth.

Sin hath no hold on it; yea, men may take
Their loves into their arms tenaciously.
For Sleep is as a chamber high and fair,
Wherein warm love makes light of cold despair;
Where wives may deem their faithless lords are nigh,
And maids may kiss false lovers for love's sake.

Thou canst not fetter it, for it is free;
No tyrant yokes it to the labouring oar.
It is a solemn region visited
By mystic radiance when the sun is fled;
Where Labour bends his aching brows no more,
And men have peace, and slaves have liberty.

See now it hath a tender bloom, like light
Viewed at the Autumn's latest outgoing.
It is the Summer of our daily sorrow,
The solstice sweet whose Winter is the morrow.
And, now, 'tis like the firstlings of the Spring,
Which win their fragrance in the snow's despite.

Faint, far-off sounds are blown unto our ears,
Faint, far-off savours steal unto our lips,
When orient dreams assemble, manifold,
Where Sleep hath throned himself on royal gold,
Then night is noontide, morning an eclipse
Where oft no comfort is but in our tears.

So man may say not to himself, "Time fills
Its even measures with matched bitterness,"
Whilst he hath sleep, a jewel without peer,
Set in the light which is its bezel here;
Whilst fall athwart the days the hours which bless,
Wherein strong forces strive with human ills.

For, though unequal with the unseen Powers,
We—who eat bread and suffer strange decay—
Yet scale their universe in dreams which make,
Mid adverse things, a heaven for our sake,
And find, beyond the precincts of the day,
The gates of an elysium which is ours.

GEORGE THOMAS LANIGAN [1846-1886]

George Thomas Lanigan, born at Three Rivers, Quebec, early abandoned telegraphy for journalism and by 1869 was Editor-in-Chief of the Montreal *Star*. In the United States he did newspaper work in Chicago, New York, Rochester and Philadelphia. In prose he published a book of fables, in verse, under the pen name "Allid," *National Ballads of Canada, Imitated and Translated from the Originals* (1865).

THE AHKOOND OF SWAT

"The Ahkoond of Swat is dead."—*Press Dispatch*

What, what, what,
What's the news from Swat?
  Sad news,
  Bad news,
Comes by the cable led
Through the Indian Ocean's bed,
Through the Persian Gulf, the Red
Sea and the Med-
Iterranean—he's dead;
The Ahkoond is dead!

For the Ahkoond I mourn.
  Who wouldn't?
He strove to disregard the message stern,
  But he Ahkoondn't.

Dead, dead, dead;
  Sorrow, Swats!
Swats wha' hae wi' Ahkoond bled,
Swats whom we had often led
Onward to a gory bed,
  Or to victory,
  As the case might be.
  Sorrow, Swats!
Tears shed,
  Shed tears like water,
Your great Ahkoond is dead!
  That Swat's the matter!

Mourn, city of Swat!
Your great Ahkoond is not,
But lain 'mid worms to rot:
His mortal part alone, his soul was caught
(Because he was a good Ahkoond)
Up to the bosom of Mahound.
Though earthly walls his frame surround
(For ever hallowed be the ground!)
And sceptics mock the lowly mound
And say, "He's now of no Ahkound!"
(His soul is in the skies!)
The azure skies that bend above his loved
Metropolis of Swat
He sees with larger, other eyes,
Athwart all earthly mysteries—
He knows what's Swat.

Let Swat bury the great Ahkoond
With a noise of mourning and of lamentation!
Let Swat bury the great Ahkoond
With the noise of the mourning of the Swattish nation!

Fallen is at length
Its tower of strength,
Its sun had dimmed ere it had nooned:
Dead lies the great Ahkoond.
The great Ahkoond of Swat
Is not.

EDWARD WILLIAM THOMSON [1849-1924]

Edward William Thomson was born in Toronto Township, the son of William and Margaret Hamilton (Foley) Thomson. He was educated at Caledonia and Brantford public schools and at Trinity College School, Weston, Ontario. He participated in the last years of the American Civil War and in the suppression of the Fenians in Canada. Then he followed surveying and civil engineering till he took up journalism in 1878. From 1879 to 1891 he was chief editorial writer of the Toronto *Globe*. From then till 1901 he was literary editor of the *Youth's Companion*, Boston, and a writer of short stories. Next came twenty years as Ottawa correspondent of the Boston *Transcript* and free-lance writing. After that he lived in Boston. His books of poetry are *When Lincoln Died and Other Poems* (1909), and *The Many-Mansioned House and Other Poems* (1909). (Cf. *Who was Who in America.*)

THE CANADIAN ROSSIGNOL

When furrowed fields of shaded brown,
  And emerald meadows spread between,
And belfries towering from the town,
  All blent in wavering mists are seen;
When quickening woods with freshening hue
  Along Mount Royal rolling swell,
When winds caress and May is new,
  Oh, then my shy bird sings so well!

Because the blood-roots flock so white,
  And blossoms scent the wooing air,
And mounds with trillium flags are dight,
  And dells with violets frail and rare;
Because such velvet leaves unclose,
  And new-born rills all chiming ring,
And blue the sun-kissed river flows,
  My timid bird is forced to sing.

A joyful flourish lilted clear,
  Four notes, then falls the frolic song,
And memories of a sweeter year
  The wistful cadences prolong:—
"A sweeter year—Oh heart too sore!—
  I cannot sing!"—Thus ends the lay.
Long silence. Then awakes once more
  His song, ecstatic with the May.

ARTHUR WENTWORTH HAMILTON EATON [1849-1937]

Arthur Wentworth Hamilton Eaton was born at Kentville, Nova Scotia, the son of William and Anna A. W. (Hamilton) Eaton, both of Puritan stock. He was educated at Dalhousie and Harvard universities. Ordained to the priesthood of the Protestant Episcopal Church, he served for a short time the parish of Chestnut Hill, Boston, and then that of New York till he retired in 1907 and took up residence in Boston, where he had a coterie of literary friends, as he had formerly had in New York. His prose works include books on theology and history, ecclesiastical and secular. His books of poetry are *Acadian Legends and Lyrics* (1889), *Acadian Ballads* (1905), *Poems of the Christian Year* (1905), *The Lotus of the Nile* (1907). (Cf. *Who was Who in America.*)

THE PHANTOM LIGHT OF THE BAIE DES CHALEURS

'Tis the laughter of pines that swing and sway
Where the breeze from the land meets the breeze from the bay;
'Tis the silvery foam of the silver tide
In ripples that reach to the forest side;
'Tis the fisherman's boat, in a track of sheen,
Plying through tangled seaweed green
O'er the Baie des Chaleurs.

Who has not heard of the phantom light
That over the moaning waves, at night,
Dances and drifts in endless play,
Close to the shore, then far away,
Fierce as the flame in sunset skies,
Cold as the winter light that lies
On the Baie des Chaleurs?

They tell us that many a year ago,
From lands where the palm and the olive grow,
Where vines with their purple clusters creep
Over the hillsides grey and steep,
A knight in his doublet, slashed with gold,
Famed, in that chivalrous time of old,
For valorous deeds and courage rare,
Sailed with a princess wondrous fair
To the Baie des Chaleurs;

That a pirate crew from some isle of the sea,
A murderous band as e'er could be,
With a shadowy sail, and a flag of night,
That flaunted and flew in heaven's sight,
Sailed in the wake of the lovers there,
And sank the ship and its freight so fair
In the Baie des Chaleurs.

Strange is the tale that the fishermen tell!
They say that a ball of fire fell
Straight from the sky, with crash and roar,
Lighting the bay from shore to shore;
Then the ship, with a shudder and groan,
Sank through the waves to the caverns lone
Of the Baie des Chaleurs.

That was the last of the pirate crew;
But many a night a black flag flew
From the mast of a spectre vessel, sailed
By a spectre band that wept and wailed
For the wreck they had wrought on the sea, on the land,
For the innocent blood they had spilt on the sand
  Of the Baie des Chaleurs.

This is the tale of the phantom light
That fills the mariner's heart, at night,
With dread as it gleams o'er his path on the bay,
Now by the shore, then far away,
Fierce as the flame in sunset skies,
Cold as the winter moon that lies
  On the Baie des Chaleurs.

ISABELLA VALANCY CRAWFORD [1850-1887]

Isabella Valancy Crawford, the daughter of cultured parents, Dr. Stephen Dennis and Sydney (Scott) Crawford, was born in Dublin, Ireland. While the father visited Australia in 1857 to consider the possibility of settling there, seven of his children died. In 1858 the family came to Ontario and lived successively at Paisley (1858-1864, during which period two more children died), Lakefield, Peterborough, and, after the father's death in 1875, in Toronto. There, to support herself and her mother, Isabella wrote indefatigably till her death from heart failure. She published verse and stories in newspapers and one volume, *Old Spookses' Pass, Malcolm's Katie, and Other Poems* (1884). The posthumous volume *Collected Poems* (1905), edited by John William Garvin (1859-1935), contains an introduction by Ethelwyn Wetherald (1857-1940). (Cf. Katherine Hale (Mrs. J. W. Garvin), *Isabella Valancy Crawford* (1923) and *Canadian Who was Who,* vol. 2 (1938).)

LOVE'S LAND

Oh, Love builds on the azure sea,
  And Love builds on the golden sand,
And Love builds on the rose-winged cloud,
  And sometimes Love builds on the land!

Oh, if Love build on sparkling sea,
  And if Love build on golden strand,
And if Love build on rosy cloud,
  To Love these are the solid land!

Oh, Love will build his lily walls,
  And Love his pearly roof will rear,
On cloud, or land, or mist, or sea—
  Love's solid land is everywhere!

LAUGHTER

Laughter wears a lilied gown—
 She is but a simple thing;
Laughter's eyes are water-brown,
Ever glancing up and down
 Like a woodbird's restless wing.

Laughter slender is and round—
 She is but a simple thing;
And her tresses fly unbound,
And about her brow are found
 Buds that blossom by Mirth's spring.

Laughter loves to praise and play—
 She is but a simple thing—
With the children small who stray
Under hedges, where the May
 Scents and blossoms richly fling.

Laughter coyly peeps and flits—
 She is but a simple thing—
Round the flower-clad door, where sits
Maid who dimples as she knits,
 Dreaming in the rosy spring.

Laughter hath light-tripping feet—
 She is but a simple thing;
Ye may often Laughter meet
In the hayfield, gilt and sweet,
 Where the mowers jest and sing.

Laughter shakes the bounteous leaves—
 She is but a simple thing—
On the village ale-house eaves,
While the angered swallow grieves
 And the rustic revellers sing.

Laughter never comes a-nigh—
 She's a wise though simple thing—
Where men lay them down to die;
Nor will under stormy sky
 Laughter's airy music ring.

THE CITY TREE

I stand within the stony, arid town,
  I gaze for ever on the narrow street,
I hear for ever passing up and down
  The ceaseless tramp of feet.

I know no brotherhood with far-locked woods,
  Where branches bourgeon from a kindred sap,
Where o'er mossed roots, in cool, green solitudes,
  Small silver brooklets lap.

No emerald vines creep wistfully to me
  And lay their tender fingers on my bark;
High may I toss my boughs, yet never see
  Dawn's first most glorious spark.

When to and fro my branches wave and sway,
  Answ'ring the feeble wind that faintly calls,
They kiss no kindred boughs, but touch alway
  The stones of climbing walls.

My heart is never pierced with song of bird;
  My leaves know nothing of that glad unrest
Which makes a flutter in the still woods heard
  When wild birds build a nest.

There never glance the eyes of violets up,
  Blue, into the deep splendour of my green;
Nor falls the sunlight to the primrose cup
  My quivering leaves between.

Not mine, not mine to turn from soft delight
  Of woodbine breathings, honey sweet and warm:
With kin embattled rear my glorious height
  To greet the coming storm!

Not mine to watch across the free, broad plains
  The whirl of stormy cohorts sweeping fast,
The level silver lances of great rains
  Blown onward by the blast!

Not mine the clamouring tempest to defy,
  Tossing the proud crest of my dusky leaves—
Defender of small flowers that trembling lie
  Against my barky greaves!

Not mine to watch the wild swan drift above,
  Balanced on wings that could not choose between
The wooing sky, blue as the eye of love,
  And my own tender green!

And yet my branches spread, a kingly sight,
  In the close prison of the drooping air;
When sun-vexed noons are at their fiery height
  My shade is broad, and there

Come city toilers, who their hour of ease
  Weave out to precious seconds as they lie
Pillowed on horny hands, to hear the breeze
  Through my great branches die.

I see no flowers, but as the children race
  With noise and clamour through the dusty street,
I see the bud of many an angel face,
  I hear their merry feet.

No violets look up, but, shy and grave,
  The children pause and lift their crystal eyes
To where my emerald branches call and wave
  As to the mystic skies.

THE AXE OF THE PIONEER

High grew the snow beneath the low-hung sky,
And all was silent in the wilderness.

"Bite deep and wide, O Axe, the tree,
What doth thy bold voice promise me?"

"I promise thee all joyous things
That furnish forth the lives of Kings!

"For every silver ringing blow
Cities and palaces shall grow!"

"Bite deep and wide, O Axe, the tree,
Tell wider prophecies to me."

"When rust hath gnawed me deep and red,
A nation strong shall lift its head!"

"Bite deep and wide, O Axe, the tree,
Bright seer, help on thy prophecy!"

Max smote the snow-weighed tree and lightly laughed,
"See, friend," he cried to one that looked and smiled,

"My axe and I, we do immortal tasks;
We build up nations—this my axe and I!"

GEORGE FREDERICK CAMERON [1854-1885]

George Frederick Cameron, of Scottish ancestry, was born at New Glasgow, Nova Scotia, and was educated at the local high school, Boston University (Law), and Queen's University. The family moved to Boston in 1869, and the poet remained in the United States till 1882, holding a position in a law office after completing his course but devoting himself largely to literature. For the last three years of his life he was editor of the Kingston *News*. His poems, *Lyrics on Freedom, Love and Death* (1887), were collected and published by his brother, Charles J. Cameron. Because of his excellence of form and his cosmopolitan sympathy with suffering mankind, his poetry is not of Canada merely but of the world. (Cf. *Five Canadian Poets* (1954), by Arthur S. Bourinot.)

STANDING ON TIPTOE

Standing on tiptoe ever since my youth,
Striving to grasp the future just above,
I hold at length the only future—Truth,
And Truth is love.

I feel as one who being awhile confined
Sees drop to dust about him all his bars;—
The clay grows less, and, leaving it, the mind
Dwells with the stars.

AH ME! THE MIGHTY LOVE

Ah me! the mighty love that I have borne
To thee, sweet Song! A perilous gift was it
My mother gave me that September morn,
When sorrow, song and life were at one altar lit.

A gift more precious than the priest's: his lore
Is all of books and to his books extends;
And what they see and know he knows—no more,
And with their knowing all his knowing ends.

A gift more perilous than the painter's: he
In his divinest moments only sees
The inhumanities of colour; we
Feel each and all the inhumanities.

IN AFTER DAYS

I will accomplish that and this,
And make myself a thorn to Things—
Lords, councillors and tyrant kings—
Who sit upon their thrones and kiss

The rod of Fortune; and are crowned
The sovereign masters of the earth
To scatter blight and death and dearth
Wherever mortal man is found.

I will do this and that, and break
The backbone of their large conceit,
And loose the sandals from their feet,
And show 'tis holy ground they shake.

So sang I in my earlier days,
Ere I had learned to look abroad
And see that more than monarchs trod
Upon the form I fain would raise.

Ere I, in looking toward the land
That broke a triple diadem,
That grasped at Freedom's garment hem,
Had seen her, sword and torch in hand,

A freedom-fool: ere I had grown
To know that Love is freedom's strength—
France taught the world that truth at length!—
And Peace her chief foundation stone.

Since then, I temper so my song
That it may never speak for blood;
May never say that ill is good;
Or say that right may spring from wrong:

Yet am what I have ever been—
A friend of Freedom, staunch and true,
Who hate a tyrant, be he—you—
A people,—sultan, czar, or queen!

And then the Freedom-haters came
   And questioned of my former song,
   If *now* I held it right, or wrong:
And still my answer was the same:—

The good still moveth towards the good:
   The ill still moveth towards the ill:
   But who affirmeth that we will
Not form a nobler brotherhood

When communists, fanatics, those
   Who howl their "*vives*" to Freedom's name
   And yet betray her unto shame,
Are dead and coffined with her foes.

WILLIAM HENRY DRUMMOND (1854-1907]

William Henry Drummond, the son of George and Elizabeth Morris (Loden) Drummond, was born near Mohill, Ireland. When he was two years old, the family moved to Tawley for about seven years, and then, after briefly revisiting Mohill, came to Canada when the son was twelve years old. The father soon died, and the mother heroically managed, with the help of what the boy could earn as a telegrapher, to continue his education at Montreal High School and at Bishop's College, Lennoxville, from which he graduated in medicine in 1884. His professional practice, first in the country and then in Montreal, richly supplemented his earlier knowledge of French-Canadian life, in the interpretation of which, through the medium of his dialect poems, he occupies a unique position. His poems interpreting Irish-Canadian life, overshadowed by those on French-Canadian themes, have not yet received adequate recognition. His poems are found in: *The Habitant* (1897); *Phil-o-Rum's Canoe* (1898) (containing "Madeleine Vercheres"); *Johnnie Courteau* (1901); *The Voyageur* (1905); *The Great Fight* (1908), edited with a memoir by his widow, before marriage May Isabel Harvey; and two collected editions, *Poetical Works* (1912) and *Complete Poems* (1926), containing Drummond's Preface and the Introduction in French by Louis Fréchette (1839-1908) to *The Habitant*, a "memorial poem" by the American doctor and poet, Silas Weir Mitchell (1829-1914), and an appreciation by Neil Munro (1864-1930), a Scottish writer, who also used the pen name "Mr. Incognito," who met Drummond in Scotland during the latter's visit to the British Isles in 1901, and who visited the Drummonds in Montreal in 1902 after touring in Canada. (Cf. John Ford Macdonald (1878-), *Makers of Canadian Literature* (1923), and *Canadian Who was Who* (vol. 1, 1934).)

MADELEINE VERCHÈRES

I've told you many a tale, my child, of the old heroic days
Of Indian wars and massacres, of villages ablaze
With savage torch, from Ville Marie to the Mission of Trois Rivières
But never have I told you yet, of Madeleine Verchères.

Summer had come with its blossoms, and gaily the robin sang
And deep in the forest arches the axe of the woodman rang,
Again in the waving meadows, the sun-browned farmers met,
And out on the green St. Lawrence, the fisherman spread his net.

And so through the pleasant season, till the days of October came
When children wrought with their parents, and even the old and lame
With tottering frames and footsteps, their feeble labours lent
At the gathering of the harvest, le bon Dieu himself had sent.

For news there was none of battle, from the forts on the Richelieu
To the gates of the ancient city, where the flag of King Louis flew.
All peaceful the skies hung over the seigneurie of Verchères,
Like the calm that so often cometh, ere the hurricane rends the air.

And never a thought of danger had the Seigneur sailing away,
To join the soldiers of Carignan, where down at Quebec they lay,
But smiled on his little daughter, the maiden Madeleine,
And a necklet of jewels promised her, when home he should come again.

And ever the days passed swiftly, and careless the workmen grew
For the months they seemed a hundred, since the last war-bugle blew.
Ah! little they dreamt on their pillows, the farmers of Verchères,
That the wolves of the southern forest had scented the harvest fair.

Like ravens they quickly gather, like tigers they watch their prey.
Poor people! with hearts so happy, they sang as they toiled away,
Till the murderous eyeballs glistened, and the tomahawk leaped out
And the banks of the green St. Lawrence echoed the savage shout.

"O mother of Christ, have pity," shrieked the women in despair.
"This is no time for praying," cried the young Madeleine Verchères,
"Aux armes! aux armes! les Iroquois! quick to your arms and guns,
Fight for your God and country and the lives of the innocent ones."

And she sped like a deer of the mountain, when beagles press close behind
And the feet that would follow after, must be swift as the prairie wind.
Alas! for the men and women, and little ones that day
For the road it was long and weary, and the fort it was far away.

But the fawn had outstripped the hunters, and the palisades drew near,
And soon from the inner gateway the war-bugle rang out clear;
Gallant and clear it sounded, with never a note of despair,
'Twas a soldier of France's challenge, from the young Madeleine Verchères.

"And this is my little garrison, my brothers Louis and Paul?
With soldiers two—and a cripple? may the Virgin pray for us all.
But we've powder and guns in plenty, and we'll fight to the latest breath
And if need be for God and country, die a brave soldier's death.

"Load all the carabines quickly, and whenever you sight the foe
Fire from the upper turret, and the loopholes down below.
Keep up the fire, brave soldiers, though the fight may be fierce and long
And they'll think our little garrison is more than a hundred strong."

So spake the maiden Madeleine, and she roused the Norman blood
That seemed for a moment sleeping, and sent it like a flood
Through every heart around her, and they fought the red Iroquois
As fought, in the old-time battles, the soldiers of Carignan.

And they say the black clouds gathered, and a tempest swept the sky
And the roar of the thunder mingled with the forest tiger's cry,
But still the garrison fought on, while the lightning's jagged spear
Tore a hole in the night's dark curtain, and showed them a foeman near.

And the sun rose up in the morning, and the colour of blood was he,
Gazing down from the heavens on the little company.
"Behold! my friends!" cried the maiden, "'tis a warning lest we forget,
Though the night saw us do our duty, our work is not finished yet."

And six days followed each other, and feeble her limbs became,
Yet the maid never sought her pillow, and the flash of the carabines' flame
Illumined the powder-smoked faces, aye, even when hope seemed gone
And she only smiled on her comrades, and told them to fight, fight on.

And she blew a blast on the bugle, and lo! from the forest black,
Merrily, merrily ringing, an answer came pealing back.
Oh! pleasant and sweet it sounded, borne on the morning air,
For it heralded fifty soldiers, with gallant De la Monniere.

And when he beheld the maiden, the soldier of Carignan,
And looked on the little garrison that fought the red Iroquois
And held their own in the battle, for six long weary days
He stood for a moment speechless, and marvelled at woman's ways.

Then he beckoned the men behind him and steadily they advance,
And, with carabines uplifted, the veterans of France
Saluted the brave young Captain so timidly standing there
And they fired a volley in honour of Madeleine Verchères.

And this, my dear, is the story of the maiden Madeleine.
God grant that we in Canada may never see again
Such cruel wars and massacres, in waking or in dream,
As our fathers and mothers saw, my child, in the days of the old regime.

THE WRECK OF THE *JULIE PLANTE*

(*A Legend of Lac St. Pierre*)

On wan dark night on Lac St. Pierre,
  De win' she blow, blow, blow,
An' de crew of de wood-scow *Julie Plante*
  Got scar't an' run below—
For de win' she blow lik' hurricane,
  Bimeby she blow some more,
An' de scow bus' up on Lac St. Pierre
  Wan arpent from de shore.

De captinne walk on de front deck,
  An' walk de hin' deck too—
He call de crew from up de hole,
  He call de cook also.
De cook she's name was Rosie,
  She come from Montreal,
Was chambermaid on lumber-barge
  On de Grande Lachine Canal.

De win' she blow from nor'-eas'-wes',
  De sout' win' she blow too,
W'en Rosie cry, "Mon cher captinne,
  Mon cher, w'at I shall do?"
De captinne t'row de beeg ankerre,
  But still de scow she dreef:
De crew he can't pass on de shore
  Becos' he los' hees skeef.

De night was dark lak' wan black cat,
  De wave run high an' fas',
W'en de captinne tak' de Rosie girl
  An' tie her to de mas'.
Den he also tak' de life-preserve,
  An' jomp off on de lak',
An' say, "Good-bye, my Rosie dear,
  I go drown for your sak'!"

Nex' mornin' very early
  'Bout ha'f pas' two—t'ree—four—
De captinne—scow—an' de poor Rosie
  Was corpses on de shore.
For de win' she blow lak' hurricane,
  Bimeby she blow some more,
An' de scow bus' up on Lac St. Pierre
  Wan arpent from de shore.

Moral

Now all good wood-scow sailor-man,
  Tak' warning by dat storm,
An' go an' marry some nice French girl
  An' leev on wan beeg farm.
De win' can blow lak' hurricane,
  An' s'pose she blow some more,
You can't get drown' on Lac St. Pierre
  So long you stay on shore.

JOHNNIE COURTEAU

Johnnie Courteau of de mountain,
  Johnnie Courteau of de hill—
Dat was de boy can shoot de gun,
Dat was de boy can jomp an' run,
  An' it's not very offen you ketch heem still—
    Johnnie Courteau

Ax dem along de reever,
  Ax dem along de shore,
Who was mos' bes' fightin' man
From Managance to Shaw-in-i-gan?
  De place w'ere de great beeg rapide roar—
    Johnnie Courteau!

Sam' t'ing on ev'ry shaintee
  Up on de Mekinac:
Who was de man can walk de log,
W'en w'ole of de reever she's black wit' fog,
  An' carry de beeges' load on hees back?
    Johnnie Courteau!

On de rapide you want to see heem
  If de raf' she's swingin' roun,
An' he's yellin', "Hooraw Bateese! good man!"
W'y de oar come double on hees han'
  W'en he's makin' dat raf' go flyin' down—
    Johnnie Courteau!

An' Tête de Boule chief can tole you
  De feller w'at save hees life,
W'en beeg moose ketch heem up a tree,
Who's shootin' dat moose on de head, sapree!
  An' den run off wit' hees Injun wife?
    Johnnie Courteau!

An' he only have pike pole wit' heem
  On Lac a la Tortue,
W'en he meet de bear comin' down de hill,
But de bear very soon is get hees fill!
  An' he sole dat skin for ten dollar too—
    Johnnie Courteau!

Oh, he never was scare for not'ing
  Lak de ole coureurs de bois,
But w'en he's gettin' hees winter pay
De bes' t'ing sure is kip out de way;
  For he's goin' right off on de Hip Hooraw!
                    Johnnie Courteau!

Den pullin' hees sash aroun' heem
  He dance on hees botte sauvage,
An' shout, "All aboar' if you want to fight!"
Wall! you never can see de finer sight
  W'en he go lak dat on de w'ole village!
                    Johnnie Courteau!

But Johnnie Courteau get marry
  On Philomene Beaurepaire:
She's nice leetle girl was run de school
On w'at you call Parish of Sainte Ursule,
  An' he see her off on de pique-nique dere—
                    Johnnie Courteau!

Den somet'ing come over Johnnie
  W'en he marry on Philomene,
For he stay on de farm de w'ole year roun',
He chop de wood an' he plough de groun',
  An' he's quieter feller was never seen—
                    Johnnie Courteau!

An' ev'ry wan feel astonish,
  From La Tuque to Shaw-in-i-gan,
W'en dey hear de news was goin' aroun',
Along on de reever up an' down,
  How wan leetle woman boss dat beeg man—
                    Johnnie Courteau!

He never come out on de evening
No matter de hard we try,
'Cos he stay on de kitchen an' sing hees song:
    "A la claire fontaine,
      M'en allant promener,
      J'ai trouvé l'eau si belle
      Que je m'y suis baigner!
      Il y a longtemps que je t'aime,
      Jamais je ne t'oublierai."
Rockin' de cradle de w'ole night long,
Till baby's asleep on de sweet bimeby—
                    Johnnie Courteau!

An' de house, wall! I wish you see it:
  De place she's so nice an' clean
Mus' wipe your foot on de outside door,
You're dead man sure if you spit on de floor,
  An' he never say not'ing on Philomene—
    Johnnie Courteau!

An' Philomene watch de monee
  An' put it all safe away
On very good place; I dunno w'ere,
But anyhow nobody see it dere,
  So she's buyin' new farm de noder day—
    Madame Courteau!

LEETLE BATEESE

You bad leetle boy, not moche you care
How busy you're kipin' your gran'père
  Tryin' to stop you ev'ry day
  Chasin' de hen aroun' de hay—
  W'y don't you geev' dem a chance to lay?
    Leetle Bateese!

Off on de fiel' you foller de plough,
Den w'en you're tire you scare de cow,
  Sickin' de dog till dey jomp de wall,
  So de milk ain't good for not'ing at all—
  An' you're only five an' a half dis fall,
    Leetle Bateese!

Too sleepy for sayin' de prayer tonight?
Never min', I s'pose it'll be all right.
  Say dem tomorrow—ah! dere he go!
  Fas' asleep in a minute or so—
  An' he'll stay lak dat till de rooster crow,
    Leetle Bateese!

Den wake us up right away tout de suite
Lookin' for somet'ing more to eat,
  Makin' me t'ink of dem long leg crane—
  Soon as dey swaller, dey start again;
  I wonder your stomach don't get no pain,
    Leetle Bateese!

But see heem now lyin' dere in bed,
Look at de arm onderneat' hees head;
If he grow like dat till he's twenty year
I bet he'll be stronger dan Louis Cyr,
An' beat all de voyageurs leevin' here,
Leetle Bateese!

Jus' feel de muscle along hees back,
Won't geev' heem moche bodder for carry pack
On de long portage, any size canoe;
Dere's not many t'ing dat boy won't do,
For he's got double-joint on hees body too,
Leetle Bateese!

But leetle Bateese! please don't forget
We rader you're stayin' de small boy yet;
So chase de chicken an' mak' dem scare,
An' do w'at you lak wit' your ole gran'père,
For w'en you're beeg feller he won't be dere—
Leetle Bateese!

WILLIAM DOUW LIGHTHALL [1857-]

Descended from three prominent Dutch families of New York, Dr. Lighthall was born in Hamilton, Ontario. He distinguished himself in English at Montreal High School and at McGill University, from which he graduated also in law. An outstanding lawyer, he has found time to take a great interest in cultural pursuits. He has achieved success in the novel, has edited an anthology, *Songs of the Great Dominion: Voices from the Forests and Waters, the Settlements and Cities of Canada* (1889), of which a slightly shortened edition with a different title was published in the "Canterbury Poets Series," and has published his collected poems under the title *Old Measures* (1922). (Cf. *Leading Canadian Poets*, ed. by W. P. Percival (1948).)

THE CAUGHNAWAGA BEADWORK SELLER

Kanawâki—"By the Rapid,"—
Low the sunset midst thee lies;
And from the wild Reservation
Evening's breeze begins to rise.
Faint the Kônoronkwa chorus
Drifts across the current strong;
Spirit-like the parish steeple
Stands thy ancient walls among.

Kanawâki—"By the Rapid,"—
  How the sun amidst thee burns!
Village of the Praying Nation,
  Thy dark child to thee returns.
All day through the pale-face city,
  Silent, selling beaded wares,
I have wandered with my basket,
  Lone, excepting for their stares!

They are white men; we are Indians;
  What a gulf their stares proclaim!
They are mounting; we are dying;
  All our heritage they claim.
We are dying, dwindling, dying,
  Strait and smaller grows our bound;
They are mounting up to heaven
  And are pressing all around.

Thou art ours,—little remnant,
  Ours through countless thousand years—
Part of the old Indian world,
  Thy breath from far the Indian cheers.
Back to thee, O Kanawâki!
  Let the rapids dash between
Indian homes and white men's manners—
  Kanawâki and Lachine!

O my dear! O Knife-and-Arrows!
  Thou art bronzed, thy limbs are lithe;
How I laugh as through the crosse-game,
  Slipst thou like red elder withe.
Thou art none of these pale-faces!
  When with thee I'll happy feel,
For thou art the Mohawk warrior
  From thy scalp-lock to thy heel.

Sweet the Kônoronkwa chorus
  Floats across the current strong;
Clear behold the parish steeple
  Rise the ancient walls among.
Speed us deftly, noiseless paddle;
  In my shawl my bosom burns!
Kanawâki—"By the Rapid,"—
  Thine own child to thee returns.

ETHELWYN WETHERALD [1857-1940]

Agnes Ethelwyn Wetherald, daughter of Rev. William Wetherald, was born at Rockwood, Ontario, and educated at the Friends' Boarding School, Union Springs, New York, and at Pickering College, Ontario. After working for a while on the staff of the Toronto *Globe*, the "Bel Thistlewaite" of the Woman's Department, she engaged in free-lance writing for the rest of her active life. She was joint author of a novel, and five books of verse preceded a complete edition of her poems, *Lyrics and Sonnets* (1931), with an introduction by J. W. Garvin (1859-1935). (Cf. *Leading Canadian Poets* (1948), ed. by W. P. Percival.)

THE HOUSE OF THE TREES

Ope your doors and take me in,
  Spirit of the wood;
Wash me clean of dust and din—
  Clothe me in your mood.

Take me from the noisy light
  To the sunless peace,
Where at midday standeth Night,
  Signing Toil's release.

All your dusty twilight stores
  To my senses give;
Take me in and lock the doors—
  Show me how to live.

Lift your leafy roof for me,
  Part your yielding walls;
Let me wander lingeringly
  Through your scented halls.

Ope your doors and take me in,
  Spirit of the wood;
Take me—make me next of kin
  To your leafy brood.

WOODLAND WORSHIP

Here 'mid these leafy walls
  Are sylvan halls,
And all the Sabbaths of the year
  Are gathered here.

Upon their raptured mood
My steps intrude,
Then wait—as some freed soul might wait
At heaven's gate.

Nowhere on earth—nowhere
On sea or air,
Do I as easily escape
This earthly shape.

As here upon the white
And dizzy height
Of utmost worship, where it seems
Too still for dreams.

IN APRIL

When spring unbound comes o'er us like a flood
My spirit slips its bars,
And thrills to see the trees break into bud
As skies break into stars.

And joys that earth is green with eager grass,
The heavens grey with rain,
And quickens when the spirit breezes pass,
And turn and pass again.

And dreams upon frog melodies at night,
Bird ecstasies at dawn,
And wakes to find sweet April at her height
And May still beckoning on.

And feels its sordid work, its empty play,
Its failures and its stains
Dissolved in blossom dew, and washed away
In delicate spring rains.

WILLIAM E. MARSHALL [1859-1923]

William Edward Marshall, son of James Noble Shannon and Adelaide Amelia (Allison) Marshall, was born at Liverpool, Nova Scotia, and educated there and at Mount Allison Academy, Sackville, New Brunswick. Called to the bar in Nova Scotia in 1881, he practised law in Bridgewater. From 1898 on he was registrar of deeds for the district of Lunenburg. He published *A Legend of Venice* (1907), *A Book of Verse* (1908, 1909), and *Brookfield and Other Poems* (1919). (Cf. *Canadian Who was Who*, vol. 2 (1938), and *Five Canadian Poets* (1954) by Arthur S. Bourinot.)

TO A MAYFLOWER

Hath the rude laugh of Boreas frighted thee,
My dainty one, that thou hast sought to hide
Thy loveliness from the young Spring, whose bride
Thou art, and, like a novice, ecstasy
Of life renounce, in this dark monast'ry
Of mossy cells? Nay, my pale beauty, chide
Me not, that I have mocked thy holy pride
With ardent praise of so rare modesty!
For I am come to claim thee, pretty flower,
As a sweet solace for my lady's eyes,—
That thou—thy vigil past—all in a bower
Of love, may'st blush and bloom in glad surprise;
Happy that, unawares, thy worth was known,
And all thy fragrance saved for Love alone.

From BROOKFIELD

But see this happy village festival,
Where all the country folk are gathered round
Responsive to the clear, vibrating call
Of one uplifted voice,—whose echoes sound
Above the hill-tops now. This toil-won ground
Is holy; here the burning bush flamed high
One hundred years ago, when faith was crowned
In the first settler's log hut built near by,
And love, in that rude home, was blessed with children's cry.

Not that the Venturer grew rich or great,
Or seemed a hero or was honoured more
By those who followed him to conquer fate
In the far wilderness; nor that he bore
Himself as one who paid for other's score;
But that among the forest immigrants,
He was the first life-bringer to explore
These hills, where the shy Indian had his haunts,
And prove the settler's worth, beyond the body's wants. . . .

ALBERT DURRANT WATSON [1859-1926]

Albert Durrant Watson, son of William Youle and Mary (Aldred) Watson, was born at Dixie, Ontario. After graduation from the Toronto Normal School, he taught for a while, and then studied medicine at Victoria University (then at Cobourg) and at Edinburgh University. During a long medical practice in Toronto he wrote philosophical prose and philosophical poetry of distinction. His books in the latter field are: *Wing of the Wild Bird and Other Poems* (1908); *Love and the Universe* (1913); *Heart of the Hills* (1917); *The Dream of God* (1922); *Woman: a Poem* (1923); and *Complete Poems* (1923). (Cf. Lorne Pierce, *Albert Durrant Watson* (1924).)

A HYMN FOR CANADA

Lord of the lands, beneath Thy bending skies,
On field and flood, where'er our banner flies,
Thy people lift their hearts to Thee,
Their grateful voices raise:
May our Dominion ever be
A temple to Thy praise.
Thy will alone let all enthrone;
Lord of the lands, make Canada Thine own!

Almighty Love, by Thy mysterious power,
In wisdom guide, with faith and freedom dower;
Be ours a nation evermore
That no oppression blights,
Where justice rules from shore to shore,
From Lakes to Northern Lights.
May Love alone for wrong atone;
Lord of the lands, make Canada Thine own!

Lord of the worlds, with strong eternal hand,
Hold us in honour, truth, and self-command;
The loyal heart, the constant mind,
The courage to be true,
Our wide-extending Empire bind,
And all the earth renew.
Thy name be known through every zone;
Lord of the worlds, make all the lands Thine own!

SOUL LIFTED

Crowd back the hills and give me room,
Nor goad me with the sense of things;
Earth cramps me like a narrow tomb,
Your sunlight is too dense for wings;
Away with all horizon-bars;
Push back the mountains and the stars.

PRIEST AND PAGAN

He deemed his task a solemn one,
And kneeled in solemn garb to pray;
Made much of symbols, ancient rites,
Of holy book and sacred day.

I, on the grass beneath the pine—
A pagan to my finger-tips,
Accounting every flower divine,
Breathed incense from its petal lips.

And God, in His almighty Love,
Knowing our need, and nothing loath,
Leaned kindly from His heavens above,
And poured His blessing on us both.

BREEZE AND BILLOW

A fair blue sky,
A far blue sea,
Breeze o'er the billows blowing!
The deeps of night o'er the waters free
With mute appeal to the soul of me
In billows and breezes flowing;

The stars that watch
While sunbeams sleep,
Breeze o'er the billows blowing!
The soft-winged zephyrs that move the deep
And rock my barque in a dreamy sweep;
The moonlight softly glowing;

The glint of wave,
The gleam of star,
Breeze o'er the billows blowing!
The surf-line cadence of beach and bar,
The voice of nature near and far,
The night into morning growing,

And I afloat
With canvas free,
Breeze o'er the billows blowing!
At one with the heart of eternity,
The fair blue sky and the far blue sea,
And the breeze o'er the billows blowing.

S. FRANCES HARRISON [1859-1935]

Mrs. Susie Frances (Riley) Harrison, who frequently used the pen name "Seranus," daughter of John Byron Riley, was born in Toronto and educated in that city and in Montreal. She wrote both fiction and poetry, achieving more distinction in the latter, notably for her mastery of the highly technical form known as the villanelle. Volumes of verse are: *Pine, Rose, and Fleur-de-lis* (1891, 1896); *In Northern Skies and Other Poems* (1912); *Songs of Love and Labour* (1925); *Later Poems and New Villanelles* (1928); *Penelope and Other Poems* (1932); and *Four Ballads and a Play* (n.d.).

CHATEAU PAPINEAU

The red-tiled towers of the old Chateau,
  Perched on the cliff above our bark,
Burn in the western evening glow.

The fiery spirit of Papineau
  Consumes them still with its fever spark.
The red-tiled towers of the old Chateau!

Drift by and mark how bright they show,
  And how the mullioned windows—mark!
Burn in the western evening glow!

Drift down, or up, where'er you go,
  They flame from out the distant park,
The red-tiled towers of the old Chateau.

So was it once with friend, with foe;
  Far off they saw the patriot's ark
Burn in the western evening glow.

Think of him now! One thought bestow
  As, blazing against the pine trees dark,
The red-tiled towers of the old Chateau
Burn in the western evening glow!

HELENA COLEMAN [1860-1953]

Miss Helena Coleman, of Toronto, was born at Newcastle, Ontario, the daughter of Rev. Francis and Emmeline Maria (Adams) Coleman. She was educated at Ontario Ladies' College, Whitby, where she also taught. She has published *Songs and Sonnets* (1906), *Marching Men* (1917), *Sheila and Others* (1920), and *Songs* (1937).

MORE LOVELY GROWS THE EARTH

More lovely grows the earth as we grow old,
More tenderness is in the dawning spring,
More bronze upon the blackbird's burnished wing;
And richer is the autumn cloth-of-gold;
A deeper meaning, too, the years unfold,
Until to waiting hearts each living thing
For very love its bounty seems to bring,
Intreating us with beauty to behold.

Or is it that with years we grow more wise
And reverent to the mystery profound—
Withheld from careless or indifferent eyes—
That broods in simple things the world around,
More conscious of the Love that glorifies
The common ways and makes them holy ground?

AS DAY BEGINS TO WANE

Encompassed by a thousand nameless fears,
I see life's little day begin to wane,
And hear the well-loved voices call in vain
Across the narrowing margin of my years;
And as the Valley of the Shadow nears,
Such yearning tides of tenderness and pain
Sweep over me that I can scarce restrain
The gathering flood of ineffectual tears.

Yet there are moments when the shadows bring
No sense of parting or approaching night,
But, rather, all my soul seems broadening
Before the dawn of unimagined light—
As if within the heart a folded wing
Were making ready for a wider flight.

"RICHARD SCRACE" [1860-1952]

Mrs. J. B. Williamson, who used the pen name "Richard Scrace," was born in Guelph, Ontario, the daughter of Charles John Buckland. Eight of her early years were spent in California. After her marriage she lived in Evanston, Illinois. She published privately in Toronto, in collaboration with her son, O. T. G. Williamson, *Duet for Cello and Drum* (1947), Foreword by Judith Robinson.

AT THE PLACE OF THE ROMAN BATHS

I have come down to the garden
Of the wide spreading cedar;
The great limbs stretch out,
Make an archway over the road,—
The dark green boughs are the roof
Of a pavilion of dreams.

I watch the man, grey-haired, silent,
Whetting his blade:
Moving with slow tedious movements,
Cutting a swath,
Resting; then mowing again.

I shall watch for the men and the chariots:
They come from as far off as the Tor,
They will come from beyond the hill where Arthur lies.
The men of the fens will come out and stare,
Eyeing the dark Romans with their soft robes,
Shapely sandals, circlets of gold:
The dust of their wheels is as smoke
The trappings of their horses shine as stars;
They pass by to the pillared pools,
In the somnolent water
Resting, in body and soul:
In dreaming rest to lie,
Slaves to minister to them,
Bringing rare unguents
When from the water they step out,
To be wrapped in fair linens,
Swathed in white woollens,
Spun by the Roman maidens,
Then shall they go swiftly to Diana's temple,
Make oblation, and pray the goddess
For all gracious gifts
Of victory, in love and war.

. . .

I watch the man, grey-haired and silent,
Mowing:
Wiping the scythe blade with fresh cut grass;
Then, mowing again.

THE GIPSIES

I saw them chase the Gipsies
Out of the little town,
And it made me think of autumn leaves,
Red and yellow and brown.

Their yellow eardrops dangled
Like flowers in country lanes,
And beads like wild fruit, red and blue,
Hung round their necks in chains.

And like an autumn sunset
Their scarlet flounces flared;
To left and right their bright eyes roved
Like birds by hunters scared.

The constable rode proudly,
The idle ones turned round,
But they could not follow the wild folk
Whither they were bound.

I think they had a pattern
Of leaf and feather and stone,
This handful of bright-eyed wild things
Like leaves from a wild tree blown.

They are gathered in some green hollow
And laughing now and then;
The Gipsy folk in Arcady,
They laugh at wiser men.

JOHN FREDERIC HERBIN [1860-1923]

John Frederic Herbin, son of John and Marie (Robicheau) Herbin, was born at Windsor, Nova Scotia, and taught in Colorado for a time before entering Acadia University, from which he graduated in 1890. He spent the rest of his life as a jeweller at Wolfville, Nova Scotia. His prose includes historical writing and fiction. His books of poems are *Canada and Other Poems* (1891) and *The Marshlands* (1899).

THE DIVER

Like marble, nude, against the purple sky,
In ready poise, the diver scans the sea,
Gemming the marsh's green placidity
And mirroring the fearless form on high.
Behold the outward leap—he seems to fly!
His arms like arrow-blade just speeded free;
His body like the curving bolt, to be
Deep driven till the piercing flight shall die.
Sharply the human arrow cleaves the tide,
Only a foaming swell to mark his flight;
While shoreward moves the silent ring on ring.
And now the sea is stirred and broken wide
Before the swimmer's passage free and light,
And bears him as a courser bears a king.

HAYING

From the soft dyke-road, crooked and waggon-worn,
Comes the great load of rustling scented hay,
Slow-drawn with heavy swing and creaky sway
Through the cool freshness of the windless morn.
The oxen, yoked and sturdy, horn to horn,
Sharing the rest and toil of night and day,
Bend head and neck to the long hilly way
By many a season's labour marked and torn.
On the broad sea of dyke the gathering heat
Waves upward from the grass, where road on road
Is swept before the tramping of the teams.
And while the oxen rest beside the sweet
New hay, the loft receives the early load,
With hissing stir, among the dusty beams.

SIR CHARLES G. D. ROBERTS [1860-1943]

Sir Charles George Douglas Roberts, son of Rev. George Goodridge and Emma Wetmore (Bliss) Roberts, was born at Douglas, New Brunswick, and spent most of the first fourteen years of his life at Westcock, near the mouth of the Tantramar. He was educated at Fredericton Grammar School while George Robert Parkin (1846-1922), later knighted, was headmaster, and at the University of New Brunswick. After teaching for several years, he was for a brief period editor of the Toronto *Week*. From 1885 to 1895 he was a professor at the University of King's College, Windsor, Nova Scotia. From 1897 to 1907 he lived in New York. He then went abroad and settled in England in 1911. He served in the First World War. From 1925 on he lived in Toronto. In prose he wrote novels, animal stories that won for him the title "poet laureate of the animal world," travel literature, and history. His poems deal with classical themes, with Canadian nature in vivid descriptions and thoughtful lyrics, and with love. *Selected Poems* (1936) contains his own choice from thirteen preceding volumes. Later he published *Twilight over Shaugamauk* (1937) and *Canada Speaks of Britain* (1941). (Cf. J. Cappon (1855-1939), *Roberts and the Influences of his Time* (1905) and *Charles G. D. Roberts* (1923); Elsie May Pomeroy (1886-), *Sir Charles G. D. Roberts* (1943); *Leading Canadian Poets*, ed. by W. P. Percival (1948).)

AUTOCHTHON

I

I am the spirit astir
To swell the grain
When fruitful suns confer
With labouring rain;
I am the life that thrills
In branch and bloom;
I am the patience of abiding hills,
The promise masked in doom.

II

When the sombre lands are wrung,
And storms are out,
And giant woods give tongue,
I am the shout;
And when the earth would sleep,
Wrapped in her snows,
I am the infinite gleam of eyes that keep
The post of her repose.

III

I am the hush of calm,
I am the speed,
The flood-tide's triumphing psalm,
The marsh-pool's heed;
I work in the rocking roar
Where cataracts fall;
I flash in the prismy fire that dances o'er
The dew's ephemeral ball.

IV

I am the voice of wind
  And wave and tree,
Of stern desires and blind,
  Of strength to be;
I am the cry by night
  At point of dawn,
The summoning bugle from the unseen height,
  In cloud and doubt withdrawn.

V

I am the strife that shapes
  The stature of man,
The pang no hero escapes,
  The blessing, the ban;
I am the hammer that moulds
  The iron of our race,
The omen of God in our blood that a people beholds,
  The foreknowledge veiled in our face.

KINSHIP

Back to the bewildering vision
And the borderland of birth;
Back into the looming wonder,
The companionship of earth;

Back unto the simple kindred—
Childlike fingers, childlike eyes,
Working, waiting, comprehending,
Now in patience, now surprise;

Back unto the faithful healing
And the candour of the sod—
Scent of mould and moisture stirring
At the secret touch of God;

Back into the ancient stillness
Where the wise enchanter weaves,
To the twine of questing tree-root,
The expectancy of leaves;

Back to hear the hushed consulting
Over bud and blade and germ,
As the Mother's mood apportions
Each its pattern, each its term;

Back into the grave beginnings
Where all wonder-tales are true,
Strong enchantments, strange successions,
Mysteries of old and new;

Back to knowledge and renewal,
Faith to fashion and reveal,
Take me, Mother,—in compassion
All thy hurt ones fain to heal.

Back to wisdom take me, Mother;
Comfort me with kindred hands;
Tell me tales the world's forgetting,
Till my spirit understands.

Tell me how some sightless impulse,
Working out a hidden plan,
God for kin and clay for fellow,
Wakes to find itself a man.

Tell me how the life of mortal,
Wavering from breath to breath,
Like a web of scarlet pattern
Hurtles from the loom of death.

How the caged bright bird, desire,
Which the hands of God deliver,
Beats aloft to drop unheeded
At the confines of forever:

Faints unheeded for a season,
Then outwings the farthest star,
To the wisdom and the stillness
Where thy consummations are.

THE UNKNOWN CITY

There lies a city inaccessible,
Where the dead dreamers dwell.

Abrupt and blue, with many a high ravine
And soaring bridge half seen,
With many an iris cloud that comes and goes
Over the ancient snows,
The imminent hills environ it, and hold
Its portals from of old,
That grief invade not, weariness, nor war,
Nor anguish evermore.

White-walled and jettied on the peacock tide,
With domes and towers enskied,
Its battlements and balconies one sheen
Of ever-living green,
It hears the happy dreamers turning home
Slow-oared across the foam.

Cool are its streets with waters musical
And fountains' shadowy fall.
With orange and anemone and rose,
And every flower that blows
Of magic scent or unimagined dye,
Its gardens shine and sigh.

Its chambers, memoried with old romance
And faëry circumstance,—
From any window love may lean some time
For love that dares to climb.
This is that city babe and seer divined
With pure, believing mind.
This is the home of unachieved emprize.
Here, here the visioned eyes
Of them that dream past any power to do,
Wake to the dream come true.
Here the high failure, not the level fame,
Attests the spirit's aim.
Here is hope fulfilled each hope that soared and sought
Beyond the bournes of thought.

The obdurate marble yields; the canvas glows;
Perfect the column grows;
The chorded cadence art could ne'er attain
Crowns the imperfect strain;
And the great song that seemed to die unsung
Triumphs upon the tongue.

AFOOT

Comes the lure of green things growing,
Comes the call of waters flowing,—
  And the wayfarer Desire
Moves and wakes and would be going.

Hark the migrant hosts of June
Marching nearer noon by noon!
  Hark the gossip of the grasses
Bivouacked beneath the moon!

Hark the leaves their mirth averring;
Hark the buds to blossom stirring;
  Hark the hushed, exultant haste
Of the wind and world conferring!

Hark the sharp, insistent cry
Where the hawk patrols the sky!
  Hark the flapping, as of banners,
Where the heron triumphs by!

Empire in the coasts of bloom
Humming cohorts now resume,—
  And desire is forth to follow
Many a vagabond perfume.

Long the quest and far the ending
Where my wayfarer is wending,—
  When Desire is once afoot,
Doom behind and dream attending!

Shuttle-cock of indecision,
Sport of chance's blind derision,
  Yet he may not fail nor tire
Till his eyes shall win the Vision.

In his ears the phantom chime
Of incommunicable rhyme,
  He shall chase the fleeting camp-fires
Of the Bedouins of Time.

Farer by uncharted ways,
Dumb as Death to plaint or praise,
  Unreturning he shall journey,
Fellow to the nights and days:

Till upon the outer bar
Stilled the moaning currents are,
  Till the flame achieves the zenith,
Till the moth attains the star,

Till, through laughter and through tears,
Fair the final peace appears,
  And about the watered pastures
Sink to sleep the nomad years!

THE SOLITARY WOODSMAN

When the grey lake-water rushes
Past the dripping alder-bushes,
  And the bodeful autumn wind
In the fir-tree weeps and hushes,—

When the air is sharply damp
Round the solitary camp,
  And the moose-bush in the thicket
Glimmers like a scarlet lamp,—

When the birches twinkle yellow,
And the cornel bunches mellow,
  And the owl across the twilight
Trumpets to his downy fellow,—

When the nut-fed chipmunks romp
Through the maples' crimson pomp,
  And the slim viburnum flushes
In the darkness of the swamp,—

When the blueberries are dead,
When the rowan clusters red,
  And the shy bear, summer-sleekened,
In the bracken makes his bed,—

On a day there comes once more
To the latched and lonely door,
  Down the wood-road striding silent,
One who has been here before.

Green spruce branches for his head,
Here he makes his simple bed,
  Couching with the sun, and rising
When the dawn is frosty red.

All day long he wanders wide
With the grey moss for his guide,
  And his lonely axe-stroke startles
The expectant forest-side.

Toward the quiet close of day
Back to camp he takes his way,
  And about his sober footsteps
Unafraid the squirrels play.

On his roof the red leaf falls,
At his door the bluejay calls,
And he hears the wood-mice hurry
Up and down his rough log walls;

Hears the laughter of the loon
Thrill the dying afternoon,—
Hears the calling of the moose
Echo to the early moon.

And he hears the partridge drumming,
The belated hornet humming,—
All the faint, prophetic sounds
That foretell the winter's coming.

And the wind about his eaves
Through the chilly night-wet grieves,
And the earth's dumb patience fills him,
Fellow to the falling leaves.

THE SOWER

A brown, sad-coloured hillside, where the soil
Fresh from the frequent harrow, deep and fine,
Lies bare; no break in the remote sky-line,
Save where a flock of pigeons streams aloft,
Startled from feed in some low-lying croft,
Or far-off spires with yellow of sunset shine;
And here the Sower, unwittingly divine,
Exerts the silent forethought of his toil.
Alone he treads the glebe, his measured stride
Dumb in the yielding soil; and though small joy
Dwell in his heavy face, as spreads the blind
Pale grain from his dispensing palm aside,
This plodding churl grows great in his employ;—
Godlike, he makes provision for mankind.

THE POTATO HARVEST

A high bare field, brown from the plough, and borne
Aslant from sunset; amber wastes of sky
Washing the ridge; a clamour of crows that fly
In from the wide flats where the spent tides mourn
To yon their rocking roosts in pines wind-torn;
A line of grey-snake-fance, that zigzags by
A pond, and cattle; from the homestead nigh
The long deep summonings of the supper horn.

Black on the ridge, against that lonely flush,
A cart, and stoop-necked oxen; ranged beside
Some barrels; and the day-worn harvest-folk,
Here emptying their baskets, jar the hush
With hollow thunders. Down the dusk hillside
Lumbers the wain; and day fades out like smoke.

THE SALT FLATS

Here clove the keels of centuries ago,
  Where now unvisited the flats lie bare.
  Here seethed the sweep of journeying waters, where
No more the tumbling floods of Fundy flow;
And only in the samphire pipes creep slow
  The salty currents of the sap. The air
  Hums desolately with wings that seaward fare,
Over the lonely reaches, beating low.
The wastes of hard and meagre weeds are thronged
With murmurs of a past that time has wronged;
  And ghosts of many an ancient memory
Dwell by the brackish pools and ditches blind,
In these low-lying pastures of the wind,
  These marshes pale and meadows by the sea.

IN THE WIDE AWE AND WISDOM OF THE NIGHT

In the wide awe and wisdom of the night
I saw the round world rolling on its way,
Beyond significance of depth or height,
Beyond the interchange of dark and day.
I marked the march to which is set no pause,
And that stupendous orbit, round whose rim
The great sphere sweeps, obedient unto laws
That utter the eternal thought of Him.
I compassed time, outstripped the starry speed,
And in my still Soul apprehended space,
Till weighing laws which these but blindly heed,
At last I came before Him face to face,—
And knew the Universe of no such span
As the august infinitude of man.

O SOLITARY OF THE AUSTERE SKY

O Solitary of the austere sky,
Pale presence of the unextinguished star,
That from thy station where the spheres wheel by,
And quietudes of infinite patience are,
Watchest this wet, grey-visaged world emerge,—
Cold pinnacle on pinnacle, and deep
On deep of ancient wood and wandering surge,—
Out of the silence and the mists of sleep;
How small am I in thine august regard!
Invisible,—and yet I know my worth!
When comes the hour to break this prisoning shard,
And reunite with Him that breathed me forth,
Then shall this atom of the Eternal Soul
Encompass thee in its benign control!

TANTRAMAR REVISITED

Summers and summers have come, and gone with the flight of the swallow;
Sunshine and thunder have been, storm, and winter, and frost;
Many and many a sorrow has all but died from remembrance,
Many a dream of joy fall'n in the shadow of pain.
Hands of chance and change have marred, or moulded, or broken,
Busy with spirit or flesh, all I most have adored;
Even the bosom of Earth is strewn with heavier shadows,—
Only in these green hills, aslant to the sea, no change!
Here where the road that has climbed from the inland valleys and woodlands,
Dips from the hill-tops down, straight to the base of the hills,—
Here, from my vantage-ground, I can see the scattering houses,
Stained with time, set warm in orchards, meadows, and wheat,
Dotting the broad bright slopes outspread to southward and eastward,
Wind-swept all day long, blown by the south-east wind.
Skirting the sunbright uplands stretches a riband of meadow,
Shorn of the labouring grass, bulwarked well from the sea,
Fenced on its seaward border with long clay dykes from the turbid
Surge and flow of the tides vexing the Westmoreland shores.
Yonder, toward the left, lie broad the Westmoreland marshes,—
Miles on miles they extend, level, and grassy, and dim,
Clear from the long red sweep of flats to the sky in the distance,
Save for the outlying heights, green-rampired Cumberland Point;
Miles on miles outrolled, and the river-channels divide them,—
Miles on miles of green, barred by the hurtling gusts.

Miles on miles beyond the tawny bay is Minudie.
There are the low blue hills; villages gleam at their feet.
Nearer a white sail shines across the water, and nearer
Still are the slim, grey masts of fishing boats dry on the flats.
Ah, how well I remember those wide red flats, above tide-mark
Pale with scurf of the salt, seamed and baked in the sun!
Well I remember the piles of blocks and ropes, and the net-reels
Wound with the beaded nets, dripping and dark from the sea!
Now at this season the nets are unwound; they hang from the rafters
Over the fresh-stowed hay in upland barns, and the wind
Blows all day through the chinks, with the streaks of sunlight, and sways them
Softly at will; or they lie heaped in the gloom of a loft.
Now at this season the reels are empty and idle; I see them
Over the lines of the dykes, over the gossiping grass.
Now at this season they swing in the long strong wind, thro' the lonesome
Golden afternoon, shunned by the foraging gulls.
Near about sunset the crane will journey homeward above them;
Round them, under the moon, all the calm night long,
Winnowing soft grey wings of marsh-owls wander and wander,
Now to the broad, lit marsh, now to the dusk of the dike.
Soon, thro' their dew-wet frames, in the live keen freshness of morning
Out of the teeth of the dawn blows back the awakening wind.
Then, as the blue day mounts, and the low-shot shafts of the sunlight
Glance from the tide to the shore, gossamers jewelled with dew
Sparkle and wave, where late sea-spoiling fathoms of drift-net
Myriad-meshed, uploomed sombrely over the land.

Well I remember it all. The salt, raw scent of the margin;
While, with men at the windlass, groaned each reel, and the net,
Surging in ponderous lengths, uprose and coiled in its station;
Then each man to his home,—well I remember it all!

Yet, as I sit and watch, this present peace of the landscape,—
Stranded boats, these reels empty and idle, the hush,
One grey hawk slow-wheeling above yon cluster of haystacks,—
More than the old-time stir this stillness welcomes me home.
Ah, the old-time stir, how once it stung me with rapture,—
Old-time sweetness, the winds freighted with honey and salt!
Yet will I stay my steps and not go down to the marshland,—
Muse and recall far off, rather remember than see,—
Lest on too close sight I miss the darling illusion,
Spy at their task even here the hands of chance and change.

O EARTH, SUFFICING ALL OUR NEEDS

O Earth, sufficing all our needs, O you
With room for body and for spirit too,
  How patient while your children vex their souls
Devising alien heavens beyond your blue!

Dear dwelling of the immortal and unseen,
How obstinate in my blindness have I been,
  Not comprehending what your tender calls,
Veiled promises and re-assurance, mean.

Not far and cold the way that they have gone
Who through your sundering darkness have withdrawn;
  Almost within our hand-reach they remain
Who pass beyond the sequence of the dawn.

Not far and strange the Heaven, but very near,
Your children's hearts unknowingly hold dear.
  At times we almost catch the door swung wide.
An unforgotten voice almost we hear.

I am the heir of Heaven—and you are just.
You, you alone I know—and you I trust.
  I have sought God beyond His farthest star—
But here I find Him, in your quickening dust.

THE ICEBERG

  I was spawned from the glacier,
A thousand miles due north
Beyond Cape Chidley;
And the spawning,
When my vast, wallowing bulk went under,
Emerged and heaved aloft,
Shaking down cataracts from its rocking sides,
With mountainous surge and thunder
Outraged the silence of the Arctic sea.

  Before I was thrust forth
A thousand years I crept,
Crawling, crawling, crawling irresistibly,
Hid in the blue womb of the eternal ice,
While under me the tortured rock
Groaned,
And over me the immeasurable desolation slept.

Under the pallid dawning
Of the lidless Arctic day
Forever no life stirred.
No wing of bird—
Of ghostly owl low winnowing
Or fleet-winged ptarmigan fleeing the pounce of death,—
No foot of backward-glancing fox
Half glimpsed, and vanishing like a breath,—
No lean and gauntly stalking bear,
Stalking his prey.
Only the white sun, circling the white sky.
Only the wind screaming perpetually.

And then the night—
The long night, naked, high over the roof of the world,
Where time seemed frozen in the cold of space,—
Now black, and torn with cry
Of unseen voices where the storm raged by,
Now radiant with spectral light
As the vault of heaven split wide
To let the flaming Polar cohorts through,
And close ranked spears of gold and blue,
Thin scarlet and thin green,
Hurtled and clashed across the sphere
And hissed in sibilant whisperings,
And died.
And then the stark moon, swinging low,
Silver, indifferent, serene,
Over the sheeted snow.

But now, an Alp afloat,
In seizure of the surreptitious tide,
Began my long drift south to a remote
And unimagined doom.
Scornful of storm,
Unjarred by thunderous buffeting of seas,
Shearing the giant floes aside,
Ploughing the wide-flung ice-fields in a spume
That smoked far up my ponderous flanks,
Onward, I fared,
My ice-blue pinnacles rendering back the sun
In darts of sharp radiance;
My bases fathoms deep in the dark profound.

And now around me
Life, and the frigid waters all aswarm.
The smooth wave creamed
With tiny capelin and the small pale squid,—
So pale the light struck through them.
Gulls and gannets screamed
Over the feast, and gorged themselves, and rose,
A clamour of weaving wings, and hid
Momently my face.
The great bull whales
With cavernous jaws agape,
Scooped in the spoil, and slept,
Their humped forms just awash, and rocking softly,—
Or sounded down, down to the deeps, and nosed
Along my ribbed and sunken roots,
And in the green gloom scattered the pasturing cod.

And so I voyaged on, down the dim parallels,
Convoyed by fields
Of countless calving seals
Mild-featured, innocent-eyed, and unforeknowing
The doom of the red flenching knives.
I passed the storm-racked gate
Of Hudson Strait,
And savage Chidley where the warring tides
In white wrath seethe forever.
Down along the sounding shore
Of iron-fanged, many-watered Labrador
Slow weeks I shaped my course, and saw
Dark Mokkowic and dark Napiskawa,
And came at last off lone Belle Isle, the bane
of ships and snare of bergs.
Here, by the deep conflicting currents drawn,
I hung,
And swung,
The inland voices Gulfward calling me
To ground amid my peers on the alien strand
And roam no more.
But then an off-shore wind,
A great wind fraught with fate,
Caught me and pressed me back,
And I resumed my solitary way.

Slowly I bore
South-east by bastioned Bauld,
And passed the sentinel light far-beaming late
Along the liners' track,
And slanted out Atlanticwards, until
Above the treacherous swaths of fog
Faded from the view the loom of Newfoundland.

Beautiful, ethereal
In the blue sparkle of the gleaming day,
A soaring miracle
Of white immensity,
I was the cynosure of passing ships
That wondered and were gone,
Their wreathed smoke trailing them beyond the verge.
And when in the night they passed—
The night of stars and calm,
Forged up and passed, with churning surge
And throb of huge propellers, and long-drawn
Luminous wake behind,
And sharp, small lights in rows,
I lay a ghost of menace chill and still,
A shape pearl-pale and monstrous, off to leeward,
Blurring the dim horizon line.

Day dragged on day,
And then came fog,
By noon, blind-white,
And in the night
Black-thick and smothering the sight.
Folded therein I waited,
Waited I knew not what
And heeded not,
Greatly incurious and unconcerned.
I heard the small waves lapping along my base,
Lipping and whispering, lisping with bated breath
A casual expectancy of death.
I heard remote
The deep, far carrying note
Blown from the hoarse and hollow throat
Of some lone tanker groping on her course.

Louder and louder rose the sound
In deepening diapason, then passed on,
Diminishing, and dying,—
And silence closed around.
And in the silence came again
Those stealthy voices,
That whispering of death.

And then I heard
The thud of screws approaching.
Near and more near,
Louder and yet more loud,
Through the thick dark I heard it,—
The rush and hiss of waters as she ploughed
Head on, unseen, unseeing,
Toward where I stood across her path, invisible.
And then a startled blare
Of horror close re-echoing,—a glare
Of sudden, stabbing searchlights
That but obscurely pierced the gloom;
And there
I towered, a dim immensity of doom.

A roar
Of tortured waters as the giant screws,
Reversed, thundered full steam astern.
Yet forward still she drew, until,
Slow answering desperate helm,
She swerved, and all her broadside came in view,
Crawling beneath me;
And for a moment I saw faces, blanched,
Stiffly agape, turned upward, and wild eyes
Astare; and one long, quavering cry went up
As a submerged horn gored her through and through,
Ripping her beam wide open;
And sullenly she listed, till her funnels
Crashed on my steep,
And men sprang, stumbling, for the boats.

But now, my deep foundations
Mined by those warmer seas, the hour had come
When I must change.
Slowly I leaned above her,
Slowly at first, then faster,
And icy fragments rained upon her decks.

Then my enormous mass descended on her,
A falling mountain, all obliterating,—
And the confusion of thin, wailing cries,
The babel of shouts and prayers
And shriek of steam escaping
Suddenly died.
And I rolled over,
Wallowing,
And once more came to rest,
My long hid bases heaved up high in air.

And now, from fogs emerging,
I traversed blander seas,
Forgot the fogs, the scourging
Of sleet-whipped gales, forgot
My austere origin, my tremendous birth,
My journeyings, and that last cataclysm
Of overwhelming ruin.
My squat, pale, alien bulk
Basked in the ambient sheen;
And all about me, league on league outspread,
A gulf of indigo and green.
I laughed in the light waves laced with white,—
Nor knew
How swiftly shrank my girth
Under their sly caresses, how the breath
Of that soft wind sucked up my strength, nor how
The sweet, insidious fingers of the sun
Their stealthy depredations wrought upon me.

Slowly now
I drifted, dreaming.
I saw the flying-fish
With silver gleaming
Flash from the peacock-bosomed wave
And flicker through an arc of sunlit air
Back to their element, desperate to elude
The jaws of the pursuing albacore.

Day after day
I swung in the unhasting tide.
Sometimes I saw the dolphin folk at play,
Their lithe sides iridescent-dyed,
Unheeding in their speed
That long grey wraith,
The shark that followed hungering beneath.

Sometimes I saw a school
Of porpoise rolling by
In ranked array,
Emerging and submerging rhythmically,
Their blunt black bodies heading all one way
Until they faded
In the horizon's dazzling line of light.
Night after night
I followed the low, large moon across the sky,
Or counted the large stars on the purple dark,
The while I wasted, wasted and took no thought,
In drowsed entrancement caught;—
Until one noon a wave washed over me,
Breathed low a sobbing sigh,
Foamed indolently, and passed on;
And then I knew my empery was gone;
As I, too, soon must go.
And well content I was to have it so.

Another night
Gloomed o'er my sight,
With cloud, and flurries of warm, wild rain.
Another day,
Dawning delectably
With amber and scarlet stain,
Swept on its way,
Glowing and shimmering with heavy heat.
A lazing tuna rose
And nosed me curiously,
And shouldered me aside in brusque disdain,
So had I fallen from my high estate.
A foraging gull
Stooped over me, touched me with webbed pink feet,
And wheeled and skreeled away,
Indignant at the chill.

Last I became
A little glancing globe of cold
That slid and sparkled on the slow-pulsed swell.
And then my fragile, scintillating frame
Dissolved in ecstasy
Of many coloured light,
And I breathed up my soul into the air
And merged forever in the all-solvent sea.

ARCHIBALD LAMPMAN [1861-1899]

Archibald Lampman, son of Rev. Archibald and Susannah (Gesner) Lampman, was born at Morpeth, Ontario, and educated at Trinity University, Toronto. From 1883 on he was in the Post Office Department of the Civil Service at Ottawa. He devoted his spare time to poetry and excelled in vivid description of the part of the Canadian scene with which he was well acquainted, as is shown by the contents of *Among the Millet* (1888), *Lyrics of Earth* (1893), *Alcyone* (1899), and *The Poems of Archibald Lampman* (1900), with a memoir by Duncan Campbell Scott (1862-1947), who also wrote an introduction to another volume of selections, *Lyrics of Earth* (1925), served as joint editor with E. K. Brown of *At the Long Sault and Other Poems* (1943), and edited with an introduction *Selected Poems of Archibald Lampman* (1947). (Cf. Norman Gregor Guthrie (1877-1929), "John Crichton," *The Poetry of Archibald Lampman* (1927); C. Y. Connor, *Archibald Lampman: A Canadian Poet of Nature* (1929); *Five Canadian Poets* (1954) by Arthur S. Bourinot.)

AMONG THE MILLET

The dew is gleaming in the grass,
  The morning hours are seven,
And I am fain to watch you pass,
  Ye soft white clouds of heaven.

Ye stray and gather, part and fold;
  The wind alone can tame you;
I think of what in time of old
  The poets loved to name you.

They called you sheep, the sky your sward,
  A field without a reaper;
They called the shining sun your lord,
  The shepherd wind your keeper.

Your sweetest poets I will deem
  The men of old for moulding
In simple beauty such a dream,
  And I could lie beholding,

Where daisies in the meadow toss,
  The wind from morn till even,
For ever shepherd you across
  The shining field of heaven.

THE TRUTH

Friend, though thy soul should burn thee, yet be still.
Thoughts were not meant for strife, nor tongues for swords.
He that sees clear is gentlest of his words,
And that's not truth that hath the heart to kill.
The whole world's thought shall not one truth fulfil.
Dull in our age, and passionate in our youth,
No mind of man hath found the perfect truth,
Nor shalt thou find it; therefore, friend, be still.
Watch and be still, nor hearken to the fool,
The babbler of consistency and rule:
Wisest is he, who, never quite secure,
Changes his thoughts for better day by day:
Tomorrow some new light will shine, be sure,
And thou shalt see thy thought another way.

A THUNDERSTORM

A moment the wild swallows like a flight
Of withered gust-caught leaves, serenely high,
Toss in the wind-rack up the muttering sky.
The leaves hang still. Above the weird twilight,
The hurrying centres of the storm unite
And spreading with huge trunk and rolling fringe,
Each wheeled upon its own tremendous hinge,
Tower darkening on. And now from heaven's height,
With the long roar of elm-trees swept and swayed,
And pelted waters, on the vanished plain
Plunges the blast. Behind the wild white flash
That splits abroad the pealing thunder-crash,
Over bleared fields and gardens disarrayed,
Column on column comes the drenching rain.

AFTER THE SHOWER

The shower hath past, ere it hath well begun.
The enormous clouds are rolling up like steam
Into the illimitable blue. They gleam
In summits of banked snow against the sun.
The old dry beds begin to laugh and run,
As if 'twere spring. The trees in the wind's stir
Shower down great drops, and every gossamer
Glitters a net of diamonds fresh-spun.

The happy flowers put on a spritelier grace,
Star-flower and smilacina creamy-hued,
With little spires of honey-scent and light,
And that small, dainty violet, pure and white,
That holds by magic in its twisted face
The heart of all the perfumes of the wood.

THE DAWN ON THE LIEVRE

Up the dark-valleyed river stroke by stroke
We drove the water from the rustling blade;
And when the night was almost gone we made
The Oxbow bend; and there the dawn awoke;
Full on the shrouded night-charged river broke
The sun, down the long mountain valley rolled
A sudden, swinging avalanche of gold,
Through mists that sprang and reeled aside like smoke.
And lo! before us, toward the East upborne,
Packed with curled forest, bunched and topped with pine,
Brow beyond brow, drawn deep with shade and shine,
The mount; upon whose golden sunward side,
Still threaded with the mountain mist, the morn
Sat like some glowing conqueror satisfied.

HEAT

From plains that reel to southward, dim,
The road runs by me white and bare;
Up the steep hill it seems to swim
Beyond, and melt into the glare.
Upward half-way, or it may be
Nearer the summit, slowly steals
A hay-cart, moving dustily
With idly clacking wheels.

By his cart's side the wagoner
Is slouching slowly at his ease,
Half-hidden in the windless blur
Of white dust puffing to his knees.
This wagon on the height above,
From sky to sky on either hand,
Is the sole thing that seems to move
In all the heat-held land.

Beyond me in the fields the sun
  Soaks in the grass and hath his will;
I count the marguerites one by one;
  Even the buttercups are still.
On the brook yonder not a breath
  Disturbs the spider or the midge.
The water-bugs draw close beneath
  The cool gloom of the bridge.

Where the far elm-tree shadows flood
  Dark patches in the burning grass,
The cows, each with her peaceful cud,
  Lie waiting for the heat to pass.
From somewhere on the slope near by
  Into the pale depth of the noon
A wandering thrush slides leisurely
  His thin, revolving tune.

In intervals of dream I hear
  The cricket from the droughty ground;
The grasshoppers spin into mine ear
  A small, innumerable sound.
I lift mine eyes sometimes to gaze;
  The burning sky-line blinds my sight;
The woods far off are blue with haze;
  The hills are drenched in light.

And yet to me not this or that
  Is always sharp or always sweet:
In the sloped shadow of my hat
  I lean at rest and drain the heat;
Nay, more, I think some blessèd power
  Hath brought me wandering idly here.
In the full furnace of this hour
  My thoughts grow keen and clear.

THE VIOLINIST

In Dresden, in the square one day,
  His face of parchment, seamed and grey,
With wheezy bow and proffered hat,
  An old blind violinist sat.

Like one from whose worn heart the heat
  Of life had long ago retired,
He played to the unheeding street
  Until the thin old hands were tired.

Few marked the player how he played,
Or how the child beside his knee
Besought the passers-by for aid
So softly and so wistfully.

A stranger passed. The little hand
Went forth, so often checked and spurned.
The stranger wavered, came to stand,
Looked round with absent eyes and turned.

He saw the sightless, withered face,
The tired old hands, the whitened hair,
The child with such a mournful grace,
The little features pinched and spare.

"I have no money, but," said he,
"Give me the violin and bow.
I'll play a little, we shall see,
Whether the gold will come or no."

With lifted brow and flashing eyes
He faced the noisy street and played.
The people turned in quick surprise,
And every foot drew near and stayed.

First from the shouting bow he sent
A summons, an impetuous call;
Then some old store of grief long pent
Broke from his heart and mastered all.

The tumult sank at his command,
The passing wheels were hushed and stilled;
The burning soul, the sweeping hand
A sacred ecstasy fulfilled.

The darkness of the outer strife,
The weariness and want within,
The giant wrongfulness of life,
Leaped storming from the violin.

The jingling round of pleasure broke,
Gay carriages were drawn anear,
And all the proud and haughty folk
Leaned from their cushioned seats to hear.

And then the player changed his tone,
　And wrought another miracle
Of music, half a prayer, half moan,
　A cry exceeding sorrowful.

A strain of pity for the weak,
　The poor that fall without a cry,
The common hearts that never speak,
　But break beneath the press and die.

Throughout the great and silent crowd
　The music fell on human ears,
And many kindly heads were bowed,
　And many eyes were warm with tears.

"And now your gold," the player cried,
　"While love is master of your mood";
He bowed, and turned, and slipped aside,
　And vanished in the multitude.

And all the people flocked at that,
　The money like a torrent rolled,
Until the grey old battered hat
　Was bursting to the brim with gold.

And loudly as the giving grew,
　The question rose on every part,
If any named or any knew
　The stranger with so great a heart.

Or what the moving wonder meant,
　Such playing never heard before;
A lady from her carriage leant,
　And murmured softly, "It was Spohr."

THE LARGEST LIFE

I

I lie upon my bed and hear and see.
　The moon is rising through the glistening trees;
　And momently a great and sombre breeze,
With a vast voice returning fitfully,
Comes like a deep-toned grief, and stirs in me,
　Somehow, by some inexplicable art,
　A sense of my soul's strangeness, and its part
In the dark march of human destiny.

What am I, then, and what are they that pass
  Yonder, and love and laugh, and mourn and weep?
What shall they know of me, or I, alas!
  Of them? Little. At times, as if from sleep,
We waken to this yearning, passionate mood,
And tremble at our spiritual solitude.

II

Nay, never once to feel we are alone,
  While the great human heart around us lies:
To make the smile on other lips our own,
  To live upon the light in others' eyes:
To breathe without a doubt the limpid air
  Of that most perfect love that knows no pain:
To say—"I love you"—only, and not care
  Whether the love come back to us again,
Divinest self-forgetfulness, at first
  A task, and then a tonic, then a need;
To greet with open hands the best and worst,
  And only for another's wound to bleed:
This is to see the beauty that God meant,
Wrapped round with life, ineffably content.

III

There is a beauty at the goal of life,
  A beauty growing since the world began,
Through every age and race, through lapse and strife,
  Till the great human soul complete her span.
Beneath the waves of storm that lash and burn,
  The currents of blind passion that appall,
To listen and keep watch till we discern
  The tide of sovereign truth that guides it all;
So to address our spirits to the height,
  And so attune them to the valiant whole,
That the great light be clearer for our light,
  And the great soul the stronger for our soul:
To have done this is to have lived, though fame
Remember us with no familiar name.

COMFORT OF THE FIELDS

What would'st thou have for easement after grief,
  When the rude world hath used thee with despite,
  And care sits at thy elbow day and night,
Filching thy pleasures like a subtle thief?

To me, when life besets me in such wise,
'Tis sweetest to break forth, to drop the chain,
And grasp the freedom of this pleasant earth,
To roam in idleness and sober mirth,
Through summer airs and summer lands, and drain
The comfort of wide fields unto tired eyes.

By hills and waters, farms and solitudes,
To wander by the day with wilful feet;
Through fielded valleys wide with yellowing wheat;
Along grey roads that run between deep woods,
Murmurous and cool; through hallowed slopes of pine,
Where the long daylight dreams, unpierced, unstirred,
And only the rich-throated thrush is heard;
By lonely forest brooks that froth and shine
In bouldered crannies buried in the hills;
By broken beeches tangled with wild vine,
And log-strewn rivers murmurous with mills.

In upland pastures, sown with gold, and sweet
With the keen perfume of the ripening grass,
Where wings of birds and filmy shadows pass,
Spread thick as stars with shining marguerite;
To haunt old fences overgrown with brier,
Muffled in vines, and hawthorns, and wild cherries,
Rank poisonous ivies, red-bunched elder-berries,
And pièd blossoms to the heart's desire,
Grey mullein towering into yellow bloom,
Pink-tasselled milkweed, breathing dense perfume,
And swarthy vervain, tipped with violet fire.

To hear at eve the bleating of far flocks,
The mud-hen's whistle from the marsh at morn;
To skirt with deafened ears and brain o'erborne
Some foam-filled rapid charging down its rocks
With iron roar of waters; far away
Across wide-reeded meres, pensive with noon,
To hear the querulous outcry of the loon;
To lie among deep rocks, and watch all day
On liquid heights the snowy clouds melt by;
Or hear from wood-capped mountain-brow the jay
Pierce the bright morning with his jibing cry.

To feast on summer sounds; the jolted wains,
  The thresher humming from the farm near by,
  The prattling cricket's intermittent cry,
The locust's rattle from the sultry lanes;
Or in the shadow of some oaken spray,
  To watch, as through a mist of light and dreams,
  The far-off hayfields, where the dusty teams
Drive round and round the lessening squares of hay,
  And hear upon the wind, now loud, now low,
With drowsy cadence half a summer's day,
  The clatter of the reapers come and go.

Far violet hills, horizons filmed with showers,
  The murmur of cool streams, the forest's gloom,
  The voices of the breathing grass, the hum
Of ancient gardens overbanked with flowers;
Thus, with a smile as golden as the dawn,
  And cool fair fingers radiantly divine,
  The mighty mother brings us in her hand,
For all tired eyes and foreheads pinched and wan,
Her restful cup, her beaker of bright wine;
  Drink, and be filled, and ye shall understand!

WILLIAM WILFRED CAMPBELL [1861-1918]

William Wilfred Campbell, son of Rev. Thomas Swaniston and Matilda Frances (Wright) Campbell, was born at Kitchener (then Berlin), Ontario. He was educated at Upper Canada College, Owen Sound, the University of Toronto, and the Episcopal Divinity School, Cambridge, Massachusetts. After a little more than five years of pastoral work in New England, at Fredericton, New Brunswick, and at Southampton, Ontario, he entered the Civil Service, Ottawa. For a while he helped conduct a literary department of the Toronto *Globe.* He wrote two novels, a descriptive work on the Canadian lake region, collaborated with the painter Thomas Mower Martin (1838-1934) in *Canada* (1907) and with Rev. George Bryce (1844-1931) in *The Scot in Canada* (1911, 2v.). He began to write poetry during his New England days. His published volumes are: *Lake Lyrics* (1889); *The Dread Voyage* (1893); *Beyond the Hills of Dream* (1899); *Collected Poems* (1906, 1922) (with a memoir by W. J. Sykes); *Sagas of Vaster Britain* (1914); *War Lyrics* (1915); and, in the field of tragedy in verse, *Mordred* and *Hildebrand* (1895), later included, with *Daulac* and *Morning*, in *Poetical Tragedies* (1908). He also edited *The Oxford Book of Canadian Verse* (1913). (Cf. *Canadian Who was Who*, vol. 1 (1934); Carl Frederick Klinck (1908-   ), *Wilfred Campbell: A Study in Late Victorian Provincialism* (1942), originally a Columbia doctoral dissertation; *Leading Canadian Poets* (1948), ed. by W. P. Percival.)

VAPOUR AND BLUE

Domed with the azure of heaven,
  Floored with a pavement of pearl,
Clothed all about with a brightness,
  Soft as the eyes of a girl.

Girt with a magical girdle,
  Rimmed with a vapour of rest—
These are the inland waters,
  These are the lakes of the west.

Voices of slumberous music,
  Spirits of mist and flame,
Moonlit memories left here
  By gods who long ago came.

And vanishing left but an echo
  In silence of moon-dim caves,
Where haze-wrapt the August night slumbers,
  Or the wild heart of October raves.

Here where the jewels of nature
  Are set in the light of God's smile,
Far from the world's wild throbbing,
  I will stay me and rest awhile.

And store in my heart old music,
  Melodies gathered and sung
By the genies of love and beauty
  When the heart of the world was young.

INDIAN SUMMER

Along the line of smoky hills
  The crimson forest stands,
And all the day the blue-jay calls
  Throughout the autumn lands.

Now by the brook the maple leans
  With all his glory spread,
And all the sumachs on the hills
  Have turned their green to red.

Now by great marshes wrapt in mist,
  Or past some river's mouth,
Throughout the long, still autumn day
  Wild birds are flying south.

HOW ONE WINTER CAME IN THE LAKE REGION

For weeks and weeks the autumn world stood still,
  Clothed in the shadow of a smoky haze;
The fields were dead, the wind had lost its will,
And all the lands were hushed by wood and hill,
  In those grey, withered days.

Behind a mist the blear sun rose and set,
  At night the moon would nestle in a cloud;
The fisherman, a ghost, did cast his net;
The lake its shores forgot to chafe and fret,
  And hushed its caverns loud.

Far in the smoky woods the birds were mute,
  Save that from blackened tree a jay would scream,
Or far in swamps the lizard's lonesome lute
Would pipe in thirst, or by some gnarled root
  The tree-toad trilled his dream.

From day to day still hushed the season's mood,
  The streams stayed in their runnels shrunk and dry;
Suns rose aghast by wave and shore and wood,
And all the world, with ominous silence, stood
  In weird expectancy.

When one strange night the sun like blood went down,
  Flooding the heavens in a ruddy hue;
Red grew the lake, the sere fields parched and brown,
Red grew the marshes where the creeks stole down,
  But never a wind-breath blew.

That night I felt the winter in my veins,
  A joyous tremor of the icy glow;
And woke to hear the North's wild vibrant strains,
While far and wide, by withered woods and plains,
  Fast fell the driving snow.

THE HILLS AND THE SEA

Give me the hills and wide water,
  Give me the heights and the sea;
And take all else, 'tis living
  And heaven enough for me.
For my fathers of old they were hillsmen,
  My sires they were sons of the sea.

Give me the uplands of purple,
  The sweep of the vast world's rim,
Where the sun dips down, or the dawnings
  Over the earth's edge swim;
With the days that are dead, and the old earth-tales,
  Human, and haunting, and grim.

Give me where the great surfs landward
  Break on the iron-rimmed shore,
Where winter and spring are eternal,
  And the miles of the sea-sand their floor;
Where wind and vastness, for ever
  Walk by the red dawn's door.

Back from the grime of this present,
  This slavery worse than all death,
Let me stand out alone on the highlands,
  Where there's life in the brave wind's breath;
Where the one wise word and the strong word
  Is the word that the great hush saith.

BEREAVEMENT OF THE FIELDS

In memory of Archibald Lampman, who died February 10, 1899.

Soft fall the February snows, and soft
Falls on my heart the snow of wintry pain;
For never more, by word or field or croft,
Will he we knew walk with his loved again;
No more, with eyes adream and soul aloft,
In those high moods where love and beauty reign,
Greet his familiar fields, his skies without a stain.

Soft fall the February snows, and deep
Like downy pinions from the moulting breast
Of the all-mothering sky, round his hushed sleep,
Flutter a million loves upon his rest,
Where once his well-loved flowers were fain to peep,
With adder-tongue and waxen petals prest,
In young spring evenings reddening down the west.

Soft fall the February snows, and hushed
Seems life's loud action, all its strife removed,
Afar, remote, where grief itself seems crushed,
And even hope and sorrow are reproved;
For he whose cheek erstwhile with hope was flushed,
And by the gentle haunts of being moved,
Hath gone the way of all he dreamed and loved.

Soft fall the February snows, and lost,
This tender spirit gone with scarce a tear,
Ere, loosened from the dungeons of the frost,
Wakens with yearnings new the enfranchised year,
Late winter-wizened, gloomed, and tempest-tost;
And Hesper's gentle, delicate veils appear,
When dream anew the days of hope and fear.

And Mother Nature, she whose heart is fain
Yea, she who grieves not, neither faints nor fails,
Building the seasons, she will bring again
March with rudening madness of wild gales,
April and her wraiths of tender rain,
And all he loved—this soul whom memory veils,
Beyond the burden of our strife and pain.

Not his to wake the strident note of song,
Nor pierce the deep recesses of the heart,
Those tragic wells, remote, of might and wrong;
But, rather, with those gentler souls apart,
He dreamed like his own summer days along,
Filled with the beauty born of his own heart,
Sufficient in the sweetness of his song.

Outside this prison-house of all our tears,
Enfranchised from our sorrow and our wrong,
Beyond the failure of our days and years,
Beyond the burden of our saddest song,
He moves with those whose music filled his ears,
And claimed his gentle spirit from the throng,—
Wordsworth, Arnold, Keats, high masters of his song.

Like some rare Pan of those old Grecian days,
Here in our hours of deeper stress reborn,
Unfortunate thrown upon life's evil ways,
His inward ear heard ever that satyr horn
From Nature's lips reverberate night and morn,
And fled from men and all their troubled maze,
Standing apart, with sad, incurious gaze.

And now, untimely cut, like some sweet flower
Plucked in the early summer of its prime,
Before it reached the fullness of its dower,
He withers in the morning of our time;
Leaving behind him, like a summer shower,
A fragrance of earth's beauty, and the chime
Of gentle and imperishable rhyme.

Songs in our ears of winds and flowers and buds
And gentle loves and tender memories
Of Nature's sweetest aspects, her pure moods,
Wrought from the inward truth of intimate eyes
And delicate ears of him who harks and broods,
And, nightly pondering, daily grows more wise,
And dreams and sees in nightly solitudes.

Soft fall the February snows, and soft
He sleeps in peace upon the breast of her
He loved the truest; where, by wood and croft,
The wintry silence folds in fleecy blur
About his silence, while in glooms aloft
The mighty forest fathers, without stir,
Guard well the rest of him, their rare sweet worshipper.

BLISS CARMAN [1861-1929]

Bliss Carman, son of William and Sophia Mary (Bliss) Carman, was born at Fredericton, New Brunswick. His education, begun by his father, was continued at Fredericton Grammar School while George Robert Parkin (1846-1922), later knighted, was headmaster, at the University of New Brunswick, at Edinburgh University, and at Harvard University. His life was varied by frequent change of residence and by travel. From journalistic and editorial work (1890-1895) and from lectures to students on Canadian literature was largely derived the material of his five volumes of essays. His poetry falls into three periods. That of the first period, up to *Behind the Arras* (1895), is decidedly romantic. That of the second, up to the *Pipes of Pan* (1902-1905, 1906), is decidedly rationalistic. The third period strikes the happy balance between the two extremes of the earlier periods and achieves genuine classicism. *Ballads and Lyrics* (1923) makes a selection from six of his previous thirteen titles. After that came *Far Horizons* (1925), *Wild Garden* (1929), *Sanctuary* (1929), *Poems* (1931), *The Music of Earth* (1939). He collaborated in poetry with Richard Hovey and in pageants and masques with Mrs. Mary Perry King. He edited *The World's Best Poetry* (1904, 10 vols.) and *The Oxford Book of American Verse* (1927), on a second edition of which he was at work when he died. (Cf. Odell Shepard, *Bliss Carman* (1923); James Cappon (1855-1939), *Bliss Carman and the Literary Currents and Influences of his Time* (1930); *Canadian Who was Who*, vol. 1 (1934); Muriel Miller (now Mrs. Julian Miner) (1908-   ), *Bliss Carman: A Portrait* (1935); Percival, as above.)

THE SHIPS OF YULE

When I was just a little boy,
Before I went to school,
I had a fleet of forty sail
I called the Ships of Yule;

Of every rig, from rakish brig
And gallant barkentine,
To little Fundy fishing boats
With gunwales painted green.

They used to go on trading trips
Around the world for me,
For though I had to stay on shore
My heart was on the sea.

They stopped at every port to call
From Babylon to Rome,
To load with all the lovely things
We never had at home;

With elephants and ivory
Bought from the King of Tyre,
And shells and silk and sandal-wood
That sailor men admire;

With figs and dates from Samarkand,
And squatty ginger-jars,
And scented silver amulets
From Indian bazaars;

With sugar-cane from Port of Spain,
And monkeys from Ceylon,
And paper lanterns from Pekin,
With painted dragons on;

With cocoanuts from Zanzibar,
And pines from Singapore;
And when they had unloaded these
They could go back for more.

And even after I was big
And had to go to school,
My mind was often far away
Aboard the Ships of Yule.

THE GRAVE-TREE

Let me have a scarlet maple
  For the grave-tree at my head,
With the quiet sun behind it,
  In the years when I am dead.

Let me have it for a signal,
  Where the long winds stream and stream,
Clear across the dim blue distance,
  Like a horn blown in a dream;

Scarlet when the April vanguard
  Bugles up the laggard Spring,
Scarlet when the bannered Autumn,
  Marches by unwavering.

It will comfort me with honey
  When the shining rifts and showers
Sweep across the purple valley
  And bring back the forest flowers.

It will be my leafy cabin,
  Large enough when June returns
And I hear the golden thrushes
  Flute and hesitate by turns.

And in fall, some yellow morning,
  When the stealthy frost has come,
Leaf by leaf it will befriend me
  As with comrades going home.

Let me have the Silent Valley
  And the hill that fronts the east,
So that I can watch the morning
  Redden and the stars released.

Leave me in the Great Lone Country,
  For I shall not be afraid
With the shy moose and the beaver
  There within my scarlet shade.

I would sleep, but not too soundly,
  Where the sunning partridge drums,
Till the crickets hush before him
  When the Scarlet Hunter comes.

That will be in warm September,
  In the stillness of the year,
When the river-blue is deepest
  And the other world is near.

When the apples burn their reddest
  And the corn is in the sheaves,
I shall stir and waken lightly
  At a football in the leaves.

It will be the Scarlet Hunter
  Come to tell me time is done;
On the idle hills for ever
  There will stand the idle sun.

There the wind will stay to whisper
  Many wonders to the reeds;
But I shall not fear to follow
  Where my Scarlet Hunter leads.

I shall know him, in the darkling
  Murmur of the river bars,
While his feet are on the mountains
  Treading out the smouldering stars.

I shall know him, in the sunshine
  Sleeping in my scarlet tree,
Long before he halts beside it
  Stooping down to summon me.

Then fear not, my friends, to leave me
  In the boding autumn vast;
There are many things to think of
  When the roving days are past.

Leave me by the scarlet maple,
  When the journeying shadows fail,
Waiting till the Scarlet Hunter
  Pass upon the endless trail.

THRENODY FOR A POET

Not in the ancient abbey,
  Nor in the city ground,
Not in the lonely mountains,
  Nor in the blue profound,
Lay him to rest when his time is come
And the smiling mortal lips are dumb;

But here in the decent quiet
  Under the whispering pines,
Where the dogwood breaks in blossom
  And the peaceful sunlight shines,
Where wildbirds sing and ferns unfold,
When spring comes back in her green and gold.

And when that mortal likeness
  Has been dissolved by fire,
Say not above the ashes,
  "Here ends a man's desire."
For every year when the bluebirds sing,
He shall be part of the lyric spring.

Then dreamful-hearted lovers
  Shall hear in wind and rain
The cadence of his music,
  The rhythm of his refrain,
For he was a blade of the April sod
That bowed and blew with the whisper of God.

THE OLD GREY WALL

Time out of mind I have stood
  Fronting the frost and the sun,
That the dream of the world might endure,
  And the goodly will be done.

Did the hand of the builder guess,
  As he laid me stone by stone,
A heart in the granite lurked,
  Patient and fond as his own?

Lovers have leaned on me
  Under the summer moon,
And mowers laughed in my shade
  In the harvest heat at noon.

Children roving the fields
  With early flowers in spring,
Old men turning to look,
  When they heard a bluebird sing,

Have seen me a thousand times
  Standing here in the sun,
Yet never a moment dreamed
  Whose likeness they gazed upon.

Ah, when will ye understand,
  Mortals who strive and plod—
Who rests on this old grey wall
  Lays a hand on the shoulder of God!

HACK AND HEW

Hack and Hew were the sons of God
  In the earlier earth than now;
One at His right hand, one at His left,
  To obey as he taught them how.

And Hack was blind, and Hew was dumb,
  But both had the wild, wild heart;
And God's calm will was their burning will,
  And the gist of their toil was art.

They made the moon and the belted stars,
  They set the sun to ride;
They loosed the girdle and veil of the sea,
  The wind and the purple tide.

Both flower and beast beneath their hands
  To beauty and speed outgrew—
The furious, fumbling hand of Hack,
  The glorying hand of Hew.

Then, fire and clay, they fashioned a man,
  And painted him rosy brown;
And God Himself blew hard in his eyes:
  "Let them burn till they smoulder down!"

And "There!" said Hack, and "There!" thought Hew,
  "We'll rest, for our toil is done."
But "Nay," the Master Workman said,
  "For your toil is just begun.

"And ye who served me of old as God
  Shall serve me anew as man,
Till I compass the dream that is in my heart,
  And perfect the vaster plan."

And still the craftsman over his craft
  In the vague, white light of dawn,
With God's calm will for his burning will,
  While the mounting day comes on,

Yearning, wind-swift, indolent, wild,
  Toils with those shadowy two—
The faltering, restless hand of Hack,
  And the tireless hand of Hew.

DAFFODIL'S RETURN

What matter if the sun be lost?
  What matter though the sky be grey?
There's joy enough about the house,
  For Daffodil comes home today.

There's news of swallows on the air,
  There's word of April on the way;
They're calling flowers within the street,
  And Daffodil comes home today.

Oh, who would care what fate may bring,
  Or what the years may take away!
There's life enough within the hour,
  For Daffodil comes home today.

I LOVED THEE, ATTHIS, IN THE LONG AGO

I loved thee, Atthis, in the long ago,
When the great oleanders were in flower
In the broad herded meadows full of sun.
And we would often at the fall of dusk
Wander together by the silver stream,
When the soft grass-heads were all wet with dew
And purple-misted in the fading light.
And joy I knew and sorrow at thy voice,
And the superb magnificence of love,—
The loneliness that saddens solitude,
And the sweet speech that makes it durable,—
The bitter longing and the keen desire,
The sweet companionship of quiet days
In the slow ample beauty of the world,
And the unutterable glad release
Within the temple of the holy night.
O Atthis, how I loved thee long ago
In that fair perished summer by the sea!

LOW TIDE ON GRAND-PRÉ

The sun goes down and over all
  These barren reaches by the tide
Such unelusive glories fall,
  I almost dream they yet will bide
  Until the coming of the tide.

And yet I know that not for us,
  By any ecstasy of dream,
He lingers to keep luminous
  A little while the grievous stream,
  Which frets, uncomforted of dream;—

A grievous stream, that to and fro,
  Athrough the fields of Acadie
Goes wandering, as if to know
  Why one belovèd face should be
  So long from home and Acadie!

Was it a year or lives ago
  We took the grasses in our hands,
And caught the summer flying low
  Over the waving meadow-lands,
  And held it there between our hands?

The while the river at our feet—
  A drowsy inland meadow stream—
At set of sun the after-heat
  Made running gold, and in the gleam
  We freed our birch upon the stream.

There down along the elms at dusk
  We lifted dripping blade to drift,
Through twilight scented fine like musk,
  Where night and gloom awhile uplift,
  Nor sunder soul and soul adrift.

And that we took into our hands—
  Spirit of life or subtler thing—
Breathed on us there, and loosed the bands
  Of death, and taught us, whispering,
  The secret of some wonder-thing.

Then all your face grew light, and seemed
  To hold the shadow of the sun;
The evening faltered, and I deemed
  That time was ripe, and years had done
  Their wheeling underneath the sun.

So all desire and all regret,
  And fear and memory were naught;
One to remember or forget
  The keen delight our hands had caught;
  Morrow and yesterday were naught.

The night has fallen, and the tide . . .
  Now and again comes drifting home,
Across these aching barrens wide,
  A sigh like driven wind or foam:
  In grief the flood is bursting home!

OVERLORD

Lord of the grass and hill,
Lord of the rain,
White Overlord of will,
Master of pain,

I who am dust and air
Blown through the halls of death,
Like a pale ghost of prayer,—
I am thy breath.

Lord of the blade and leaf,
Lord of the bloom,
Sheer Overlord of grief,
Master of doom,

Lonely as wind or snow,
Through the vague world and dim,
Vagrant and glad I go;
I am thy whim.

Lord of the storm and lull,
Lord of the sea,
I am thy broken gull,
Blown far alee.

Lord of the harvest dew,
Lord of the dawn,
Star of the paling blue
Darkling and gone,

Lost on the mountain height
Where the first winds are stirred,
Out of the wells of night
I am thy word.

Lord of the haunted hush,
Where raptures throng,
I am thy hermit thrush,
Ending no song.

Lord of the frost and cold,
Lord of the North,
When the red sun grows old
And day goes forth,

I shall put off this girth,—
Go glad and free,
Earth to my mother earth,
Spirit to thee.

VESTIGIA

I took a day to search for God,
And found him not. But as I trod
By rocky ledge, through woods untamed,
Just where one scarlet lily flamed,
I saw his footprint in the sod.

Then suddenly, all unaware,
Far off in the deep shadows, where
A solitary hermit thrush
Sang through the holy twilight hush—
I heard His voice upon the air.

And even as I marvelled how
God gives us Heaven here and now,
In a stir of wind that hardly shook
The poplar trees beside the brook—
His hand was light upon my brow.

At last with evening as I turned
Homeward, and thought what I had learned
And all that there was still to probe—
I caught the glory of His robe
Where the last fires of sunset burned.

Back to the world with quickening start
I looked and longed for any part
In making saving Beauty be . . .
And from that kindling ecstasy
I knew God dwelt within my heart.

FREDERICK GEORGE SCOTT [1861-1944]

Frederick George Scott was born in Montreal and educated at Bishop's College, Lennoxville, Quebec. From 1889 on, he had a notable record in the Anglican Church as rector of St. Matthew's, Quebec (1889-1934), as canon of the Cathedral (1906-1925), and as Archdeacon of Quebec (1925-1944). He distinguished himself in the chaplain service during and after the First World War. His prose includes a personal account of that war and a novel. *Poems, Old and New* (1900) was his fourth volume of verse. Other comprehensive volumes are *Selected Poems* (1933), and *Collected Poems* (1934). These were followed by *Poems* (1936). (Cf. Percival as above.)

THE UNNAMED LAKE

It sleeps among the thousand hills
  Where no man ever trod,
And only nature's music fills
  The silences of God.

Great mountains tower above its shore,
  Green rushes fringe its brim,
And o'er its breast for evermore
  The wanton breezes skim.

Dark clouds that intercept the sun
  Go there in Spring to weep.
And there, when Autumn days are done,
  White mists lie down to sleep.

Sunrise and sunset crown with gold
  The peaks of ageless stone,
Where winds have thundered from of old
  And storms have set their throne.

No echoes of the world afar
  Disturb it night or day,
But sun and shadow, moon and star,
  Pass and repass for aye.

'Twas in the grey of early dawn
  When first the lake we spied,
And fragments of a cloud were drawn
  Half down the mountain side.

Along the shore a heron flew,
  And from a speck on high,
That hovered in the deepening blue,
  We heard the fish-hawk's cry.

Among the cloud-capt solitudes
  No sound the silence broke,
Save when, in whispers down the woods,
  The guardian mountains spoke.

Through tangled brush and dewy brake,
  Returning whence we came,
We passed in silence, and the lake
  We left without a name.

DAWN

The immortal spirit hath no bars
  To circumscribe its dwelling-place;
My soul hath pastured with the stars
  Upon the meadow-lands of space.

My mind and ear at times have caught,
  From realms beyond our mortal reach,
The utterance of eternal thought
  Of which all nature is the speech.

And high above the seas and lands,
  On peaks just tipped with morning light,
My dauntless spirit mutely stands
  With eagle wings outspread for flight.

IN THE WOODS

This is God's house—the blue sky is the ceiling,
  This wood the soft, green carpet for His feet,
Those hills His stairs, down which the brooks come stealing,
  With baby laughter making earth more sweet.

And here His friends come, clouds and soft winds sighing,
  And little birds whose throats pour forth their love,
And spring and summer, and the white snow lying
  Pencilled with shadows of bare boughs above.

And here come sunbeams through the green leaves straying,
  And shadows from the storm-clouds overdrawn,
And warm, hushed nights, when mother earth is praying
  So late that her moon-candle burns till dawn.

Sweet house of God, sweet earth so full of pleasure,
  I enter at thy gates in storm or calm;
And every sunbeam is a joy and treasure,
  And every cloud a solace and a balm.

JOHN PLUMMER DERWENT LLWYD [1861-1933]

John Plummer Derwent Llwyd was born in Manchester, England, and educated at Toronto (Trinity), Oxford, and Berlin universities. After serving various churches in the states of Illinois, Nebraska, and Washington, he was vice-provost of his alma mater from 1909 to 1912, and then Dean of Nova Scotia till his death. In prose he wrote of the life and work of John of Bethsaida. His poetic works are *The Vestal Virgin* (1920), a closet drama set in Rome in the early second century, *Sonnet Sequence on the Spring* (1925), and *Poems of Nature, Childhood, and Religion* (1928).

From THE VESTAL VIRGIN

LUCIO (*lover of Nysia*):

The night is soft with summer; yon faint arch
Of mystic silver heralds the moonrise;
And all the air is spicéd with rich breath
From shrubs and flowers unnumbered; as if earth
A mighty mother conscious of her children
Sent forth her soul in sympathy with lovers:
It is a night for all high things to prosper—
A night when faith soars higher, and the creed
Of Pagan gods gives place to noble dreams:
A night for hearts to cleave in tenderness,
But more for hearts to spill with sacrifice.
I cannot hold a base thought in this hour . . .

NYSIA:

I cannot tell the time when love began.
There was no first or last, 'twas as the tide
Swells up in silence round some sleeper on a rock,
Some tired child weary with summer play,
That knows not, feels not, till she wakes to find
The sea her cradle, and the mighty flood
Sweeping her past resistance to new shores
And worlds undreamt of. So it came to me,
Came and remained, a dawn from Paradise:
We never spoke, we simply looked and trembled
And we knew . . .

ALBERT E. S. SMYTHE [1861-1947]

Albert Ernest Stafford Smythe was born near Gracehill, Ireland, and educated at Ballymena Model School and Belfast Institute. After a brief period in journalism in Belfast, he spent about eleven years in commercial work in Chicago. From there he came to Toronto in 1889. He was employed on the editorial staffs of the Toronto *Globe* and the Toronto *World*, of the latter of which he became editor-in-chief, and conducted a column, "Crusts and Crumbs," in the *Sunday World*. From 1928 to 1934 he was editor of the Hamilton *Herald*. He also edited *The Lamp*, journal of the Theosophical Society of Canada (which he founded in 1891), and was honorary editor of *The Canadian Theosophist*. His belief in the spiritual oneness of the universe finds felicitous expression in his poetry, *Poems Grave and Gay* (1891) and *The Garden of the Sun* (1923). (Cf. *Canadian Author and Bookman*, December, 1947, p. 29.)

ANASTASIS

What shall it profit a man
To gain the world—if he can—
And lose his soul, as they say
In their uninstructed way?

The whole of the world in gain;
The whole of your soul! Too vain
You judge yourself in the cost.
'Tis you—not your soul—is lost.

Your soul! If you only knew—
You would reach to the Heaven's blue,
To the heartmost centre sink,
Ere you severed the silver link,

To be lost in your petty lust
And scattered in cosmic dust.
For your soul is a Shining Star
Where the Throne and the Angels are.

And after a thousand years,
With the salve of his bottled tears,
Your soul shall gather again
From the dust of a world of pain

The frame of a slave set free—
The man that you ought to be,
The man you may be tonight
If you turn to the Valley of Light.

GILBERT PARKER [1862-1932]

Sir Horatio Gilbert Parker, son of Joseph Parker, was born at Camden East, Ontario, and educated at Ottawa Normal School and Trinity University, Toronto. After serving as a journalist in Australia from 1885 to 1889, he went to England and turned to fiction and, later, to politics. He is chiefly noted as an historical novelist. His poems are found in *A Lover's Diary* (1894, 1901), and *Embers* (1908).

THE WORLD IN MAKING

When God was making the world,
(*Swift was the wind and white was the fire*)
The feet of His people danced the stars;
There was laughter and swinging bells,
And clanging iron and breaking breath,
The hammers of heaven making the hills,
The vales, on the anvils of God.
(*Wild is the fire and low is the wind*)

When God had finished the world,
(*Bright was the fire and sweet was the wind*)
Up from the valleys came song,
To answer the morning stars;
And the hand of man on the anvil rang,
His breath was big in his breast, his life
Beat strong 'gainst the walls of the world.
(*Glad is the wind and tall is the fire*)

PAULINE JOHNSON [1862-1913]

Emily Pauline Johnson, Tekahionwake (the smoky haze of Indian Summer), daughter of George Henry Martin and Emily S. (Howells) Johnson, was born at "Chiefswood", on the Grand River Reserve of the Six Nations Indians, Brantford, Ontario, and attended Brantford Central Public School. Her triumphant sixteen years' series of recitals began in 1892 with Frank Yeigh as manager. For nearly a decade Walter Jackson McRaye (1877-1946) toured with her, acting as her business manager and sharing the programme with her as an interpreter of Henry Drummond's French-Canadian poems. Her prose includes two volumes of juvenile stories, almost entirely of Indian life, and *Legends of Vancouver* (1911, 1922), tales told to her for the first time to any English-speaking person by the late Chief Joe Capilano. She had made jingles before she could use a pen and had read Shakespeare, Byron, Scott, and Longfellow before she was twelve years of age. By that time she was writing creditable poems. In her poetic development her outlook broadens from the Indian to the Canadian to the Imperial to the cosmopolitan. Her books of poetry are *White Wampum* (1895), *Canadian Born* (1903), and the collected poems, entitled *Flint and Feather* (1912), of which there have been sixteen editions, the second with the introduction by T. Watts-Dunton. (Cf. Walter Jackson McRaye, *Town Hall Tonight* (1929), *Pauline Johnson and her Friends* (1947); Mrs. W. Garland Foster (1875-   ) (now Mrs. Patrick Hanley), *The Mohawk Princess—Tekahionwake* (1931); Percival as above.)

SHADOW RIVER

(*Muskoka*)

A stream of tender gladness,
Of filmy sun, and opal-tinted skies;
Of warm midsummer air that lightly lies
In mystic rings,
Where softly swings
The music of a thousand wings
That almost tones to sadness.

Midway 'twixt earth and heaven,
A bubble in the pearly air, I seem
To float upon the sapphire floor, a dream
Of clouds of snow,
Above, below,
Drift with my drifting, dim and slow,
As twilight drifts to even.

The little fern-leaf, bending
Upon the brink, its green reflection greets,
And kisses soft the shadow that it meets
With touch so fine,
The border line
The keenest vision can't define;
So perfect is the blending.

The far fir trees that cover
The brownish hills with needles green and gold,
The arching elms o'erhead, vinegrown and old,
Repictured are
Beneath me far,
Where not a ripple moves to mar
Shades underneath, or over.

Mine is the undertone;
The beauty, strength and power of the land
Will never stir or bend at my command;
But all the shade
Is marred or made,
If I but dip my paddle blade;
And it is mine alone.

O! pathless world of seeming!
O! pathless life of mine whose deep ideal
Is more my own than ever was the real.
For others Fame
And Love's red flame,
And yellow gold: I only claim
The shadows and the dreaming.

THE SONG MY PADDLE SINGS

West wind, blow from your prairie nest,
Blow from the mountains, blow from the west.
The sail is idle, the sailor too;
O! wind of the west, we wait for you.
Blow, blow!
I have wooed you so,
But never a favour you bestow.
You rock your cradle the hills between,
But scorn to notice my white lateen.

I stow the sail, unship the mast:
I wooed you long, but my wooing's past;
My paddle will lull you into rest.
O! drowsy wind of the drowsy west,
Sleep, sleep,
By your mountain steep,
Or down where the prairie grasses sweep!
Now fold in slumber your laggard wings,
For soft is the song my paddle sings.

August is laughing across the sky,
Laughing while paddle, canoe and I,
Drift, drift,
Where the hills uplift
On either side of the current swift.

The river rolls in its rocky bed;
My paddle is plying its way ahead;
Dip, dip,
While the waters flip
In foam as over their breast we slip.

And oh, the river runs swifter now;
The eddies circle about my bow.
Swirl, swirl!
How the ripples curl
In many a dangerous pool awhirl!

And forward far the rapids roar,
Fretting their margin for evermore.
Dash, dash,
With a mighty crash,
They seethe, and boil, and bound, and splash.

Be strong, O paddle! be brave, canoe!
The reckless waves you must plunge into.
Reel, reel,
On your trembling keel,
But never a fear my craft will feel.

We've raced the rapid, we're far ahead!
The river slips through its silent bed.
Sway, sway,
As the bubbles spray
And fall in tinkling tunes away.

And up on the hills against the sky,
A fir tree rocking its lullaby,
Swings, swings,
Its emerald wings,
Swelling the song that my paddle sings.

THE CORN HUSKER

Hard by the Indian lodges, where the bush
Breaks in a clearing, through ill-fashioned fields,
She comes to labour, when the first still hush
Of autumn follows large and recent yields.

Age in her fingers, hunger in her face,
Her shoulders stooped with weight of work and years,
But rich in tawny colouring of her race,
She comes a-field to strip the purple ears.

And all her thoughts are with the days gone by,
Ere might's injustice banished from their lands
Her people, that today unheeded lie,
Like the dead husks that rustle through her hands.

THE TRAIL TO LILLOOET

Sob of fall, and song of forest, come you here on haunting quest,
Calling through the seas and silence, from God's country of the west.
Where the mountain pass is narrow, and the torrent white and strong,
Down its rocky-throated canyon, sings its golden-throated song.

You are singing there together through the God-begotten nights,
And the leaning stars are listening above the distant heights
That lift like points of opal in the crescent coronet
About whose golden setting sweeps the trail to Lillooet—

Trail that winds and trail that wanders, like a cobweb hanging high,
Just a hazy thread outlining midway of the stream and sky,
Where the Fraser River canyon yawns its pathway to the sea;
But half the world has shouldered up between its song and me.

Here, the placid English August, and the sea-encircled miles;
There, God's copper-coloured sunshine beating through the lonely aisles,
Where the waterfalls and forest voice for ever their duet,
And call across the canyon on the trail to Lillooet.

DUNCAN CAMPBELL SCOTT [1862-1947]

Duncan Campbell Scott, born in Ottawa, was the son of Rev. William Scott, a Methodist minister, and so attended various public schools before entering Stanstead College. In 1879 he was appointed a clerk in the Department of Indian Affairs, Ottawa. He was made Deputy Superintendent General in 1913, a position he filled till his retirement. His prose work includes two volumes of distinctive short stories, a biography of John Graves Simcoe, one-act plays, and the critical work mentioned in the comment on Archibald Lampman. His excellent *Collected Poems* (1926) was his eighth volume of poetry. This was followed by *The Green Cloister* (1935), *The Circle of Affection* (1947), containing also some prose, and the posthumously published *Selected Poems* (1951), edited by E. K. Brown (1905-1951). (Cf. also Brown's *On Canadian Poetry* (1943, 1944), Percival as above, and *Five Canadian Poets* (1954) by Arthur S. Bourinot.)

AT THE CEDARS

You had two girls—Baptiste—
One is Virginie—
Hold hard—Baptiste!
Listen to me.

The whole drive was jammed
In that bend at the Cedars,
The rapids were dammed
With the logs tight rammed
And crammed; you might know
The Devil had clinched them below.

We worked three days—not a budge,
"She's as tight as a wedge, on the ledge,"
Says our foreman;
"Mon Dieu! boys, look here,
We must get this thing clear."
He cursed at the men
And we went for it then;
With our cant-dogs arow,
We just gave he-yo-ho;
When she gave a big shove
From above.

The gang yelled and tore
For the shore,
The logs gave a grind
Like a wolf's jaws behind,
And as quick as a flash,
With a shove and a crash,
They were down in a mash,
But I and ten more,
All but Isaàc Dufour,
Were ashore.

He leaped on a log in the front of the rush,
And shot out from the bind
While the jam roared behind;
As he floated along
He balanced his pole
And tossed us a song.
But just as we cheered,
Up darted a log from the bottom,
Leaped thirty feet square and fair,
And came down on his own.

He went up like a block
With the shock,
And when he was there
In the air,
Kissed his hand
To the land;
When he dropped
My heart stopped,
For the first logs had caught him
And crushed him;
When he rose in his place
There was blood on his face.

There were some girls, Baptiste,
Picking berries on the hillside,
Where the river curls, Baptiste,
You know—on the still side
One was down by the water,
She saw Isaàc
Fall back.

She did not scream, Baptiste,
She launched her canoe;
It did seem, Baptiste,
That she wanted to die too,
For before you could think
The birch cracked like a shell
In that rush of hell,
And I saw them both sink—

Baptiste!—
He had two girls,
One is Virginie,
What God calls the other
Is not known to me.

RAPIDS AT NIGHT

Here at the roots of the mountains,
Between the sombre legions of cedars and tamaracks,
The rapids charge the ravine:
A little light, cast by foam under starlight,
Wavers about the shimmering stems of the birches:
Here rise up the clangorous sounds of battle,
Immense and mournful.
Far above curves the great dome of darkness
Drawn with the limitless lines of the stars and the planets.
Deep at the core of the tumult,
Deeper than all the voices that cry at the surface,
Dwells one fathomless sound,
Under the hiss and cry, the stroke and the plangent clamour.

O human heart that sleeps,
Wild with rushing dreams and deep with sadness!

The abysmal roar drops into almost silence,
While over its sleep play in various cadence
Innumerous voices crashing in laughter;
Then rising calm, overwhelming,
Slow in power,
Rising supreme in utterance,
It sways and reconquers and floods all the spaces of silence,
One voice, deep with the sadness,
That dwells at the core of all things.

There by a nest in the glimmering birches,
Speaks a thrush as if startled from slumber,
Dreaming of Southern ricefields,
The moted glow of the amber sunlight,
Where the long ripple roves among the reeds.

Above curves the great dome of darkness,
Scored with the limitless lines of the stars and the planets;
Like the strong palm of God,
Veined with the ancient laws,
Holding a human heart that sleeps,
Wild with rushing dreams and deep with the sadness,
That dwells at the core of all things.

ON THE WAY TO THE MISSION

They dogged him all one afternoon,
Through the bright snow,
Two whitemen servants of greed;
He knew that they were there,
But he turned not his head;
He was an Indian trapper;
He planted his snow-shoes firmly,
He dragged the long toboggan
Without rest.

The three figures drifted
Like shadows in the mind of a seer;
The snow-shoes were whisperers
On the threshold of awe;
The toboggan made the sound of wings,
A wood-pigeon sloping to her nest.

The Indian's face was calm.
He strode with the sorrow of fore-knowledge,
But his eyes were jewels of content
Set in circles of peace.

They would have shot him;
But momently in the deep forest,
They saw something flit by his side;
Their hearts stopped with fear.
Then the moon rose.
They would have left him to the spirit,
But they saw the long toboggan
Rounded well with furs,
With many a silver fox-skin,
With the pelts of mink and of otter.

They were the servants of greed;
When the moon grew brighter
And the spruces were dark with sleep,
They shot him.
When he fell on a shield of moonlight
One of his arms clung to his burden;
The snow was not melted:
The spirit passed away.

Then the servants of greed
Tore off the cover to count their gains;
They shuddered away into the shadows,
Hearing each the loud heart of the other.
Silence was born.

There in the tender moonlight,
  As sweet as they were in life,
Glimmered the ivory features,
  Of the Indian's wife.

In the manner of Montagnais women
  Her hair was rolled with braid;
Under her waxen fingers
  A crucifix was laid.

He was drawing her down to the Mission,
  To bury her there in spring,
When the bloodroot comes and the windflower
  To silver everything.

But as a gift of plunder
  Side by side were they laid,
The moon went on to her setting
  And covered them with shade.

THE FORSAKEN

I

Once in the winter
Out on a lake
In the heart of the north-land,
Far from the Fort
And far from the hunters,
A Chippewa woman
With her sick baby,
Crouched in the last hours
Of a great storm.

Frozen and hungry,
She fished through the ice
With a line of the twisted
Bark of the cedar,
And a rabbit-bone hook
Polished and barbed;
Fished with the bare hook
All through the wild day,
Fished and caught nothing;
While the young chieftain
Tugged at her breasts,
Or slept in the lacings
Of the warm *tikanagan.*
All the lake-surface
Streamed with the hissing
Of millions of iceflakes
Hurled by the wind;
Behind her the round
Of a lonely island
Roared like a fire
With the voice of the storm
In the deeps of the cedars.
Valiant, unshaken,
She took of her own flesh,
Baited the fish-hook,
Drew in a grey-trout,
Drew in his fellows,
Heaped them beside her,
Dead in the snow.
Valiant, unshaken,
She faced the long distance,
Wolf-haunted and lonely,
Sure of her goal
And the life of her dear one:
Tramped for two days,
On the third in the morning,
Saw the strong bulk
Of the Fort by the river,
Saw the wood-smoke
Hang soft in the spruces,
Heard the keen yelp
Of the ravenous huskies
Fighting for whitefish:
Then she had rest.

II

Years and years after,
When she was old and withered,
When her son was an old man
And his children filled with vigour,
They came in their northern tour on the verge of winter,
To an island in a lonely lake.
There one night they camped, and on the morrow
Gathered their kettles and birch-bark,
Their rabbit-skin robes and their mink-traps,
Launched their canoes and slunk away through the islands,
Left her alone forever,
Without a word of farewell,
Because she was old and useless,
Like a paddle broken and warped,
Or a pole that was splintered.
Then, without a sigh,
Valiant, unshaken,
She smoothed her dark locks under her kerchief,
Composed her shawl in state,
Then folded her hands ridged with sinews and corded with veins,
Folded them across her breasts spent with the nourishing of children,
Gazed at the sky past the tops of the cedars,
Saw two spangled nights arise out of the twilight,
Saw two days go by filled with the tranquil sunshine,
Saw, without pain, or dread, or even a moment of longing:
Then on the third great night there came throng and in thronging
Millions of snowflakes out of a windless cloud;
They covered her close with a beautiful crystal shroud,
Covered her deep and silent.
But in the frost of the dawn,
Up from the life below,
Rose a column of breath
Through a tiny cleft in the snow,
Fragile, delicately drawn,
Wavering with its own weakness,
In the wilderness a sign of the spirit,
Persisting still in the sight of the sun
Till day was done.
Then all light was gathered up by the hand of God and hid in His
breast,
Then there was born a silence deeper than silence,
Then she had rest.

THE HALF-BREED GIRL

She is free of the trap and the paddle,
The portage and the trail,
But something behind her savage life
Shines like a fragile veil.

Her dreams are undiscovered,
Shadows trouble her breast,
When the time for resting cometh
Then least is she at rest.

Oft in the morns of winter,
When she visits the rabbit snares,
An appearance floats in the crystal air
Beyond the balsam firs.

Oft in the summer mornings
When she strips the nets of fish,
The smell of the dripping net-twine
Gives to her heart a wish.

But she cannot learn the meaning
Of the shadows in her soul,
The lights that break and gather,
The clouds that part and roll,

The reek of rock-built cities,
Where her father dwelt of yore,
The gleam of loch and shealing,
The mist on the moor,

Frail traces of kindred kindness,
Of feud by hill and strand,
The heritage of an age-long life
In a legendary land.

She wakes in the stifling wigwam,
Where the air is heavy and wild,
She fears for something or nothing
With the heart of a frightened child.

She sees the stars turn slowly
Past the tangle of the poles,
Through the smoke of the dying embers,
Like the eyes of dead souls.

Her heart is shaken with longing
For the strange, still years,
For what she knows and knows not,
For the wells of ancient tears.

A voice calls from the rapids,
Deep, careless and free,
A voice that is larger than her life
Or than her death shall be.

She covers her face with her blanket,
Her fierce soul hates her breath,
As it cries with a sudden passion
For life or death.

BELLS

Slow bells at dawn—
What mean ye by your tolling?
Bells in the growing light,
Knolling afar,

Loitering in leisured sequence,
Where the ringing seraphim
Shake you out of heaven,
From the morning star.

Echoes are in my soul,—
Consonances and broken melodies,—
Survivals frayed and remembrances
Vanished and irretrievable.

What know ye of life,
Or of perished hours or years,
Ye tones that are born in air
And throb in air and die,
Leaving no traces anywhere,
Save tremors in the quickened pool of tears
Within the windless deeps of memory?

ECSTASY

The shore-lark soars to his topmost flight,
Sings at the height where morning springs,
What though his voice be lost in light,
The light comes dropping from his wings.

Mount, my soul, and sing at the height
Of thy clear flight in the light and the air.
Heard or unheard in the night in the light
Sing there! Sing there!

IN THE SELKIRKS

The old grey shade of the mountain
Stands in the open sky,
Counting, as if at his leisure,
The days of Eternity.

The stream comes down from its sources,
Afar in the glacial height,
Rushing along through the valley
In loops of silver light.

"What is my duty, O Mountain?
Is it to stand like thee?
Is it, O flashing Torrent,
Like thee—to be free?"

The man utters the questions,
He breathes—he is gone!
The mountain stands in the heavens,
The stream rushes on.

JEAN BLEWETT [1862-1934]

Mrs. Jean (McKishnie) Blewett, daughter of John and Janet (McIntyre) McKishnie, was born at Scotia, Ontario, and educated at St. Thomas Collegiate Institute. For years she was associated with the Toronto *Globe*, as contributor, member of the staff, and editor of the "Homemaker's Department." Her one novel is *Out of the Depths* (1890). In verse she published *Heart Songs* (1897), *The Cornflower and Other Poems* (1906), and *Poems* (1922).

AT QUEBEC

Quebec, the grey old city on the hill,
Lies with a golden glory on her head,
Dreaming throughout this hour so fair—so still—
Of other days and all her mighty dead.
The white doves perch upon the cannons grim,
The flowers bloom where once did run a tide
Of crimson, when the moon rose pale and dim
Above the battlefield so grim and wide.

Methinks within her wakes a mighty glow
Of pride, of tenderness—her stirring past—
The strife, the valour, of the long ago
Feels at her heartstrings. Strong, and tall, and vast,
She lies, touched with the sunset's golden grace,
A wondrous softness on her grey old face.

PHILLIPS STEWART [1864-1892]

Thomas Brown Phillips Stewart, a native of Ontario, was educated at Brampton High School and the University of Toronto. Ill health caused the melancholy tone of *Poems* (1887). (Cf. *Canadian Who was Who*, vol. 2 (1938).)

HOPE

In shadowy calm the boat
  Sleeps by the dreaming oar,
The green hills are afloat
Beside the silver shore.

Youth hoists the white-winged sail,
  Love takes the longing oar—
The oft-told fairy tale
  Beside the silver shore.

Soft lip to lip, and heart
  To heart, and hand to hand,
And wistful eyes depart
  Unto another strand.

And lovely as a star
  They tremble o'er the wave,
With eager wings afar
  Unto the joys they crave.

In a sweet trance they fare
  Unto the wind and rain,
With wind-tossed waves of hair,
  And ne'er return again.

And at the drifting side,
  Changed faces in the deep
They see, and changing tide,
  Like phantoms in a sleep.

Slow hands furl the torn sail
Without one silver gleam,
And sad, and wan, and pale,
They gaze into a dream.

ELIZABETH ROBERTS MACDONALD [1864-1922]

Mrs. Jane Elizabeth Gostwycke (Roberts) MacDonald, who married her cousin Samuel Roberts MacDonald, was born at Westcock, New Brunswick, the daughter of Rev. George Goodridge and Emma Wetmore (Bliss) Roberts. She published *Poems* (1891) and *Dream Verses and Others* (1906), and *Northland Lyrics* (1899) contains poems by her and by her brothers William Carman Roberts and Theodore Goodridge Roberts. (Cf. Lloyd Roberts, *The Book of Roberts* (1923).)

THE SUMMONS

The wind voice calls and calls you;
Heart of the woods, return!
The little paths remember,
Lonely among the fern.

The autumn fields await you,
Soul of my song, Hilaire;
Their purple pennons signal,
Their golden banners flare.

The solemn sunset gladness,
Like some great organ's roll;
The moonlight's white enchantment,
Awakening the soul—

They call you home to Dreamhurst,
Out of the world's great glare;
Your woods and I are waiting,
Heart of my heart, Hilaire!

ANNIE CHARLOTTE DALTON [1865-1938]

Mrs. Annie Charlotte (Armitage) Dalton and her husband, Willie Dalton, natives of Huddersfield, England, settled in Vancouver in 1904. There she wrote: *The Marriage of Music* (1910); *Flame and Adventure* (1924); *Songs and Carols* (1925); *The Ear Trumpet* (1926); *The Silent Zones* (1927); *The Call of the Carillon* (1928); *The Amber Riders* (1929); *The Neighing North* (1931); and *Lilies and Leopards* (1935). For "Wheat and Barley" she was posthumously awarded the Tweedsmuir medal for the best poem appearing in *Canadian Poetry Magazine* during 1937. (Cf. *Canadian Author and Bookman*, September, 1946, pp. 42-44.)

THE ROBIN'S EGG

The drenched earth has a warm, sweet radiance all her own;
The wakening chestnut flings upon the air
Her crumpled loveliness of leaf.
Lovely and brief,
The daffodil stands deep
In arabis full-blown—
There, early honey gatherers come.

Gold dawns along the spare,
Sleek buds of leopard's-bane,
Beneath the autumn-planted dog-wood still asleep;
Lovely and vain,
The slim, young plum
Flaunts her white bridal veil
Beyond the garden pale.

Fallen, fallen amongst the daffodils,
A robin's egg half-crushed—
Bluer than any sky could be,
Blue with a tense divinity
As if some god had brushed,
Impatiently, a jewel from his hand—
Ah! who shall understand
This radiant mystery!

A moment, and the beauty of our garden has rushed
Away; my heart with some strange rapture fills—
This rapture of this robin's blue
Holds all my soul in thrall,
As if I heard and knew
Some strange, sweet, foreign call;
As if I saw and knew
Some secret in the robin's precious blue.

This scrap of jelly which should be,
Potentially,
A singing robin in our tree—
I sorrow for its tiny life, but still,
Intoxicating, leaps the thrill
That ravishes, that satisfies my soul,
Soothes me, and makes me whole—

So strangely are we made! If I could tell
Whence this pure rapture, this dumb spell—
So strangely are we made that I must know
Why this small thing doth move me so;
Why, for an amulet, I fain would beg
The turquoise of some robin's egg.

FOR AN ESKIMO

Come, let us sing! it is the time for summer,
  Here is no darkness in the noon of night;
Bring forth the drum and fetch the skilful drummer,
  It is the summer and we need no light.
    Bring forth the drum
    That eager folk may come
      And with us sing the grace,
  The crown and glory of our Northern race,
        Eatna!

  Fair as the mellow moon is she,
    Gentle stars attending,
  Fierce as the summer sun can be
    From the sky descending,
Bright as the river flashing into foam
  When the ice is broken,
Steadfast as he who drives the harpoon home
  With a word unspoken;
Fair, fierce, and bright; steadfast as the bravest—
Shine, Golden North! on the queen thou gavest.

  Our huts are far away;
    The winter's hunting done,
  We come a while to play
    Beneath the strengthening sun.
Young men, go build the dance-house! Take your knives
To cut fair blocks and shape the great snow dome;
Too soon the welcome trading-ship arrives
  And all the goodly company go home.
Short is the summer, fretful as the spring,
Put on your building-coats and mittens whilst we sing.

The wild fowl darken now the sun
To each other crying,
Little rivers to the gulches run,
The solid sea is sighing.
Soon will the dainty flowers be blooming
In the genial air,
Soon will the riven ocean booming,
Beat the beaches bare.

Fast, fast the young men work—now we shall go
Into the dazzling dance-house built of snow;
Now those who may not dance will sing and beat
Time for the dancers' nimble shoeless feet,
And all their songs shall be of Eatna's fame,
None but her praises call the dancing game,
And she herself twirl round
The hollow beaten ground.

She is not here, but in this windless calm
What woe can threaten her and our undoing?
She is not here—what over-hidden harm
Can stay the staunch outgoing
Of one who would the stricken prey recover
From tearing tooth of bear or bitter gale,
Of one who will not any task give over,
Who cannot fail?
She is not here—we know not what we fear—
Make no delay,
Let us away!

Stay! O Stay!
Eatna! Eatna!
She comes! She comes! Beat loud the drums—
"Eho! Eho! Eho-o-o!" she's crying,
Over the echoing ice she's flying—
Eho! Eho! Eho-o-o!
Hath she not many a beast
To grace our dancing feast?
Her joyful dogs give voice to us replying.
Eatna! Eatna!
Fear-denying
Death-defying
Eatna!

TO THE YOUNG MAN JESUS

Where is the word of Your youth and beauty,
Your young courage and Your desire to roam?
Where is the song of Your gay companions,
 Your laughter, and joy at home?
We have been fed with tales of bearded men.

The old still sit in their high seats,
Weaving thin webs of silver and gold;
The old still kill, and eat strange meats—
Strange are the ways of the old.

We would see You, Jesus!
Not as the old men see,
But, as Youth would have You,
Young eternally.

Not in the Temple confounding
The Wise with sacred themes,
But as a young deer bounding
Over secret streams.

Not as a Seer unsealing
Fault unconfessed,
But as a bird wide-wheeling
About a nest.

Not on a crude cross panting—
Pale remove—
But on this rich earth wanting
Life and Love.

For You were Life indeed,
And Life was rough;
For You were Love indeed,
And Love was not enough.

For You were Youth discrowned
And thrown to Death,
For You were Truth unfound
Of Nazareth.

The old sat in high seats
Weaving webs of gold;
The old ate strange meats—
Strange were the ways of the old.

Alas for youth and beauty so
Put to shame!
Alas for the Young companions
Who cried Your name!
We have been fed with tales of bearded men.

THE NEIGHING NORTH

He knows not bit nor bridle, his nostrils are flaming,
He calls—do you hear him—the Ghost of the North?
With his hoofs he is pounding the reach and the tundra,
With his wings he is shifting the Way of the Stars;
He calls—do you hear him—the Neighing North?

There where no horse may live, he is calling the horsemen,
He stands in tossed splendour and neighs at their world;
In his eyes lurk the lightnings, from his teeth rolls the thunder,
And the wind of his Spirit like a whirlwind is blowing
Invincible strength to the "chafferers and chatterers."

He calls to the heroes who care not for danger,
To the Men of the North who for death have no caring,
From the North to the North comes the challenging answer,
And he lifts his proud head in his scorn of their weakness,
With his beauty he closes the eyes of the ocean,
With his lonely wild grace breaks the heart of the sailor.

In his youth he would browse through the vale of fair lilies,
There where now moose in the stream chew the stems of the lilies;
In his youth he would soar—joyously soar with Apollo,
There, where now flushed as the sky, the Valkyrior are riding,
Seeking to snare brave men's souls for the banquet of Odin.

He calls—do you hear him—the Ghost of the North?
From the North to the North comes the challenging answer,
From the East to the West go the shining Armadas,
From the West to the East fly the scarlet Armadas,
He calls—do they hear him—they wheel to the North!

With his hoofs he is pounding the reach and the tundra,
With his wings he is toppling the ships from the skies,
But under his feet come new conquerors creeping,
And a Voice from the depth of his Kingdom defies him,
A Voice that is stronger than his, that is crying—
"Thule? Thule? There's no Ultima Thule for man!"

THE SOUNDING PORTAGE

The wind roars and the river roars;
  Strange footsteps hurrying by,
To the roaring wind and the roaring stream
  Tumultuously reply.

The wind sinks and the river sinks;
  And the footsteps dwindling by,
With the fainting wind and the falling stream,
  Pause, hesitate, and die.

This is the Sounding Portage where
  A mort of years ago,
Fur-trappers bound for the hunting-ground
  Came tramping to and fro.

The red men first with their birch canoes,
  The white men next prevail;
Together, they in hardship tread
  An immemorial trail.

Here, by the camp-fire, tales are told,
  And stranger things are said,
How the highway then is a by-way now
  And portage for the dead.

The hurrying sounds make a man's flesh creep;
  Though he strive to laugh and joke,
When the steps draw nigh, none make reply,
  And the scarlet embers smoke.

The steps draw nigh and the rapid roars,
  The listeners breathe a prayer,
They think they hear faint words of cheer
  From struggling mortals there.

When the stars come out with a rapturous shout,
  The nodding campers peer
Through the fringe of trees to the ghostly stream,
  And lose in sleep their fear.

But the wind roars and the river roars,
  And the footsteps hurrying by,
To the roaring wind and the roaring stream
  Tumultuously reply.

Then the wind sinks and the river sinks
  With the footsteps dwindling by,
But the fainting wind and the falling stream
  Like them can never die.

It is dawn and the deer are drinking,
  For the hasty camp is gone;
And the wind roars and the stream roars
  As the tramping dead move on.

VIRNA SHEARD [-1943]

Virginia (Stanton) Sheard, Mrs. (Dr.) Charles Sheard, daughter of Eldridge Stanton, was born in Cobourg, Ontario, and educated there and in Toronto. She was a successful writer of both juvenile and adult fiction and published six books of verse: *The Miracle and Other Poems* (1913); *Carry On* (1917); *The Ballad of the Quest* (1922); *Candle Flame* (1926); *Fairy Doors* (1932); and *Leaves in the Wind* (1938). (Cf. Clara Thomas, *Canadian Novelists* (1946).)

THE YAK

For hours the princess would not play or sleep
  Or take the air;
Her red mouth wore a look it meant to keep
  Unmelted there;
(Each tired courtier longed to shriek, or weep,
  But did not dare.)

Then one young duchess said: "I'll to the King,
  And short and flat
I'll say, 'Her Highness will not play or sing
  Or pet the cat;
Or feed the peacocks, or do anything—
  And that is that'."

So to the King she went, curtsied, and said,
  (No whit confused):
"Your Majesty, I would go home! The court is dead.
  Have me excused;
The little princess still declines,"—she tossed her head—
  "To be amused."

Then to the princess stalked the King: "What ho!" he roared,
"What may you lack?
Why do you look, my love, so dull and bored
With all this pack
Of minions?" She answered, while he waved his sword:
"I want a yak."

"A yak!" he cried (each courtier cried "Yak! Yak!"
As at a blow)
"Is that a figure on the zodiac?
Or horse? Or crow?"
The princess sadly said to him: "Alack
I do not know."

"We'll send the vassals far and wide, my dear!"
Then quoth the King:
"They'll make a hunt for it, then come back here
And bring the thing;—
But warily,—lest it be wild, or queer,
Or have a sting."

So off the vassals went, and well they sought
On every track,
Till by and by in old Tibet they bought
An ancient yak.
Yet when the princess saw it, she said naught
But: "Take it back!"

And what the courtiers thought they did not say
(Save soft and low),
For that is surely far the wisest way
As we all know;
While for the princess? She went back to play!
Tra-rill-a-la-lo!
Tra-rill-a-la-lo!
Tra-rill-a-la-lo!

PETER McARTHUR [1866-1924]

Peter McArthur, "the sage of Ekfrid," son of Peter and Catherine (McLennan) McArthur, was born at Ekfrid, Ontario, and educated there, at Strathroy Collegiate Institute, and at University College, Toronto. After leaving the University in 1889, he first tried teaching and then joined the staff of the Toronto *Mail and Empire.* From 1890 to 1908, except for two years in London, England (1902-1904), he was engaged in journalistic work in New York. He then retired to his old home on the farm and became a regular contributor of articles on farm life to the Toronto *Globe.* During 1910-1911 he published his own periodical, *Ourselves,* in St. Thomas, Ontario. He wrote biography, delightfully humorous essays, and *The Prodigal and Other Poems* (1907). (Cf. W. A. Deacon, *Peter McArthur* (1924).)

EARTHBORN

Hurled back, defeated, like a child I sought
The loving shelter of my native fields,
Where Fancy still her magic sceptre wields,
And still the miracles of youth are wrought.
'Twas here that first my eager spirit caught
The rapture that relentless conflict yields,
And, scorning peace and the content that shields,
Took life's mild way, unguarded and untaught.
Dear Mother Nature, not in vain we ask
Of thee for strength! The visioned victories
Revive my heart, and golden honours gleam:
For here, once more, while in thy love I bask,
My soul puts forth her rapid argosies
To the uncharted ports of summer dream.

SUGAR WEATHER

When snow-balls pack on the horses' hoofs
  And the wind from the south blows warm,
When the cattle stand where the sunbeams beat
  And the noon has a dreamy charm,
When the icicles crash from the dripping eaves
  And the furrows peep black through the snow,
Then I hurry away to the sugar bush,
  For the sap will run, I know.

With auger and axe and spile and trough
  To each tree a visit I pay,
And every boy in the country-side
  Is eager to help today.
We roll the backlogs into their place,
  And the kettles between them swing,
Then gather the wood for the roaring fire
  And the sap in pailfuls bring.

A fig for your arches and modern ways,
  A fig for your sheet-iron pan,
I like the smoky old kettles best
  And I stick to the good old plan;
We're going to make sugar and taffy tonight
  On the swing pole under the tree,
And the girls and the boys for miles around
  Are all sworn friends to me.

The hens are cackling again in the barn,
  And the cattle beginning to bawl,
And neighbours, who long have been acting cool,
  Now make a forgiving call;
For there's no love-feast like a taffy pull,
  With its hearty and sticky fun,
And I know the whole world is at peace with me,
  For the sap has commenced to run.

TOM MacINNES [1867-1951]

Thomas Robert Edward MacInnes, "Canada's picaresque poet," son of Thomas Robert and Martha Elinor MacInnes, was born at Dresden, Ontario, and educated at the High School and St. Louis Brothers College, New Westminster, British Columbia, at Trinity College School, Port Hope, Ontario, and at the University of Toronto. He was called to the Bar in British Columbia in 1893. From 1896 to 1910 he held various government appointments that brought him into contact with different parts of the Canadian Northwest, especially British Columbia and Yukon. He drafted the Canadian Immigration Act. As a result of travel in China, he was well informed on Oriental matters, even to the extent of writing a book on Chinese philosophy. After his return from China in 1922 he spent most of the rest of his life in Vancouver. His *Complete Poems* (1923) was his fifth volume of poems. It was followed by *High Low Along* (1934) and *In the Old of My Age* (1948), an amazing accomplishment for an octogenarian in its intellectual vigour, critical acumen, experimentation in form, and the grasp of human experience revealed in its seven groups of poems. (Cf. William Arthur Deacon, in *Leading Canadian Poets* (1948).)

BALLADE OF FAITH

I think between my cradle-bars
  Of a summer night there fell to me
Some pale religion of the stars,
  While an old Moon lookt weirdly
  At me thro' an apple-tree
And fixt my faith in a fair One
  Fading out of memory:
But I would that I knew where my Lord is gone!

Things there are by night I know
  That in the day I ne'er detect:
Stars that shine from long ago
  Until bewildered I suspect
  The obvious World is not correct,
And fear to lean too much upon
  The showings of mere intellect:
But I would that I knew where my Lord is gone!

In my own fashion I persist:
  No counsel of despair I brook:
Neither for priest nor pessimist,
  Nor the jealous God nor his black Book:
  My early faith I've not forsook
For the low things that pass anon:
  With eyes unspoiled to the stars I look—
But I would that I knew where my Lord is gone!

And caring less how the World esteems
  Me or my doing, I go on
With incommunicable dreams—
  But I would that I knew where my Lord is gone!

TO WALT WHITMAN

I

Hello there, Walt!
Out of sight on the old Highway
I hear your song:
I hear the words that you have said for me:
I, a sayer of words, sing out hello to you:
And you are not so very far ahead but you will hear my words also.

II

Words, Walt, words!
Your words, anybody's words, and the words of the rolling worlds!
But under all the one Word never uttered.

III

O comrade mine!
Accepting all, eager for all, taking no denial!
Good-will shines in you, through you, from you,
Splendid as the sun!

IV

O eagle-eyed! O Titan-heart!
I look with you to the heights of old philosophies:
Looking above and beyond them, shouting ahoy
To wonders weaving out of Wonder endless in the still Eterne!

V

But mostly, Walt,
I watch you saunter down with huge, rejoicing tread,
Tramping America:
Noting New York and its enormity:
Swinging an axe in the Oregon forests:
Bellowing songs to the sea.

VI

Your catalogs I read unedified:
Your lines that lumber humorless as Jewish genealogy:
Your divine average is not divine:
And for all your rant and brag about your States, Who cares?
But the coming of the lilacs, Walt,
And the call of mating birds,
And the smell of June, with its berries,
And the feel of the harvest air,
And supple-bodied youth, and clean red blood, and the ripe, white
 quiver of the grown girl's breast,
And all the easy, common joys of life to be had for the asking,
The beautiful, bountiful flow of things in every land:
Simple, copious, unrestrained forever:
The sky and the stars and the winds of God, and the lovely faces
 behind the masque of Death:—
For chanting these my hat goes off to you,
Old stalwart out of days primeval,
Earth-born and generous!

VII

Down South:
And the tide is coming in:
I watch you fishing from the edge of the old dock:
And a darky sitting by you in the sunshine:
I listen to your lazy chat:
Careless there, smoking a corn-cob pipe:
Blowing blue incense up to the round blue sky:
Breathing the absolute now.

VIII

O but the Ocean played great tunes for you in octaves run too deep
For your dull-eared compatriots to hear!

IX

I tell you, Walt,
This world lies sick for want of men like you!
Resistant, unconforming, singular,
Against the moulding and compression of the average:
Against the drag to the level, and the blatherskite commune.

X

Here's to you, Walt!
To you, and all good tramps of Adam following!
Singing at sun-up through the morning air,
Free of all stifling unions,
Striking the trail of the great companions,
Forever on their own!

CHINATOWN CHANT

I go down to Dupont Street
  See my very good friend:
I have something good to eat
  With my very good friend:
Feel so blue and want some fun,
Play fantan with Wun Fat Bun,
He thinks me just Number One,
  He my very good friend.

  Yum poi—I no care!
  Yum poi—you no care!
Sometime good time alla time maybe!
  We no care—yum poi!

Hello, how do, come in, sit down!
  You my very good friend!
You come best place in Chinatown,
  You my very good friend!
Too much cold and rain in street,
You look sick, me stand you treat,
Fix up something good to eat
  For my very good friend.

Yum poi—I no care!
Yum poi—you no care!
Sometime good time alla time maybe!
We no care—yum poi!

S'pose you like some extra-dry,
You my very good friend:
S'pose you like some laichee-guy,
You my very good friend!
Birdnest soup and some shark-fin,
Bamboo-stick in chicken-wing,
Mushroom stew with everything
For my very good friend.

Yum poi—I no care!
Yum poi—you no care!
Sometime good time alla time maybe!
We no care—yum poi!

Plenty eat and plenty drink
For my very good friend!
You stay here all night, I think,
You my very good friend!
I lock fast big outside door,
Have best time you had before,
Sing-song girlie come some more
For my very good friend.

Yum-poi—I no care!
Yum-poi—you no care!
Sometime good time alla time maybe!
We no care—yum poi!

Sing-song girlie dance for you,
Sing, my very good friend!
No more now you feel so blue,
Sing, my very good friend!
Too much drink and too much fun
Just enough for Number One,
You know nothing when you done—
O my very good friend.

Yum poi—I no care!
Yum poi—you no care!
Sometime good time alla time maybe!
We no care—yum poi!

THE MODERNISTS

(*Villanelle*)

How very modern once they were
  In Nineveh and Babylon—
Maybe earlier in Ur!

Arrantly they play upon
  A single string to make a tune—
Declaring it the paragon!

Youngsters of the New Moon,
  With bubble ponderosity
Would pin a permanent on Noon!

Witless of how brief may be
  The consummated, smart, elated
Click of their modernity!

Or late or soon evaluated,
  Fine Art is of no epoch drawn,
And Beauty's like the sky—undated!

Now they're here and now they're gone!
  How very modern once they were
In Nineveh and Babylon—
  Maybe earlier in Ur!

THE VELVET SONNETEERS

The velvet sonneteers of days gone by
  Were nice in choice of things to sing about:
  Tho' life for them was grim enough, no doubt,
They had for its romance the single eye
When Art was in command. I wonder why
  Fine writers of the rhymeless modern rout
  Push corrugated prose in stanzas out—
So scant of sense or tune to satisfy?
Up from the wrack of these downcrashing years,
  When agonies of war at last are o'er,
  Let Art again for her own sake restore
Those artful lines whose every twist appears
  Revealing of her loveliness the more!
Let sing again the velvet sonneteers!

ALAN SULLIVAN [1868-1947]

Edward Alan Sullivan, son of Right Reverend Edward and Frances Mary (Renaud) Sullivan, was born in Montreal and educated there and at the University of Toronto. As an explorer, and engineer in the construction of railways and canals, he became an authority on the Canadian North. His literary output includes numerous novels, short stories, and some pleasing poems. (Cf. Clara Thomas, *Canadian Novelists* (1946).)

THE WHITE CANOE

There's a whisper of life in the grey dead trees,
  And a murmuring wash on the shore,
And a breath of the south in the loitering breeze,
  To tell that a winter is o'er.
While, free at last from its fetters of ice,
  The river is clear and blue,
And cries with a tremulous, quivering voice
  For the launch of the White Canoe.

Oh, gently the ripples will kiss her side,
  And tenderly bear her on;
For she is the wandering phantom bride
  Of the river she rests upon;
She is loved with a love that cannot forget,
  A passion so strong and true
That never a billow has risen yet
  To peril the White Canoe.

So come when the moon is enthroned in the sky,
  And the echoes are sweet and low,
And Nature is full of the mystery
  That none but her children know.
Come, taste of the rest that the weary crave,
  But is only revealed to a few:
When there's trouble on shore, there's peace on the wave,
  Afloat in the White Canoe.

SUPPLIANT

Grant me, dear Lord, the alchemy of toil,
  Clean days of labour, dreamless nights of rest,
And that which shall my weariness assoil,
  The Sanctuary of one beloved breast;

Laughter of children, hope and thankful tears,
  Knowledge to yield, with valour to defend
A faith immutable, and steadfast years
  That move unvexed to their mysterious end.

ERNEST FEWSTER [1868-1947]

Dr. Ernest Philip Fewster, son of Philip and Mary (Woolley) Fewster, was born in Berkshire, England, and attended schools in Wiltshire, Reading, and South Kensington. In the United States he studied at Dunham-Hering Medical College, Chicago, and at the University of Chicago. He practised medicine on Vancouver Island till 1911, when he moved to Vancouver. He published a book of essays, *My Garden Dreams* (1926), and was joint author with Mrs. Alice M. Winlow of *Poems of Armageddon* (First World War), and author of *White Desire* (1930, 2 edd.), *The Immortal Dweller* (1938), *Litany Before the Dawn of Fire* (1942), and *The Wind and the Sea* (1946).

THE PEARLY EVERLASTING

Flower of the shining Summer,
Love of the Autumn day,
Sea-grey leaves defiant
When blustering Fall winds play.

Child of the joy of nature,
Faring o'er hill and glade
Where wilding winds may kiss you,
Vagrant and unafraid.

Time with a touch impatient
Falters before your will.
Like a quiet catch of laughter
You thread the woodlands still.

'Mid the Fireweed's ragged pillars
And the Bracken's brown distress,
Like broken pools of moonlight
Soft flutters your pearl-grey dress.

Older than Spring's old music,
Older than Summer skies,
Along the lonely ranges
Your sturdy challenge flies.

Shattered the comely beauty
Where the sun's great riot ran,
But you are left like memory,
Or hope, in the heart of man.

THE CLIFF ROSE

Rose to the roseburst break of day
Where cliff meets the bending sky—
Aglow to twilight's fading fire
Where the sunset colours lie.

Poised on the perilous edge of light
From passionate life out-blown,
On the weathered face of the mountain wall
Slender and fair, alone.

Beyond the reach of the eager hand,
Greeting the day's bright crown
With the tender sway of a cradled bud
Or a petal fluttering down.

Hung like a flame 'tween cliff and sky
Where never a foot hath trod,
Thy pure grace blooms as a kiss of Earth
Upheld to the lips of God.

J. D. LOGAN [1869-1929]

John Daniel Logan, son of Charles and Elizabeth G. (Rankin) Logan, was born at Antigonish, Nova Scotia, and educated at Pictou Academy and Dalhousie and Harvard universities. After five years of teaching, he took up advertising. Then came journalistic work, first as literary and music critic for the *Sunday World*, Toronto, and then on the staff of the Toronto *Daily News*. During the First World War he enlisted as a private. In the winter of 1915-1916 he gave at Acadia University, Wolfville, Nova Scotia, the first series of lectures on Canadian literature to be given in any Canadian university. After serving for some time as Assistant Canadian Archivist in Halifax, he spent his last years in educational work in the United States. In prose he contributed critical works and discussions of affairs. His books of poems are: *Preludes, Sonnets, and Other Verses* (1906); *Songs of the Makers of Canada and Other Homeland Lyrics* (1911); *Insulters of Death* (1916); *The New Apocalypse* (1919); and *Twilight Litanies* (1920).

HELIODORE

O world that turneth as a vane that veers!
In what pure Isles beyond the sensual sight
Dwells Heliodore, whose presence was the light
Of Life's obscure probationary spheres?
We pledged her—fervently—our fairest years;
But she is fled; and, like the Eremite,—
Companion of the Caves and black-browed Night,—
We feed on Dust and drink the Cup of Tears.
Is there no boon upon the empty earth
For us, O World!—no other gift of bliss?
Ah, if of Love there be no second birth,
And for our longing lips no lips to kiss,
Grant us this saving boon—if nothing more—
Dear dreams of our first Love—lost Heliodore!

ALEXANDER LOUIS FRASER [1870-1954]

Alexander Louis Fraser, son of Hugh and Charlotte (Dillman) Fraser, was born at Blue Mountain, Nova Scotia, and educated at Pictou Academy, Pine Hill Divinity Hall, and New College, Edinburgh. He filled various Presbyterian and United Church pastorates in the Maritime Provinces. After his retirement he lived in Halifax. His books of poems are: *Sonnets and Other Verses* (1909); *At Life's Windows* (1910); *Fugitives* (1912); *The Indian Bride* (1915); *Aftermath* (1919); *God's Wealth and Other Poems* (1922); *The Drained Cup and Other Poems* (1925); *By Cobequid Bay* (1927); *People of the Street* (1929); *By Eastern Windows* (1932); *Ruth and Other Poems* (1946); and *Moose River Mines and Other Poems* (1949).

BY COBEQUID BAY

[*Masstown, N.S.*]

Like a forsaken theatre art thou,
    The lights extinguished and the actors gone,
  Where once Wit, Gaiety and Beauty shone.
Twice fourscore years since their departing bow,
Who to the Fleur-de-lis had kept their vow.
  From Plenty-laden field and velvet lawn,
  And garden of the dead all were withdrawn,
As Fundy's tide swept round their Grief-draped prow.

Where once light-sandalled Happiness was glad,
  With Home and sylvan voices everywhere,
Moved marshalled men, each visage passing sad,
  Leaving their humble cross-crowned house of prayer;
And lingering by this strand today one hears
A wail of sorrow down the time-washed years.

FRANCIS SHERMAN [1871-1926]

Francis Joseph Sherman, son of Louis Walsh and Alice (Maxwell) Sherman, was born at Fredericton, where he attended the Grammar School while Parkin was headmaster and studied for a while at the University of New Brunswick. He left the University before graduating to take up banking, in which he achieved notable success. In addition to some work in collaboration, he published *Matins* (1896), poems of fine workmanship, and two booklets of sonnets, *In Memorabilia Mortis* (1896) and *A Prelude* (1897). *The Complete Poems of Francis Sherman*, edited with a memoir by Lorne Pierce, and a foreword by Sir Charles G. D. Roberts, was published in 1935. (Cf. H. G. Wade, *An Acadian Singer* (1930); *Canadian Who was Who*, vol. 1 (1934).)

IN MEMORABILIA MORTIS

I marked the slow withdrawal of the year.
Out on the hills the scarlet maples shone—
The glad, first herald of triumphant dawn.
A robin's song fell through the silence—clear
As long ago it rang when June was here.
Then, suddenly, a few grey clouds were drawn
Across the sky; and all the song was gone,
And all the gold was quick to disappear.
That day the sun seemed loth to come again;
And all day long the low wind spoke of rain,
Far off, beyond the hills; and moaned, like one
Wounded, among the pines: as though the Earth
Knowing some giant grief had come to birth,
Had wearied of the Summer and the Sun.

THE BUILDER

Come and let me make thee glad
In this house that I have made!
Nowhere (I am unafraid!)
Canst thou find its like on Earth:
Come, and learn the perfect worth
Of the labour I have had.

I have fashioned it for thee,
Every room and pictured wall;
Every marble pillar tall,
Every door and window-place;
All were done that thy fair face
Might look kindlier on me.

Here, moreover, thou shalt find
Strange, delightful, far-brought things:
Dulcimers, whose tightened strings,
Once, dead women loved to touch;
(Deeming they could mimic much
Of the music of the wind!)

Heavy candlesticks of brass;
Chess-men carved of ivory;
Mass-books written perfectly
By some patient monk of old;
Flagons wrought of thick, red gold,
Set with gems and coloured glass;

Burnished armour, once some knight
(Dead, I deem, long wars ago)
Its great strength was glad to know
When his Lady needed him:
(Now that both his eyes are dim
Both his sword and shield are bright!)

Come, and share these things with me,
Men have died to leave us!
We shall find life glorious
In this splendid house of love;
Come, and claim thy part thereof,—
I have fashioned it for thee!

THE HOUSE OF COLOUR

Fine gold is here; yea, heavy yellow gold,
Gathered ere Earth's first days and nights were fled;
And all the walls are hung with scarfs of red,
Broidered in fallen cities, fold on fold;
The stainèd window's saints are aureoled;
And all the textures of the East are spread
On the pavèd floor, whereon I lay my head,
And sleep, and count the coloured things of old.
Once, when the hills and I were all aflame
With envy of the pageant in the West
(Except the sombre pine-trees—whence there came
Continually, the sigh of their unrest),
A lonely crow sailed past me, black as shame,
Hugging some ancient sorrow to his breast.

LET US RISE UP AND LIVE

Let us rise up and live! Behold, each thing
Is ready for the moulding of our hand.
Long have they all awaited our command;
None other will they ever own for king.
Until we come no bird dare try to sing,
Nor any sea its power may understand;
No buds are on the trees; in every land
Year asketh year some tidings of some Spring.
Yea, it is time,—high time we were awake!
Simple indeed shall life be unto us.
What part is ours?—To take what all things give;
To feel the whole world growing for our sake;
To have sure knowledge of the marvellous;
To laugh and love.—*Let us rise up and live!*

MARIAN OSBORNE [1871-1931]

Mrs. Marian (Francis) Osborne, daughter of George Grant Francis, a native of Wales, was born in Montreal and educated at Sacred Heart Convent there, at Hellmuth College, London, Ontario, and at Trinity College, Toronto. As Mrs. Charles Lambert Bath she spent five years in Wales. Her second husband was Col. Henry C. Osborne. Long a resident of Toronto, she lived in Ottawa for the last eleven years of her life. She wrote ballets, plays for stage and screen, and lyrics for songs. Books of poetry are *Poems* (1914), *The Song of Israfel and Other Poems* (1923), *Flight Commander Stork and Other Verses* (1925), children's verse, and *Sappho and Phaon* (1926), a lyrical drama. (Cf. *Canadian Who was Who*, vol. 1 (1934).)

WHITE VIOLET

White Violet within the close-drawn wood,
  Nun-like and pale and shy,
  Child-sweet in purity;
These silent hidden places suit you best
Where God gives sheltered rest.

White Violet within the close-drawn wood,
  Why is your heart so crushed?
  "When night was dark and hushed
A guilty soul could find no peace within
And told me of his sin."

White Violet within the close-drawn wood,
Why do you shuddering sigh
And fear each passer-by?
"A fleck of blood has glazed my upturned face
The murderer to trace."

White Violet within the close-drawn wood,
Why do you fade so soon?
There was no heat at noon.
"My purity was all I had to give
And now . . . I dare not live."

THE TRINITY

Truth, Beauty, Love, in these are formed a ring
Embracing most of virtue. To attain
To love we must be one in heart and brain
With all existence. Beauty sweeps each string
Weaving fair harmonies, through everything
Interpreting herself in joy and pain.
Truth is the crystal clear by which we gain
The vision pure of life and reasoning.

And every sin against this Trinity
Wrongs all the world and not ourselves alone.
Our acts are like the pebbles that we fling
Into the placid lake, and no more see;
Yet far from us their influence is shown
In outward circles ever widening.

LYON SHARMAN [1872-]

Abbie Mary (Lyon) Sharman, Mrs. Henry Burton Sharman, daughter of Reverend and Mrs. David N. Lyon, was born in Hangchow and lived there for seven years. She was educated at Wooster College, Ohio, and at the University of Chicago. For some time she reviewed books for the weekly literary supplement of the Chicago *Evening Post.* The Sharmans went to Winnipeg in 1910 and later moved to Toronto and then to California. Mrs. Sharman has written stories and sketches of Oriental life, biographical material, and two books of poetry, *The Sea Wall and Other Verse* (1925), and *Town and Forest* (1942).

OLD MAN POT

Like any of us—you or me—
He lived with his family, met his relatives,
Spoke to acquaintances, who one and all
Made free with his useful everyday name,
But stupidly took no pains to know
His uncommon soul. He was an artist
In porcelains; maker of monochrome jars,
Egg-shell winecups, celadon plates.
Of hundreds who knew him few could divine
The skill he spent on an apple-green glaze,
On fish-roe crackle, or millet-grained surface,
On patterns incised, or figures in relief,
On tints of sea-water or liquid dawn;
So he dreamed of those who would love his work
For its beauty, long after the ewers of wine
And bowls of food had ceased to be offered
By good but unaesthetic descendants,
Before his decaying, ancestral tablet.
When in the paste of his jars he pencilled
His mark in Mohammedan blue or vermilion,
He wrote himself down, he the maker,
As "Old Man Pot, Hiding in the Jar."

There lay a hint of an ancient story,
Told by the common folk over and over,
A happy legend of a good magician,
("Old Man Pot," the children call him),
Who busied himself daily with wonders,
But disappeared at night from his friends
By secretly making himself so small
He could hide in a pot hung by the doorway.
The artist who made the marvellous porcelain,
The etched celadon and blue rice-bowls,
Knew that the tale would surely outlive
Both his thinnest cups and his staunchest jars;
So he signed himself for the knowing in art—
His true kinsfolk who would understand,
As far down the ages as you and me—
Not as Wang or Lo, whom everyone knew,
And even the catalogues would forget,
But, as "Old Man Pot, Hiding in the Jar":—
As if he would say—"I'm another magician,
Whose prank it is to belittle myself,
And hide away in these beautiful jars."

JOHN McCRAE [1872-1918]

John McCrae, son of Lieut.-Col. David and Janet Simpson (Eckford) McCrae, was born in Guelph, Ontario. After graduating in Arts and Medicine from the University of Toronto, he served in the South African War. From 1900 to 1914 he had a notable medical record in Montreal hospitals. During the last four years of his life he served as a medical officer in the First World War. He had been writing verse during his professional career, and after his death a collected edition, *In Flanders Fields and Other Poems* (1918), was published, with "An Essay in Character" by Sir Andrew Macphail (1864-1938). (Cf. A. E. Byerly, *The McCraes of Guelph* (1932).)

IN FLANDERS FIELDS

In Flanders fields the poppies blow
Between the crosses, row on row,
That mark our place; and in the sky
The larks, still bravely singing, fly
Scarce heard amid the guns below.

We are the Dead. Short days ago
We lived, felt dawn, saw sunset glow,
Loved and were loved, and now we lie
   In Flanders fields.

Take up our quarrel with the foe:
To you from failing hands we throw
The torch; be yours to hold it high.
If ye break faith with us who die
We shall not sleep, though poppies grow
   In Flanders fields.

JAMES B. DOLLARD [1872-1946]

The Rev. James B. Dollard, son of Michael and Anastasia (Quinn) Dollard, was born at Mooncoin, Ireland, and educated at Kilkenny College, at the Grand Seminary of Montreal, and at Laval University. Except for nine years as Parish Priest of Uptergrove, Ontario, he served in Toronto parishes. He published a volume of short stories. His books of poems are *Irish Mist and Sunshine* (1902), *Poems* (1910), *Irish Lyrics and Ballads* (1917), and *The Bells of Old Quebec and Other Poems* (1920).

THE FAIRY HARPERS

As I walked the heights of Meelin on a tranquil autumn day,
The fairy host came stealing o'er the distant moorland grey.
   I heard like sweet bells ringing,
   Or a grove of linnets singing,
And the haunting, wailful music that the fairy harpers play!

Like thunder of deep waters when vast-heaving billows break,
Like soughing of the forest when ten thousand branches shake,
  Like moaning of the wind,
  When the night falls bleak and blind,
So wild and weird the melodies the fairy minstrels make.

The sunbeams flecked the valley, and the cloud-shapes ranged the hill,
The thistle-down scarce drifted in the air so calm and still.
  But along the slopes of Meelin
  Came the ghostly music pealing,
With sad and fitful cadences that set my soul a-thrill!

Then wan and wistful grew the sky o'er Meelin's summit lone,
And weeping for the days gone by, my heart grew cold as stone,
  For I heard loved voices calling
  Beyond the sunlight falling
On Meelin's mournful mountain where the magic harps make moan!

JESSE EDGAR MIDDLETON [1872-]

Jesse Edgar Middleton, son of Rev. Eli and Margaret (Agar) Middleton, was born in Pilkington township, Ontario, and educated at Strathroy Collegiate, Dutton High School, and Ottawa Normal School. He taught school for three years, read proof in Cleveland, Ohio, entered journalism in Quebec, served as music critic on the Toronto *Mail and Empire*, and was for years on the staff of the Toronto *News*. He has written history, fiction, drama, ballad opera, light verse, and war poems. His book of verse is *Sea Dogs and Men at Arms: A Canadian Book of Songs* (1918).

JESOUS AHATONHIA

[Huron Christmas Carol, *circa* 1641]

'Twas in the moon of winter time when all the birds had fled
That Mighty Gitshi Manitou sent angel-choirs instead.
  Before their light the stars grew dim
  And wand'ring hunters heard the hymn
    "Jesus, your King is born,
    Jesus is born;
    In Excelsis Gloria!"

Within a lodge of broken bark the tender Babe was found.
A ragged robe of rabbit-skin enwrapped His beauty 'round;
  And as the hunter braves drew nigh
  The angel song ran loud and high
    "Jesus, your King is born,
    Jesus is born;
    In Excelsis Gloria!"

The earliest moon of winter time is not so round and fair
As was the ring of glory on the helpless Infant there,
While Chiefs from far before Him knelt
With gifts of fox and beaver pelt.
"Jesus, your King is born,
Jesus is born;
In Excelsis Gloria!"

O children of the forest free, O sons of Manitou,
The Holy Child of earth and heav'n is born today for you.
Come, kneel before the radiant Boy
Who brings you beauty, peace and joy.
"Jesus, your King is born,
Jesus is born;
In Excelsis Gloria!"

NOTE: This is an interpretation rather than a translation of Saint Jean de Brébeuf's original Huron, as sung to this day in a French version in the Province of Quebec.

HERBERT T. J. COLEMAN [1872-]

Herbert Thomas John Coleman, son of Francis T. and Elizabeth A. Coleman, was born in Carlington township, Ontario, and educated at the University of Toronto and Columbia University. He has had a distinguished career as an educator in schools and universities (University of Colorado, University of Toronto, and Queen's University), and from 1920 till 1940 was Professor of Philosophy and Dean of the Faculty of Arts and Sciences at the University of British Columbia. In prose he has written on the history of education in Ontario, and on leisure in the form of a Platonic dialogue. His poems include juvenile verse and serious poetry: *The Poet Confides* (1928); *Cockle-Shell and Sandal-Shoon* (1928); *A Rhyme for a Penny* (1930); *Israel in the Wilderness: A Dramatic Cantata* (1934); *Patricia Ann: The Story of a Doll* (1936).

COCKLE-SHELL AND SANDAL-SHOON

Life is a pilgrimage, they say;
At times upon the broad highway,
At times by narrow paths that creep
Painfully o'er mountains steep.
We reach the summit as we may.
Life is a pilgrimage, they say.

Life is a pilgrimage, they say;
But with stout staff of truth alway
We never need be faint of heart,
Nor from the pilgrim path depart,
Even though the skies be heavy and grey.
Life is a pilgrimage, they say.

Life is a pilgrimage, they say.
At times there may be toll to pay
Of our heart's blood; this, life may ask
If we should choose the higher task.
The valiant do not shun the fray.
Life is a pilgrimage, they say.

Life is a pilgrimage, they say.
He that is wise takes time to stay
For worship at some wayside shrine
Of common things that are divine.
The pilgrim heart has need to pray.
Life is a pilgrimage, they say.

Life is a pilgrimage, they say.
At times the heavens are blue, and gay
About our feet are summer flowers
Dancing with the shining hours.
Such joys as these cannot betray
Though life's a pilgrimage, they say.

Life is a pilgrimage, they say.
And when we reach the close of day
Travel-stained and journey-worn,
A voice shall whisper, "Rest till morn!
Rest till the night has passed away."
Life is a pilgrimage, they say.

THE POET CONFIDES

Sometimes I write with the stub of a pencil
On the back of an old envelope,
Or an odd scrap of paper
That I fish up out of an inside pocket.
And sometimes I write on decent paper
With pen and ink.
But always I write (when I write truly)
With my heart's blood.

And it is not I that write,
At least it is not the man
Who bears a conventional name,
And sometimes wears evening clothes,
And has a street address and a telephone number,
And is mentioned in Who's Who.

The one who writes is a very different person,
He has been warmed by the suns of a million summers,
And chilled by the frosts of a million winters,
And gone naked in the jungle,
And followed dim trails through primeval forests,
And suffered indescribable agonies and experienced unimaginable
joys,
Before streets or telephones or the banalities of publicity were ever
thought of.

No! I am not the person you take me for,
But so different, indeed, that you might not care to shake hands
with me if you saw me truly,
Yet I hope you could pity me even if you could not love me,
For I am the soul of man.

WILMOT B. LANE [1872-]

Wilmot Burkmar Lane, son of Freeman and Sarah Eliza Lane, was born in Perth, Ontario, and educated at Napanee Collegiate Institute, University of Toronto, University of Wisconsin, and Cornell University. Between 1899 and 1913 he taught in the United States (Cornell University, Mount Union College, Randolph Macon College). From 1913 to 1940 he was Professor of Ethics at Victoria College, Toronto. In prose he has written on philosophy and psychology. His books of poems are *Quinté Songs and Sonnets* (1925), *Quebec* (1936), a poem on the capture of the title city in 1759, and *The Closed Book: An Epic of the Soul's Quest* (1943).

OWNING

Who owns the moonlit skies, the purple dawn,
The dust of stars that fleck the Milky Way,
Dominions vast in filmy galaxy?
Whose is the splendour of the sea's green lawn,
Its rhythms of curve and fleecy mains wind-drawn?
And whose the voiceless hills that peak the sky
Like index fingers of eternity?
The same that owns the sunset ere 'tis gone.
Who holds the skies and pencilled trees in mind
Of love no title deeds can make nor bind,
He, only, owns. His soul can grasp the theme
And love the utmost lines of nature's dream,
Can sense the marvels of the birds and trees,
Night and her thousand eyes and gleaming seas.

GEORGE HERBERT CLARKE [1873-1953]

George Herbert Clarke, son of George K. M. and Anne (Mann) Clarke, was born at Gravesend, England, and educated at private schools in England and at Woodstock College and McMaster University in Ontario. Four years (1897-1901) in Chicago were followed by forty-two years as a Professor of English, twenty-four in various American universities and eighteen at Queen's University. His activities have included British publicity work, editorial work, and criticism. His poetry books are *At the Shrine and Other Poems* (1914), *The Hasting Day* (1930), *Halt and Parley* (1934), *Collected Poems* (1947), and *Selected Poems* (1954), edited and with an Introduction by George Whalley, and a Memoir by W. O. Raymond. He was awarded the Seranus Memorial Prize for poetry in 1937 and the Lorne Pierce Medal of the Royal Society of Canada in 1943.

OVER SALÈVE

[*Geneva*]

Over Salève I heard a skylark singing
  Blessèd be Beauty, Beauty! He soared and swirled,
In very ecstasy of flight outflinging
  His breathless music on a broken world.
Joy, the sole faith of that so tiny flyer
  Twining unnumbered notes in psalms of praise,
Lifted him up on high and ever higher
  Till the blue heaven hid him from my gaze.
Still he adored, flooding the sky and mountain
  With delicate waves of sound more silver-sweet
Than the pure flowing of a pebbled fountain
  To desert-farers fainting in the heat.
Beggar am I for Beauty's least caress;
The little lark knows all her loveliness.

HALT AND PARLEY

Good Toll-Gate keeper, kindle a light!
The Sun has fallen: full sudden the Night:
(He seemeth some ancient anchorite
Who broodeth, and heedeth us not.)

He heeds.

Stay by the Gate and tell your needs!

Sir, we would learn the lawful toll.

How many travellers?

Body and Soul.

How long have you journeyed together thus?

All Day, and nothing shall sunder us.

How have you fared? Was the roadway rough?

Some miles were stony and steep enough.

But why have you toiled and suffered so?
And whither is it that you would go?

Our goal is a vision that vanisheth.
To pause is to perish: devouring Death
Would slow our pulses and choke our breath . . .

Tollman, teach us your name! A sage
Are you, acquaint with our pilgrimage?

No sage, yet mayhap wiser than Man,
Torn with a doubt since Time began:
Man the afraid, infirm, impure!
Yet how he can love and how endure,—
Endure to the end and arise again,
Victorious victim of passion and pain . . .

Motley the breed that mount to my Gate:
They fear their fate, yet they face their fate.
Of Radiant Heat and Primal Slime
Engendered, hither they creep and climb,—
Ether and earth, perverse, sublime! . . .

The Ongoer made me His Deputy here:
Who payeth may pass, though he reckon it dear,—
His quittance from clumsy, cumbering gear.

You are Death?

I am Death, Devourer and Foe
Or Friend and Deliverer: how may ye know? . . .

Slowly the Gate swings for entrance—and end:
The shrouded way waits, unposted, unkenned;
Time's phantasies fade: the Reals impend. . . .

Let the toll be taken!

Nay, gallantly dare
The dark passage, Soul! Body's paid the full fare—
Poor clod—while you've parried and parleyed out there.

FOG-HORN

Slow the moon rises, wraith of a moon long drowned,
And clouds of her cold breath, obscuring her,
Curtain the sea and shadowily stir,
Pale shreds of mist floating in phantom round—
Intangible sheaves bound but to be unbound—
While the gulls wheel and churlishly confer,
And the low whine of the wind is a harbinger
Of the strange sound that stills all other sound.

Urgent it comes, vibrant and hoarse and urgent,
Far in that wilderness of fog and foam,
Cleaving the deep and climbing the hollow height;
Mournful it surges, ceases; then, resurgent,
Cries of the soul that it hath a homeless home. . . .
And ever the waste, and the dank mist, and night!

SANTA MARIA DEL FIORE

Summits and vales, slim cypresses and pines—
Arno and April and the Apennines!

And Giotto's captive dream (what dream has ending?)
Lifting his Florence up to God for friending.

Her dream enfolded his. She willed and waited,
Conceived her popes and princes, and created.

Mother and Muse was she of mighty singers;
Grave Dante drank her breast; the beauty-bringers

In cell and cloister felt her mood and fashioned
Mystic Madonnas palely unimpassioned,

With cherubean Babes and saints immortal,
High men and humble kneeling at the portal.

She was the pale Madonna, hers the story
Of pilgrim lords at pause before her glory.

And for the Babe she showed them Beauty solely
The while they worshipped: "Holy, O Thou holy!"

Fear was her fault, too cold a doubt of duty,
Of brows that burned, of hearts that beat, for Beauty.

So Florence fell. Yet, strangely sweet and vernal,
Beauty is born again in her eternal.

Summits and vales, slim cypresses and pines—
Arno and April and the Apennines!

ARTHUR STRINGER [1874-1950]

Arthur John Arbuthnott Stringer, son of Hugh Arbuthnott Stringer, was born in Chatham, Ontario, and educated in London, Ontario, and at the University of Toronto and at Oxford University. He held editorial positions with the Montreal *Herald*, the American Press Association, and *Success*. His works include biography, criticism, fiction (adult and juvenile), and plays for stage and screen. His verse ranges from epigrams almost to epics in form, on classical, Irish, Canadian, and mystical themes, in sixteen volumes, some of them with second editions. (Cf. Victor Lauriston, (1881-), *Arthur Stringer, Son of the North* (1941), in *Makers of Canadian Literature*, and *Postscript to a Poet* (1941), and Percival as above.)

MORNING IN THE NORTH-WEST

Grey countries and grim empires pass away,
And all the pomp and glory of citied towers
Goes down to dust, as Youth itself shall age.
But oh the splendour of this autumn dawn,
This passes not away! This dew-drenched Range,
This infinite great width of open space,
This cool keen wind that blows like God's own breath
On life's once drowsy coal, and thrills the blood,
This brooding sea of sun-washed solitude,
This virginal vast dome of opal air—
These, these endure, and greater are than grief!
Still there is strength: and life, oh, life is good!
Still hearts adventurous seek outward trails,
Still life holds up its tattered hope!

For here
Is goodly air, and God's own greenness spread!
Here youth audacious fronts the coming day
And age on life ne'er mountainously lies!
Here are no huddled cities old in sin,
Where coil in tangled languors all the pale
Envenomed mirths that poisoned men of old,
Where peering out with ever-narrowing eyes
Reptilious Ease unwinds its golden scales
And slimes with ugliness the thing it eats!
Here life takes on a glory and a strength
Of things still primal, and goes plunging on!
And what care I of time-encrusted tombs,
What care I here of all the ceaseless drip
Of tears in countries old in tragedy?
What care I here for all Earth's creeds outworn,
The dreams outlived, the hopes to ashes turned,
In that old East so dark with rain and doubt?
Here life swings glad and free and rude, and I
Shall drink it to the full, and go content!

SAPPHO'S TOMB

I

In an old and ashen island,
Beside a city grey with death,
They are seeking Sappho's tomb!

II

Beneath a vineyard ruinous
And a broken-columned temple
They are delving where she sleeps!
There between a lonely valley
Filled with noonday silences
And the headlands of soft violet
Where the sapphire seas still whisper,
Whisper with her sigh;
Through a country sad with wonder
Men are seeking vanished Sappho,
Men are searching for the tomb
Of muted song!

III

They will find a Something there,
In a cavern where no sound is,
In a room of milky marble
Walled with black amphibolite
Over-scored with faded words
And stained with time!

IV

Sleeping in a low-roofed chamber,
With her phials of perfume round her,
In a terra-cotta coffin
With her image on the cover,
Childish echo of her beauty
Etched in black and gold barbaric—
Lift it slowly, slowly, seekers,
Or your search will end in dust!

V

With a tiny nude Astarte,
Bright with gilt and gravely watching
Over grass-green malachite,
Over rubies pale, and topaz,
And the crumbled dust of pearls!

VI

With her tarnished silver mirror,
And her rings of beaten gold,
With her robes of faded purple,
And the stylus that so often
Traced the azure on her eyelids,—
Eyelids delicate and weary,
Drooping, over-wise!
And at her head will be a plectron
Made of ivory, worn with time,
And a flute and gilded lyre
Will be found beside her feet,
And two little yellow sandals,
And crude serpents chased in silver
On her ankle rings—
And a cloud of drifting dust
All her shining hair!

VII

In that lost and lonely tomb
They may find her;
Find the arms that ached with rapture,
Softly folded on a breast
That for evermore is silent;
Find the eyes no longer wistful,
Find the lips no longer singing,
And the heart, so hot and wayward
When that ashen land was young,
Cold through all the mists of time,
Cold beneath the Lesbian marble
In the low-roofed room
That drips with tears!

THE SOD-BREAKER

Solemn and slow they move
As one together,
Plowman and plow and straining team,
Dark-shadowed on the ground-swells,
Ant-like against the wash
Of tawny light.
They wheel and crawl again
Across the pulsing prairie-rim
Where the plowshare tears implacably
At the tangled roots of life
And the mould-board hides away
Bunch-grass and crocus-bloom and prairie-rose
And leaves blank waves of black.

Silent and utterly alone
The plowman widens that long aisle
Of umber loam and emptiness.
Yet not alone he goes,
And still majestical he moves
Along each conquering furrow
That flings its promise back
Where a thousand sheaves of grain
Like a thousand girls with golden hair
Are singing at his side!

ROBERT NORWOOD [1874-1932]

Robert Winkworth Norwood, son of Joseph W. and Edith (Harding) Norwood, was born at New Ross, Nova Scotia, and educated at Coaticook Academy, Quebec, Bishop's College, Lennoxville, Quebec, University of King's College, Windsor, Nova Scotia, while Roberts was teaching there, and Columbia University. As an Anglican pastor he held four charges in Nova Scotia and one each in Montreal, London, Ontario, Philadelphia, and New York. He wrote four books of religious prose. His lyric poems appeared in *Driftwood* (1898), a joint volume with C. W. Vernon (1871-1934), *His Lady of the Sonnets* (1915), *The Piper and the Reed* (1917), *The Modernists* (1918), and *Mother and Son* (1925). His two poetic tragedies are *The Witch of Endor* (1916) and *The Man of Kerioth* (1919). *Bill Boram* (1921) is his contribution to Canadian narrative poetry. *Issa* (1931) is a mystical spiritual autobiography in poetic form. (Cf. *Who was Who*, vol. 2 (1938); Albert Durrant Watson, *Robert Norwood* (1923), in Makers of Canadian Literature.)

THE MAN OF KERIOTH

[*Act V*]

MARY: But, this I found:
A world not ready for this lover-man,
Confusing him with images of clay
On temple tables, seeking for a sign—
A manifesting of his power—his power!
God! how the stupid people miss the path
That winds past every garden gate to heaven.
His power! Oh, it is upon his mouth
And in his eyes—the touch—the way of him!
Supreme and tender miracle of man,
What do they, asking you for any sign?

BARTIMAEUS: Ay, you know Christ!

MARY: And of these foolish men,
Judas is first. Oh, what has blinded him
That he can miss the sun on Jesus' hair!

BARTIMAEUS: He pays the price strong men must pay on whom
The fretting business of the world depends.
Listen—a parable of four men, told
By Persian Magi: "When God made the world
Four angels watched him turn the star in space—
The first said: Give to me, O God, thy star!
The second: Tell me, God, how it was made!

The third: Why is there any world at all?
The fourth knelt to adore and went away
To make another like God's golden star."
These souls are known in human history·
The man of business, then the scientist,
The sage and poet. Judas is the first,
And we the last—only as men rise up
From holding and accounting for a star
To that pure worship of the beautiful
In holy art of giving like the Christ's,
Will they no longer clamour for a sign—
The sign will be the service of their love.

MARY: The way to Christ must be as you have said—
Past any need that holds one bound by love
Of builded things and faith in ancient law,
Customs and forms. A spirit must be free
To tread the upper air of day with him.

WILLIAM TALBOT ALLISON [1874-1941]

William Talbot Allison was born at Unionville, Ontario, and educated at Victoria College, Toronto, and Yale University. After eight years as a Presbyterian clergyman (1902-1910), he became a professor of English, first at Wesley College, Winnipeg, Manitoba, from 1910 to 1920, and then at the University of Manitoba till 1941. For more than twenty years he was literary editor of the Winnipeg *Tribune.* His prose includes editorial work, criticism, and essays. His verse collection is *The Amber Army and Other Poems* (1909). (Cf. *This for Remembrance* (1949), edited by his son, Carlyle Allison, editor of the Winnipeg *Tribune.*)

O AMBER DAY, AMID THE AUTUMN GLOOM

O amber day, amid the autumn gloom,
With languid lids drooping on eyes of dream,
How many ancient poets in their bloom
Have sung the strange, sad wonder of thy gleam!

O splendid softness of the iron days,
Mistress between the haunts of life and death,
The poets of our time entune thy praise,
And love the sweet nepenthe of thy breath.

And so to them, lost in thy purple eyes,
Come visions of the Vallombrosan groves,
Where flaming dawns, and mellow evening skies,
And falling leaves saw old unhappy loves.

HELEN MERRILL EGERTON

Helen (Merrill) Egerton, Mrs. Frank Egerton, daughter of Edwards and Caroline (Wright) Merrill, was born at Napanee, Ontario, and educated at the schools of Picton and at Ottawa Ladies' College.

SANDPIPERS

Morning on the misty highlands,
On the outer shining islands;
Gulls their grey way seaward winging
To the blinking zones of blue;
South winds in the sallows singing
Where I wander far with you,
Little pipers, careless, free,
On the sandlands by the sea.

All day, on the amber edges
Of the pools and silver ledges
Of the sedgelands in the sun,
Restlessly the pipers run—

Weet, a-weet, a-weet, a-weet!
Sun and wind and sifting sand,
Joy of June on sea and land—
Weet, a-weet, a-weet, weet weet!

Evening on the fading highlands,
On the outer amber islands;
Grey wings folded in the sedges,
In the glimmer of a star
Where the lights of Algol are
Shining on a world's white edges.

Moonlight on the sombre forelands,
On the outer, silver shorelands;
Peaceful mists that pale and drift
Seaward like a phantom fleet,
Through a sapphire, shadowed rift.

Weet, a-weet, a-weet, weet weet!
Night, and stars, and empty hushes,
Darkness in the purple rushes—
Weet, a-weet, a-weet, weet weet!

L. M. MONTGOMERY [1874-1942]

Lucy Maud (Montgomery) Macdonald, daughter of Hugh John and Clara Woolner (Macneill) Montgomery, was born at Clifton, Prince Edward Island, whence, in her early infancy, the family moved to Cavendish. She attended the Cavendish school and spent a year each at Prince of Wales College and Dalhousie University. She worked for a while on the Halifax *Chronicle* and then lived with her widowed grandmother at Cavendish, spending some time in teaching and a great deal in mastering the art of fiction, in which field she published more than a score of books, of which about half consisted of the eight Anne books and the three Emily books. After her marriage to Rev. Ewan Macdonald in 1911, she lived in Ontario, at Leaskdale, at Norval, and in Toronto. Her one volume of poetry is *The Watchman and Other Poems* (1916). (Cf. *Canadian Author and Bookman*, September, 1944, p. 24.)

OFF TO THE FISHING GROUND

There's a piping wind from a sunrise shore
Blowing over a silver sea,
There's a joyous voice in the lapsing tide
That calls enticingly;
The mist of dawn has taken flight
To the dim horizon's bound,
And with wide sails set and eager hearts
We're off to the fishing ground.

Ho, comrades mine, how that brave wind sings
Like a great sea-harp afar!
We whistle its wild notes back to it
As we cross the harbour bar.
Behind us there are the homes we love
And hearts that are fond and true,
And before us beckons a strong young day
On leagues of glorious blue.

Comrades, a song as the fleet goes out,
A song of the orient sea,
We are the heirs of its tingling strife,
Its courage and liberty!
Sing as the white sails cream and fill,
And the foam in our wake is long,
Sing till the headlands black and grim
Echo us back our song!

Oh, 'tis a glad and heartsome thing
To wake ere the night be done
And steer the course that our fathers steered
In the path of the rising sun.
The wind and welkin and wave are ours
Wherever our bourne is found,
And we envy no landsman his dream and sleep
When we're off to the fishing ground!

J. E. H. MacDONALD [1874-1932]

James E. H. MacDonald was born in Durham, England, and came to Canada in 1887. He studied painting at the Hamilton Art School and at Ontario School of Art, Toronto. A member of the Group of Seven, he achieved distinction in art and for the last three years of his life was Principal of the Ontario College of Art. His poetry is preserved in *West by East and Other Poems* (1933). (Cf. *Canadian Who was Who*, vol. 2 (1938); E. R. Hunter, *J. E. H. MacDonald* (1940).)

KITCHEN WINDOW

I glance from humble toil and see
The star-gods go in heavenly pride;
Bright Sirius glittering through a tree
Orion with eternal stride.

And as I watch them in the blue
With shading hand against the glass,
I know not if their work I do,
Or if for me they rise and pass.

GALLOWS AND CROSS

I saw one hung upon a cross
That every man might see
If sinless God could pardon sin
All men might pardoners be.

I saw the gallows lifted high
And in the cruel rope
The twisted law and sin of man
Strangled the Saviour's hope.

I heard a tortured spirit cry
Upon the darkened cross;
And heavy was the lowered sky
With sin and pain and loss.

FLORENCE RANDAL LIVESAY [1874-1953]

Florence Hamilton (Randal) Livesay, Mrs. J. F. B. Livesay, daughter of Stephen and Mary Louisa (Andrews) Randal, was born at Compton, Quebec, and educated at Compton Ladies' College (now King's Hall). A year of teaching in New York was followed by seven years as editor of the Woman's Page of the Ottawa *Evening Journal*, a year of teaching in Boer Concentration Camps, and several years of journalism in Winnipeg, three years on the staff of the Winnipeg *Telegram* and then as editor of the Children's Department of the Winnipeg *Free Press*. In prose she wrote material for magazines, a book of fiction, and a memoir for her edition of her husband's autobiography. In verse she was noted for her translations and interpretations of Ukrainian poetry and for her original poems as found in *Shepherd's Purse* (1923).

TIM, THE FAIRY

The little shrivelled and humpbacked creature!
A changeling, shure! And they fed him right
When they gave him food on the end of a shovel.
I'd have taken a lilac twig and laced him,
And him gibberin' there like a little imp.

They sold his knitting, they taught him weaving,
His darning was fine enough for a queen;
Folks treasured hooked rugs his fingers knotted;
'Twas something to see, and they came to see him,
And brought sick lambs, that they'd get a "cure."

Wisha, will he spin and weave for the fairies?
They like good workers. And he was that.
Belike if his mother had kept him idle? . . .
But it's no good talking of things that's past.

For at last, wan day, they called and beckoned. . . .
His mother found him, and thought him asleep—
Lard save us! And Tim there *away* two hours,
Slippin' down a bit in his barrel-chair,
With the quarest smile on his wizened face!

THE VIOLIN CALLS

Clouds in the sky at twilight,
  Storm in the air, and cries. . . .
"Fiddler, play for the dying,
  Play as the old man dies!

"Call up the hosts of the fairies;
They will escort old Tim.
See how they gather, the phantom
Grey wings enfolding him!"

"*Bold on the moor stood the fairies,*
Bold and undaunted." The song,
Piercing and sweet on the fiddle,
Draws him along and along.

Rain-beat and crashing of thunder,
Sighing of chords faint and low,
To Ireland, on cloud-riven pinions
The Dead and the Fairies go.

ISABEL ECCLESTONE MacKAY [1875-1928]

Mrs. Isabel Ecclestone (Macpherson) MacKay, daughter of Donald McLeod and Priscilla (Ecclestone) Macpherson and wife of Peter J. MacKay, was born in Woodstock, Ontario, and educated at the Collegiate Institute there. From 1909 till her death she made her home in Vancouver. She wrote short stories, novels, drama, folklore, and poetry. Her books of verse are *Between the Lights* (1904), *The Shining Ships and Other Verse* (1918), *Fires of Driftwood* (1922), and the posthumously published *Complete Poems* (1930).

FIRES OF DRIFTWOOD

On what long tides
Do you drift to my fire,
You waifs of strange waters?
From what far seas,
What murmurous sands,
What desolate beaches—
Flotsam of those glories that were ships!

I gather you,
Bitter with salt,
Sun-bleached, rock-scarred, moon-harried,
Fuel for my fire.

You are Pride's end.
Through all tomorrows you are yesterday.
You are waste,
You are ruin,
For where is that which once you were?

I gather you.
See! I set free the fire within you—
You awake in thin flame!
Tremulous, mistlike, your soul aspires,
Blue, beautiful,
Up and up to the clouds which are its kindred!
What is left is nothing—
Ashes blown along the shore!

HELEN—OLD

CHILD

"Great lady, were you Helen long ago?
And were you beautiful as all men say?"

HELEN

"Yea, child, my name was Helen . . . I think so . . .
Helen? . . . I thought of her but yesterday."

CHILD

"There was a song of Helen. 'World's Delight'
It named her, 'Heaven Fair' and 'Rose Divine!'"

HELEN

"A song? . . . 'Tis true one sang to me by night
Of Helen's eyes—what colour, child are mine?"

CHILD

"No colour, lady. Tell me of that host,
So splendid brave, who fought before Troy's town."

HELEN

"A host of shadows, child . . . ghost locked with ghost,
Blows falling light as sea-mist drifting down—"

CHILD

"Tell of that day which saw great Hector die,
Dragged in the dust beneath the echoing gate!"

HELEN

"Hector! . . . was that his name? I often try
To fit the names. They slip and change of late . . ."

CHILD

"But, lady, you were Helen . . . tell but one
Of those famed battles joined to make you free!"

HELEN

"All battles are the same when they are done. . . .
But Helen once saw moonlight on the sea . . ."

CHILD

"Then tell me of the happy vows you paid
When you returned—the crowds, the pageantry!"

HELEN

"Returned, you say? returned? . . . But Helen stayed
In Troy . . . I know . . . Cease, child—you trouble me!"

NORAH HOLLAND [1876-1925]

Norah Mary Holland, daughter of John H. and Elizabeth (Yeats) Holland, was born at Collingwood, Ontario, and educated at Port Dover and in Toronto. She married Lionel William Claxton, and they made their home in Toronto. (Cf. *Canadian Who was Who*, vol. 1 (1934).)

SEA SONG

I will go down to the sea again,
To the waste of waters, wild and wide;
I am tired—so tired—of hill and plain
And the dull, tame face of the country-side.

I will go out across the bar,
With a swoop like the flight of a sea-bird's wings,
To where the winds and the waters are,
With their multitudinous thunderings.

My prow shall furrow the whitening sea,
Out into the teeth of the lashing wind,
Where a thousand billows snarl and flee
And break in a smother of foam behind.

O strong and terrible Mother Sea,
Let me lie once more on your cool white breast,
Your winds have blown through the heart of me
And called me back from the land's dull rest.

For night by night they blow through my sleep,
The voice of waves through my slumber rings,
I feel the spell of the steadfast deep;
I hear its tramplings and triumphings.

And at last when my hours of life are sped,
  Let them make me no grave by hill or plain,
Thy waves, O Mother, shall guard my head;
  I will go down to my sea again.

ROBERT W. SERVICE [1876-]

Robert William Service, son of Robert and Emily (Parker) Service, was born in Preston, England. While the family lived in Glasgow, he attended Hillhead High School and the University and began his banking career. He came to Canada at the age of twenty, made his way westward from city to city, and for five years travelled back and forth along the Pacific coast, engaging in various kinds of work, and residing temporarily in every city of importance as far south as Mexico. In 1905 he joined the staff of the Bank of Commerce in Victoria, later serving in Vancouver, Kamloops, Whitehorse, and Dawson. He won three decorations in the First World War. In prose he has written two autobiographical books, several novels, and two volumes of informal philosophy. The earliest edition of *Collected Verse* (1930, 1932, 1949) was preceded by five volumes. Between the two editions of *Complete Poems* (1933, 1941) came *Bar-Room Ballads* (*1940*), and since the second edition he has published *Bathtub Ballads* (n.d.), *Songs of a Sun-Lover* (1949), *Rhymes of a Roughneck* (1950), *Lyrics of a Low Brow* (1951), and *Rhymes of a Rebel* (1952). (Cf. Percival as above.)

THE LAW OF THE YUKON

This is the law of the Yukon, and ever she makes it plain:
"Send not your foolish and feeble; send me your strong and your
    sane;
Strong for the red rage of battle; sane, for I harry them sore;
Send me men girt for the combat, men who are grit to the core;
Swift as the panther in triumph, fierce as the bear in defeat,
Sired of bulldog parent, steeled in the furnace heat.
Send me the best of your breeding, lend me your chosen ones;
Them will I take to my bosom, them will I call my sons;
Them will I gild with my treasure, them will I glut with my meat;
But the others—the misfits, the failures—I trample under my feet;
Dissolute, damned and despairful, crippled and palsied and slain,
Ye would send me the spawn of your gutters—Go! take back your
    spawn again.

"Wild and wide are my borders, stern as death is my sway;
From my ruthless throne I have ruled alone for a million years and a day;
Hugging my mighty treasure, waiting for man to come:
Till he swept like a turbid torrent, and after him swept—the scum.
The pallid pimp of the dead-line, the enervate of the pen,
One by one I weeded them out, for all that I sought was—Men.
One by one I dismayed them, frighting them sore with my glooms;
One by one I betrayed them unto my manifold dooms;
Drowned them like rats in my rivers, starved them like curs on my plains,
Rotted the flesh that was left them, poisoned the blood in their veins;
Burst with my winter upon them, searing forever their sight,
Lashed them with fungus-white faces, whimpering wild in the night;
Staggering wild through the storm-whirl, stumbling mad through the snow,
Frozen stiff in the ice-pack, brittle and bent like a bow;
Featureless, formless, forsaken, scented by wolves in their flight,
Left for the wind to make music through ribs that are glittering white;
Gnawing the black crust of failure, searching the pit of despair,
Crooking the toe in the trigger, trying to patter a prayer;
Going outside with an escort, raving with lips all afoam;
Writing a cheque for a million, drivelling feebly of home;
Lost like a louse in the burning . . . or else in the tented town
Seeking a drunkard's solace, sinking and sinking down;
Steeped in the slime at the bottom, dead to a decent world,
Lost 'mid the human flotsam, far on the frontier hurled;
In the camp at the bend of the river, with its dozen saloons aglare,
Its gambling dens a-riot, its gramophones all ablare;
Crimped with the crimes of a city, sin-ridden and bridled with lies,
In the hush of my mountained vastness, in the flush of my midnight skies.
Plague-spots, yet tools of my purpose, so natheless I suffer them thrive,
Crushing my Weak in their clutches, that only my Strong may survive.

"But the others, the men of my mettle, the men who would 'stablish my fame,
Unto its ultimate issue, winning me honour, not shame;
Searching my uttermost valleys, fighting each step as they go,
Shooting the wrath of my rapids, scaling my ramparts of snow;
Ripping the guts of my mountains, looting the beds of my creeks,
Them will I take to my bosom, and speak as a mother speaks.
I am the land that listens, I am the land that broods;
Steeped in eternal beauty, crystalline waters and woods.

Long have I waited lonely, shunned as a thing accurst,
Monstrous, moody, pathetic, the last of the lands and the first;
Visioning camp-fires at twilight, sad with a longing forlorn,
Feeling my womb o'er-pregnant with the seethe of cities unborn.
Wild and wide are my borders, stern as death is my sway,
And I wait for the men who will win me—and I will not be won in a day;
And I will not be won by weaklings, subtle, suave, and mild,
But by men with the hearts of vikings, and the simple faith of a child;
Desperate, strong and resistless, unthrottled by fear or defeat,
Them will I gild with my treasure, them will I glut with my meat.

"Lofty I stand from each sister land, patient and wearily wise,
With the weight of a world of sadness in my quiet, passionless eyes;
Dreaming alone of a people, dreaming alone of a day,
When men shall not rape my riches, and curse me and go away;
Making a bawd of my bounty, fouling the hand that gave—
Till I rise in my wrath and I sweep on their path and I stamp them into a grave.
Dreaming of men who will bless me, of women esteeming me good,
Of children born in my borders, of radiant motherhood,
Of cities leaping to stature, of fame like a flag unfurled,
As I pour the tide of my riches in the eager lap of the world."

This is the Law of the Yukon, that only the Strong shall thrive;
That surely the Weak shall perish, and only the Fit survive.
Dissolute, damned and despairful, crippled and palsied and slain,
This is the Will of the Yukon—Lo! how she makes it plain!

THE CALL OF THE WILD

Have you gazed on naked grandeur, where there's nothing else to gaze on,
Set pieces and drop-curtain scenes galore,
Big mountains heaved to heaven, which the blinding sunsets blazon,
Black canyons where the rapids rip and roar?
Have you swept the visioned valley with the green stream streaking through it,
Searched the Vastness for a something you have lost?
Have you strung your soul to silence? Then for God's sake go and do it;
Hear the challenge, learn the lesson, pay the cost.

Have you wandered in the wilderness, the sage-brush desolation,
The bunch-grass levels where the cattle graze?
Have you whistled bits of rag-time at the end of all creation,
And learned to know the desert's little ways?
Have you camped upon the foothills, have you galloped o'er the ranges,
Have you roamed the arid sun-lands through and through?
Have you chummed up with the mesa? Do you know its moods and changes?
Then listen to the wild,—it's calling you.

Have you known the Great White Silence, not a snow-gemmed twig aquiver?
(Eternal truths that shame our soothing lies.)
Have you broken trail on snowshoes? mushed your Huskies up the river,
Dared the unknown, led the way, and clutched the prize?
Have you marked the map's void spaces, mingled with the mongrel races,
Felt the savage strength of brute in every thew?
And though grim as hell the worst is, can you round it off with curses?
Then hearken to the wild,—it's wanting you.

Have you suffered, starved, and triumphed, grovelled down, yet grasped at glory,
Grown bigger in the bigness of the whole?
"Done things" just for the doing, letting babblers tell the story,
Seeing through the nice veneer the naked soul?

Have you seen God in His splendours, heard the text that nature renders
(You'll never hear it in the family pew),
The simple things, the true things, the silent men who do things?
Then listen to the wild,—it's calling you.

They have cradled you in custom, they have primed you with their preaching,
They have soaked you in convention through and through;
They have put you in a showcase; you're a credit to their teaching—
But can't you hear the wild?—it's calling you.
Let us probe the silent places, let us seek what luck betide us:
Let us journey to a lonely land I know.
There's a whisper on the night-wind, there's a star agleam to guide us,
And the wild is calling, calling . . . let us go.

"JOHN CRICHTON" [1877-1929]

Norman Gregor Guthrie, who used the pen name "John Crichton," son of Donald and Eliza Guthrie, was born in Guelph, Ontario, and educated at the collegiate institute there, at McGill University, and at Osgoode Hall. He began the practice of law in Ottawa in 1902, where he remained, chiefly as parliamentary solicitor and counsel. He was the author of a critical appreciation of Lampman's poetry and published four volumes of his own, *A Vista* (1921), *Flower and Flame* (1924), *Pillar of Smoke* (1925), and *Flake and Petal* (1928). (Cf. *Canadian Bookman*, January, 1930.)

A BED OF CAMPANULA

So I possess a perfect thing,
The blue and white of cloud and sky
Fallen to earth, slow-wavering
As little lazy winds go by.

My quiet friends, no clamour tells
Your presence: yet I almost hear
Your soundless carillons of bells
That have no music for the ear,

Float from your sweet ascending stalk,
Restful and white: faithful and blue:
While gaudier sisters crowd the walk,
You have a better thing to do.

Just to be still, and exquisite:
And as the lazy winds go by
Be for a while a little bit
Of landscape borrowed from the sky.

THEODORE GOODRIDGE ROBERTS [1877-1953]

George Edward Theodore Goodridge Roberts, son of Rev. George Goodridge and Emma Wetmore (Bliss) Roberts, was born at Fredericton, New Brunswick, and educated there at the Grammar School and the University. He had journalistic experience on the New York *Independent*, for which he was special correspondent during the Spanish-American War, and on the *Newfoundland Magazine*. He served with distinction in the First World War. He was elected a Fellow of the Royal Society of Canada, and his alma mater conferred upon him the Litt.D. *honoris causa*. His last years were spent at Digby, Nova Scotia. He wrote on historical and military subjects and published twenty-nine romantic novels. His poetry is found in *Northland Lyrics* (1899) and *The Leather Bottle* (1934). (Cf. Lloyd Roberts (1884-), *The Book of Roberts* (1923), and Percival as above.)

THE LOST SHIPMATE

Somewhere he failed me, somewhere he slipt away—
Youth, in his ignorant faith and his bright array.
The tides go out and the flooding tides come in,
And still the old years pass and the new begin—
But Youth?—
Somewhere we lost each other, last year or yesterday.

Somewhere he failed me. . . . Down at the harbour-side
I waited for him a little where the anchored argosies ride.
I thought he came. 'Twas the dawn-wind blowing free!
I thought he came. 'Twas but the shadow of me!
And Youth?—
Somewhere he turned and left me, about the turn of the tide.

Perhaps I shall find him. It may be he waits for me,
Sipping those wines we knew, beside some tropic sea.
The tides still serve, and I am out and away
To search the spicy harbours of yesterday
For Youth,
Where the lamps of the town are yellow behind the lamps of the quay.

Somewhere he left me, some time he turned away—
Youth, of the careless heart and the bright array.
Was it in Bados? God! I would pay to know.
Or was it on Spanish Hill, where the roses blow?
Shall I hear his laughter tomorrow in painted Olivio?

Somewhere I failed him, somewhere I let him depart—
Youth, who could only sleep for the morn's fresh start. . . .
The tides slipt out, the tides washed out and in,
And far and oft were we lured by the capstan's din . . .
Dear Youth,
Shall I find you south of the Gulf?—or are you dead in my heart?

FIDDLER'S GREEN

"At a place called Fiddler's Green, there do all honest Mariners take their pleasure after death; and there are Admirals with their dear Ladies and Captains of lost voyages with the Sweethearts of their youth, and tarry-handed Sailormen singing in cottage gardens."

Never again shall we beat out to sea
In rain and mist and sleet like bitter tears,
And watch the harbour beacons fade, alee,
And people all the sea-room with our fears.
Our toil is done. No more, no more do we
Square the low yards and stagger on the sea.

No more for us the white and windless day,
Undimmed, unshadowed, where the weed drifts by,
And leaden fish pass, rolling, at their play,
And changeless suns slide up a changeless sky.
Our watch is done; and never more shall we
Whistle the wind across an empty sea.

Cities we saw—white walled and glinting dome—
And palm-fringed islands dreaming on the blue.
To us more fair the kindly sights of home—
The climbing street, the window shining true.
Our voyage is done: And never more shall we
Reef the harsh topsails on a tossing sea.

Wonders we knew and beauty in far ports;
Laughter and peril 'round the swinging deep;
The wrath of God; the pomp of painted courts. . . .
The rocks sprang black!—*And we awoke from sleep.*
Our task is done, and never more shall we
Square the low yards and stagger on the sea.

Here are the hearts we love, the lips we know,
The hands of seafarers who came before.
The eyes that wept for me a night ago
Are laughing now that we shall part no more.
All grief is done; and never more shall we
Make sail at dawning for the luring sea.

THE BLUE HERON

In a green place lanced through
With amber and gold and blue;
A place of water and weeds
And roses pinker than dawn,
And ranks of lush young reeds,
And grasses straightly withdrawn
From graven ripples of sands,
The still blue heron stands.

Smoke-blue he is, and grey
As embers of yesterday.
Still he is, as death;
Like stone, or shadow of stone,
Without a pulse or breath,
Motionless and alone
There in the lily stems:
But his eyes are alive like gems.

Still as a shadow; still
Grey feather and yellow bill:
Still as an image made
Of mist and smoke half hid
By windless sunshine and shade,
Save when a yellow lid
Slides and is gone like a breath:
Death-still—and sudden as death.

"KATHERINE HALE" [1878-]

Mrs. Amelia Beers (Warnock) Garvin, Mrs. John William Garvin, daughter of James and Katherine Hale (Byard) Warnock, was born in Galt, Ontario, and educated there, at Glen Mawr School, Toronto, in New York, and abroad. She is a noted lecture-recitalist, has written literary and musical criticism, especially for the Toronto *Mail and Empire*, several volumes of creative non-fiction, and has published five books of poems: *Grey Knitting*

(1914); *The White Comrade* (1916); *Morning in the West* (1923); *The Island and Other Poems* (1935); and *The Flute and Other Poems* (1950). (Cf. Percival as above.)

LOST GARDEN

So many evenings, on the red-tiled terrace,
We used to sit and plan to make a pool
Under the tall pine trees,
Just at their very feet,
In that soft hollow of the garden's curve
Where sunlight seldom falls.

It is a place intended for a pool
Sunk deep within a basin of grey rock.
We'd grow no flowers there,
But let the pool take colour
From gorgeous vagabonds with flaming wings,
And emerald-waving boughs.

Perhaps we were not faithful to our trees;
We laid no water-shadows at their feet
In pledge of our delight. . . .
And all the lovely place
Has vanished now into a city street—
Only these lines remain!

GIANT'S TOMB IN GEORGIAN BAY

Who is the sleeping giant
That sprawls beneath this monstrous, uncouth tomb,
Bare in the searching moonlight,
Older than the hills?

Sometimes at ardent midday
In a persistent, dazzling flame of azure
The tomb becomes a castle
With ivory-coloured walls.

Then into deep crevasses
Painted webs of shadow may be flung.
There it glitters softly
In the deep blue water,
Old loneliness, old beauty,
Hiding some savage secret—power, or lust—
Out of a far-off time—
Out of the naked days.

PORTRAIT OF A CREE

Cun-ne-wa-bum—"one who looks on stars"—
(Feel the singing wind from out the western hills)
"The tip-end of a swan's wing is her fan,
With a handle of porcupine quills."
Here is the artist's name, Paul Kane;
Painting in forty-seven, at Edmonton, I see.
That was when prairies were untamed,
And untamed this young Cree.

What an incantation in her name!
Magic as her dark face underneath the stars;
There is sword-like wind about it wrapped,
And echoes of old wars.
Cun-ne-wa-bum!
When turtle shells were rattling,
And the drums beat for the dance
In the great hall of the Factor's house till dawn,
You sat without the door,
Where the firelight on the floor
Caught the red of beads upon your moccasins.

At evening through the grassy plains the wind
Came shouting down the world to meet the dawn,
And with the wind the firelight rose and fell,
Answered with flame his shrill barbaric yell,
And died like whining fiddles at his feet.
And through it all the constant sound of drums—
Did your feet move to drums?

The men from near and far,
Crees and Sarcees,
And a Blackfoot brave or two,
Made rhythm of a dance that moves like rhyme
To the rush of wind, and rattles swung in time
To the constant, constant, constant beat of drums.

No Indian woman dances in the light;
Silent they sit together out of sight.
But tonight I think this artist from the East,
Who had come to paint the natives hereabout,
Found a splendid flare of crimson on the feast
And moved near the open door,
Where the firelight on the floor
Caught the red of beads upon your moccasins.

So it is, O Cun-ne-wa-bum,
Who were wont to look on stars,
That you sit for ever here,
Like a wild lost note from far,
From the days of ancient war
And of towered stockade and guns
In the Edmonton of seventy years ago.
In your buckskin and your beads
(Feel the sudden wind from out the western hills)
The tip-end of a swan's wing for your fan
With a handle of porcupine quills.

ETERNAL MOMENT

Here through our little world of outward sense,
Moves a batik of bright objective things,
A figured curtain that forever swings
Before the dark abyss that beckons hence.
And, whirling in a mechanistic dance,
Are flying figures that some power flings
To rotate as they may to snarl of strings
Or the uncertain, faulty flutes of chance.
But just suppose that once, before the end,
Amid the blinding whirl we sudden find
Enfolding beauty and the answering mind,
The quivering lover and the blessèd friend—
Can we be sure that such a deathless kiss
Holds nothing from beyond the dark abyss!

FREDERICK NIVEN [1878-1944]

Frederick John Niven was born in Valparaiso, Chile, the son of somewhat itinerant Scots, John and Jane (Barclay) Niven, who took him back to Scotland at an early age. In Glasgow he attended Hutchesons' and the Glasgow School of Art. After a short period in library work, he came to Canada in 1891 and spent some time in railway and lumber camps in British Columbia. This experience gave him material for a series of articles in the Glasgow *Weekly Herald* when he returned to Scotland. He worked at journalism in Glasgow and London till 1912, and then he and his wife, the former Mary Pauline Thorne-Quelch, toured Canada, commissioned to write articles on the Canadian West. During the First World War he was with the Ministry of Information in London. The couple came to Canada again in 1920 for a visit, decided to stay, and made their home at Kootenay

Lake, British Columbia. His prose includes Scottish and Canadian fiction, historical and descriptive writing, and an autobiography. His books of verse are *Maple-Leaf Songs* (1917) and *A Lover of the Land and Other Poems* (1925). (Cf. *Canadian Author and Bookman*, March, 1944.)

INDIAN DANCE

When they had pitched their smoked tepees
  In horse-shoe curve upon the plain,
I strolled into the Indian camp—
  And straightway was a boy again.
The years between were crumbled dust;
  A dream of youth had come to pass:
I smoked a calumet with five
  Tall red men in the sun-dried grass.
Yet coming back to Now and Town,
  Interrogated where I'd been,
"Just looking at the Indian camp,"
  I said, with most nonchalant mien.
For who believes in miracles?
  Or why proclaim so much as half
Our happy lunacies to one
  Who would, not understanding, laugh?
But there was deeper miracle
  At night, when stars and fires were lit
And wind-borne rhythms came to Town
  As though to cast a spell on it.
Out to the Indian camp I went—
  And far beyond my boyhood then:
Greece was not dreamt; Rome had not been:
  Young wonder filled the hearts of men.
There's something lost in organ-peals
  Or witchery of violins;
These Indians had not quite forgot
  Who danced in deer-skin moccasins.
Where had I heard these lilts before,
  That plaintive cry, that dying fall?
Or did they but remind me of
  The wind in trees, a wild-fowl's call?
It seemed I knew it all of old,
  So long ago the world was young
When to such drum-throbs once I danced
  And heard these weird cadenzas sung.

There was a moon I marvelled at;
There was a new and clamant shore;
Dark eyes looked questioning in mine
A million years ago and more.
Back through a million years and more
I crept, but tom-toms in my brain
Still pulsed through tattered memories,
To Now and Town returned again.
"Where have you been to all this time?"
How could I tell? 'Twas best perchance
To counterfeit a yawn and say:
"Just looking at the Indian dance."

FRANK OLIVER CALL [1878-]

Frank Oliver Call, son of Lorenzo and Sarah (Hungerford) Call, was born at West Brome, Quebec, and educated at Stanstead College, at Bishop's College, at the universities of Marburg and Paris, and at McGill. He made an eminent contribution to education, from 1898 to 1908 as master of languages and principal in important secondary schools and from 1908 till his retirement at Bishop's College. In prose he contributed *The Spell of French Canada* (1926) and *The Spell of Acadia* (1930) to Page's "Spell" series, and wrote *The Life of Marguerite Bourgeoys* (1930). His books of poetry are *In a Belgian Garden* (1916), *Acanthus and Wild Grape* (1920), *Simples and Other Sonnets* (1923), *Blue Homespun* (1924), and *Sonnets for Youth* (1944). *Blue Homespun*, which won the David Prize of the Province of Quebec, is especially notable for its sympathetic and realistic interpretation of *habitant* life in Quebec.

AN OLD HABITANT

He sits in silence on his porch at night
And looks into the gloom. The low winds mutter
Across dark level fields, and poplars utter
Low sighing sounds. Along the horizon's height
His barns rise darkly in the waning light;
Within the house, behind the half-closed shutter,
A flickering candle burns, and white moths flutter
Against the casement in their blundering flight.
Attracted by the glow of village lamps,
The younger folk have left him with his pipe,
Listening to the wind and crickets' call.
He only thinks: The sun has dried the swamps,
The frost has touched the corn, and oats are ripe,
And in the orchard fruit begins to fall.

BLUE HOMESPUN

Beyond the doorway of the tiny room
The yellow autumn sunshine died away
Into the shadows of the waning day;
Wrapped in the twilight stood old Marie's loom,
A shapeless mass of timbers in the gloom;
But one small window cast a golden ray
Upon a bench where sky-blue homespun lay,
Lighting the dusk-like sheaves of chicory bloom.
Above the loom the Holy Virgin hung,
Blue-robed and smiling down; and old Marie,
After the evening angelus had rung,
Arose and touched the picture lovingly
With rough brown hand, then turned and looked once more
Upon her sky-blue cloth, and closed the door.

LILIAN LEVERIDGE [1879-1953]

Lilian Leveridge, of Carrying Place, Ontario, has published six books of pleasing verse: *Over the Hills of Home and Other Poems* (1918); *A Breath of the Woods* (1927); *Hero Songs of Canada* (1927); *The Blossom Trail* (1932); a mimeographed volume, *Still Waters* (1933); *Lyrics and Sonnets* (1939). In 1945 she won second and fourth prizes in the Macnab poetry competition.

THE FIRST ROBIN

A tawny gleam in the sunlight,
  And the flash of a ruddy breast
Amid the glooms of the hemlocks
  That crowd to the hill's high crest;
A torrent of song comes pouring,
  Like a brook from the ice unbound,
While the listening hills and the valleys
  In echoes give back the sound.

As I wake in the misty dawning
  Gone is the hemlock hill,
Gone are the tossing pine plumes,
  And the whispering winds are still;
But there on a roof a robin
  Is singing his heart away,
Bearing me back to the sunshine
  Of a far-off golden day.

A whistle comes clear as a robin's,
  Blithe, and so full of cheer,
I know ere a gay smile greets me
  A laddie I love draws near.
Oh, strange that a note of minor
  From the heart of that song should creep!
Dear lad! do the robins whistle
  On that cross-crowned hill where you sleep?

I am back in the heart of the city;
  'Mid the housetops smoky and grim
The bird sings over and over
  The notes of his morning hymn.
And something I catch of its meaning:
  There's a song in my soul today,
Of the life that blossoms in Spring land,
  And never shall fade away.

HARRY AMOSS [1880-]

Dr. Harry Edwin Amoss, son of James and Annie (Hockey) Amoss, was born at Corinth, Ontario, and educated at Queen's University and the University of Toronto. He has had a distinguished educational career, first as a teacher in the public schools and finally as Superintendent of Professional Training in the Ontario Department of Education. He has written short stories and magazine articles and a number of books to remove drudgery from educational subjects. His service in the First World War is reflected in his first book of poetry, *The Prayer of the Good Trouper* (1933). His *Sunday-Monday: Selected Poems* (1947) shows content varying from humour and fantasy to profound thought and originality of expression secured by successful experimentation with established forms, especially the sonnet.

RIDING

Oh, how my pulse pipes to go riding, go riding
  With Ellen this morning across the green lea;
The boat on the river is gliding, is gliding,
  But a brush with the breezes for Ellen and me.

The hoof times the heart that goes dashing, goes dashing,
  As hedges and hillocks we take side by side,
Or through the tall thickets go crashing, go crashing,
  And ring the loud laughter as singing we ride.

A fig for your lovers a-strolling, a-strolling
With whispers and kisses beneath the soft moon,
And tears that ask answers consoling, consoling,
And vows that will vanish like dew 'neath the noon.

I know that she loves me forever, forever,
What use, then, of kisses, of sighs and of fears?
When afar we may gallop, together, together,
With wind-blown blushes that never bring tears.

PEDAGOGICAL PRINCIPLES

A measuring worm with a hump on his back
Went over and over a leafy track,
Surveying out doughnuts of annular size,
Triangular trifles, and circular pies.
He paced off proportionate polygons sweet,
And trisected rectangles—sure nice to eat.
But alas, while computing his n'th angulation,
He humped a parabola, died of starvation.
Though measuring is magnificent and science you can't spurn,
Eating is the business of a plain common worm.

The Pedagogue Person, where Bill went to school
For reading and writing and 'rithmetic's rule,
Tapped his intelligence, took his M.A.,
And found his I.Q. in a ouija-board way,
Scaled his achievement, and plotted the curve
His mechanical aptitude made with his nerve
Computed objectively, alpha test, four.
But, Bill in the world made no wonderful score;
For the Pedagogue Person who made the 'pilation
Forgot to teach spelling and multiplication.
Though measuring is magnificent and science you can't fool,
Learning is the business of the boy and girl in school.

WILSON MacDONALD [1880-   ]

Wilson Pugsley MacDonald, son of Alexander and Anna Maria (Pugsley) MacDonald, was born at Cheapside, Ontario, and educated at the public schools of Port Dover, at Woodstock College, and at McMaster University. For a number of years he lived a life of great variety. For some time he has made his home in Toronto, where, in the spring of 1953, the Wilson MacDonald Poetry Society was organized in his honour. He has written plays and a musical comedy. His poetry shows marked versatility in theme and in treatment, but it is unified by the quest for beauty. His books of poems are: *The Song of the Prairie Land* (1918, 1923); *The Miracle Songs of Jesus* (1921, 1923); *Out of the Wilderness* (1926 and 5 later edd.); *Ode on the Diamond Jubilee of Confederation* (1927); *Caw Caw Ballads* (1930); *A Flagon of Beauty* (1931); *Paul Marchand* (1933); *Song of the Undertow* (1935); *Comber Cove* (1937); *Greater Poems of the Bible* (1943); *The Way Out* (1947); and *The Lyric Year* (1952). (Cf. *Leading Canadian Poets* (1948) ed. by W. P. Percival.)

THE TOLL-GATE MAN

They tore down the toll-gate
  By the songless mill,
But the grey gate-man
  Takes toll there still;
And he takes from all
  Whether or not they will.

Few people see him,
  With his moonlit hair,
Taking with ghost palms
  The old, slim fare.
But the whole night long
  He waits sadly there.

In winter on the snow
  I can hear his shoes
Crunching me welcome,
  Crunching me adieus:
But wherever he goes
  He leaves no clews.

Strange coin I pay him,
  Minted in my soul—
Tears I caught long ago
  In a silver bowl,
Sighings for a lost love:
  These I pay for toll.

Strangely does his hand come
  Out of the thin wind,
And strangely is the night air
  About his shoulders pinned.
So white his hair is you would think
  His soul had never sinned.

The fool goes by him,
  In a blazing car,
Sighing: "How lonely
  These crossroads are."
But the old gate-man
  Will follow him far.

Follow him until he pays
  As men paid of old;
But not with cold silver
  And not with warm gold,
But with that treasure
  Which is life to hold.

On dark, wet nights
  In the slanting rain
The gate-man bends
  With an old, old pain;
But on warm, clear nights
  He grows straight again.

They tore down the toll-gate
  By the songless mill,
But the grey gate-man
  Takes toll there still;
You can see his moonlit hair
  From the next far hill.

EXIT

Easily to the old
  Opens the hard ground:
But when youth grows cold,
  And red lips have no sound,
Bitterly does the earth
  Open to receive
And bitterly do the grasses
  In the churchyard grieve.

Cold clay knows how to hold
  An agèd hand;
But how to comfort youth
  It does not understand.
Even the gravel rasps
  In a dumb way
When youth comes homing
  Before its day.

Elizabeth's hair was made
  To warm a man's breast,
Her lips called like roses
  To be caressed;
But the grim Jester
  Who gave her hair to lie
On the coldest lover
  Under the cold sky.

But Elizabeth never knew
  Nor will learn now,
How the long wrinkle comes
  On the white brow;
Nor will she ever know,
  In her robes of gloom,
How chill is a dead child
  From a warm womb.

O clay, so tender
  When a flower is born!
Press gently as she dreams
  In her bed forlorn.
They who come early
  Must weary of their rest—
Lie softly, then, as light
  On her dear breast.

Unflowered is her floor
  Her roof is unstarred.
Is this then the ending—
  Here, shuttered and barred?
Nay, not the ending;
  She will awake
Or the heart of the earth
  That enfolds her will break.

Easily to the old
  Opens the hard ground:
But when youth grows cold,
  And red lips have no sound,
Bitterly does the earth
  Open to receive
And bitterly do the grasses
  In the churchyard grieve.

IN A WOOD CLEARING

I

All night I wearied utterly of the pillow of darkness
In hope of the dawn, knowing it should bring me,
In one soft word, a joy that is past understanding.
Now stirs the morning breeze with thoughts of the clover
Bent by the bees, with thoughts of the balsam-trees;
But I go with dreams sweeter by far—with dreams of a maiden
Sloping to loveliness up from her finger-tips.

High in the wilderness there is a clearing
That gluts itself all day with the sunshine.
Here is the rain soonest forgotten; here the slim shadows
Of bending trees run in and away again,
Like children at play. Here I come this high morning,
Robed in the freshness of dawn, and here I wait
In a delicious confusion, knowing not whether
'Tis my heart that beats or her step that falls
On the wood mosses of grey, green, and silver.

And here, splashed by sun, I sit wondering
Which shall bend lower the head of the clover—
The bee or the wind: the transparent dragon-flies,
Hovering, watch with me, and the birch leaves applaud,
Their green-gloved fingers joyously clapping.
She comes now out of the wood, her long hair tossing
Darkness out of its tangle. The woodpecker thumps
On the tree to out-distance my heart.
Now I know who taught the willow its grace
And the flower its abundance of sweetness—now I know
Where the curve in the wind found its pattern.

II

All day we sat in a clearing, under a great tree,
Holding the leash of the runaway hours in our hands.
Sometimes we shut our eyes and offered vague guesses
Which was the voice of the lake at our feet,
And which was the cry of the cool, liquid poplar—
That mimic of water. Thus we were startled by dusk
Ere we were quite aware the young dawn had departed.
How easily slips night into the forest; it is black wine
Into black wine. What a fine tussle with light in this clearing
Hath darkness! Proudly it gains this place.

It was she who spoke first of the home-going—
Perhaps, in a woman's way, just to be sure in her heart
That I was reluctant to leave her. So we stayed:
Stayed till the bronze moon grew pale from its climbing,
Stayed till the night was an octoroon lovely to see.
The air was so silent that even the whip-poor-wills dared not sing;
Nor could we hear aught save the rhythmic advance of our hearts
And the wash of her hair that fell about me like rain.

IN THE FAR YEARS

What have I to give?
Nothing that you can take.
You have no lips for that bread
Which my hands can make;
That pure, living bread
Which the gods break.

It is a strong bread
That few mortals favour;
But somewhere in the far years
You will catch its flavour:
Like a sweet incense
Will rise its old savour.

But not for you; another
Clad in white apparel,
Will catch up her dark hair
In a clasp of beryl
And carry that bread past your door,
Singing a sweet carol.

JUNE

The world is white with cherry-trees,
a holy light on faery seas;
my garden's full of merry bees
  and sweet with robin-rune.
My cheek is washed by fragrant sighs,
and roses stain my vagrant eyes,
as I go wandering paradise,
  in June, in lovely June.

The day's astir with musk and myrrh,
and night's a purr of gossamer.
I cannot see for blossom-blur
  the silver-riding moon.
Strawberry rugs beneath me spread,
and apple-bloom is overhead—
a canopy of white and red,
  in June, in gentle June.

The lilacs speak their scented words
the orioles are demented birds;
the cattle, in tree-tented herds,
  lie, shadow-cool, at noon.
The grass is lush on field and lawn,
and larks, that pealed the flush of dawn,
to higher chancels now have gone
  to tell the joy of June.

The hands of peace and love are here,
and bring surcease from woe and fear.
The cooing breeze and dove are here
  and they together croon.
A thousand weddings rouse the dells
with song of Canterbury-bells.
The meadows throng with nectar-wells
  to quench the thirst of June.

When June is over I shall flee—
as drunk a rover as a bee
who sips the clover's ecstasy
  and trips a rigadoon.
Nor shall December's cold desires
wash out the embers of these fires
or make me unremember choirs
  that sang for me in June.

THE SONG OF THE SKI

Norse am I when the first snow falls;
Norse am I till the ice departs.
The fare for which my spirit calls
Is blood from a hundred viking-hearts.

The curved wind wraps me like a cloak;
The pines blow out their ghostly smoke.
I'm high on the hill and ready to go—
A wingless bird in a world of snow:
Yet I'll ride the air
With a dauntless dare
That only a child of the north can know.

The bravest ski has a cautious heart
And moves like a tortoise at the start,
But when it tastes the tang of the air
It leaps away like a frightened hare.
The day is gloomy, the curtains half-drawn,
And light is stunted as at the dawn;
But my foot is sure and my arm is brawn.

I poise on the hill and I wave adieu
(My curving skis are firm and true)
The slim wood quickens, the air takes fire
And sings to me like a gypsy's lyre.
Swifter and swifter grows my flight:
The dark pines ease the unending white.
The lean, cold birches, as I go by,
Are like blurred etchings against the sky.

One am I for a moment's joy
With the falling star and the plunging bird.
The world is swift as an Arab boy;
The world is sweet as a woman's word.
Never came such a pure delight
To a bacchanal or a sybarite:
Swifter and swifter grows my flight,
And glad am I, as I near the leap,
That the snow is fresh and the banks are deep.

Swifter and swifter on I fare,
And soon I'll float with the birds on air.
The speed is blinding; I'm over the ridge,
Spanning space on a phantom bridge,
The drifts await me; I float, I fall:
The world leaps like a lunging carp.
I land erect and the tired winds drawl
A lazy rune on a broken harp.

MOONLIGHT ON LAKE SYDENHAM

The dawn came wild with rain, and all day long
  The storm ran over the lake with furious feet,
Waking the silent shores to lovely song
  And cooling the high meadows, brown with heat.
And now pale light descends,
  With sandals white as frost, this daring stair
  Down which the storm-cloud tumbled through the air,
And to the wounded lake sweet ministering sends,
  As though she were the ghost of that cold rain
  In chaste repentance come to earth again.

The fragrance of a rose at noonday sings
  In language louder than a spoken word;
And if your ear is tuned to soundless things
  The silent tread of moonlight can be heard.
For with that hidden ear
  I catch the rhythmic marching of the stars—
  White-helmed Arcturus and red-hooded Mars—
Treading the same high roadways year by year.
  And I have heard in winter, blow on blow,
  The chisels of the frost against the snow.

The workers sit around me everywhere,
  Shaping the fragrant beauty of each hour.
At noon I hear their hammers of warm air
  Welding the golden armor of a flower.
With tireless hands they toil
  In maple groves or hawthorne-haunted lanes;
  And, in their glad employ, the bugling rains
Arouse the lovely sleepers of the soil.
  And I can see their axes fall as one,
  At even, against the rose-bush of the sun.

Sunlight is fire to warm our cooling faith;
  And moonlight shall restore our broken dreams:
She moves across the world, a lovely wraith,
  Beatifying rocks and lakes and streams.
And something in her eyes
  Betrays a sorrow for the moonless days
  When, in a flood of warm, revealing rays,
The evening's cool romancing droops and dies,
  To be restored again on cloudless nights
  When that Pale Traveller treads her jewelled heights.

Beneath the granite glory of these shores
  I carve the flameless water with my blade;
While high above the hills the night-wind roars
  Until the cloistral forest is dismayed.
And soon my frail craft turns
  From overhanging gloom of rock and brake,
  And moth-like seeks the silver-flaming lake
Where the dropped candle of the high moon burns.
  And troubadours of many a wandering choir
  Sing at my prow upon this sea of fire.

When waters are turned by ploughmen of the breeze
  The grain of light upon them yieldeth well;
But when those seeds invade the gloom of trees
  They darken and wither swiftly where they fell.
And I too feel at night
  The black repulse of woods, and flee their gloom
  For that high, roofless Temple where the doom
Of darkness dies on billows rich with light.
  And here, afar from slumbering bird and tree,
  My restless spirit joins the unsleeping sea.

There is a universal loneliness
  Where deep goes calling sadly unto deep;
And, as the darkness grows, the planets press
  In closer ranks along the shores of sleep.
And this same lonely heart
  Is in the serried pine, and mortal man,
  Who climbs an overcrowded caravan
And fears the woodland, silent and apart;
  Nor knows the balm for loneliness is found
  In herbs that in the wilderness abound.

How fine this Limner, who can leave His dyes—
  The blue of noon and evening's crimson blush—
And etch the glory of these lakes and skies
  With naught but black and silver on His brush.
Far from a reeded shoal
  Floats down the dauntless laughter of the loon:
  I hear it while the drapery of the moon
Falls, through the lonely night, about my soul;
  And wait until some frail star is withdrawn
  To light the first thin taper of the dawn.

JOHN GRAYDON

I own John Graydon's place—
His elm trees moving with a lovely grace
As slow and stately as a minuet,
His great lawns wearing shadows like black lace,
Too lovely to forget.
A beggar am I, or vagabond of verse,
With neither script nor guinea in my purse,
With neither land nor honour of men, and yet,
Unknown to all the scullions of his race,
I own John Graydon's place.

John Graydon bought with gold
These ivied walls, magnificent and old,
This roadway guarded by dark, granite towers,
These moon-cooled urns that, uncomplaining, hold
The ashes of dead flowers,
And watch the dawn-like roses come and go,
And these warm hawthorne hedges white as snow,
These fountains, cool against the sunburnt hours,
These beds, where blue forget-me-nots unfold,
John Graydon bought with gold.

John Graydon paid the cost;
But what he gained with power of gold, he lost.
I bought his lands with love, and they are mine—
These acres where the moonlight lies like frost
On grass and tree and vine.
And, though I stand afar, my spirit sees
The falling streams of beauty in his trees:
I hear his roses speak, his lilacs call;
And mine are all these gardens of cool shade
For which John Graydon paid.

Comrade, the world is yours:
Her gardens fountains, valleys, hills and moors;
And for each lonely aching of your soul
There is a balm that ever heals and cures.
The amber sunlight filling high her bowl,
The pomp of purple asters are for you,
And heavy roses wet with crimson dew:
For you the march of stars, the ocean's roll.
And you can own, as I, these gardens old
John Graydon bought with gold.

SISTER MAURA [1881-]

Rev. Sister Maura, Mary Power, who has also used the pen name "Mary Seton," was born in Halifax, the daughter of Lawrence G. and Susan (O'Leary) Power. She was educated at Sacred Heart Convent, Mount Saint Vincent College, where she has been Professor of English since 1925, University of London, Dalhousie University, and University of Notre Dame, where she taught for five summers (1921-1925). She has also taught at Fordham University and Boston College. Her prose includes magazine articles and works of literary criticism. Her dramatic writing in the form of miracle, morality, and mystery plays and of the masque illustrates her lyrical gift as well, which is further exemplified in *Rhyme and Rhythm* (1932), *Breath of the Spirit* (1937), *Rhythm Poems* (1944), *A Sheaf of Songs* (n.d., ca. 1949).

THE BLESSING OF ST. FRANCIS

"The Lord bless thee and keep thee; the Lord show
His face to thee and have mercy on thee; the Lord
turn His countenance to thee and give thee peace."

Seven times the centuple wheels of life have whirled
  Since Francis in his brave abandonment
Committed his young way to a free world
  And the great hand of God; above him bent
The pitying sky; he saw in the sun and moon
  And the light of stars, the smile of God, and heard
His voice in the music of the sea, the croon
  Of the wilful wind, and the joyous lilt of a bird:
He loved in every soul drawing human breath
  The Spirit of the Maker, Whose best peace
Followed his shining steps to the bourne of death
  And filled the orbit of his life's increase.
Trust, mercy, peace—all those who love him will
Know in their lives his triple blessing still.

DEIRDRE'S SONG AT SUNRISE

Hail to thee, beautiful, mighty, and golden!
  Rise in thy splendour and gladden the earth;
Banish the darkness, all good things embolden;
  Shine, O life-giver, that joy may have birth.

Hail to thee, mighty and golden,
Lord of the days new and olden,
  Shine, that our joy may have birth.

Winter lies slain by the gold-gleaming arrows;
Far hast thou driven his coldness and dearth.
Hail to thee, victor whose peace no foe harrows!
Shine on in splendour and gladden the earth.

Shine on, O mighty and golden,
Lord of the days new and olden,
Shine on and gladden the earth

CLAIRE HARRIS MacINTOSH [1882-]

Mrs. Claire (Harris) MacIntosh, daughter of Rev. Canon Voorhees E. and Mrs. Harris, was born at Londonderry, Nova Scotia, and educated in the public schools of Amherst and at Edgehill School for Girls, Windsor, Nova Scotia. She has received an award for her work in advancing the cause of drama, has written plays and stories for children, songs, both words and music, and three books of poems, *Attune with Spring in Acadie* (1931), *Phantom Pirates* (1941), and *The Spirit of the Bluenose and Other Poems* (1951).

THE BARN IN WINTER

Winter winds howled and the great barn creaked
While a nibbling mouse in a feed-bag squeaked.
Gone were the rays of the setting sun
Which had gleamed through curtains of cob-web spun.
Snug in their stalls were the bedded cattle
And I heard them low and their tie-chains rattle.
Little pigs fed from a mother sow
And a fatted calf from a spotted cow.

Small was the door in the big barn door
Where a lantern gleamed on the straw-strewn floor,
Showing a Collie that wagged his tail
For the pat and the words that never fail.
Animals stirred but their home was warm
And they worried not at the winter storm.
Rhythmic the swish as the milk pails filled
And the beasties dozed and the barn was stilled,

Save soothing sounds as the cattle slept
And a farm horse pawed while the barn cat crept
Stealthily, peering with eyes that gleamed.
When the great storm passed then the moonlight streamed
In through the rafters, over the hay,
On a blinking fowl, in a witching way.
Then came a sound like an ancient horn;—
'Twas a crowing cock as he hailed the morn.

THE *BLUENOSE*

The fishing schooner *Bluenose* was built in Lunenburg, Nova Scotia, and launched in 1921. She spent the summer fishing on the Grand Banks and in October of the same year defeated seven Nova Scotian schooners off Halifax, winning the honour of representing Canada in an International race. Later, off Halifax, she defeated the schooner *Elsie* and brought home the championship which, although many attempts were made, was never taken from her. She was the undisputed champion of Fishing Schooners.

The picture of the *Bluenose* is on Canadian 10-cent pieces and a special 50-cent stamp was issued.

On January 29, 1946, the *Bluenose* struck a reef off Haiti and sank. Her memory will linger long after the passing of wooden ships.

THE SPIRIT OF THE *BLUENOSE*

Beneath the deep my broken timbers lie
But I, in spirit, ocean depths defy
And soar above the glory of the sea
I loved. Reefs wrecked but did not conquer me
For memory, insistent, with me stays,
Forgetting not my very early days.
Cradled where deep seas reflect the skies
Or greet the tempests with wild, strident cries.
My lullaby, the screams of gulls in race
For ocean food. I dreamed and grew apace.
"Both strong and great my infant protégé"
Designer Roue said, "You'll grow to be,
With Scotian skipper, venturesome and brave
And triumph over ocean's wildest wave."
And soon with splash, much spirit and acclaim
They christened me *Bluenose*—an honoured name,
And I was launched with Angus as my guide.
We twain, with fishing crew, upon the tide. . . .

And now I think of *Marty*—good old Mart—
And how we jockeyed and he won the start.
Then down the harbour to the Inner Buoy
We raced. Again we sped, with shouts of joy,
For Shut In Island where I had the luck;
Although at times the race was "nip and tuck."
With scuppers all awash, the wind a blow
And Angus shouting madly "grow wind grow"
We took the homeward stretches, spirits high—
The skipper reassuring with his cry.

The wind-god heard, touched seeming lazy sail
Ballooning it to meet a rising gale.
Amid wild cheers we (Angus, crew and I)
Had won and all new comers could defy.
True sportsmen that they were, they came—and went,
Acknowledging that I to them now meant
The fleetest schooner fishermen to sail
And champion racer in slow wind or gale.

And *now* I hide in billows, where fog lies,
The swelling of the tide or other guise,
And visit haunts I loved—old fishing grounds,
Where Northern Lights rejoice in crackling sounds.
I glory in the moonlight on the sea,
A shooting star,—perhaps saluting me!
Sometimes I whistle with the breeze and sing
Sea music with the billows as they fling
About the fishing craft and give them zest
While I come close atop a briny crest.
I, on a ghost cloud often seek home town
Where ships are ships and where I won renown.
And so deep waters frothed with crested foam
Are now my haunting grounds where I may roam
For I am outward bound where lightnings flash,
The heavens rage with thunder, breakers crash.

Once more recalling soft, sweet summer nights,
The sea reflecting charm of star-dipped lights
Which soothed my soul,—yes, soul of wooden ship.
With Sea I shared the glory of each trip.
I listened to the siren songs she sang,
Enjoyed her moods and salt, breath-taking tang.
Though on her lowly bed she bids me lie,
My conquering spirit sails and will not die.

A. M. STEPHEN (1882-1942]

Alexander Maitland Stephen, son of Alexander and Margaret (Whiteford) Stephen, was born near Hanover, Ontario, and educated at Walkerton Collegiate Institute. He wrote two novels, two books of plays on Canadian themes, edited two anthologies of Canadian poetry, and published four volumes of poems: *The Rosary of Pan* (1923), *The Land of Singing Waters*

(1927), *Brown Earth and Bunch Grass* (1931), and *Vérendrye, a Poem of the New World* (1935). He advanced the cause of Canadian poetry also by giving lecture-recitals, in which he was very favourably received. (Cf. *Who's Who among North American Authors*, vol. 6, and Percival as above.)

CAPILANO

Capilano, in the canyon,
  Where the ghost of wintry moons
Chills the silence of the twilights
  And the night wind softly croons,
Do your dark firs whisper secrets
  Old as Earth's forgotten runes?

Gleam and ripple, glint and shimmer—
  Are the shafts your rapids throw
Rays of those lost suns that glimmer
  Where the tides of time o'erflow?

When the storm wind bears your challenge
  And your rock-bound bugles ring,
When the voices, in your torrent,
  With the lust of battle sing,
Then we know the valley places
  Wait the bannered hosts of Spring.

Flashing, foaming, in the gloaming
  Of your shadowy mists of green;
Murmuring, dreaming, thro' the gleaming
  Of the sheer-cleft, grey ravine;
Onward, seaward, bear the summons
  Of the watchers cold and keen—
Stars above your snowy summits
  In the purple Night's demesne!

Sing, till all the listening alders
  Leaning, robed in opal mist,
Burgeon into leaf and blossom
  By your silver magic kissed!
Sing, till brown and red of bracken
  Hear the cadence of your lyre
And, thro' thickets dank and sodden,
  Breaks the trillium's white desire!

Capilano, in the canyon,
  Where the snows of Winter meet
Fires of Spring and heat of Summer
  And the waning seasons greet
Life renewed in Love's alembic,
  Hope reborn and promise sweet,
Follow we your chant triumphal!
  Hear the great sea-breakers roar
Where your song is lost in thunders
  And your dreaming is no more!

BRING TORCHES

Tear down the Ivory Tower!
Let the day strip your house of dream!
Bring torches—
Light the dark with their gleam!

Sink deep the word of the past!
Set your lip to the breath that glows!
Strive onward
With the wind as it blows!

Hearken! . . . The sound of an Age!
Mark the cliff where the waves of time,
In thunder,
Break as they climb!

Not sweet as the flute of a bird
Are the tunes of the flame and steel.
Can linnets
Hum the song of the wheel?

Tear down the Ivory Tower,
For life is greater than dream!
Bring torches—
Light the dark with their gleam!

LOUISE MOREY BOWMAN [1882-1944]

Louise (Morey) Bowman, daughter of Samuel Foote and Lily Louise (Dyer) Morey, was born in Sherbrooke, Quebec, and educated by private tutors, at Dana Hall, Wellesley, Massachusetts, and by travel in Europe. In 1909 she married Archibald Abercromby Bowman. They lived in Toronto for ten years and then moved to Montreal. Mrs. Bowman has written short stories of distinction in addition to her poetry: *Moonlight and Common Day* (1922); *Dream Tapestries* (1924), for which she won the David Award of the Quebec Government; *Characters in Cadence* (1938), in the vivid manner of the Imagists.

SEA LAVENDER

My Puritan Grandmother!—I see her now,
With placid brow,
Always so sure
"That no things but the right things shall endure!"
Sombrely neat, so orderly and prim,
Always a little grim,
Austere but kind. . . .
Smooth-banded hair and smoothly-banded mind.
But let me whisper it to you today—
I know it now—
That deep in her there was a flame at play.
Beneath that brow
The blue-grey eyes sought beauty, found it too
Most often by the ocean's passionate blue.
Her sea-beach treasures—shells and coloured weed
Gathered and hoarded with glad human greed—
They warm my heart today with insight new.
How vividly I see her, frail and old,
A tiny, black-clothed figure on the beach,
Compactly wrapped against the sea-wind's cold,
Patiently waiting till waves let her reach
Some sandy strip, where purple, amber, green,
Her lacy sea-weed treasures could be seen.
(She pressed and mounted them—frail tangled things!
Handled by her, fit to trim fairies' wings.)
So I recall her,
Searching salt-sea pools
For Beauty's shadow.
All her rigid rules,
And cold austereness with a storm-tossed child,
Melt into airs of evenings, warm and mild.
And I find revelation, sweet indeed
In her dear treasures of sea shells and weed.

SHE PLANS HER FUNERAL

Bring to me then all passionate, crimson flowers
And lay them on my breast.
They shall be symbols of the love-lit hours—
And Love is best.
Folk who would believe in Immortality,
Why should they pass in panoply of woe?
I would be linked with colour and ecstasy
That day I go.

Linked with glad dancers, their white limbs set free,
And rhythmical through veils of filmy green,
With children, rose-flushed with a mystic glee—
All these I mean
To leave as wishes for my funeral day.
But, lest I burden those I leave behind,
Let me add, hastily, that any way
They care to manage—
Will be to my mind! . . .
Yet I crave mightily for that last hour
At least one dancer and one crimson flower.

MARJORIE PICKTHALL [1883-1922]

Marjorie Lowry Christie Pickthall, daughter of Arthur C. and Helen (Mallard) Pickthall, who brought her to Canada when she was six years old, was born in Gunnersbury, England, and educated at Bishop Strachan School, Toronto. From 1912 to 1919 she lived in England, after that in Victoria and Vancouver, British Columbia. She began to write at an early age. Her prose works include two novels and a book of short stories of distinction. Her poetry, which ranks her very high among Canadian poets, is found in *Drift of Pinions* (1912), *The Lamp of Poor Souls and Other Poems* (1917), *The Wood Carver's Wife and Later Poems* (1922), *Little Songs* (1925), and *Complete Poems* (1927, 1936 [New Ed. with a few poems not previously included]). (Cf. J. D. Logan, *Marjorie Pickthall* (1922); Lorne Pierce, *Marjorie Pickthall: a Book of Remembrance* (1925), *Marjorie Pickthall: a Memorial Address* (1943); *Canadian Who was Who*, vol. 2 (1938).)

PÈRE LALEMENT

I lift the Lord on high,
Under the murmuring hemlock boughs, and see
The small birds of the forest lingering by
And making melody.
These are mine acolytes and these my choir,
And this mine altar in the cool green shade,
Where the wild soft-eyed does draw nigh
Wondering, as in the byre
Of Bethlehem the oxen heard Thy cry
And saw Thee, unafraid.

My boatmen sit apart,
Wolf-eyed, wolf-sinewed, stiller than the trees.
Help me, O Lord, for very slow of heart
And hard of faith are these.

Cruel are they, yet Thy children. Foul are they,
Yet wert Thou born to save them utterly.
Then make me as I pray
Just to their hates, kind to their sorrows, wise
After their speech, and strong before their free
Indomitable eyes.

Do the French lilies reign
Over Mont Royal and Stadacona still?
Up the St. Lawrence comes the spring again,
Crowning each southward hill
And blossoming pool with beauty, while I roam
Far from the perilous folds that are my home,
There where we built St. Ignace for our needs,
Shaped the rough roof tree, turned the first sweet sod,
St. Ignace and St. Louis, little beads
On the rosary of God.

Pines shall Thy pillars be,
Fairer than those Sidonian cedars brought
By Hiram out of Tyre, and each birch-tree
Shines like a holy thought.
But come no worshippers; shall I confess,
St. Francis-like, the birds of the wilderness?
O, with Thy love my lonely head uphold,
A wandering shepherd I, who hath no sheep;
A wandering soul, who hath no scrip, nor gold,
Nor anywhere to sleep.

My hour of rest is done;
On the smooth ripple lifts the long canoe;
The hemlocks murmur sadly as the sun
Slants his dim arrows through.
Whither I go I know not, nor the way,
Dark with strange passions, vexed with heathen charms,
Holding I know not what of life or death;
Only be Thou beside me day by day,
Thy rod my guide and comfort, underneath
Thy everlasting arms.

LITTLE SONGS

When the little Grecian cities went a-warring each with each,
From the olive on the headland to the plume-grass on the beach,
They set their gates in order and they raised their seaward towers
To songs as brief as morning and as strange as ocean-flowers.

On many a lost endeavour, on many a far retreat,—
White cattle in the oak-wood, white villa in the wheat,—
Between the harsh north-easter and the lonely British foam,
The Legions sang of summer on the little roofs of Rome.

When David tired of marching in battle for the Lord
When the dew was on his harness and the dark was on his sword,
The bearded captains listened with many a listening star,
When he sang of little pastures where the quiet waters are.

When the Master was grown weary of calling men from sin,
He went homeward in the twilight and His Mother let Him in,
And while the doves were nesting and her Son sat by her knee,
She sang Him little harvest songs of pleasant Galilee.

And when I climb to heaven by many a stair of gold,
They'll tell of little evenings along the lambing-fold,
And, in the streets unlit of sun, men will go singing still
Of little dawns of springtime above an English hill.

THE IMMORTAL

Beauty is still immortal in our eyes.
When sways no more the spirit-haunted reed,
When the wild grape shall build
No more her canopies,
When blows no more the moon-grey thistle seed,
When the last bell has lulled the white flocks home,
When the last eve has stilled
The wandering wind and touched the dying foam,
When the last moon burns low, and spark by spark
The little worlds die out along the dark.

Beauty that rosed the moth-wing, touched the land
With clover horns and delicate faint flowers,
Beauty that bade the showers
Beat on the violet's face,
Shall hold the eternal heavens within their place
And hear new stars come singing from God's hand.

SWALLOW SONG

O little hearts, beat home, beat home,
  Here is no place of rest;
Night darkens on the falling foam
  And on the fading west.
O little wings, beat home, beat home,
Love may no longer roam.

Oh, Love has touched the fields of wheat,
  And Love has crowned the corn;
And we must follow Love's white feet
  Through all the ways of morn:
Through all the silver roads of air
We pass and have no care.

The silver roads of Love are wide,
O winds that turn, O stars that guide.
Sweet are the ways that Love hàth trod
Through the clear skies that reach to God;
But in the cliff-grass Love builds deep
A place where wandering wings may sleep.

A MOTHER IN EGYPT

Is the noise of grief in the palace over the river
  For this silent one at my side?
There came a hush in the night, and he rose with his hands aquiver
  Like lotus petals adrift on the swing of the tide.

O small soft hands, the day groweth old for sleeping!
  O small still feet, rise up for the hour is late!
Rise up, my son, for I hear them mourning and weeping
  In the temple down by the gate.

Hushed is the face that was wont to brighten with laughter
  When I sang at the mill,
And silence unbroken shall greet the sorrowful dawns hereafter,
  The house shall be still.

Voice after voice takes up the burden of wailing,—
  Do you heed, do you hear, in the high-priest's house by the wall?
But mine is the grief, and their sorrow is all unavailing.
  Will he wake at their call?

Something I saw of the broad, dim wings half folding
  The passionless brow.
Something I saw of the sword the shadowy hands were holding,—
  What matters it now?

I held you close, dear face, as I knelt and harkened
  To the wind that cried last night like a soul in sin,
When the broad, bright stars dropped down and the soft sky darkened,
  And the Presence moved therein.

I have heard men speak in the market-place of the city,
Low-voiced, in a breath,
Of a god who is stronger than ours, and who knows not changing
nor pity,
Whose anger is death.
Nothing I know of the lords of the outland races,
But Amun is gentle and Hathor the Mother is mild,
And who would descend from the light of the peaceful places
To war on a child?

Yet here he lies, with a scarlet pomegranate petal
Blown down on his cheek.
The slow sun sinks to the sand like a shield of some burnished
metal,
But he does not speak.
I have called, I have sung, but he neither will hear nor waken;
So lightly, so whitely he lies in the curve of my arm,
Like a feather let fall from the bird that the arrow hath taken.
Who could see him, and harm?

"The swallow flies home to her sleep in the eaves of the altar,
And the crane to her nest,"
So do we sing o'er the mill, and why, ah, why should I falter,
Since he goes to his rest?
Does he play in their flowers as he played among these with his
mother?
Do the gods smile downward and love him and give him their
care?
Guard him well, O ye gods, till I come; lest the wrath of that Other
Should reach to him there!

BEGA

From the crowded belfry calling,
Hear my soft, ascending swells;
Hear my notes like swallows falling;
I am Bega, least of bells.
When great Turkeful rolls and rings
All the storm-touched turret swings,
Echoing battle, loud and long.

When great Tatwin wakening roars
To the far-off shining shores,
All the seamen know his song.
I am Bega, least of bells:
In my throat my message swells.
I with all the winds athrill,
Murmuring softly, murmuring still:
"God around me, God above me,
God to guard me, God to love me."

I am Bega, least of bells,
Weaving wonder, wind-born spells.
High above the morning mist,
Wreathed in rose and amethyst.

Still the dreams of music float,
Silver from my silver throat,
Whispering beauty, whispering peace.
When great Tatwin's golden voice
Bids the listening land rejoice,
When great Turkeful rings and rolls
Thunder down to trembling souls,
Then my notes like curlews flying,
Lifting, falling, sinking, sighing,
Softly answer, softly cease.
I with all the airs at play
Murmuring, sweetly murmuring, say:
"God around me, God above me,
God to guard me, God to love me."

THE BRIDEGROOM OF CANA

"There was a marriage in Cana of Galilee. . . . And both Jesus was called, and His disciples, to the marriage."

Veil thine eyes, O belovèd, my spouse,
Turn them away,
Lest in their light my life withdrawn
Dies as a star, as a star in the day,
As a dream in the dawn.

Slenderly hang the olive leaves
Sighing apart;
The rose and silver doves in the eaves
With a murmur of music bind our house.
Honey and wine in thy words are stored,
Thy lips are bright as the edge of a sword
That hath found my heart,
That hath found my heart.

Sweet, I have waked from a dream of thee,—
And of Him.
He who came when the songs were done.
From the net of thy smiles my heart went free
And the golden lure of thy love grew dim.
I turned to them asking, "Who is He,
Royal and sad, who comes to the feast
And sits Him down in the place of the least?"
And they said, "He is Jesus, the carpenter's son."

Hear how my harp on a single string
Murmurs of love.
Down in the fields the thrushes sing
And the lark is lost in the light above,
Lost in the infinite, glowing whole,
As I in thy soul,
As I in thy soul.

Love, I am fain for thy glowing grace
As the pool for the star, as the rain for the rill.
Turn to me, trust to me, mirror me
As the star in the pool, as the cloud in the sea.
Love, I looked awhile in His face
And was still.

The shaft of the dawn strikes clear and sharp;
Hush, my harp.
Hush, my harp, for the day is begun,
And the lifting, shimmering flight of the swallow
Breaks in a curve on the brink of morn,
Over the sycamores, over the corn,
Cling to me, cleave to me, prison me
As the mote in the flame, as the shell in the sea,
For the winds of the dawn say, "Follow, follow
Jesus Bar-Joseph, the carpenter's son."

EBB TIDE

(*The Sailor's Grave at Clo-oose, Vancouver Island*)

Out of the winds' and the waves' riot,
Out of the loud foam,
He has put in to a great quiet
And a still home.

Here he may lie at ease and wonder
Why the old ship waits,
And hark for the surge and the strong thunder
Of the full Straits.

And look for the fishing fleet at morning,
Shadows like lost souls,
Slide through the fog where the seal's warning
Betray the shoals,

And watch for the deep-sea liner climbing
Out of the bright West,
With a salmon-sky and her wake shining
Like a tern's breast,—

And never know he is done for ever
With the old sea's pride,
Borne from the fight and the full endeavour
On an ebb tide.

E. J. PRATT [1883-]

Edwin John Pratt, son of John and Fanny Pratt, was born at Western Bay, Newfoundland, and was educated at the Methodist College, St. John's, and at Victoria College, Toronto. He has been the recipient of four honorary degrees and has been made a C.M.G. From 1921 till his retirement in 1952 he taught English at Victoria College, his alma mater. His critical work includes the editing of two novels and two plays. In the field of Canadian narrative poetry, in which he has three times won the Governor-General's Medal, he is unparalleled in quantity and in quality. His *Collected Poems* (1944) was his thirteenth book of poetry. Since then he has published *They Are Returning* (1945), *Behind the Log* (1947), and *Towards the Last Spike* (1952), the latest to win the Governor-General's Award. (Cf. W. E. Collin, *The White Savannahs* (1936); E. K. Brown, *On Canadian Poetry* (1943, 1944); C. F. Klinck and H. W. Wells, *Edwin J. Pratt, The Man and His Poetry* (1947); John Sutherland, *E. J. Pratt: A Major Contemporary Poet* (1952, *Northern Review*, vol. 5, nos. 3, 4); Percival as above).

THE GROUND-SWELL

Three times we heard it calling with a low,
Insistent note; at ebb-tide on the noon;
And at the hour of dusk, when the red moon
Was rising and the tide was on the flow;
Then, at the hour of midnight once again,
Though we had entered in and shut the door
And drawn the blinds, it crept up from the shore
And smote upon a bedroom window-pane;
Then passed away as some dull pang that grew
Out of the void before Eternity
Had fashioned out an edge for human grief;
Before the winds of God had learned to strew
His harvest-sweepings on a winter sea
To feed the primal hungers of a reef.

THE ICE-FLOES

Dawn from the foretop! Dawn from the barrel!
A scurry of feet with a roar overhead;
The master-watch wildly pointing Northward,
Where the herd in front of *The Eagle* was spread!

Steel-planked and sheathed like a battleship's nose,
She battered her path through the drifting floes;
Past slob and growler we drove, and rammed her
Into the heart of the patch and jammed her.
There were hundreds and thousands of seals, I'd swear,
In the stretch of that field—"white harps" to spare
For a dozen such fleets as had left that spring
To share in the general harvesting.
The first of the line, we had struck the main herd;
The day was ours, and our pulses stirred
In that brisk, live hour before the sun,
At the thought of the load and the sweepstake won.

We stood on the deck as the morning outrolled
On the fields its tissue of orange and gold,
And lit up the ice to the north in the sharp,
Clear air; each mother-seal and its "harp"
Lay side by side; and as far as the range
Of the patch ran out we saw that strange,

And unimaginable thing
That sealers talk of every spring—
The "bobbing-holes" within the floes
That neither wind nor frost could close;
Through every hole a seal could dive,
And search, to keep her brood alive,
A hundred miles it well might be,
For food beneath that frozen sea.
Round sunken reef and cape she would rove,
And though the wind and current drove
The ice-fields many leagues that day,
We knew she would turn and find her way
Back to the hole, without the help
Of compass or log, to suckle her whelp—
Back to that hole in the distant floes,
And smash her way up with her teeth and her nose.
But we flung those thoughts aside when the shout
Of command from the master-watch rang out.

Assigned to our places in watches of four—
Over the rails in a wild carouse,
Two from the port and starboard bows,
Two from the broadsides—off we tore,
In the breathless rush for the day's attack,
With the speed of hounds on a caribou's track.
With the rise of the sun we started to kill,
A seal for each blow from the iron bill
Of our gaffs. From the nose to the tail we ripped them,
And laid their quivering carcasses flat
On the ice; then with our knives we stripped them
For the sake of the pelt and its lining of fat.

With three fathoms of rope we laced them fast,
With their skins to the ice to be easy to drag,
With our shoulders galled we drew them, and cast
Them in thousands around the watcher's flag.
Then, with our bodies begrimed with the reek
Of grease and sweat from the toil of the day,
We made for *The Eagle*, two miles away,
At the signal that flew from her mizzen peak.
And through the night, as inch by inch
She reached the pans with the harps piled high,
We hoisted them up as the hours filed by
To the sleepy growl of the donkey-winch.

Over the bulwarks again we were gone,
With the first faint streaks of a misty dawn;
Fast as our arms could swing we slew them,
Ripped them, "sculped" them, roped and drew them
To the pans where the seals in pyramids rose
Around the flags on the central floes,
Till we reckoned we had nine thousand dead
By that time the afternoon had fled;
And that an added thousand or more
Would beat the count of the day before.
So back again to the patch we went
To haul, before the day was spent,
Another load of four "harps" a man,
To make the last the record pan.

And not one of us saw, as we gaffed, and skinned,
And took them in tow, that the north-east wind
Had veered off-shore; that the air was colder;
That the signs of recall were there to the south,
The flag of *The Eagle*, and the long, thin smoulder
That drifted away from her funnel's mouth.
Not one of us thought of the speed of the storm
That hounded our tracks in the day's last chase
(For the slaughter was swift, and the blood was warm)
Till we felt the first sting of the snow in our face.

We looked south-east, where, an hour ago,
Like a smudge on the sky-line, some one had seen
The Eagle, and thought he had heard her blow
A note like a warning from her sirene.
We gathered in knots, each man within call
Of his mate, and slipping our ropes, we sped,
Plunging our way through a thickening wall
Of snow that the gale was driving ahead.
We ran with the wind on our shoulder; we knew
That the night had left us this only clew
Of the track before us, through each wail
That grew to the pang of a shriek from the gale,
Some of us swore that *The Eagle* screamed
Right off to the east; to the others it seemed
On the southern quarter and near, while the rest
Cried out with every report that rose
From the strain and the rend of the wind on the floes
That *The Eagle* was firing her guns to the west.

And some of them turned to the west, though to go
Was madness—we knew it and roared, but the notes
Of our warning were lost as a fierce gust of snow
Eddied, and strangled the word in our throats.
Then we felt in our hearts that the night had swallowed
All signals, the whistle, the flare, and the smoke
To the south; and like sheep in a storm we followed
Each other; like sheep huddled and broke.

Here one would fall as hunger took hold
Of his step; here one would sleep as the cold
Crept into his blood, and another would kneel
Athwart the body of some dead seal,
And with knife and nails would tear it apart,
To flesh his teeth in its frozen heart.
And another dreamed that the storm was past,
And raved of his bunk and brandy and food,
And *The Eagle* near, though in that blast
The mother was fully as blind as her brood.
Then we saw, what we feared from the first—dark places
Here and there to the left of us, wide, yawning spaces
Of water; the fissures and cracks had increased
Till the outer pans were afloat, and we knew,
As they drifted along in the night to the east,
By the cries we heard, that some of our crew
Were borne to the sea on those pans and were lost.
And we turned with the wind in our faces again,
And took the snow with its lancing pain,
Till our eye-balls cracked with the salt and the frost;
Till only iron and fire that night
Survived on the ice as we stumbled on;
As we fell and rose and plunged—till the light
In the south and the east disclosed the dawn,
And the sea heaving with floes—and then,
The Eagle in wild pursuit of her men.

And the rest is as a story told,
Or a dream that belonged to a dim, mad past,
Of a March night and a north wind's cold,
Of a voyage home with a flag half-mast;
Of twenty thousand seals that were killed
To help to lower the price of bread;
Of the muffled beat . . . of a drum . . . that filled
A nave . . . at our count of sixty dead.

THE SEA CATHEDRAL

Vast and immaculate; no pilgrim bands,
In ecstasy before the Parian shrines,
Knew such a temple built by human hands,
With this transcendent rhythm in its lines.
Like an epic on the North Atlantic stream
It moved—and fairer than a Phidian dream.

Rich gifts unknown to kings were duly brought,
At dawn and sunset and at cloudless noons,
Gifts from the sea-gods, and the sun who wrought
Cascades and rainbows; flung them in festoons
Over the spires, with emerald, amethyst,
Sapphire and pearl out of their fiery mist.

Within the sunlight—vast, immaculate!
Beyond all reach of earth in majesty,
It passed on southward slowly to its fate—
To be drawn down by the inveterate sea.
Without one chastening fire made to start
From altars built around its polar heart.

BURIAL AT SEA

[From *The Roosevelt and the Antinoe*]

From every quarter came the night confounding
The unhorizoned sea with sky and air,
And to the crew of the *Antinoe*—despair.
At ten o'clock the *Roosevelt* bugle sounding
From the saloon stairway a call to prayer!

With separated phrase and smothered word
An immemorial psalm became a blurred
Bulwark under erosion by the sea.
Beneath the maddening crashes of the wind
Crumbled the grammar of the liturgy.

God of all comfort . . .
humbly beseeching thee . . .
We do acknowledge . . . . sinned . . .
Most merciful . . . confess . . . grievously . . .
Who spreadest out the heavens, crownest the years.
. . . . . Grant us we pray thee . . . . .
Who commandest the seas and they do obey thee.
Nigh unto all . . . .
. . . . our distresses and fears.
. . . . A father to the fatherless.

Followed the fragments of great passages:
I am the Resurrection. . . . . We
. . . commit . . . bodies to the deep . . .
Corruptible. . . . . . Of those who sleep . . .
. . . . shall put on immortality.

And then brief tributes to the seamen drowned,
While Miller and his men were ranged around,
Bandaged in head and wrist, with arms in sling,
And others who had come, despite the warning,
To take their places were envisaging
The job that lay before them in the morning.

Meanwhile outside, echoing the ritual—
Now unto Him who is able to do . . . .
Exceeding abundantly . . . a wild antiphonal
Of shriek and whistle from the shrouds broke through,
Blending with thuds as though some throat had laughed
In thunder down the ventilating shaft;
And the benediction ended with the crack
Of a stanchion on the starboard beam, the beat
Of a loose block, with the fast run of feet,
Where a flying guy careered about the stack;

Then following the omen of a lull,
The advent of a wave which like a wall
Crashed down in volleys flush against the hull,
Lifting its white and shafted spume to fall
Across the higher decks; and through it all,
As on the dial of the telegraph,
Governed by derelict and hurricane,
Rang *Stop*, *Full Speed Astern* or *Slow* or *Half*,
The irregular pulse and cough of the engine strain
The quick smite of the blades against a wave,
And always threat, escape, threat, then the brave
Lift of the keel, and still that breathless sink,
Dividing up the seconds, nearing the brink
Of a grey, unplumbed precipice and grave.

Within this hour a priest clothed with the whole
Habiliment and dignity of office—
Black cassock, surplice white and purple stole—
Feeling that from an older faith would come
The virtue of a rubric yet unspoken
For the transition of a soul, a crumb

Of favour from a cupboard not bereft
Of all by the night's intercessions, left
His room; climbed the stairs; pushed through a door
Storm-wedged, and balancing along the floor
Of the deck to where a davit stood, he placed
His grip securely on a guy rope there.
Lifting up a crucifix, he faced
The starboard quarter, looking down the waste
Of the waters casting back the flickering light
Of the steamer, where two bodies without wrap
Of shroud, deprived of their deck funeral rite,
Swung to the rune of the sea's stern foster-lap.

Ego vos absolvo . . . . . . ab omnibus
Peccatis et censuris . . . .
. . . . in nomine
Patris et Filii et Spiritus . . . . .
Sancti . . . . Attende Domine
. . . . et miserere
Hear . . . O stella maris . . . Mary.

But no Gennesaret of Galilee
Conjured to its level by the sway
Of a hand or a word's magic was this sea,
Contesting with its iron-alien mood,
Its pagan face, its own primordial way,
The pale heroic suasion of a rood.
And the absolving Father, when the ship
Righted her keel between two giant rolls,
Recrossed himself, and letting go his hold,
Returned to berth, murmuring *God rest their souls.*

And now throughout the middle of the night,
The *Roosevelt* took the hurricane, hove-to.
Into her own defence the captain knew
Must enter all the sinews of her fight—
Her searchlight ripping fissures as through dark
Parchment where at times the freighter, set
In a frame of tossing silver, showed the stark
And streaming edges of her silhouette,
Battered but yet miraculously afloat,
Heaving, subsiding with her lathered flank,
Like a bison smitten from the loin to shank,
Surrendering to the wolves about her throat.

EROSION

It took the sea a thousand years,
A thousand years to trace
The granite features of this cliff,
In crag and scarp and base.

It took the sea an hour one night,
An hour of storm to place
The sculpture of these granite seams
Upon a woman's face.

INVISIBLE TRUMPETS BLOWING

[From *Brébeuf and His Brethren*]

And sometimes the speech
Of Brébeuf struck out, thundering reproof to his foes,
Half-rebuke, half-defiance, giving them roar for roar.
Was it because the chancel became the arena,
Brébeuf a lion at bay, not a lamb on the altar,
As if the might of a Roman were joined to the cause
Of Judaea? Speech they could stop for they girdled his lips,
But never a moan could they get. Where was the source
Of his strength, the home of his courage that topped the best
Of their braves and even out-fabled the lore of their legends?
In the bunch of his shoulders which often had carried a load
Extorting the envy of guides at an Ottawa portage?
The heat of the hatchets was finding a path to that source.
In the thews of his thighs which had mastered the trails of the
Neutrals?
They would gash and beribbon those muscles. Was it the blood?
They would draw it fresh from its fountain. Was it the heart?
They dug for it, fought for the scraps in the way of wolves.
But not in these was the valour or stamina lodged;
Nor in the symbol of Richelieu's robes or the seals
Of Mazarin's charters, nor in the stir of the *lilies*
Upon the Imperial folds; nor yet in the words
Loyola wrote on a table of lava-stone
In the cave of Manresa—not in these the source—
But in the sound of invisible trumpets blowing
Around two slabs of board, right-angled, hammered
By Roman nails and hung on a Jewish hill.

From THE CACHALOT

Where Cape Delgado strikes the sea,
A cliff ran outward slantingly
A mile along a tossing edge
Of water towards a coral ledge,
Making a sheer and downward climb
Of twenty fathoms where it ended,
Forming a jutty scaur suspended
Over a cave of murk and slime.
A dull reptilian silence hung
About the walls, and fungus clung
To knots of rock, and over boles
Of lime and basalt poisonous weed
Grew rampant, covering the holes
Where crayfish and sea-urchins breed.
The upper movement of the seas
Across the reefs could not be heard;
The nether tides but faintly stirred
Sea-nettles and anemones.
A thick festoon of lichens crawled
From crag to crag, and under it
Half-hidden in a noisome pit
Of bones and shells a kraken sprawled.
Moveless, he seemed, as a boulder set
In pitch, and dead within his lair,
Except for a transfixing stare
From lidless eyes of burnished jet,
And a hard spasm now and then
Within his viscous centre, when
His scabrous feelers intertwined
Would stir, vibrate, and then unwind
Their ligatures with easy strength
To tap the gloom, a cable length;
And finding no life that might touch
The mortal radius of their clutch,
Slowly relax, and shorten up
Each tensile tip, each suction cup,
And coil again around the head
Of the mollusc on its miry bed,
Like a litter of pythons settling there
To shutter the Gorgonian stare.

But soon the squid's antennae caught
A murmur that the waters brought—

No febrile stirring as might spring
From a puny barracuda lunging
At a tuna's leap, some minor thing,
A tarpon or a dolphin plunging—
But a deep consonant that rides
Below the measured beat of tides
With that vast, undulating rhythm
A sounding sperm whale carries with him.
The kraken felt that as the flow
Beat on his lair with plangent power,
It was the challenge of his foe,
The prelude to a fatal hour;
Nor was there given him more than time,
From that first instinct of alarm,
To ground himself in deeper slime,
And raise up each enormous arm
Above him, when, unmeasured, full
On the revolving ramparts, broke
The hideous rupture of a stroke
From the forehead of the bull.
And when they interlocked, that night—
Cetacean and cephalopod—
No Titan with Olympian god
Had ever waged a fiercer fight;
Tail and skull and teeth and maw
Met sinew, cartilage, and claw,
Within those self-engendered tides,
Where the Acherontic flood
Of sepia, mingling with the blood
Of whale, befouled Delgado's sides.
And when the cachalot out-wore
The squid's tenacious clasp, he tore
From frame and socket, shred by shred,
Each gristled, writhing tentacle,
And with serrated mandible
Sawed cleanly through the bulbous head;
Then gorged upon the fibrous jelly
Until, finding that six tons lay
Like Vulcan's anvil in his belly,
He left a thousand sharks his prey,
And with his flukes, slow-labouring, rose
To a calm surface where he shot
A roaring geyser, steaming hot,
From the blast-pipe of his nose.

One hour he rested, in the gloom
Of the after-midnight; his great back
Prone with the tide and, in the loom
Of the Afric coast, merged with the black
Of the water; till a rose shaft, sent
From Madagascar far away,
Etched a ripple, eloquent
Of a freshening wind and a fair day.

GEORGE FREDERICK CLARKE [1883-]

George Frederick Clarke, son of Abram Edwin and Maria Lucy (Harris) Clarke, was born at Woodstock, New Brunswick, was educated there and at Medical-Chirurgical College, Philadelphia, and is a dental surgeon in his native town. He is the author of numerous animal stories, six juvenile novels, one or more of which can be read by adults, and *The Saint John and Other Poems* (1933).

THE SAINT JOHN

Where have they gone,
De Monts and Champlain,
Gallant adventurers who sailed into the west
To search for a passage to Cathay
And discovered and named you, Saint John?
The Malecites now no more
Make canoes of birchen bark,
Or elm, as in days of yore,
Nor fashion their arrows of flint.
Stockade and wigwam and warriors
Are one with the age-old dust
That nurtures the blood-root and violet,
The Linnaea and anemone;
But you, my river, flow on, flow on to the sea;
Past island, intervale, upland
Where the stately elms stand guard alone.
Oh, my river, you have seen the passing of spruce and pine,
And the hemlock, too, has gone to the housing of man.
Those who gave you your name—
De Monts and Champlain,
Do they know, do they sorrow with me
When they see the elm trees standing alone?

Do they hear the wind in the leaves,
And the bobolink's joyous and rollicking lay,
The lilt of the river over the bars,
And the leap of the salmon in play?
I hope so:
For I, too, some day, years hence in the centuries unmade,
Should love to lie in the grass under the elm tree's shade,
Listening to the song of the bobolink and the thrush,
Content, with De Monts and Champlain,
With this, for Cathay.

GERTRUDE MACGREGOR MOFFATT [1884-1923]

Gertrude (MacGregor) Moffatt, Mrs. Thomas E. Moffatt, daughter of Rev. Daniel Arthur and Augusta J. (Hull) MacGregor, was born in Stratford, Ontario, and educated at Moulton College, Toronto, and McMaster University. Her collected poems, edited by B. K. Sandwell (1876-), appeared as *A Book of Verses* (1924). (Cf. *Canadian Who was Who*, vol. 1 (1934).)

ALL NIGHT I HEARD

All night I heard the singing rain,
On early leaf and apple-bloom,
Like fragrance of a low refrain,
The lyric of a faint perfume.

And through my dreams it seemed to me
A sweet confusion, all night long,
Of music falling fragrantly,
And flowers that opened in a song.

CECIL FRANCIS LLOYD [1884-1938]

Cecil Francis Lloyd, born at Stonelea House, Herefordshire, England, came to Canada in 1896. He was educated at Queen's University, Kingston, Ontario, and at London University. He worked for a business firm in Winnipeg from 1897 till a few years before his death and during his last years tried to live by his pen. He published two books of essays. His marked poetic gift is well exemplified in *Landfall: The Collected Poems of Cecil Francis Lloyd* (1935). (Cf. *Canadian Poetry Magazine*, October, 1938.)

MARCH WINDS

I hear enormous noises in the night
Pass through the house to die into the dark,
Setting my wild heart shuddering with fright,
Like some old tale of witch or goblin. Hark!
Surely that was a foot upon the floor,
And hark again, a dreadful moan of pain;
A ghostly hand is troubling my door,
That was a sigh that passed, I heard it plain.
Primeval terrors darkly stir along
The current of my blood and lift my hair;
Around my bed mysterious faces throng,
Demonic, ah but one of them is fair;
She smiles at me, I'll slumber like a child,
Though on the plains the winds of March blow wild.

TRUTH

No heavier lies the everlasting snow
On Alps or Andes than upon my tongue
The pain of silence, yet I surely know
The vast abyss whence all great words have sprung.
If I should lay a steady hand in yours
And to the passion of your words reply
With just a syllable, the thing endures
Beyond the steadfast beauty of the sky:
And as the tenderness of dawn and eve
Turns the suspended avalanche to gold,
I would that for your sake you should believe
My heart is warm although my words are cold.
Lacking the facile power of easy breath,
For life, I give you love, that fears no death.

LLOYD ROBERTS [1884-]

William Harris Lloyd Roberts, son of Sir Charles George Douglas and Mary Isabel (Fenety) Roberts, was born at Fredericton, New Brunswick, and educated by private tutors and at King's College School, Windsor, Nova Scotia, and Fredericton schools. Between 1904 and 1913 he engaged in a variety of journalistic work. From 1913 to 1920 he was in the Canadian Civil Service in Ottawa. From 1925 to 1939 he was the parliamentary correspondent of the *Christian Science Monitor*. For the next four years he was R.C.M.P. Liaison and Public Relations Officer. In addition to his writing, he has given lecture-recitals on poetry across Canada. He has written radio scripts, articles, naval history, short stories, *The Book of Roberts* (1923), and three books of poems: *England Over Seas* (1914); *Along the Ottawa* (1927); and *I Sing of Life: Selected Poems of Lloyd Roberts* (1937).

ONE MORNING WHEN THE RAIN-BIRDS CALL

The snows have joined the little streams and slid into the sea;
The mountainsides are damp and black and steaming in the sun;
But Spring who should be with us now is waiting timidly
For Winter to unbar the gates and let the rivers run.

It matters not how green the grass is lifting through the mould,
How strong the sap is climbing out to every naked bough,
That in the towns the market stalls are bright with jonquil gold,
And over marsh and meadowland the frogs are fluting now.

For still the waters groan and grind beneath the icy floor,
And still the winds are hungry-cold that leave the valley's mouth.
Expectantly each day we wait to hear the sullen roar,
And see the blind and broken herd retreating to the south.

One morning when the rain-birds call across the singing rills,
And the maple buds like tiny flames shine red among the green,
The ice will burst asunder and go pounding through the hills—
An endless grey procession with the yellow floods between.

Then the Spring will no more linger, but come with joyous shout,
With music in the city squares and laughter down the lane;
The thrush will pipe at twilight to draw the blossoms out,
And the vanguard of the summer host will camp with us again.

DEEP DARK RIVER

Deep dark river drifting through the night,
Stabbed with cold stars and the cold moon's light,
Quickened with the north wind and the draining snow,
What strange dreams stir in thy turgid flow!

I can see the black silt of far-drowned places,
And the white froth of rapids like drowned faces,
And the red and purple stains of sunsets burning,
And the endless grey rains of winter's turning.

I can hear the bobcat scream, the cow moose calling,
The dull reverberant crash of rampike falling,
And from the portage trail below Deschênes
The pulse of paddles and *A la Claire Fontaine.*

I hear the ghost waves lapping on a million beaches,
I hear the ghost laughter of loons down lonely reaches,
The sighing of spent winds in the matted spruce
And the sudden honk and splash of arrow-stricken goose.

And always I hear the stir of men slipping
Down to the Chaudière, their thin blades dripping,
Catch the long low wraith of a bark canoe
And the wild sweet chansons of a phantom crew.

Strange smells are loosed by the hurrying prows—
Wood-smoke, trade rum, dried balsam boughs;
Strange smells steeped from the drip of years
And dyed with the stuff of dead dreams and tears.

Into the wash and waste of thy brave débris,
Drifting through the dark night toward a dark sea,
Into thy silent keeping receive from me
The gleam of one more broken dream, O Ottawa!

THE FRUIT RANCHER

He sees the rosy apples cling like flowers to the bough:
He plucks the purple plums and spills the cherries on the grass;
He wanted peace and silence,—God gives him plenty now—
His feet upon the mountain and his shadow on the pass.

He built himself a cabin from red cedars of his own;
He blasted out the stumps and twitched the boulders from the soil;
And with an axe and chisel he fashioned out a throne
Where he might dine in grandeur off the first fruits of his toil.

His orchard is a treasure-house alive with song and sun,
Where currants ripe as rubies gleam and golden pippins glow;
His servants are the wind and rain whose work is never done,
Till winter rends the scarlet roof and banks the halls with snow.

He shouts across the valley, and the ranges answer back;
His brushwood smoke at evening lifts a column to the moon;
And dim beyond the distance where the Kootenai snakes black,
He hears the silence shattered by the laughter of the loon.

ANDREW MERKEL [1884-]

Andrew Doane Merkel, son of Andrew DeB. and Margaret J. (Thomas) Merkel, was born at Morley, New York, and educated at Acacia Villa Seminary, Horton, Nova Scotia, at Davenport School, Saint John, New Brunswick, at St. Andrew's School, Annapolis Royal, Nova Scotia, and at the University of King's College, Windsor, Nova Scotia. His journalistic career took him to various cities between 1907 and 1918. From 1918 till his retirement in 1947 he was Atlantic Superintendent of the Canadian Press. He now lives at historic Port Royal. He has published a history of the famous racing schooner the *Bluenose* and two volumes of verse, *The Order of Good Cheer* (1944) and *Tallahassee* (1945).

From TALLAHASSEE

Ann stood and watched the combers race to shore.
It was her joy to see them lift and curl,
And break in tumult, down the line, to pour
Their seething volume on the sands, and swirl
About her ankles, icy cold. The girl,
An only child, was scarce sixteen, but she
Was one with all that stretch of flashing sea.

It was her only playmate, since her home,
Huddled against a grove that fringed the beach,
Was sentinel for miles of raging foam.
So to the sea she went for whispered speech,
And marked in roar and hiss, and weird screech
Of hungry gulls, far off, all that she knew
Of love and life and death and false and true.

MARY MATHESON [1885-]

Mrs. Mary (Naismith) Matheson has been publishing poetry from Vancouver since 1926, but some of the most appealing poems are concerned with the Canadian prairies, especially with Alberta. Her books of verse are: *Destiny* (1926); *Destiny and Other Poems* (1927); *To a Prairie Rose and Other Poems* (1933); *Shining Wings* (1936); *Smiling Through* (1941); *Out of the Dusk* (1941); *The Moving Finger and Other Poems* (1944); and *I Seek My Way* (1949).

EVENING

When you have come, the house is emptied quite
Of all the drab disguises of the day,
Faint sunbeams creep across the room and light
The shadows gathered while you were away;
Each sombre silence leaves his chair, that Cheer
May be enthroned and crownèd in his place;
The muffled clock gives forth a ticking clear,
And through the house there is no longer trace
Of aught I dreaded in those haunting hours
When so remote to me seemed your return;
But now you've come my garden's wreathed in flowers,
And glowing fires on inner altars burn.
What meets it that we spend the day apart
If, when night falls, all is so changed, dear heart?

AFTERWARD

With gentle step I came at last
To where we sat long years ago;
I touched his fingers as I passed,
And called his name—so soft and low.

I moved the leaves above his head,
And smoothed his ruffled, dark-brown hair;
I wondered why he thought me dead,
And why the look of dull despair.

I wished that I might tell him how
I lived a fuller life than he;
I placed cool hands upon his brow;
Then when I thought he looked at me—

He merely moved the lips I'd heard
And said it was the wind that stirred.

LAURA E. McCULLY [1886-1924]

Laura Elizabeth McCully, daughter of Dr. S. E. and Helen (Fitzgibbon) McCully, was born in Toronto, and educated at the University of Toronto. She was a journalist and the author of *Mary Magdalene and Other Poems* (1914). (Cf. *Canadian Who was Who*, vol. 1 (1934).)

CANOE SONG AT TWILIGHT

Down in the west the shadows rest,
  Little grey wave, sing low, sing low,
With a rhythmic sweep o'er the gloomy deep
  Into the dusk of the night we go:
    And the paddles dip and lift and slip,
    And the drops fall back with a pattering drip:
The wigwams deep of the spirits of sleep
Are pitched in the gloom on the headland steep.
  Wake not their silence as you go,
  Little grey wave, sing low, sing low!

From your porch on high where the clouds go by,
  Little white moon, look down, look down,
'Neath night's shut lid the stars are hid,
  And the last late bird to his nest has flown.
    The slow waves glide and sink and slide
    And rise in ripples along the side;
The loons call low in the marsh below,
Night weaves about us her magic slow,—
  Ere the last faint gleam in our wake be gone,
  Little white moon, look down, look down.

BEATRICE REDPATH

Beatrice (Peterson) Redpath, Mrs. William Redpath, daughter of Mr. and Mrs. Alexander Peterson (the latter born Langlois), was born in Montreal and educated there in private schools till she was seventeen. She lived in Goderich, Ontario, for five years. In 1910 she married and lived in Toronto for a long time, later moving to Oakville, Ontario. She has written notable short stories and published two books of poems, *Drawn Shutters* (1914) and *White Lilac* (1919).

THE STAR

I think God sang when He had made
A bough of apple bloom,
And placed it close against the sky
To whiten in the gloom.

But, oh, when He had hung a star
Above a blue, blue hill,
I think God in His ecstasy
Was startled . . . and was still.

BUT I SHALL WEEP

Dearest, when your lovely head
Droops, and they shall call you dead,
I shall know that you have found
Somewhere . . . somewhere out of sound
Unsurpassed security.
There, wherever you may be,
You shall know all loveliness,
All that you gave voice to bless.
In your wide mysterious night
All that brought you dear delight
Shall be near for your content,
For your long assuagement.

All you loved you still shall keep
With you in your curious sleep,
Remembering only what you will,
Remembering, dear, remembering still
Old and cherished ecstasies.
Stars that hang in quiet trees,
Apple blooms and silver light,
Wings that beat against the night,
Little gardens where the bees
Go humming.
Dearest, all of these
Shall be with you in your sleep,
But I shall weep . . . I shall weep.

KATHRYN MUNRO TUPPER

Kathryn (Munro) Tupper, Mrs. John Freeman Tupper, who writes under her maiden name, was born at Orangedale, Cape Breton, the daughter of James J. and Katherine A. (Macdonald) Munro, and educated at Sydney Academy. She took a business course later, and became a reporter of the Nova Scotia Supreme Court. She has twice won prizes for poetry, in which field she has published *Forfeit and Other Poems* (1926), *Under the Maples* (1930), *Whiskers in Lilac Town* (1934), *New Moon* (1938), and *Tanager Feather* (1950).

FALLEN LEAVES

Borne on a whispered sigh,
The leaves come down,
The timid, trembling leaves,
Each lovely face turned upward to the sky.

Forgotten now the challenge of the morn
That sang across the fields of tasselled corn!

The age-enduring sun,
The regnant moon,
Those vigilants, the stars,
For you no more their cosmic benison.

But in the dark when little night-winds creep,
You stir and listen in your dreamless sleep.

SARA E. CARSLEY [1887-]

Sara Elizabeth (Keatley) Carsley, Mrs. William Early Carsley, daughter of William J. and Sarah Julia (Mahaffy) Keatley, was born at Lurgan, Ireland, and educated at Methodist College, Queen's College, and Royal University, Belfast. For a long time she taught Latin in Central High School, Calgary, Alberta, and now lives in Victoria, British Columbia. She is the winner of an award for a one-act play and of five awards for poetry. Her verse publications are *Alchemy and Other Poems* (1935); *Little Boats of Britain* (1941), a ballad of Dunkirk; *The Artisan* (1941).

THE LITTLE BOATS OF BRITAIN
[*A Ballad of Dunkirk*]

On many a lazy river, in many a sparkling bay,
The little boats of Britain were dancing, fresh and gay;
The little boats of Britain, by busy wharf and town,
A cheerful, battered company, were trading up and down.

A voice of terror through the land ran like a deadly frost:
"King Leopold has left the field, our men are trapped and lost.
No battle-ship can reach the shore, through shallows loud with foam;
Then who will go to Dunkirk town, to bring our armies home?"

From bustling wharf and lonely bay, from river-side and coast,
On eager feet came hurrying a strange and motley host,
Young lads and grandsires, rich and poor, they breathed one frantic prayer:
"O send us with our little boats to save our armies there!"

Never did such a motley host put out upon the tide:
The jaunty little pleasure-boats in gaudy, painted pride,
The grimy tugs and fishing-smacks, the tarry hulks of trade,
With paddle, oar, and tattered sail, went forth on their Crusade.

And on that horror-haunted coast, through roaring bomb and shell,
Our armies watched around them close the fiery fangs of hell,
Yet backward, backward to Dunkirk they grimly battled on,
And the brave hearts beat higher still, when hope itself was gone.

And there beneath the bursting skies, amid the mad uproar,
The little boats of Britain were waiting by the shore;
While from the heavens, dark with death, a flaming torrent fell,
The little boats undaunted lay beside the wharves of hell.

Day after day, night after night, they hurried to and fro;
The screaming planes were loud above, the snarling seas below.
And haggard men fought hard with sleep, and when their strength
was gone,
Still the brave spirit held them up, and drove them on and on.

And many a grimy little tramp, and skiff of painted pride
Went down in thunder to a grave beneath the bloody tide,
But from the horror-haunted coast, across the snarling foam,
The little boats of Britain brought our men in safety home.

Full many a noble vessel sails the shining seas of fame,
And bears, to ages yet to be, an unforgotten name:
The ships that won Trafalgar's fight, that broke the Armada's
pride,—
And the little boats of Britain shall go sailing by their side!

PORTRAIT OF A VERY OLD MAN

The thrusting glance grows dim,
Falters the fiery tread;
Once life was wine to him,
That now is bread.

Beauty was once the prize
He sought by field and stream;
But now the questing eyes
Are fixed in dream.

At every pool of fate
His eager thirst drank deep;
The heart insatiate
Is quenched with sleep.

All knowledge he desired,
All ecstasy, all mirth;
He, who to heaven aspired,
Needs only earth.

MARY JOSEPHINE BENSON [1887-]

Mary Josephine (Trotter) Benson, Mrs. (Dr.) H. W. Benson, daughter of Rev. John E. and Jane (Morphy) Trotter, was born at Port Hope, Ontario, and educated in the schools there. She has written advertising copy, edited a magazine supplement, conducted a magazine department, and contributed articles to newspapers. Since publishing her book of poems, *My Pocket Beryl* (1921), she has won a poetry prize for "The Bitter Lover."

SMOKING FLAX

The erubescent flax curls crisp and dry
To spend itself in blackness where its smoke
Has spread and spired, like mortals who invoke
God's patience on man's dullness—who would cloak
Dead offerings in fires from the sky.

But not in vain the aspiring lapsing flame,
Smoke-smothered for the damps amid its fire,
Ascends thus feebly, spark-starred, high and higher,
Charring the while it leaps its quivering pyre,
Feeling for Heaven with its sightless aim.

For He Who bosomed in the boulder's breast
The spark to kindle fireside or fane
Will not, capricious, quench in high disdain
Man's smoking sacrifice of heart and brain—
Clay of his mould and to his image prest!

ARTHUR L. PHELPS [1887-]

Arthur L. Phelps, son of Leonard and Elizabeth (Yonge) Phelps, was born at Columbus, Ontario, and educated at Victoria College, Toronto. He was Professor of English and Head of the Department at United College, University of Manitoba, from 1921 to 1945, Supervisor of the International Service of the CBC till 1947, and Professor of English at McGill University till his retirement in 1953. His prose includes two books of creative non-fiction and two of criticism. His verse is found in *Poems* (1921), and *A Bobcaygeon Chap-Book* (1922).

THE WALL

The wall should be low, as to say,
"Not a barrier this, but for beauty."
For beauty of stone upon stone,
Built through seasons,
Through sunshine and in grey windy weather,
Set up for the vine and the berry,
For the beauty of green upon grey,
For the beauty of orange and crimson,
Set up for the bird in November,
And the first storm-tossed sparrow in April:
A wall to mark generations,
If the weather
And change can be kindly;
A wall, as to say,
"Here is beauty, here is hope, here is peace."

JOHN COULTER [1888-]

John William Coulter, son of Francis and Annie (Clements) Coulter, was born in Belfast, Ireland, and educated there at the Model School and at the School of Art and School of Technology, with similar studies at Manchester University. While living in London, he was for three years associated with John Middleton Murry in the editing of the literary quarterly *The New Adelphi* and was active as a radio and magazine critic of drama and other forms of literature and of painting. He is the author of one novel, of highly successful drama, of criticism in dialogue form, of biography in dramatic form, of librettos for two operas, and of one book of poems, *The Blossoming Thorn* (1946).

MORNING BUS

The very old lady in the front seat mutters to herself.

Old woman, old and bent and worn,
A twisted thorn rough winds have shorn,
Your dream-crazed eyes see not our day
But seek some far, forgotten way
Sunk beyond time, and timeless grown,
Ghost among ghosts, you ride alone.

And blonde girl fluttering and unsure
Feigning now bold and now demure,
Soon shall you find that certain clue
Will draw love's diffident eyes to you,
And all the universe will sing
And all your ways be blossoming spring.

The bus stops. The blonde girl gets out. A bland youth gets in and takes her place.

And bland youth with your insolent grace,
A colt unbroken, on your face
Falls yet no shadow of dark wings,
For you another morning brings
The headlines in the morning paper,
Your favourite comic's latest caper.

A timid schoolchild gets in and looks around apprehensively as though we were all robbers.

And pale child, do your covert eyes
Conceal some timorous surmise
Of danger in a familiar place,
Some folly or frenzy in our face,
That "single face" of Spender's verse,
Fit figurehead for Charon's hearse?

I too have fears, hearing folk chatter
Of everything that makes no matter,
Or of what matters never a word
But what's most banal or absurd
Or lying, and grieve to think how they
Darken our intellectual day.

The man on the opposite seat tilts his bowler hat, clenches his fists and juts his jaw.

And shrewd man with the hard and sly
Surmise of business in your eye,
Planning your predatory day,
The impersonal slaying of your prey
By registered letter, has your writ
The seal of Beelzebub on it?

Perhaps by mutual consent
Of flocks and pastors what was meant
By that unrealistic Master,
In view of his personal disaster,
Were better read: What others do
To others may be done by you.

(And public charity may atone
For every private injury done.)

Several blank-faced persons of both sexes sit scanning the paper impassively.

Is it for you the race has been:
Prophet and hero, king and queen?
For you have saint and scholar wrought
High disciplines of spirit and thought?
For you our blossoming youth has died
With the spear of Calvary in its side?

(A generation crucified
That the Golden Calf be glorified.)

I catch sight of my own censorious face in the driver's mirror.

Ah, rhymster, is not railing so
Your folly? Must the river flow
As the reeds blow? Or may we plead
Mankind but history's slave, the steed
Drawn by the chariot while the bit
Drags in the mouth that bleeds on it?

And rhymster, turn your gaze within
And meditate on your own sin:
Is Pegasus a policeman's horse?
The purpose of a poet's curse
Such truncheoning of unruly times
In petulant moralising rhymes?

The bus stops, and waits.

And "Hi," I hear the driver shout,
"Ain't this the stop where you get out?"

HYMAN EDELSTEIN [1889-]

Hyman Edelstein was born in Dublin, Ireland, and educated there at the High School and University. He settled in Montreal in 1912, where he edited English-Jewish journals. He now lives in Ottawa. Besides contributing to Jewish periodicals in Canada and the United States, and writing a novel under the pen name of Don Synge, he has published in verse *Canadian Lyrics and Other Poems* (1915, 1921), *Spirit of Israel* (1942), *Last Mathematician* (1949), and *Spirit of Israel and Other Poems* (1950). In verse also is his comment on his son's letters in *All Quiet in Canada—and Why* (1944). He delightfully captures the spirit of Canada in his poems on nature and interprets the message of the Book to the world in the Spirit-of-Israel volumes, the latter of which was awarded a substantial monetary prize and was ranked by the Publication Committee of the Canadian Jewish Congress as worthy of the highest award of the Congress in 1950.

LAST MATHEMATICIAN

(*Any Poet*)

He mightn't have had wherewith to buy
A bottle of ink or a new nib for his pen:
It didn't matter to one who trod
The aery vasts of God . . .
With dauntless step stalking the blackest night
He'd plunge his pen into the ink of space
To flood with every drop and galvanize
Earth's dark alilt with aeons of light:
And, as Poet, always the Ultimate Mathematician,
Penetrate through to That Original Mind;
Read readily the parabola of the heavens
By no "maximum" or "minimum" confined;
Espy its axis of symmetry—the Milky Way:
And so interpret for us the graph of the universe
Plotted with stars. . . .

PALIMPSEST

God 'graves His cryptic script with inexorable pen
His ink the intermixt mortar-blood of cities and men
Deep across earth's breast
Dateless palimpsest
Of man His hieroglyph . . . He writes, and a little later thereon
With a little tilt of His hand
Sprinkles and spreads His blotter of sand
And lo! that mound?—that dust-embossed blur?
. . . Is it *Codex Ur?* Or *Codex Babylon?*

INDIAN NIGHT TABLEAU

(*Northern Lights*)

Lo! yon phantom army marching across Heaven,
Silhouettes of Braves crawling stealthily towards their foe,
Now retreating—flitting like shadows,
Now advancing through woods of subdued moonlight,
And with a bound—torches are flung—stockades afire—guns blazing,
Panorama of ghostly Indian battles
Re-fought in Canadian skies.

LAURA GOODMAN SALVERSON [1890-]

Laura Goodman Salverson, Mrs. George Salverson, a native of Winnipeg, supplemented private instruction by study in Western United States. She began to publish at the age of twelve and is the author of seven novels, one of which was awarded the Governor-General's Medal for fiction, an autobiography that received similar recognition as creative non-fiction, and a book of poems, *Wayside Gleams* (1935). She has written extensively for the radio, Little Theatre plays, and magazines, and has had several lyrics set to music. *Immortal Rock* won the Ryerson Fiction Award in 1954.

PREMONITION

"Why stand you, gentle mother,
So lonely and so still,
Your eyes, with fear and longing,
Upon yon distant hill?"
"I wait my son, O stranger;
Perchance, ere sun be set
His steps may lead him homeward
From blue Genesareth."
"But why these tears, O mother,
When earth is still so sweet
And snowy doves come drifting
To garland round your feet?"
"You cannot know, O stranger,
What dwells within my heart—
The bitter-sweet remembrance
That makes the tears to start."
"But why the troubled vigil?
Youth needs must find its star,
And follow it, thereafter,
Howso' it lead afar."
"My heart is heavy, stranger,
With some impending loss;
Last night I dreamed my lilies
Were twined about a cross!"

IF A MAID BE FAIR

When a maid is sweet and fair,
Wondrous fair,
Is there aught in earth or air,
Or of sea will bring her care?
When a maid is young and fair,
O, so fair?

Love's a tyrant, maiden fair,
So beware!
With his trailing grief and care,
Long will haunt thee ev'ry-where;
Pretty maid, be wise, beware,
O, take care!

BERNARD FREEMAN TROTTER [1890-1917]

Bernard Freeman Trotter, son of Dr. Thomas and Ellen (Freeman) Trotter, was born in Toronto and educated at Horton Academy, Wolfville, Nova Scotia, Woodstock College, Ontario, and McMaster University. He was killed in the First World War within five months after crossing from England to France. His poems, with an introduction by W. S. W. McLay, a former Professor of English and Dean at McMaster University, were published under the title *A Canadian Twilight: and Other Poems of War and Peace* (1917).

THE POPLARS

Oh, a lush green English meadow—it's there that I would lie—
A skylark singing overhead, scarce present to the eye,
And a row of wind-blown poplars against an English sky.

The elm is aspiration, and death is in the yew,
And beauty dwells in every tree from Lapland to Peru;
But there's magic in the poplars when the wind goes through.

When the wind goes through the poplars and blows them silver white,
The wonder of the universe is flashed before my sight:
I see immortal visions: I know a god's delight.

I catch the secret rhythm that steals along the earth,
That swells the bud, and splits the burr, and gives the oak its girth.
That mocks the blight and canker with its eternal birth.

It wakes in me the savour of old forgotten things,
Before "reality" had marred the child's imaginings:
I can believe in fairies—I see their shimmering wings.

I see the clear vision of that untainted prime,
Before the fool's bells jangled in and Elfland ceased to chime,
That sin and pain and sorrow are but a pantomime—

A dance of leaves in ether, of leaves threadbare and sere,
From whose decaying husks at last what glory shall appear
When the white winter angel leads in the happier year.

And so I sing the poplars; and when I come to die
I will not look for jasper walls, but cast about my eye
For a row of wind-blown poplars against an English sky.

EDNA JAQUES [1891-]

Edna Jaques was born at Collingwood, Ontario, the daughter of Capt. Charles A. and Ellen (Donohue) Jaques. She was educated in the public schools of Ontario and of Saskatchewan, the family having moved to the latter province when she was eleven years old. She has had a wide experience in journalism, and in extension lecturing. She has been called the Poet Laureate of the Home. She writes to the song her kettle sings. She has published a dozen volumes of poems, some of them running into several editions. Written in 1918 in answer to Colonel McCrae's immortal poem, "In Flanders Now" was read at the unveiling of the tomb of the Unknown Soldier in Washington, D.C. It was printed on a card with the Belgium National Anthem and sold in the United States by the Federation of Women's Clubs. A million dollars were raised and used for the restoration of the Louvain Library.

IN FLANDERS NOW

We have kept faith, ye Flanders' dead,
Sleep well beneath those poppies red
That mark your place.
The torch your dying hands did throw,
We've held it high before the foe,
And answered bitter blow for blow,
In Flanders' fields.

And where your heroes' blood was spilled,
The guns are now forever stilled
And silent grown.
There is no moaning of the slain,
There is no cry of tortured pain,
And blood will never flow again,
In Flanders' fields.

Forever holy in our sight
Shall be those crosses gleaming white,
That guard your sleep.
Rest you in peace, the task is done,
The fight you left us we have won,
And Peace on Earth has just begun,
In Flanders now.

FRANCES BEATRICE TAYLOR [1891-]

Frances Beatrice Taylor, daughter of Robert Leslie and Mary Chipman (Smith) Taylor, was born at Brussels, Ontario, and educated by her father. In 1919 she became editor of the "Women's Department" of the London *Free Press.* She has written musical, dramatic, and literary criticism, general articles, and short stories, has had two plays produced, and has published one book of prose and one volume of verse, *White Winds of Dawn* (1924).

THE HUSBANDMAN

God of the vineyard's royal store,
Whose fingers press the purple wine,
Forget, forget not, I implore,
This field of mine.

God of the rolling meadow-land,
Lord of the year's unwritten page,
Lies in the hollow of Thy hand
My heritage.

God of the harvest's golden grain,
God of the heights, I pray Thee, speed
The former and the latter rain,
On this, my seed.

A WEDGWOOD BOWL

Hid in a maze of quaintly-fashioned things,
  Flagons and urns of ancient pottery;
Great peacocks spreading wide, barbaric wings,
  Beryl, and jade, and lapis lazuli,
Smooth chests of cedar and of sandalwood,
  Tapestries wrought in Tyre and Babylon,
And here, a Pilgrim's staff, a carven Rood,—
  A royal Chalice whence the wine is gone.

There, then, I found it; as a garden grows
  Among her roses rue and mignonette,
But wearing subtler sweetness than the rose,
  So, in the splendid chaos surely set,—
Cool as the moon against an opal-stone,
  Hollowed like silk by some diviner's stroke;
And by a master-finger lightly strown,
  A circling wreath of little, dancing folk.

AGNES FOLEY MACDONALD

Agnes Mary (Foley) Macdonald, Mrs. Angus L. Macdonald, daughter of John Foley, was born in Halifax and educated there, mostly at Mount Saint Vincent College. Ever since her student days with Rev. Sister Maura as her English teacher she has been writing lyrics of fine finish. Twenty-two of these have been garnered in *Once and Again* (1950). "Eternal" won first place in the competition for the Halifax Bicentenary edition of the *Nova Scotia Book of Verse.*

ETERNAL

She said: The world is empty that we loved,
Sunset and moonrise are no more the same
As when we stood together, breathing deep
The loveliness of earth. All unprepared
For your too-swift departure, I am now
More desolate than when I stood alone
Before your coming. With you went the rose,
The shining waters and the friendly winds.

He said: I have not gone; I still may stand
Beside you when the night is warm with stars.
My voice will call you in the morning wind
That blows in from the sea. And you will know
My step upon the grass some August eve.
For, knowing love, you own all lovely things;
And when you touch your forehead to the rose,
You'll feel my hand in blessing on your brow.

NORMA E. SMITH [-1948]

Norma Ethel Smith, daughter of Isaiah and Grace Edden (Saunders) Smith, was born in Halifax, Nova Scotia, and educated in the city schools. During the last twenty-five years of her life she was Secretary of the Nova Scotia College of Art. She contributed feature articles, fiction, and verse to many newspapers and magazines in Canada, the United States, and England. The quality of her poetry is well exemplified in *The Hill and Far-Away* (n.d.).

EVANGELINE

You did not leave this fruited land,
The apple and the painted pear,
The meadows crossed by henna paths,
The glory of the rounded year.

This eve the whirr of irised wings
Blends with the stockdoves' drowsy croon,
Across the dykes a vesper bell
Rings in the broad benignant moon.

As silently as steals a dream
Down purple aisles of healing sleep,
You steal in kirtle blue and white,
And in your eyes a dream lies deep.

The grass blades hold their heads erect,
So light your foot beside the gate,
While stars like clover leaves astir
Warn you that Gabriel may be late.

You never left these wedded fields,
The marshes' golden lace between,
I've caught a glimpse of your small hand
On one red rose, Evangeline!

Just now I thought I heard you laugh,
As leaves laugh silverly in rain;
No matter where death holds you fast,
Tonight you walk these fields again.

JOHN A. B. McLEISH [1892-]

John A. B. McLeish was born in Calgary and educated in Winnipeg and in Montreal, where he graduated with honours from McGill University. He has had journalistic experience on the Montreal *Gazette*, and is now doing outstanding educational work in the Province of Quebec. He has contributed articles, stories, and verse to periodicals and has published two books of poems, *Ode in a Winter Evening and Other Poems* (1938) and *Not Without Beauty* (1948).

NOT WITHOUT BEAUTY

Who will say a word for a country town of a sultry summer night?
The full-cheeked moon, fat as a Chinese lantern and as bright,
Squats placidly above the old bank in the square,
And suffuses a sort of ripe complacency into the summer evening air.
In the sleepy-browed town that it looks down at there is no great
to-do:
A few cars will go wheezing along in the drowsy-eyed street,
After a first premonitory cough or two;
And down at the corner the young folks will meet
And fill the warm night with high chatter there, standing around,
In the blaze of a corner café's lighted window, old familiar ground
(O, chatter nonsensically on, for youth's hours are fleet!)

And some will get weary of talking and go off then in pairs as they
please,
Off and down the long street past the church and the school with
few people to greet,
Where the placid ubiquitous moon blows his cheeks through the lace
of the trees;
And the barber-shop's half-dozen cronies will talk the night out,
Supreme Court men in all but the name as they sweatingly sit in
their chairs,
Judgment-makers . . . no topic too small or too great to be held
forth about,
Nothing under the sun or the curious moon that pauses and stares.
Then the shrill-shrilling shrill-shrilling mail train breaks the soft of
the night with its cry,
And if you will stand on this corner here by the hotel you can see all
the townfolks go by
To the post-office moot, a communal exchange-place any day of the
year . . .
(Best of all on this earth-smelling night made for troubadour's
songs)
Hear the back-chat and kidding of youths, see the horse-play of
boys,
Hear the settled and quick steps, the low voices and all the familiar
noise,
Hear the laughter and serious comments, the howdos and solongs,
Hear the multitudinous footsteps retreat, and a trickle of sound in
the place of the surge in, the full-hearted surge in the street.
And if you will stand there at midnight and watch for a time,
You will see the hotel close its eyes and the straggling town-talkers
depart,
Hear the clock in the square clear its throat, give its chime,
And wheeze back again to the reticent hush of the town's slumbering
heart.
Then (O, then!) the night wind is alone with its play,
Like a huge unseen kitten it catches a scrap of stray paper and tosses
and turns it and scrapes it along the dry street and carries it
out and away.
Then (O, then!) both the sound and the fleet-footed player are gone,
And the interested indolent moon is alone, is alone, with the night
and its own,
And the street slumbers on.

KENNETH LESLIE [1892-]

Kenneth Leslie, son of Robert J. and Rebecca (Starrat) Leslie, was born at Pictou, Nova Scotia, and educated at Dalhousie, Nebraska, and Harvard universities. He has edited the *Protestant* for a number of years, in New York and elsewhere. His poetry is found in *Windward Rock* (1934), *Such a Din!* (1935), *Lowlands Low* (1936), and *By Stubborn Stars* (1938), for the last of which he won the Governor-General's Medal.

HALIBUT COVE HARVEST

The kettle sang the boy to a half-sleep;
and the stir, stir of the kettle's lid
drummed a new age
into the boy's day-dream.
His mind strove with the mind of steam
and conquered it
and pressed it down and shaped it
to the panting giant
whose breath lies heavy on the world.

This is a song of harvest;
the weather thickens with a harsh wind
on this salt-seared coast;
offshore a trawler, smoke-smearing the horizon,
reaps the sea.

Here on the beach
in the cove of the handliner
rain flattens the ungathered dulse
and no cheek reddens to the rain.
From the knock-kneed landing
a faltering path is lost among the rocks
to a door that is closed with a nail.
Seams widen and the paint falls off in curling flakes
from the brave, the bold so little time ago,
the dory high and dry,
anchored in hungry grass.

This is the song of harvest:
the belching trawler raping the sea,
the cobweb ghosts against the window
watching the wilderness uproot the doorsill with a weed.

GUY MASON [1893-]

Guy Mason, son of James William and Barbara Ann Frances (Cashman) Mason, was born and went to school at Tangier, Nova Scotia. From 1910 till 1914 he engaged in teaching, first in the public schools and then at the School for the Blind, Halifax. He entered Dalhousie University in 1914, to which he returned after serving from 1916 till 1919 in the First World War and after. He spent 1920 to 1929 in the West, mainly in teaching, with time out to attend Normal College in Regina and to graduate in Arts from the University of Manitoba. He returned to Nova Scotia in 1929, taught for two years in Halifax, and then entered upon his present work as teacher of English at the Provincial Normal College, Truro. His books of poetry are *The Cry of Insurgent Youth* (1927) and *Spendthrifts* (1928).

ADVENTURE

A cloying sea envelopes man at birth,
  And he may dwell within its weltering flow,
And feel not, all his days, the blighting dearth
  Of pure life-strengthening air. But some below

The surface may not freely breathe, and raise
  Their heads above to fill the lack that mars
Existence. Deeply breathing, in amaze
  They see a far horizon, rimmed with stars.

From yearning pangs that torture as they please,
  No opiate now the adventurous soul can save;
And few of godlike strength, may soon with ease
  Arise, breast-high, to meet the rushing wave;

Or, bold in faith, emerge, and walk, as He
Who lightly trod the Galilean sea.

INDEPENDENCE

Let us return from Ilium, and no more
  Together wander through the Grecian seas;
Let us for ever close the vine-clad door
  On those first lovers beneath Eden's trees;

Let Italy's seer a lonely vigil keep,
  Watching for Beatrice from the farther shore;
While proud Verona's love-slain children sleep
  With other lovers who have loved of yore;

Pile high the well-worn volumes; let the dust
  Be jealous guardian. We shall need no lore
But what Love teaches, and henceforth may trust
  In Love alone. On his wings let us soar,

Till highest heaven's highest mount we greet,
  And find a hundred Edens at our feet.

ARTHUR S. BOURINOT [1893-]

Arthur Stanley Bourinot, of Ottawa, "Poet Laureate of the Laurentians," son of Sir John George and Isabelle (Cameron) Bourinot, was born in Ottawa and educated there at the public schools and Collegiate Institute, at the University of Toronto, and at Osgoode Hall. After serving in the First World War, he practised law, first with a company and then by himself, from 1927 to 1929, was later counsel for a life insurance company and is now retired. He has done some editorial and critical work, has been editor of *Canadian Poetry Magazine* since 1948, was appointed editor of *Canadian Author and Bookman* in 1953, has several times acted as judge for the Governor-General's annual literary awards, has won two poetry prizes, and was made a Fellow of the Royal Society of Literature in 1950. He has published more than twenty books and brochures of poetry, and a prose work, *Five Canadian Poets* (1954). *Selected Poems* (1935) with an introduction by Sir Andrew Macphail was the seventh. The eleventh, *Under the Sun and Other Poems* (1939), won the Governor-General's Medal. *Collected Poems* (1947) has been followed by *Treasures of the Snow* (1950), and *This Green Earth* (1953). His work is found in many anthologies and text books, and some of his lyrics have been set to music. (Cf. *Educational Record*, October, 1947; *Dalhousie Review*, 1949; *Ottawa Journal*, August 15, 1953.)

NICOLAS GATINEAU

Delve deep amongst the musty muniments
The archives of the Courts at Trois Rivières
The old Notarial files of Montreal
Sneeze with the long lying dust and tire your eyes
With scanning of old script, perchance you'll find
The name of Nicolas Gatineau, Sieur de Plessis,
Greffier of the Court, tabellion,
Once with the Hundred Associates, trader of furs,
The penner of dry documents, a scrivener
Of legal terms; and were that all, you'd say
"Why tempt the dusty sneeze, the tired eyes
To find perhaps a deed to one La Salle?"
But is that all? The record shows scant else
And yet the fact remains, the fact remains
A great and lovely river bears his name
And sings it to the sun and to the stars.

Tiring of musty tomes he roamed the woods,
Coursed with the *Coureur de Bois* the lakes and streams
To hoard himself small gold, a patrimony,
That he might turn again to his Belle France
And live his life in safe and quiet content.
Fate intervened and wrote a different tale
Marked "*finis*" to the life of Gatineau;
But it's not told in musty tome or deed
What mishap, what chance accident upset
His long-laid plans, but legend says
The great and lovely river took his life,
Not satisfied nor sated took his name
And bears it to this day, a good return,
Fair interest on the investment of a life,
More profit than he ever hoped to gain—
The increment of immortality.

TOM THOMSON

It was a grey day
with a drizzle of rain,
something of fey
in the air
as though the lake,
the islands,
the sky
were watching,
waiting,
waiting for what?
A sense of doom
in the air
with silence everywhere
as though a god
had spoken,
and then a loon laughed
and the spell was broken,
the spell was broken.

And Tom Thomson laughed
and his friends laughed
as he launched his canoe
from the dock
and paddled away
with his lures and his lines
to befool the old trout

they had lost so often
in the bay in the river
below Joe Lake Dam;
and he turned
with a wave of his hand
and was gone.
And a loon laughed
and the old trout
waited in the bay
and the sky and lake watched
but he never came
was never seen again
till his body floated
on the surface
eight days later.

What happened?
No one knows,
no one will ever know;
no one knows
except perhaps the old trout
below Joe Lake Dam
and the lake
and the islands
the loon and the sky
that watched and waited;
no one knows.

And in far off Shoreham,
A. Y. Jackson, painting again,
after a "blighty" in France
heard of the upturned canoe
on the lake
and his dreams of camping
and fishing and painting
once more with his friend
came to an end,
as all dreams come
to an end,
as all dreams come
to an end.

Legend has it in Algonquin
Tom Thomson
watches and looks
from the headland
above the bay
on Canoe Lake,
his palette and brushes
and panels in hand
painting the symphony
of the seasons
of his beloved land
he never finished;
the unfolding year,
the folding leaf,
the gathered sheaf,
the winter snow,
the bright bateaux,
painting, painting;
and the great trout
waits in the river
below Joe Lake Dam
and the loon laughs
and sky and lake watch
and only his voice is still
on land and lake
but his spirit is awake
throughout the land he loved
kindling youth to slake
their thirst in beauty.
His spirit is awake,
a torch and a token,
as though a god had spoken;
his spirit is awake,
his spirit is awake.

JOHNNY APPLESEED

"Orchards," said Johnny Appleseed,
"Let there be orchards, yes, indeed,
Orchards, orchards, everywhere,
I've got these orchards in my hair,
Orchards to bloom, orchards to bear,
And apple trees
To scent the breeze
In blossom time."

And so he tramped from east to west
Planting seeds with zeal and zest,
He sowed them here, he sowed them there,
He planted apples everywhere.
He had no place to lay his head,
He could not earn his daily bread,
The sky the only roof he had
And yet his simple heart was glad
For he was doing what he knew
Life had taught him best to do;
And he could lay him down at night,
The stars his only candle-light,
And watch them travel who knows where
Or were they growing in the air,
The same as seeds that he had scattered,
Then fall asleep, for nothing mattered.
His clothes were threadbare, full of holes,
His shoes were sadly lacking soles,
Upon his head an old tin pan
And people said, "There goes a man
Who talks with animals and birds,
He seems to know their very words."
And he could tell about the weather,
His face was tanned as saddle leather,
And little children loved his stories
Of apple trees and morning glories
Of centipedes and blowing whales,
Of Indians he'd tell tall tales,
And they would gather at his knee
And wonder what the yarn would be.
When he came by no dogs did bark,
Something he had, a friendly spark
That miracles worked, and when he laughed
Dogs wagged their tails and people chaffed.

The apple seeds that he would sow
They couldn't help but prosper, grow
And apple trees sprang far and near
To show that Johnny had been here.
"His witness trees," he said with pride,
"You'll find them 'cross the country side."

And settlers clearing near a glade
At noon would lie beneath the shade
Of apple trees that he had planted,
And take it more or less for granted,
Enjoy a friendly, home like feeling
Thinking of days back east when stealing
Apples was but boyish fun
And rise refreshed for work begun.
And so it went from year to year
Till Appleseed was in the seer
And dawned the day that he must die
He laid him down beneath the sky
Within an orchard of his trees
In blossom time, on every breeze
The fragrance of the bloom was blown,
The very bloom that he had sown,
His broken helmet on the grass,
The warrior is home at last.
Some apple seeds lay at his side,
He scattered them before he died.
They did not move him from the spot,
For him no cemetery plot,
He loved the fellowship of trees,
The gnarled roots touched gnarled knees,
A winding sheet of barrel staves
That had held apples all their days.
And so he chose his place of rest,
An orchard, for he loved it best.

"Orchards," said Johnny Appleseed,
"Let there be orchards, yes, indeed,
Orchards, orchards, everywhere,
I've got these orchards in my hair,
Orchards to bloom, orchards to bear,
And apple trees
To scent the breeze
In blossom time."

WINTER SKETCH

Winter owl skirts hemlock tree,
Unfurls his shadow on the snow,
A rabbit scurries frantically,
Pine grosbeaks busily come and go,

A partridge breaks his buried bed
And hurtles through the solitude
And then the silence of the dead
Is held within the listening wood.

WHAT FAR KINGDOM

The soil is quick with dust of men
Who will not walk the earth again.

Each handful that is downward cast
Is particled of lives long past.

One cannot grasp the shifting sands
But centuries sift through the hand.

And children dig upon the shore
The dust of some progenitor.

The man who spades a virgin soil
Disturbs cohesion with his toil.

The plough's bright blade bites straight and sure,
Commingles dust of rich and poor.

In what far kingdom do they dwell
The dead who loved the earth so well

Whose dust is blown on every breeze
To dim the chlorophyll of trees?

To what far kingdom have they gone
The men whose dust we walk upon?

SONNETS TO MY MOTHER

Some say the dead are lonely where they lie
Deep in the earth far from the wind and rain;
Over their heads the friendly feet go by,
They do not know that they have come again.
And lost to them life's laughter and the pain
Which strikes at those they left upon the earth
And past for them life's anguish, falls no dearth,
The sorrows and the sadness all are slain.
How can the dead be lonely when they rest
Amongst the innumerable hosts of earth?
The grave's unutterable silence holds them lest
They miss their friends above and friendship's mirth;
How can the dead be lonely when they sleep
Lost in a dream beyond a boundless deep?

How like a mighty mother doth the earth
Receive into her arms her children who
After long years of labour and of mirth
Of weariness with having much to do,
Return once more to her from whom they drew
The breath of life, who gave them suck at birth,
Who folds them in her breast's gigantic girth
And seals their eyes with darkness and the dew.
No favourites hath the earth; the poor and spent,
The little child who died upon the breast,
And they who strode the world magnificent
High blazoned with the pride of princely crest
Must lay them down together when they rest
And Love alone will stand omnipotent.

DARK FLOWS THE RIVER

Dark flows the river,
A witches' brew,
Hills are hot metal
Cooling to blue.

Black flows the river,
Spattered with light,
While silence watches
Coming of night.

The stars are embers,
Sparks from the blows
Struck on the anvil
Time only knows.

On flows the river
Burdened with years,
Chanting of beauty
Night only hears.

Swift flows the river
Singing its song,
Chanting to mortals,
"Life is not long

Youth with its ardour,
Age and despair
Vanish as visions,
Mist in the air."

Dark flows the river,
Down to the sea;
What of man's journey,
Where travels he?

ONLY SILENCE

Only silence
Haunts these walls,
On the stairway
No footfall,
And the rafters
Lost all laughter
Long, long ago.

But at midnight
Come the dead,
Softly, softly,
Must they tread
For no sound
Of their footfall
Reaches to
The listening wall;
Quieter than
The step of death
Is the breathing
Of their breath,
Quieter than
The panther's walk
Is the silence
Of their talk.
Only silence
Knows no fear
When the thronging
Ghosts are near
And the only
One discerning
Knows their going
And returning.
Only silence
May presage
Where they go
On pilgrimage.

Only silence
Haunts these walls,
On the stairway
No footfall,
And the rafters
Lost all laughter
Long, long ago.

WILLIAM EDWIN COLLIN [1893-]

William Edwin Collin was born in Durham, England, and educated there, at the University of Toulouse, in Spain, and at the University of Western Ontario, London, Ontario, where he has been in the Department of Romance Languages since 1923. Most of his writing has been in the field of criticism, but he has published *Monserrat and Other Poems* (1930).

MONSERRAT

White columns of towering masonry,
Vast skittles set above the gorge,
In tempests turned, washed in a sea
Of azure, baked in Summer's forge;
Though worn, yet wearing out all time.
Thou guardian of the hills, the wells,
The sleeping-river gnats, the line
Of goats on terraced-valley beds,
Eerie of souls that scorn the plain,
Who have obeyed and left their flocks
And all the bellowing herds of men
In quest of peace within thy rocks!

Thy temple shall be warm with lights
And fervent song; for saints aspire.
And in the tempest, in the heights
God is—and in the morning fire.

SANCHO

Sleepy vines on the chalk-white houses
And pergolas snore with fat bees.
In the sand the sallow hamlet drowses
Near a clump of eucalyptus trees.

Dulcinea sallies forth to the fountain.
Her round slippery heels spring out
When she stretches across the basin
Her pitcher to the water-spout.

Then, placing her jar on the margin,
She teazes her hair with her fingers,
Half aware of Sancho watching
In the gum trees how she lingers.

The tassel of his woolen shanter,
Knitted crosswise, like a rainbow,
Hangs limp on his burning shoulder.
Feet astride, bare arms akimbo,

Lured by the lines of her beauty,
In fringes and taffeta wound,
Naked curves coming out of the shadows,
He cautiously measures the ground.

Bouncing quietly over the warm sand,
Like Falstaff, thirsty and lissom,
He kisses the buds in her black eyes,
Peeps furtively into her bosom.

While his venerable master fidgets
With a battered casque on his knees,
Bemoaning distresses of maidens
In the clump of eucalyptus trees.

ELSIE LAURENCE [1893-]

Mrs. Frances Elsie (Fry) Laurence, of Edson, Alberta, who has also used the pen name "Christine Field," is the author of *XII Poems* (1929), some of which won prizes in the London *Bookman*, of *The Band Plays a March* (1936), and of *Rearguard and Other Poems* (1944).

ALONE

Thin, erect and silent,
The black robed lady
Entered the house
Of the empty rooms,
Knowing that as soon
As the friendly street
Was left behind,
Memories would close in
Upon her, and do their utmost
To crush her spirit.

What can one do?
One cannot walk the streets
For ever: one must go home;
Even though the word,
With the sharp sword of mockery
Stab one's heart.

W. W. E. ROSS [1894-]

W. W. Eustace Ross, born in Peterborough, Ontario, educated at the University of Toronto, and now geophysicist with the Agincourt Magnetic Observatory near Toronto, has published two booklets of poems, *Laconics* (1930), and *Sonnets* (1932).

THE SUMMONS

"Waken from your sleep
Though your sleep be deeper
Than the ocean's depth
Waken, heavy sleeper,
Waken from your sleep.

"Rise and greet the morning
Coming from the East
No time this for mourning
Summoned to a feast
Rise and greet the morning.

"Though your sleep be deep—
Dreams will not awaken—
One with touch as weak
As a thin reed shaken
Wakes you from your sleep.

"Waken from your sleep
Waken, heavy sleeper,
Though your dream be lost
In the sink of Lethe
Waken from your sleep.

"So do not despair
Of the upper air
And the visionary
Throng in regions airy—
Waken from your sleep.

"All is not yet lost
All can not be lost
Though your sleep be deep
In wave of memories tossed
Waken from your sleep.

"Till the break of day
Find you far away—
Dreams cannot withhold—
Waken from your sleep
Though your sleep be deep.

"Waken from your sleep.
No pity on the weeper!
Though your sleep be deeper
Than the depth of Night
Waken from your sleep!"

THE SAWS WERE SHRIEKING

The saws were shrieking
and cutting into
the clean white wood
of the spruce logs
or the tinted hemlock
that smells as sweet—
or stronger pine,
the white and the red.

A whirling saw
received the logs;
the sound was ominous
and shrill,
rising above
the duller roaring
of the mill's
machinery.

From the revolving
of the saw
came slices of clear wood,
newly sawn,
white pine and red,
or spruce and hemlock,
the sweet spruce,
and the sweet hemlock.

WATSON KIRKCONNELL [1895-]

Watson Kirkconnell, son of Thomas Allison and Bertha Gertrude (Watson) Kirkconnell, was born at Port Hope, Ontario, and educated at Lindsay Collegiate Institute, Queen's University, Toronto Conservatory of Music, and Lincoln College, Oxford. He served during the First World War. Besides other distinctions at home and abroad, he has been awarded three medals, including the Lorne Pierce Medal of the Royal Society of Canada (1942), and four honorary degrees. He taught English at Wesley (later United) College, Winnipeg, from 1922 to 1930, Classics from 1930 to 1940, and English at McMaster from 1940 to 1948, when he became President of Acadia University. He has written a biography, a large amount of literary criticism, and several books on affairs, and has translated poetry extensively from other languages in addition to writing a considerable amount of his own: *The Tide of Life and Other Poems* (1930); *The Eternal Quest* (1934); *To Horace* (1934); *The Bridgebuilders* (1938); *Lyra Sacra* (1939); *A Western Idyll* (1940); *The Flying Bull and Other Tales* (1940); *The Crow and the Nighthawk* (1943); and *Christ and Herod and Other Poems* (1947).

From THE TIDE OF LIFE

Ah, Flood of Life on which I am a wave,
A feeble wave that soon must sink to rest,
Take now the fleeting tribute of my verse,
And as my drops disperse
Leaving no remnant of my foaming crest,
Let thy strong impulse in me be exprest
In vaster billows that go surging on.
For thou hast flowed here from an ageless deep
And shalt go forward to a deep unguessed,
And though my leaping surf shall soon be gone
And the cold currents shall no longer keep
My brief vibration in their endless quest,
Yet would I feel that somewhere down that sweep
Of mighty tides I still am manifest.

Where some dim veil of streaming star-dust lay
Across the vastness of Night's nakedness,
From the slow quickening of Time's caress
There woke beneath the dull maternal play
Of cold-pulsed ebbing eons in the dark
The throbbing of a spark
Of life engendered, of a power to stay
The elemental drift of empty force
And shape the chaos to a cosmic course.

Thus in the vast abyss of pregnant murk
An immanence at work
Wrought star and planet and the ambient earth
Jagged with cataclysmic mountain whence
Flowed down the dust of crescent continents.
Here was the protean life-force brought to birth;
Here that great pulse, begotten in the void
And never since destroyed,
Appeared parturient in the viscid spume
And clotted ooze of ancient mere and fen.
Lo, I was present then!—
For this hot blood that I give body-room,
This eager will incarnate in my brain,
Own their unbroken birthright back through all
The myriad issue of that ancient strain
Spanning the age-flux of the interval;
Thus with the waxing of longeval time
Grew worms of wandering slime,
Rough massy molluscs, fish with pulsant fin,
And those vast lizards of rock-furrowed skin
That churned hot tropic leagues of slushy mire
In wallowing battles for supremacy;
Up soared the race of birds with hearts of fire;
And subtle above all in land and sea,
Far mightier in brain and craftiness,
Came those milk-breasted beasts that bear their young;
Till, from these creatures sprung,
Shaped by the primal procreative stress
Through all the long ascent that lay behind,
Arose a regent fit for sentient rule,
Emergent man, who vaguely held enshrined
Within his simian shagginess of skull
The crowning wonder of the conscious mind. . . .

Yes, what if eons gulp the Life-flood down,
And with its high renown
The race of man shall perish utterly,
Yielding to dying skies his failing breath,
While cold around his every hope shall be
The slimy polyp tentacles of death?
Shall we recoil in anguish? Nay, not so!
Life's high adventure is its own reward. . . .

THE CROW AND THE NIGHTHAWK

I

For any golfer of resource,
The most exhilarating course
I know of has been bedded down
Beside an old Ontario town.
Along the links, the player sees
A motley grove of ancient trees,
While near them, on ungodly ground,
An old distillery is found.
Back in the days when first I knew
The joys of stance and follow-through,
That course was crowded with delight
From summer dawn to summer night.
Players were many, but still more
Were all the wild birds, score on score,
Who thronged the grove and thronged the green
And every fairway in between.
Wherever sprinklers wet the ground,
The hungry robins marched around
And, with their black beaks making passes,
Dragged juicy worms from dewy grasses.
Yet some there were who said the birds
Were given to unkindly words,
For meadowlarks were far from nice
In jeering at each hook and slice,
And every golfer in the rough
Heard cheeky blackbirds give him guff.
Now two outstanding birds there were
To give the place strong character.
One was a crow, as tough and black
As any fierce demoniac
That ever haunted cave or tomb
With accents hoarse and face of doom.
The startled golfers, every one,
Knew him as "Adolf," for his fun
Seemed based on murdering the neighbours
Amid their friendly sports and labours.
He seemed to think the raven race
Entitled, for its living space,
To all the world, and thought it good
To slay the feathered brotherhood.

And so his kids, the little yeggs,
Were fed on larks' and bluebirds' eggs;
And young song-sparrows, all alive,
He took to make his youngsters thrive.
The master-race of black-plumed devils
Thus loved to murder in their revels.
The other bird of whom I spoke
Was "Hank," the nighthawk, one whose joke
It was with swooping wings to zoom
Above us in the gathering gloom,
Intent to see our golf-balls roll
Through twilight to the eighteenth hole.
He was a harmless sort of critter
In handsome uniform of feathers,
Playful in pleasant times and bitter,
And cheerful in all sorts of weathers.
Yet he had thoughts too deep for words,
A loyalty beyond all proof—
It was a nest of baby birds
Upon the old distillery roof.

II

Now, in that summer I recall,
We saw a sort of madness fall
Upon all birds of every sort
In that green-carpeted resort.
The golfers were all heavy smokers
Of every brand of cigarette.
One day the sparrows—always jokers—
Picked up some butts, left burning yet.
The smoke inhaled was good, they found,
And so they passed the word around
Till every bird on every green
Was crazy over nicotine.
A butt was scarcely tossed away
Before some feathered scavenger
Had seized the treasure where it lay
And with his little wings a-whir
Flew with it to some branch, to sit
And puff the fag out, bit by bit.
Adolf, of course, performed his share
In this new prank, so tough and rare,
Yet he had scorn for little pets
Who only took to cigarettes.

For he would choose, as regulars,
The solid butts of black cigars.
Hank liked the smaller, milder smoke,
But practised, as a kind of joke,
Dive-bombing with his fag, and roaming
With trailing sparks across the gloaming.

III

Adolf grew tougher every day,
And once, when Hank was far away,
He sought the nighthawk's nest, to kill
The little nestlings, thus to fill
Himself and all his greedy brood
With raw, dismembered flesh for food.
The raid succeeded. Hank came back
Too late to stop the dark attack.
And when, with Mrs. Hank, he went
To call on Adolf at his nest
In a tall pine-tree, there to vent
The anger of a heart distressed,
They found the crow, with happy croak,
Having an after-dinner smoke.
Making contemptuous grimaces,
He blew cigar-smoke in their faces.

IV

It was the first day of July
That saw this dirty deed of blood.
Homeward they turned, with many a sigh,
When Hank was startled by the thud
And loud report of fire-crackers
From crowds of gay, young bivouackers
Who sought with noise to celebrate
The happy birthday of their state.
His bright eyes flashed. He did not loiter,
But cruised about to reconnoitre;
Then hurtled down without a pause
And picked up in his bony claws
A lighted cracker, from whose fuse
The sparks were spitting to amuse
Small boys at play. Up soared the bird
One, two, three hundred feet, and heard
The boys and golfers roar surprise
At the strange sight before their eyes.

His ceiling reached, he turned to dive,
With sputtering bomb-load all alive:
Straight at the crow's nest and its crew,
Down, ever faster down, he flew,
And with a bang would fairly scare ye
Hit squarely on the target area,
While he, with skill of wing and eye,
Veered off in safety to the sky.
The bursting cracker filled the air
With croaks and corpses and despair.
Down from the pine we saw them go—
Scorched chunks of old and baby crow,
A rain of feathers, beaks and legs,
And wreckage of once rifled eggs.
Adolf, too tough to blow apart,
Fell shrieking down, and with a start,
We saw the battered crow expire
Four minutes later, spitting fire.
Some folk who marked him as he fell
Proclaimed this as a sign of hell;
The truth is that the blitz's jar
Had made him gulp his lit cigar,
And then in anguish writhe and hop
With poisoned flames inside his crop,
Ending a life of utter sin
With fierce heart-burnings deep within.
Then peace returned to bless the earth,
A peace unknown since Adolf's birth;
And every nest in bush and tree
Was blest with sweet serenity.
Appalled by Adolf's end obscene,
The birds abjured all nicotine.
(No nestlings, since that awful death,
Complain about their parents' breath.)
Since then, through all the feathered nation,
The proudest theme of conversation
Is the stout nighthawk's swift reproof;
While on the old distillery roof
Successive broods of little Hanks
Rise up to give their father thanks.

MARY ELIZABETH COLMAN [1895-]

Mary Elizabeth Colman, who also used the pen names "Marie Zibeth Colman" and "Mary Zibeth Colman," daughter of C. A. and Jenny (Jorand) Colman, was born in Victoria, British Columbia, and was educated by private tuition, at College de Rolle, at Central Collegiate, Winnipeg, at Victoria Normal School, and at the University of British Columbia. She has been a school librarian in Vancouver and has written magazine articles and verse and two poetry chap-books, *The Immigrants* (1928) and *For This Freedom Too and Other Poems* (1942).

WE MEN ARE OF TWO WORLDS

We men are of two worlds.
In craft frail as chambered nautilus
we come, solitary, minute,
propelled by waves that had their genesis
on shores so far beyond our knowing
that they have never dwelt in memory.
And when we reach these coasts—
inhospitable sands we never asked to see,
strewn with many a bleaching bone
and horrid skull,
where greedy fingers of the foam
advance, retreat, advance,
with promise ever unfulfilled—
forgetful whence we came
we plunge into the jungle.

. . .

A high standard of living:
a second car, you owe it to yourself,
a permanent for little Lou,
the best sorority for sister Sue,
a racoon coat for brother,
mink and silver fox for mother,
the country club for dad, and golf . . .

The Japanese invade Manchuria,
but Manchuria's far away.

Better wages, shorter hours;
the world owes us a living
and a good one too!

Swing the music hot and sweet
to the rhythm of dancing feet,
days are born to give us pleasure
nights are added for good measure . . .

The Abyssinian sky is dark
with wingèd death.

Smiles are cheap and win new friends,
use flattery to influence the great;
learn to play the piano—ten easy lessons,
or be an artist in six pleasant sessions;
twenty shades of polish for your finger tips
choose a tone to match the colour of your lips . . .

Rehearsal for world war is called in Spain,
insatiate the Nazi vampire feasts on blood.

What I can make is mine,
my cunning and my cleverness
have earned my right
to better things.
  Lebensraum!
What I can take is mine!
My arm is strong; by right of might
make way, all lesser men, for herrenvolk!

. . .

Deep in the jungle
we have forgotten whence we came
until some day at dawn perhaps,
at some street end where factories
lift blackened hands to heaven,
or in some field where autumn sun
tearing through the curtain of the rain
touches with gold and purple tenderness
some leaf forsaken tree,
there comes a moment of awareness,
of sudden recollection.
We stand upon a hill, facing the sea
and hear its cadence with delight.
Then with puzzled headshake
all is gone. There is just a factory
with black chimney stacks,
a naked tree, cold autumn rain.

Yet, seek we the hill top and we shall find,
ears open to its call shall hear again
the ocean's never silent call;
and hearing turn towards the sound,
and seeing march towards the sea
where salty winds, clean and free,
greet us from that far country whence we came.

We men are of two worlds—
how great the cost of our forgetting!
Turn, turn, have done with fear
and greed, and selfish seeking;
so shall we win to peace at last
and only so, and so to victory;
dwell in this our pleasant land
yet live in vibrant harmony
with that other, unseen world,
our spirit's home.

LENORE PRATT [1895-]

Lenore Alexandra (Tucker) Pratt, Mrs. F. Miller Pratt, daughter of James Alexander Tucker, was born in Toronto, moved to Ottawa at the age of thirteen, and is now a resident of Newfoundland. She became interested in writing verse at an early age, and her work appeared in various periodicals before the publication of *Midwinter Thaw* (1948).

MIDWINTER THAW

The rivulet with rush of sound
Spills through the prison ice that bound
It to a darkness of deep snows,
And past the thawing wood it flows,
Making music live and merry,
Racing with a frozen berry,
Tattered birch leaf, tip of fir,
Moss tuft green as midsummer
Where no summer is, but weight
Of shrunken drifts, and sky of slate
Through restless boughs, and winds that sigh;
While from nowhither comes the cry
Towards day's end of wakeful owls.
With amber eyes and feather cowls.

Track of foot and trace of claw
Blur and vanish in the thaw,
And from a dripping hemlock crest
Falls the cold remnant of a nest.

THE OLD BOAT

Beached on the meadow, close by the sea's
Accustomed lap, with wash of irises
Full on her bow,
And many a reef ahead of ox-eye daisies,
She silvers in the sun. Her prow
Is caught with a long strand of vetch,
And little agile spiders stretch
Cables from her timbers to the hay
Grown through her hull, and crickets leap
In impudence across. The spray
Of the tossed wave drives not this deep
Into the field.
Its white hand beckons all in vain:
Her fate is sealed.
The snail crawls aimlessly across her boards,
A dun moth shelters from the rain,
And on a summer day her shade affords
Haven, where the fisher's child
Gathers more treasure than his hands can hold—
Bits of blue glass, stones speckled with gold,
The wing feather of a sea-bird fiercely wild.

MARJORIE FREEMAN CAMPBELL [1896-]

Marjorie (Freeman) Campbell, Mrs. William MacFarlane Campbell, daughter of John A. and Carrie M. (Whiteside) Freeman, was born at Delhi, Ontario, and educated at the public schools of Fergus and Port Hope and the collegiate institutes of Lindsay and Hamilton and at Hamilton Normal School. She has taught school, written magazine juvenile fiction and numerous articles, a biography *Holbrook of the San* (1953), and published two poetry chap-books, *Merry-Go-Round* (1946) and *High on a Hill* (1949).

VIGIL

Although you died in a distant land
I have never known,
Have never beheld,
I could tell, if I willed, just where you lie.

I know that the sun ascends on the right
Of the long low mound
With its wooden cross,
Descends on the left in a storied sea
That must be blue, yet is gray to me.

I have watched the shadow of that cross
Through the long, long hours
Lengthen . . . contract . . . and lengthen again
On the stark, parched clods . . .
Lengthen . . . contract . . . and lengthen again
As one with ten thousand other crosses.

And I at the foot of the too-still mound,
(You who were always so restless in sleeping!)
A veiled black figure bowed in the dust,
As fixed as the crosses, mute, immobile,
An empty form in the empty silence—
God! for the shout of ten thousand laughters!

They say, "She has grown absent-minded this past while,"
Not realizing I am here no more,
That here a shadow moves about my missions,
While I, upon an unknown, well-known shore,
Keep vigil.

ONLY THE HEART

Teach me, life,
To take my friend as he is:
Confident that only he,
And God who shapes him on the potter's wheel,
Can estimate what strains and stresses,
What conditioning of circumstance
Have moulded him.

Man's eye may judge
Alone the finished form . . .
Only the heart knows its own despair!

DORIS FERNE [1896-]

Doris Maud (Napper) Ferne, Mrs. E. G. Ferne, daughter of Lt.-Col. Henry George and Bella Alice Mary (Curtis) Napper, was born in Richmond, England, and educated there privately and at Scarsdale School. She came to Canada in 1912 and lives in Victoria, British Columbia. She has written reviews, articles, songs, short stories, and an operetta, lectured and given radio broadcasts on poetry, and published two books of verse, *Ebb Tide* (1941) and *The Paschal Lamb and Other Poems* (1946).

SOUNDING

The struggle is strong and splendid
and the tide is swift and terrible
and deep as the depth of one destroyer
"overdue and must be considered lost . . .
a full complement of men aboard,
one hundred and forty-five . . .
relatives have been notified . . .
she was built in 1936 . . ."

And the men, when were the men built?
In the soundless depths of antiquity
in the still caves of a great past
where honour began and love
and a vast capacity for self-sacrifice.
Their veins the veins of England
running full tide with Shakespeare,
crimson with Drake and Raleigh.
Their limbs the limbs of children
cradled at clean hearthstones,
suckled by free women,
"Relatives who have been notified . . ."

We know the effort must be
until limbs crack and lungs burst,
for freedom is more than men
and honour than women.

The struggle is strong and splendid
and the tide is swift and terrible
and deep as the depth of one destroyer
"overdue and must be considered lost . . ."

NIJINSKY

Light as a leaping faun!
Strong as a seasoned bow!
Bring from mad shades forlorn
The art that made you so.
Give to a wondering world
Once more the shivered thrill
Of breath-stopped silence,
While you hurl
Your balanced beauty to the still
Bright radiance of perfect poise.
Your fabled leap a drift
Of snow, no weight, no noise,
That lightning spring, the stage's length,
Lifting us too—defiant of all laws—
Godlike—
Exulting in your strength—
Paying you tribute with our wild applause!

JAMES HAROLD MANNING [1897-1924]

James Harold Manning, son of Dr. James and Helen (Hanington) Manning, was born in Saint John, New Brunswick, and educated at the High School there and, after service in the First World War, at Acadia University, where he ably edited and contributed to the *Acadia Athenæum*, the literary magazine of the University. He died at Maturin, Venezuela, where he had taken a position in 1922 on the Engineering Staff of the Standard Oil Company. He edited, with a biographical sketch, *Poems* (n.d.), by his brother Frederick Charles Manning (1895-1917), killed in action. His own lyrical poetry and his verse tragedy, *What is Truth?*, were published, with a biographical sketch by James Manning, in *Courcelette and Other Poems* (1925).

From WHAT IS TRUTH?

HARGEST:

I have been,
Three separate times, in war, and from the depths
Of horrors, that to mention chills the blood,
Three times came living . . .
Twice oblivious slothfulness
Held and delayed me, till I scorned myself.
Now from this last and greatest, scourged to action,
With grim peace torn from cannon's mouth, I come
Late, with one flaming purpose. Peace is won:

To work remains. Once more the diplomats
Who laid the trains of war; the editors
Who fanned base popular rage; the czars of wealth
Who played with lives for gold, have sat unmoved,
Watching the red blood flow, and piteous waste
Of vainly glorious valor, front to front.
And yet unmoved they sit, victor and vanquished,
Half heeding tales of others' agony
Words fail to mimic, that consumes the soul
Or leaves it gasping, dims the eye, and shakes
The frame with palsy, through the toughest shield
Of matchless courage. But we seek in vain
To limit war too dangerous that a nation
Should venture it, not seeing wars are made
By men, not nations, and projecting more
Terrors for those who fight, but none at all
For those who send to war. Those erring brains
And fallible decisions wove the web.
Shall they then ride unchecked to what new strife
Revenge and pride shall spur them?

JOHN HANLON MITCHELL [1897-1953]

John Hanlon Mitchell, who used the pen name John Hanlon, son of Mr. and Mrs. Walter Mitchell (the latter born Hanlon), was born and educated in Halifax, an honours graduate of Dalhousie University. For several years he was a feature writer for the Halifax *Chronicle* and *Daily Star*, especially for the columns "The Wayfarer" and "The Gasoline Gypsy." He travelled widely and lived in London from Hitler's conquest of France till 1951. He wrote for various magazines, had two plays produced in London, and published two books of poems, *Songs* (1926) and *Other Songs* (1927).

FARM WIFE

She never climbed a mountain,
She never heard the sea,
But always watched a winding road
That wandered aimlessly
Among unshaded meadows—
A farm, a pasture, rife
With Black-eyed-Susans, level fields
Comprised her little life.

She never longed to travel,
She felt no urge to search,
Her longest journey the five miles
On Sundays to the church;
Yet, in her quiet dwelling,
In singing, sighing flow,
Came love and parting, birth and death,
And all that women know.

A CITY SONG

Baths of Rome and Babylon,
  Gleaming in the dusk,
Tepid water sweet with myrrh,
  Violet and musk.

Baths of Rome and Babylon—
  Lovely ladies there
Lazily drew amethyst
  Brushes through their hair.

But the baths of Babylon
  Never knew the gay
Laughter city fountains hear
  On a summer day,

When the little gutter waifs
  Leave the listless street,
Launch home-carven caravels,
  Paddle weary feet.

GOODRIDGE MacDONALD [1897-]

Goodridge MacDonald, son of Samuel Archibald Roberts and Jane Elizabeth Gostwycke (Roberts) MacDonald, was born at Fredericton, New Brunswick. His education was largely informal. In 1912 the family moved to the West, later living in Ottawa. The son, after a brief period in the Civil Service, joined the Army Medical Corps. He has done some free-lancing, and has been on the staff of the Montreal *Herald* for more than twenty-five years, having risen to the rank of Associate Editor. He has published *Armageddon and Other Poems* (1917), *The Dying General and Other Poems* (1946), and *Beggar Makes Music* (1950).

THE SAILOR

A greasy sky-line where the grey
Unending billows roam,—
A lifting bow-wash, breaking spray,—
These bound the sailor's home

A month or two. Then port is made
And in some Sailor Town
At 'Frisco, Rio, Adelaide,
His shillings rattle down

For wine and women—double rums,
Vermuth, or British beer;
A gold-haired wench to steal his purse
And call him "Jackie, dear ——."

Then comes the squat-nosed harbour-tug
To hail him out to sea;
The bell-buoys clang, the shore-lights flash
In sullen ecstasy,

And standing watch upon the peak,
He dreams of lips and hands,
Drugged liquor and a painted cheek,
And sighs, nor understands

That he's a dreamer—and the call
That made a fool of him
In Hamburg or in Montreal,
Still to the wide sea's rim

Must lure him on, with hint of wine
More fragrant, and of lips
Unpainted, luscious, half-divine
To men who sail in ships.

ELEGY, MONTREAL MORGUE

She served love well,
Now she lies here
In a white trough,
In a white room
Upon whose wall
A cross hangs high.

Little Picard
Unbars the door
And seven men
Slow shuffle in,
Their heavy hands
Turning their hats,
Nervously turning.

They look upon
Her quiet breasts
And folded hands,
Then shuffle out
To give a verdict.

But love, ah love, the crimson rose, flames on
With no less loveliness now she is gone;
So pluck the rose—the petals strew, my friend;
There is white quiet at the end.

LEO COX [1898-]

Leonard Cox was born in London, England, and educated in English Public Schools. He served in the First World War. He is now Managing Director of Walsh Advertising Inc., Montreal. His verse publications are: *Sheepfold* (1926); *The Wind in the Field* (1932); *River Without End* (1937); and *North Star* (1941), for which he was awarded in 1944 the David Prize of $800.

CORNFIELD

Night stilled the field, and every golden stook
Slipped, like a sobbing child, to misty sleep,
Till the dark held it in a slumber deep,
Dreaming of little deaths by reaping-hook.
Sometimes a corn-mountain stirred and shook,
When from the dewy stalks there crept a mouse
Who, solemn, from his new, dream-heavy house,
Drank in the heavens in one astonished look.
And who shall say, his bright eyes, shining so,
Responded not to the full flood of the moon
Nor knew the silver of this silent noon,
And that the rain of stars he could not know?
That in his fearful heart there was not born
A sweet surmise of grief of harassed corn?

EASTER THOUGHT

The hedgerows are wiser than I—
Under the weight of their snows,
Expectation runs high.
Gathered by dark roots below,
From the clay sleep of the floods,
Rises the stuff of the buds.

The hedgerows are wiser than I—
Of Easter never knew they,
Resurrection, or why
The heart should be stirred to-day. . . .
But the hedgerows renew their green breath
When taken each winter by death.

THE BELLS OF STE. ANNE DES MONTS

I climb the tower of Ste. Anne des Monts,
Possess the town, the mountains, and the sea;
And think how when we visitors are gone,
This shall I keep still in the heart of me:

Tomorrow morning, all along the shore,
A schoolhouse bell will ride upon the wind,
And call the innocents with song and lore,
By simple roads, to countries of the mind;

At noon the hospice bell with silver tongues,
Will tell another hour of little deeds
For aching hearts and feet, for ailing lungs,
—A blessed bell for all the body needs . . .

At seven, the angelus will shake this tower
As tenderly as it stirs the town to prayer,
Sainte Anne will gather, at this solemn hour,
The village soul and keep it very fair;

And then the wind will cease, the gulls will hide,
And time move only in the stars and tide . . .

PHILIP CHILD [1898-]

Philip Albert Child, son of William Addison and Elizabeth Helen (Harvey) Child, was born in Hamilton, Ontario, attended schools in Germany, Switzerland, and Canada, and continued his education at Trinity College, Toronto, Cambridge University, and Harvard University. He has taught

English at Trinity College (1923-1926), at the University of British Columbia (1928-1929), and again at Trinity College since 1942. He has published five novels, for two of which he shared the Ryerson fiction award, is co-author of a book on democracy, and contributed to Canadian poetry in *The Victorian House and Other Poems* (1951).

OAK

The ancient sowed an acorn from His mind
And He foreplanned that Oak should never move
A single inch from the earth where he was sown,
Should never lift his roots in wandering
To find some greener, richer growing place.
Oak does not think as we men do and try
To reach for stars, his business is with sap.
You'd say two neighbour oaks and the earth between
Were one continuous span of life, one flow
Of sap from tree to tree conducted through
Contiguous soil; you'd think each living tree
A vein and artery of Mother Earth . . .
Where Acorn falls and never moves again
There oak will stand three centuries or more
Then fall and rot to make a nourishing
For some unborn and still undreamed of oak.

But what of us, the restless ones, who sink
Our roots in soil we carry round with us
And label "mind"—who feed upon ourselves?
One foot we lift from earth and then the other
And when we jump we think we put a space
Between our separated selves and Earth:
"I separate," we think, "from other life;
I infinite," we say, and "I forever—
Ever separate I!" till seventy rings
Have girthed a growing oak and measured us.
Our fleeting summers come and then they go
And soon we fall and mix our dust for soil
To nourish unborn babes and unsown oaks.
Some olden poet long since laid to dust
Is whispering in the rustling leaves of Oak,
And in my separate mind some fallen tree,
Whose oaken soil has made and fed my blood,
Returns the whispered message of the leaves.

MACROCOSM

This heaven is too clear and bright,
Too peaceful and too infinite;
Its quiet will not stay with me,
I cannot find its boundary.

Beyond my thoughts it spreads too far
To coffin private peace and war,
It has no self-containing room
To close about my single doom.

Its round horizon lies unfurled
To float forever round the world;
Beyond my sight the cloudless sky
Is troubled with artillery.

THE BASILISK

I've forgotten what day, but late in December. . . .
I had no particular thing to conceal,
I was simply having my usual meal,
Just sitting quietly eating and drinking
And musing—but what it was I was thinking
  I can't remember. I can't remember!

How did it get behind my chair?
There wasn't even a draft at my back
But I knew that something demoniac
Had opened the door and stolen behind me
Lidlessly peering, meaning to find me—
It was there. I could feel its stare.

I did not look. I thought, "It will go
Perhaps, if I never turn my head
To see, not even once till I'm dead."
Then I thought, "If it looked just once at me
And I at it, then whatever I'd see
The thing would go away—and I'd know."

One day, because I hoped it would go,
I turned my head and looked behind
But I might as well have been stricken blind:
At the open door, in the empty hall
There was nothing. Nothing! Nothing at all!—
Why should that *horrify* me so?

LYRIC

I touched a shining mote of sand
But when I took away my hand
And looked for it, I looked in vain.
I passed a soul one busy day
But though I often went that way
I could not find that soul again.

I will not count the stars at night
For if I lost one star to sight
Its beam might not return to me;
And when the starry host sweeps by
I will not circumscribe the sky
Lest I should lose infinity.

I saw a snake devour a mouse
I heard the rats invade the house,
Two things I cannot look above:
I cannot separate the sin
From the soul that let it in
And I can only pray to love.

Each grain of sand or star or soul
Must be my witness of God's whole
And show eternity anew;
I pray to love each thing that's born
Lest starlight never see the morn
And lest the sea sands prove too few.

DANCING PARTNERS

I said to Death: "Supposing it were true
That from this drifting Inchoate
There were no life but mine to dance with you,
Your life my death one single state;
Then if the music stopped and I were dead
What would you do—I dead, I too?" . . .
Death echoed me: "If I were dead, were dead
What would you do?"

DESCENT FOR THE LOST

Judas Iscariot dour and dark
Carried the purse for Christ,
Travelling weary miles with him,
Dreaming of earthly power.
Green, green grows the grass
Behind our tired feet.

Jesus the leader who loved and bled
Took Judas' soul to keep,
Sharing Judas' troubled heart
And fending away the night.
Green, green grows the grass
Behind our tired feet.

Judas the empty one feared the night
And the vacant deeps within;
He followed Christ and looked to him,
But Judas was sick for power.
Green, green grows the grass
Behind our tired feet.

Judas' anguish was Christ's own pain,
For it was part of him.
"Judas, Judas, thou troubled soul
I cannot let thee go."
Green, green grows the grass
Behind our tired feet.

But Judas hated Jesus' love
Although he leaned on him,
"Thou severest me from what I am;
What is Thy love to me?"
Green, green grows the grass
Behind our tired feet.

Weary and weary the highway led
To a cross and a potter's field;
Judas the lost one looked and chose,
And Judas hanged himself.
Green, green grows the grass
Behind our tired feet.

What comfort now for such a one
Who chose the severed hell?
And for the one who kept his soul,
What comfort now for him?
Green, green grows the grass
Behind our tired feet.

Christ has gone down to search the earth
Where Judas' bones lie low,
Where only God can work the dust
Of field and sepulchre.
Green, green grows the grass
Behind our tired feet.

EDGAR McINNIS [1899-]

Edgar W. McInnis was born in Charlottetown, Prince Edward Island, and educated at the University of Toronto and Oxford University (as a Rhodes Scholar). He served in the First World War. He has been in the Department of History at the University of Toronto since 1928. He is an outstanding historian and writer on national and international affairs and has twice won the Governor-General's Award for academic non-fiction. While at Oxford he won the Newdigate Prize for English Verse.

FIRE BURIAL

She never could sleep in the earth, in the cold dark grave—
She who was proud and free,
She of the burnished hair,
She who was one with the sun and the sunlit sea
And the shining air;
She could never be laid in the lonely deep
Where no light stirs
And the sullen mould and the slow worm creep
Over the mouth that once was hers,
Shut now forever from song, and the eyes from laughter,
Out of the sight of the sun and the sunlit wave—
Oh, never prison her heart in the sombre grave,
In the dark of the long hereafter.

Build her an altar here
On the broad open shore,
Here where the long seas thunder
And swing to the lift of the tide.
This was her heart's own song, but now no more
Her dancing feet will follow the dancing foam,
Nor sunset shadow her eyes with a deep, still wonder—
O dreams that fade while they still are fair!—
No more will the wind etch clear
The cleanly strength of her body breasting the wind,
Nor fling her laughter into the sun, nor scatter her hair—
Spun bronze with the shadows intertwined;
Earth and the seas abide,
But this was her heart's own song, and her heart went home
Before her song had died.

She will not find it under the mouldering earth;
She will not hear in the grave
The laughing call of the wind, the surge of the wave.
Build her last altar here—
Here where the echoes of song and the shreds of mirth
Still hover about the pyre,
Blown by the fitful wind,
Blown as the flames that flicker and soar and fade
Over the husk her soul has left behind,
Over the cold still form on its glowing bier;
So may she find again
Beauty she loved, and the old delight and pain;
So let her loveliness pass from us, arrayed
In glory and gold of fire.

She was a crystal that held a flame
Burning clear in its inmost heart;
She was a chalice far too frail
For the flame that shattered its walls apart.
Life that called to her, love that came
Deep as the tide of the moonlight sea
Woke her soul to a singing splendour
Beyond the strength of her heart to hold,
And flesh was a robe as of iron mail
Prisoning wings till the wings burst free
And the body lay in its last surrender
Panoplied royal in flaming gold.

She could never be laid in the lonely dark—
She will go out as a flame into the sun,
Soaring and unconfined,
Free from the body and all the bonds that sever
Spirit from spirit, song from the singing heart;
So when the last faint spark
Blows out to sea, and fades, and the fire is done
And we depart
Into our loneliness, she will go questing on,
One with the world she loved, one with the dawn,
One with the sunlit air and the calling wind
And the sea for ever.

F. R. SCOTT [1899-]

Francis Reginald Scott, son of Archdeacon Frederick George and Amy Scott, was born in Quebec, and educated at the High School there, at Bishop's College, Lennoxville, at Magdalen College, Oxford, as Rhodes Scholar, and at McGill University. In 1940 he was awarded a Guggenheim Fellowship. He taught in public and private preparatory schools before joining the Faculty of Law at McGill in 1928. He went to Burma in 1952 as United Nations Technical Assistance Resident Representative. He has written singly and jointly on national and international affairs. In 1945 he published *Overture*, a volume of poems. He won the Guarantors' Prize of *Poetry*, (Chicago) in 1944 and the 1949-1950 poetry award of *Northern Review*.

FULL VALLEYS

Fly away, away, swallow,
  Summer is done,
Time to be gone, swallow,
  Time to be gone.

No swifter your flight than the flight
  Of warm days,
Less sudden of pain to the heart
  Than memories.

Only a fat bee crawling
  Over dry grass
Speaks of the droning and humming
  When August was.

Only the fall of a leaf
  On brown ground
Whispers of greener life
  When the heart burned.

And I would be alone now
  Under the slanting sun
Building a world of my own
  Out of things that are gone—

The first loves, and the hates,
  The spur and the goal, the hurt
Of wound and of wounding, the bright
  Roads of the heart.

For in these final days
  Long silences
Are of old words and ways
  Full valleys.

CONFLICT

When I see the falling bombs
Then I see defended homes.
Men above and men below
Die to save the good they know.

Through the wrong the bullets prove
Shows the bravery of love.
Pro and con have single stem
Half a truth dividing them.

Between the dagger and the breast
The bond is stronger than the beast.
Prison, ghetto, flag and gun
Mark the craving for the One.

Persecution's cruel mouth
Shows a twisted love of truth.
Deeper than the rack and rope
Lies the double human hope.

My good, your good, good we seek
Though we turn no other cheek.
He who slays and he who's slain
Like in purpose, like in pain.

Who shall bend to single plan
The narrow sacrifice of man?
Find the central human urge
To make a thousand roads converge?

WINDFALL

Until this poem is over, I shall not leave
This leaf, held like the heartache in my hand,
Fallen from brave contagion of the sun
Fallen from branches wounded by a wind
And resting, now, as green as when it flew
With sap in the stalk and veins stiff with show.

This small complete and perfect thing
Cut off from wholeness is my heart's suffering.
This separate part of something grown and torn
Is my heart's image that now rests on stone.

This is a leaf I talk to as a lover
And lay down gently now my poem is over.

SOMEONE COULD CERTAINLY BE FOUND

From the French of Anne Hébert

Someone could certainly be found
Who once killed me
And then walked away
On the tip of his toes
Without breaking the rhythm of his dance.

Who forgot to bring me to sleep
And left me standing
All tightly bound
On the road
My heart locked up as before
My eyes as clear
As the purest image of still water.

Who forgot to take away the beauty
From the world about me
Forgot to close my hungry eyes
After giving them this wasted passion.

SATURDAY SUNDAE

The triple-decker and the double-cone
I side-swipe swiftly, suck the coke-straws dry.
Ride toadstool seat beside the slab of morgue—
Sweet corner drug-store, sweet pie in the sky.

Him of the front-flap apron, him I sing,
The counter-clockwise clerk in underalls.
Swing low, sweet chocolate, Oh swing, swing,
While cheek by juke the jitter chatter falls.

I swivel on my axle and survey
The latex tintex kotex cutex land.
Soft kingdoms sell for dimes, Life Pic Look Click
Inflate the male with conquest girly grand.

My brothers and my sisters, two by two,
Sit sipping succulence and sighing sex.
Each tiny adolescent universe
A world the vested interests annex.

Such bread and circuses these times allow,
Opium most popular, life so small and slick,
Perhaps with candy is the new world born
And cellophane shall wrap the heretic.

RECOVERY

Now thought seeks shelter, lest the heart melt
In the iron rain, the brain bend
Under the bombs of news.
Fearfully the mind's hands dig
In the débris of thought, for the lovely body of faith.
Is she alive after this sock, does she yet breathe?

O say that she lives, she is ours, imperishable,
Say that the crypt stood.

We had no right to hope, no claim to defense.
We had played in the hanging gardens, lain in the sun
On a roof of glass. We had given no thought
To the deep soil of the base, the sunken shafts
Resting on rock. We loved the façade
More than the wall, the ivy more than the stone.
We took our gifts for our gains; we fed without ploughing.

But she lives, it is true, the eyes glow.
The lips are firm under the pain, they move,
It is our name that is spoken.

O clutch her to you, bring her triumphant forth.
Stand by her side now, scatter the panzer doubts.
She is more dear after this swift assault,
More one and alone, an ultimate.
In her sure presence only there is strength.

This sharp blow pulls the excesses down,
Strips off the ornament, tightens the nerve,
Bares limbs for movement and the forward march.
More roads are opened than are closed by bombs
And truth stands naked under the flashing charge.

CONSTANCE DAVIES WOODROW [1899-1937]

Constance (Davies) Woodrow, Mrs. John Woodrow, born and educated in England, lived in Toronto for most of her adult life. She made an excellent translation from French into English of Georges Bugnet's *Nipsya,* a novel with Indian, half-breed, and *habitant* characters, and wrote two books of poems, *The Captive Gypsy* (1926) and *The Celtic Heart* (1929), both of which show her gift for poetic phrase and lyric music.

TO A VAGABOND

But half of me is woman grown;
  The other half is child.
But half my heart loves quiet ways;
  The other half is wild.
And so to hear your gypsy song
  I dare not come again;
To-morrow, when the twilight falls,
  Your voice will lure in vain.

For all of you is vagabond
  And all of you is free;
Your feet roam still the winding trails
  That now are strange to me.
My gypsy feet are captive held
  Within a garden-space
Since I renounced the whole wide world
  For one belovèd face.

RAYMOND KNISTER [1900-1932]

Raymond Knister was born near Blenheim, Ontario. He spent several years on an Essex County farm and lived for some time in the middle-western United States. He attended rural schools and two universities, and then settled at Port Dover for serious writing. He wrote two novels, one of which was awarded first prize in a competition, and edited a volume of Canadian short stories. His *Collected Poems* (1949) contains a biographical and critical introduction by Dorothy Livesay.

STABLE-TALK

We have sweat our share;
The harrow is caught full of sod-pieces,
The bright disks are misted yellow in the wet.
Hear tardy hesitant drips from the eaves!
Let the rain work now.

We can rest today.
Let the dozy eye,
The one raised hip
Give no hint to the hours.

We are not done with toil:
Let rain work in these hours,
Wind in night's hours,
We with the sun together
Tomorrow.

BOY REMEMBERS IN THE FIELD

What if the sun comes out
And the new furrows do not look smeared?

This is April, and the sumach candles
Have guttered long ago.
The crows in the twisted apple limbs
Are as moveless and dark.

Drops on the wires, cold cheeks,
The mist, the long snorts, silence . . .
The horses will steam when the sun comes;
Crows, go, shrieking.

Another bird now; sweet . . .
Pitiful life, useless,
Innocently creeping
On a useless planet
Again.

If any voice called, I would hear?
It has been the same before.
Soil glistens, the furrow rolls, sleet shifts, brightens.

PLOWMAN'S SONG

Turn under, plow,
My trouble;
Turn under griefs
And stubble.

Turn mouse's nest,
Gnawing years;
Old roots up
For new love's tears.

Turn, plow, the clods
For new thunder.
Turn under, plow,
Turn under.

CHANGE

I shall not wonder more, then,
But I shall know.

Leaves change, and birds, flowers,
And after years are still the same.

The sea's breast heaves in sighs to the moon,
But they are moon and sea forever.

As in other times the trees stand tense and lonely,
And spread a hollow moan of other times.

You will be you yourself,
I'll find you more, not else,
For vintage of the woeful years.

The sea breathes, or broods, or loudens,
Is bright or is mist and the end of the world;
And the sea is constant to change.

I shall not wonder more, then,
But I shall know.

MARTHA OSTENSO [1900-]

Martha Ostenso, daughter of Sigurd and Lena (Tungeland) Ostenso, was born in Bergen, Norway, and educated at Brandon Collegiate, Kelvin Technical High School, Winnipeg, and the University of Manitoba. She is an outstanding novelist, her *Wild Geese* (1925), an excellent novel with a Canadian setting, having won the Pictorial Review Prize for fiction. In verse she published *A Far Land* (1924).

THE RETURN

Oh, strong and faithful and enduring
As my mother's face,
The sowing of the years has wrought
No change in you, no ill,
Wild field that I loved! The generous grace
Of ragweed and of nettle caught
In the ruddy fall of sun
And in the silvering of rain enveils you still,
And here and there a warm rut of the dun
And patient earth with small, slow life is stirring.

Your stiff, pale grass and weedy flowers
Still proudly grow
Innocent of being beautiless—
(Even a little vain,
Trusting no leafed thing could be low
That the sky-born rain would bless)
And oh! the sunny smell of you—
Of brittling stems, sweet spears long-matted lain
In spider weft and gold-pricked dust and dew
Through the dream and languidness of humming hours.

Under the blackbird swartly flying
From west to east,
Under the reach of the lark from north to south
You are my field—the same
Brown curve along the sky—even the least
Brown blade the same. To lay my mouth
On the quiet of your dew-sweet face
And hear the deep earth of you call my name—
This is to know that I have found my place—
And the empty years have ended all their crying.

ROBERT FINCH [1900-]

Robert Duer Claydon Finch, son of Edward Finch, was born at Freeport, Long Island, New York, and educated at the University of Paris. He teaches French at the University of Toronto. As early as 1924 he won a prize for poetry, and his *Poems* (1946) won the Governor-General's Award. Still better is *The Strength of the Hills* (1948), a collection of exquisitely wrought short poems, mostly reflective lyrics.

THE MOUNTAIN

There is a mountain everyone must climb,
Different for all and yet it is the same.
We start to climb before we have a name,
And nick the summit in our nick of time.

The more we climb the more its bulk looms bigger,
Its safest valley finds the steepest walls,
And it has icefields where the will will stagger,
And steps into the dark where reason reels.

But there is One, a stranger to no danger,
Who combs the wildness, answering each hail,
He is the indefatigable Ranger
And his the alpenstock that gives us skill

To climb the way that he alone could make,
Blazed with his cross and set on living rock.

THE NETWORK

Pure poetry, programme of the living heart
And broadcast from the station of the mind
Through will's control-room, may be words aligned
Memorably or speech of other sort:
The comfort of witch-hazel on a hurt,
An errand run, a raised or lowered blind,
A signature that only tea-leaves signed,
A comprehending silence, a stopped dart,
An unowed letter, an anonymous loan,
Steps climbed, space aired, reserve not disestablished,
A flame relit by match or telephone,
Fragrance remembered, sacrifice unpublished,
If love be sponsor, none is lost despite
The faulty sending or receiving set.

THE LOST TRIBE

They sit in the roots
Of regal sâl
Awaiting the fall
Of feet in boots,

Awaiting the pagan
Circular saw
And the glutton jaw
Of the lumber-wagon

That snaps its freight
Along with them
Out of their time
And up to date.

No clothes to mend,
No house to mind,
No cows to find,
No crops to tend,

By the climbing sun
They hunt for roots,
Birds' eggs and fruits,
And hunting's done.

In the swimming shade
Inertia weaves
From grassy leaves
A brief parade.

By the riding moon
They drink the power
Of the mowa flower
And dream till noon.

There are no moans
For caviare,
Sole meunière,
Or paving-stones,

Paraffin stove,
Hurricane lamp,
Cigarette, gamp,
Or gramophone-love.

No labour lash
Begins to crack
Ripping a back
To writhing hash.

If a snake strike
By the foul pool,
They only feel,
They hardly speak,

Their gentle stammer
Can combine
A noun, a sign,
No other grammar.

Stunted, weedy,
They disentangle
The netted jungle;
Frail yet speedy,

Running from drums,
Evil all round,
Evil in sound
And whence it comes,

Running from sight,
Running from touch,
Running from each
Sense, day and night,

Through sappy vine,
Through spongy morbid
Growth as rapid
As its decline,

Running, till all
By forty dead
Are simply laid
In the roots of sâl.

Their faces that
Of men whose wound
Was mortal, and
Who knew it not.

ALONE

Carry your grief alone,
No other wants it,
Each man has his own,
A fool flaunts it.

Alone, but not unique:
Bubble to bubble
Is not more like
Than trouble to trouble.

Alone, but light in the end,
For time shall whittle
It like the word of a friend
And the body's fettle.

Alone, to the end, and through
To join the solaced,
The steady journey due
To grief's ballast.

TIME'S BRIGHT SAND

Time's bright sand
Fools the shrewdest hand,
Promise and stone
Fall apart soon,

The poet stretches
For starred beaches
To wrick his neck
On a dream's wreck,

Dear lips are lost
In space or dust,
And some sun dies
Down all our skies,

And the road turns home
Until we come
Where the path undared
Has disappeared,

And we try to cry
What we meant to pray
When, seeing its gleam,
We saw no time.

DORIS HEDGES

Doris Hedges, Mrs. G. B. Hedges, of Montreal, was born at Lachine, Quebec. She rendered distinguished service in the First World War, has travelled much, is a radio commentator, and has advanced the cause of arts and crafts. She has written essays, short stories, two novels, and three books of poems: *The Flower in the Dusk* (1946); *Crisis* (1947); and *Words on a Page and Other Poems* (1949).

POET'S PROTEST

Words were meant
To catch meanings in.

You say you cannot
Prison beauty in a word,
Ephemeral things are sacred
So you say. You are afraid
Of moulds; yet no one else
Can say it better.
Why not make moulds
Of lovely words
And pour the moment in?

A poem written for one eye to see
Is not a poet's drab return
Of grist to mill
But is a string of words
Like finest jewels
Sharing infinity's meaning.

There is no wealth can buy
My word's fine purity.
This is not poetry,
It is a chant, flung skyward
Heavy with challenge.

Words were meant
To catch meanings in.

ONWARDNESS

Into the crucible of life
Man pours himself with recklessness
In fear, in anger, in revolt,
In tenderness, in love; with strong resolve
Not to be lost, nor wasted, nor destroyed.
That wish is greater than his will
More valiant than his deeds,
His thoughts unspoken, or his tears unshed,
His words of fury, or his lips turned back
In smiling. Into the crucible
Man pours himself, unknowing.
Is he dream, or fantasy, or whim,
Or mighty truth, or God Himself?
All that he asks is that the mould
Be ever filled and filled again
And that this strangest spending
Buy survival at the end of time.

FREDERICK B. WATT [1901-]

Commander Ernest Frederick Balmer Watt, son of Arthur Balmer and Mary Gertrude (Hogg) Watt, was born in Woodstock, Ontario, and educated in Edmonton, Alberta, at the Victoria High School and the University of Alberta. His naval career began in 1917. He is now with the Directorate of Naval Intelligence, Ottawa. He has had a varied experience in journalism, has made a specialty of maritime fiction, and has published four books of poems, *Boy Blue's Verses* (1918), *Vagrant* (1927), and two dealing with aspects of the Second World War, *Who Dare to Live* (1943, 1944) and *Landfall* (1946).

THE INSPECTION

They told us that the King was coming up to see the base
And "holystones and paint pots" was the order 'round the place.
They told us we must all clean up and wear our "Number Ones"
Just so the King could see what lads he had to fight the Huns.
So we were glad and for a while forgot the ruddy war
'Cause we were going to see the bloke that we were fighting for.

The T.B.D.'s all polished till they glistened in the sun,
The cruisers were as spotless as the breech-block on a gun,
The submarines looked snappy in a wicked sort of way,
And even paddle-sweepers seemed respectable and gay.
But we were awful shabby—though it wasn't quite our fault
That our small boat was in splinters and our funnel caked with salt.

We scrubbed our poor old vessel and we laid the paint on thick
On the rusted engine-casing—but the damned stuff wouldn't stick.
The place that "four inch" cracked us on our bent and battered bow
Was not well patched—we never knew how bad it looked till now.
We hadn't much to boast of in our "leg-o-mutton" sail—
It had ripped and hung in ribbons since we hit that Norway gale.

And our "Number Ones"—those uniforms had suffered our last trip
When the forecastle was flooded and we near abandoned ship.
There wasn't one good rig-out in our whole unshaven crew
For our sea-boots and our oilskins were the uniforms we knew.
There were other trawlers like us, come to rest up in the base,
And the commodore he saw us and he said, "A damned disgrace!"

Well, we did our level damn'dest while the skipper cried, "Oh, Lord,
Shine up that gun—it's all of the real Navy we've aboard."
We washed the wheelhouse windows and we got the deck all cleared—
When just before the King arrived a messenger appeared.
He brought a chit up from the base and this is how it read:
"Proceed with *Lark* and *Sea Dog* and drop anchor off the Head."

'Twas just three hours later that we heard the guns ashore
And we knew the King was come to see the lads who fought the war.
Three poor, old battered fishing ships, all mournfully we lay—
We were no sight for Royal eyes, so we'd been shoved away.

. . .

But, putting wet coal on our fires, we kind of hoped that he
Would see the smoke and know that ships still fought the war at sea.

JOSEPH EASTON McDOUGALL [1901-]

Joseph Easton McDougall, son of Douglas Howard and Adelaide (Rogers) McDougall, was born in New York and educated at St. Andrew's College, Aurora, Ontario, and the University of Toronto. He is chiefly noted for his humorous writing, examples of which have appeared in various magazines, and he has conducted a syndicated humorous column. His books of poems are *If You Know What I Mean* (1929) and *Blind Fiddler* (1936).

THE NEW HOUSE

If sometimes strangeness seems on me to fall,
Remember, it is not long that I've been roofed
By your heart's ceiling. Yesterday I moved;
Some things not yet unpacked lie in the hall.
Oh, there's no happier householder than I,
Running from room to room to catch the view,
Crying at spaciousness and colours new,
Here the green lawn and there a patch of sky!
But there must be times when I think I hear
Echoes of words one uttered here before,
And wonder what proud tenant held you dear
Before I came, whose feet have crossed this floor,
Who by this window pondered in the gloom,
Who climbed these stairs, who died within this room.

L. A. MacKAY [1901-]

Louis Alexander MacKay, who has used the pen name John Smalacombe, son of William and Martha Elma (Smalacombe) MacKay, was born at Hensall, Ontario, and educated at the University of Toronto and, as Rhodes Scholar, at Baliol College, Oxford. He was awarded a Guggenheim Fellowship in 1945. Formerly Professor of Latin at the University of British Columbia, he now fills a corresponding position at the University of California. He has been Associate Editor of the *Canadian Forum* and has published a play, a study of the sources of the *Iliad, Viper's Bugloss* (1938), satiric verse, and *The Ill-Tempered Lover and Other Poems* (1948).

ADMONITION FOR SPRING

Look away now from the high lonesome hills
So hard on the hard sky since the swift shower;
See where among the restless daffodils
The hyacinth sets his melancholy tower.

Draw in your heart from vain adventurings;
Float slowly, swimmer, slowly drawing breath.
See, in this wild green foam of growing things
The heavy hyacinth remembering death.

From THE ILL-TEMPERED LOVER

I wish my tongue were a quiver the size of a huge cask
Packed and crammed with long black venomous rankling darts.
I'd fling you more full of them, and joy in the task,
Than ever Sebastian was, or Caesar, with thirty-three swords in his heart.

I'd make a porcupine out of you, or a pin-cushion, say;
The shafts should stand so thick you'd look like a headless hen
Hung up by the heels, with the long bare red neck stretching, curving, and dripping away
From the soiled floppy ball of ruffled feathers standing on end.

You should bristle like those cylindrical brushes they use to scrub out bottles,
Not even to reach the kindly earth with the soles of your prickled feet.
And I would stand by and watch you wriggle and writhe, gurgling through the barbs in your throttle
Like a woolly caterpillar pinned on its back—man, that would be sweet!

NOW THERE IS NOTHING LEFT

Now there is nothing left of all our sorrow,
Or only this: to know that sorrow dwindles,
And broken hearts may take their place tomorrow
With love, in the routine of minor swindles.

Doubtless we still shall find that we are able
To call a ghost up, with a little trying,
And learn, like many more, that life's a cable
Twisted of tedious, small, unfinished dyings.

ROY DANIELLS [1902-]

Roy Daniells, born in London, England, was at the age of eight brought by his parents to Victoria, British Columbia. Eight years of school were followed by seven years of work at odd jobs and a return to school. He matriculated and then taught school for several years, later going on to the University of British Columbia and Toronto University, and working in some travel as well. He has taught English literature at Victoria University, the University of Manitoba, and the University of British Columbia, where he is Head of the English Department. His *Deeper into the Forest* (1948) shows mature reflection and power in imaginative expression.

BUFFALO

Black as a battering-ram the massive head
That stopped the early prairie settler dead.
A thick skull set suspicious on the trail
A mud-encrusted and bespattered tail
So well the frame from all attack defend
That bullets flattened him on either end.
Set in a show-case on the C.P.R.
The buffalo is at his best by far.
The traveller gazing on that solid brow
Thanks heaven that it is not encountered now.
But still the herdsmen, so the story goes,
His bellow hears o'er Manitoba's snows;
Still in his bog he wallows to the snout
Then snorting on the settler rushes out.
Even mighty smiths like true men must confess
His power than theirs proved very little less
And still he stands far out Fort Garry way
Strong to obstruct, tenacious to delay.

SUMMER DAYS

About the hilltop how the clouds are cool
Pausing like gods in slow processional;
One billowing, a white celestial rose,
Moves by superior choice
Buoyant toward the zenith:
Here is no sign, no shadow of death.
Harvest beneath, with wheat in rounded clumps,
Where the plump mottled pigeon pecks;
Cock pheasant runs ducking about the ricks
And wandering butterfly obliquely flits.
O but for you I were content as they.

The teeming rain steams on the warm wet road,
An overflowing runnel slants the grass,
White ruin of fallen acacia strews a lawn,
A drooped bough showers with droplets all who pass
The cloud blows over and the storm is gone,
Small ponds are overflowed.
But shattered, scattered down dark alleyways
Goes June, that last week seemed herself a flower
Bursting in beauty, in splendour and in power.
Such things my mind continually amaze.

LIONEL STEVENSON [1902-]

Arthur Lionel Stevenson, son of Henry and Mabel Rose (Cary) Stevenson, was born in Edinburgh and came to Canada in 1907. He was educated at the University of British Columbia, University of Toronto, and University of California. He has taught English in different American universities, notably at the University of Southern California since 1937. He has published biographical and critical volumes of distinction and two exquisitely wrought books of poems, *A Pool of Stars* (1926) and *The Rose of the Sea* (1932).

GULLS AND DREAMS

White ocean birds that seek the land
Before the storm—a drifting band
Dipping and rising on the gale
With wings unstirring, impotent
To stem the wind that makes them sail
Sideways as if their force were spent,—
Against the aureate sunset light
Grow vague, vanish and reappear,
One moment silhouetted clear,
The next, elusive, lost to sight.

So all the fair imaginings
That fain would flock on futile wings
To the calm haven of my mind
And leave the stress of life behind
Are caught and wafted far astray
By that eternal wind of truth,—
The breath of heaven's ageless youth
That sweeps the sophistries away,—
Till they are lost amid the glow
Which finite words cannot express
Nor mortal minds aspire to know,
The universal loveliness.

SUMMER INTERLUDE

All wisdom and renown are worth
  Less than the goal that I have won—
To lie upon unyielding earth
  And steep in golden drifts of sun.

Tense fibres now can all unloose,
  For faithful earth sustains me well;
Sinew and brain have sworn a truce
  To halt their warfare for a spell.

Life is a distant droning bee,
  Faith is the sun's warm unseen shower,
And love itself becomes for me
  The fragrance of a trodden flower.

I merge with earth as if I grew
  Deep in her breast; yet from the sun
The bright rays penetrate me through
  Till they and I dissolve in one.

A. J. M. SMITH [1902-   ]

Arthur James Marshall Smith, born in Montreal, of English parents, was educated at McGill University, where he did his M.A. thesis on the poetry of Yeats, and at Edinburgh University, on a fellowship, where he wrote his doctoral thesis on the English religious poets of the seventeenth century, under Professor Grierson, authority on John Donne. His two graduate theses exercised a pronounced influence on his own poetry and on his critical judgments of Canadian poetry since the First World War. He has edited *Seven Centuries of Verse* (1947), *The Worldly Muse; an Anthology of Serious Light Verse* (1951), and two editions of *The Book of Canadian Poetry* (1943, 1948). A selection of his verse, *News of the Phœnix* (1943), was awarded the Governor-General's Medal. (Cf. W. E. Collin and E. K. Brown, as above, and *Leading Canadian Poets*, edited by W. P. Percival (1948).)

THE FOUNTAIN

This fountain sheds her flowery spray
Like some enchanted tree of May
Immortalized in feathery frost
With nothing but its fragrance lost;
Yet nothing has been done amiss
In this white metamorphosis,
For fragrance here has grown to form,
And Time is fooled, although he storm.

Through Autumn's sodden disarray
These blossoms fall, but not away;
They rear a lattice-work of light
On which black roses twine with white;
And while chaotic darkness broods
The golden groves to solitudes,
Here shines, in this transfigured spray,
The cold, immortal ghost of day.

GOOD FRIDAY

This day upon the bitter tree
Died One who had He willed
Could have dried up the wide sea
   And the wind stilled.

It was about the ninth hour
He surrenderèd the ghost,
And His face was a faded flower
   Drooping and lost.

Who then was not afraid?
Targeted, heart and eye,
Struck, as with darts, by godhead
   In human agony.

For Him, who with a cry
Could shatter if He willed
The sea and earth and sky
   And them rebuild,

Who chose amid the tumult
Of the darkening sky
A chivalry more difficult—
   As Man to die—

What answering meed of love
Can finite flesh return
That is not all unworthy of
   The God I mourn?

THE LONELY LAND

Cedar and jagged fir
uplift sharp barbs
against the gray
and cloud-piled sky;
and in the bay
blown spume and windrift
and thin, bitter spray
snap
at the whirling sky;
and the pine trees
lean one way.

A wild duck calls
to her mate,
and the ragged
and passionate tones
stagger and fall,
and recover,
and stagger and fall,
on these stones—
are lost
in the lapping of water
on smooth, flat stones.

This is a beauty
of dissonance,
this resonance
of stony strand,
this smoky cry
curled over a black pine
like a broken
and wind-battered branch
when the wind
bends the tips of the pines
and curdles the sky
from the north.

This is the beauty
of strength
broken by strength
and still strong.

PROTHALAMIUM

Here in this narrow room there is no light;
The dead tree sings against the window-pane;
Sand shifts a little, easily; the wall
Responds a little, inchmeal, slowly, down.

My sister, whom my dust shall marry, sleeps
Alone, yet knows what bitter root it is
That stirs within her; see, it splits the heart—
Warm hands grown cold, grown nerveless, as a fin,
And lips enamelled to a hardness—
Consummation ushered in
By wind in sundry corners.

This holy sacrament was solemnized
In harsh poetics a good while ago—
At Malfy and the Danish battlements
And by that preacher from a cloud in Paul's.

No matter: each must read the truth himself,
Or, reading it, reads nothing to the point.
Now these are me, whose thought is mine, and hers,
Who are alone here in this narrow room—
Tree fumbling pane, bell tolling,
Ceiling dripping and the plaster falling,
And Death, the voluptuous, calling.

MARGOT OSBORN [1902-]

Margot Osborn, Mrs. Edith Margaret (Camp) Osborn, came to Canada as a bride from her native England. She now lives in Regina, Saskatchewan, where she takes a special interest in the production and writing of plays. She has written verse for periodicals and has published *Frosty-Moon and Other Poems* (1946).

ALWAYS THE MELTING MOON COMES

The silent tepees stand like shocked corn
in dark triangles against the moonlight.
Charcoal shadows shift, leaning awry.
The moon climbs down the western slope;
an owl in hushed flight slips by
and softly calls.

The old one stirs.
Winter falls. Bleached grass
will be buried in snow, tepees banked.
Green banners will flash in the north,
the air will sparkle with ice fragments.
Wind, shouting down from the north,
will pack the light snow,
pack it hard,
carve it in lines and ridges,
sculpture it in great curves.
The old one does not fear.

There is food.
Pemmican packed with chokecherries,
saskatoons pounded and dried,
deer meat and buffalo stored in deerskin.
There is fuel for the fire, and
robes to be wrapped in.
Why should the old one fear?

Many times have the wild geese flown southward
Many times have leaves fallen,
Many times has the frosty moon
breathed her cold breath on the world,
stilling water, changing the world to white.
But always the melting moon comes,
cracking ice,
rippling streams, bringing rain.
The white blanket of snow is withdrawn.
Grass comes with green blades,
and the crocus.
Rabbits' coats patchy and brown.
Crows shout and jeer
and the meadowlark calls.
The robes are shaken out;
chinook blows gently from the west.
The old one tells of it
"Always the melting moon comes."

BARBARA VILLY CORMACK [1903-]

Mrs. Barbara Villy Cormack, author of two distinguished novels, *Local Rag* and *The House*, has lived at Alix and Edmonton, Alberta. Her poems are found in *Seedtime and Harvest* (1942).

REPRIEVE

To some, the pattering raindrops on the roof
Beat fairy drums . . . A windswept stormy night
To others brings the thrill of tilting strength
'Gainst elemental power . . . To us upon the land . . .
How shall I write of that which brings to us
Not only hope,—but very life itself?

The woman at the door, 'neath dripping eaves,—
The boilers set, and barrels, pans and pails,
To catch the outpoured blessing as it falls,
Stands motionless . . . Within her mind a dream
That rivals all the wealth of Joseph's sheaves,—
Neat images of myriad shining jars
Filled with the promised berries from the hills,
And garden stuff, all canned and stored away
For winter's judgment . . . Streams of golden grain
To barter to the world for children's needs,—
For overalls, and unpaid bills, and boots . . .
A chance once more,—not certain, but a chance,—
To live, and eat, and hope again,—and laugh.

Behind her in the steaming kitchen hangs
A line of sodden coats and socks and caps,
Drying before the stove. Her mud tracked floor
For once awakes no wrath . . . Silent she stands.
Then in a little, men will come again,
All soaked and dank—fresh shirts, fresh socks to find . . .
The kitchen walls will echo to the sound,
That unfamiliar sound of laughter, and the jokes
That, lately, burning winds and scorching suns
Have withered to distrust, and bitterness . . .

To us upon the land there are no words,
No symbol meet to measure the reprieve . . .
One only pæan of praise that shields a prayer,
One glorious surge of joy that holds a tear,
One only song of true humility,—
"Thank God for rain!
Thank God,—thank God for rain!"

MARTHA EUGENIE PERRY

Martha Eugenie Perry, of Victoria, British Columbia, daughter of Matthew and Elizabeth (Cowan) Perry, was born at Kirkfield, Ontario, and educated in the public schools and Lindsay Collegiate Institute. She lived for brief periods in Manitoba, Saskatchewan, and Alberta, before settling in Victoria. She has edited a magazine page and written abundantly for newspapers and magazines in Canada, United States, and Great Britain. She has published a book on the deaf and the hard of hearing, fiction, drama, and four books of verse: *Hero in Ermine and Other Poems* (1939); *Hearing a Far Call* (1943); *Canteen* (1944); and *Song in the Silence and Other Poems* (1947).

THE LONELY SHELL

Far from the waves that soothed
  Its earliest day,
Spurning the tossed dark earth
  The seashell lay;
Frail in its element
  Of heavy clay.

Strange that this homestead knew
  Winged sail and prow;
Strange that this fertile field,
  Quick to the plow,
Bedded the sea in years
  Forgotten now.

Slanting the ocean depths
  The weird light fell;
Creatures of lesser life,
  Lulled to the swell,
Fashioned of pearl and rose
  This lonely shell.

THE MAINSPRING

Man may be martyred in bondage,
  Flailed to the mine and the plow;
Seeding from each murdered hostage,
  Ten will be enemies now.

Shatter his home and his city;
  Alter his intimate plan;
Know his integrity stiffen,
  Witness the growth of a man.

Will to be free is the mainspring.
  Genius of hate may reveal
Metal to bend, never break it—
  This is the ultimate steel!

THE WATER-WITCH

The twig turned in her hand and the diviner said: "Water."
The farmer smiled: "Wonderful, if true. Each summer
Drier than common we carry water from the mile-off creek."
"Incredible," the reporter murmured but the "dowser" heard:
"Even to me, but the hazel has proved right innumerable times."
She answered. "Dig here—yes—but tomorrow. And, please,
With augur or pick; power drill or dynamite may crush
The delicate veins of the water flow. Now, I must rest."

Tomorrow became today. The neighbours gathered if only to see
The "water-witch" discredited, knowing but shallow wells,
Seepage from rains, found here. And the reporter came,
Armed with the prose of statistics, and too, from a survey
Of library tomes, the colour and romance of the mysterious art
Of water divining from the pre-Christian to the atomic age.

No statue honours the first man to try
A withe to guide this emanative force—
Old as the desert yet airmen near Tripoli
Held a forked stick to trace a water course.
Cicero saw Romans "casting bits of sticks."
The use of the pruned "hazel or willow wand,"
Agricola noted in fifteen-forty-six,
Was practised by some humble vagabond
For finding water—earlier for mines.
Mediæval monks plied the divining rod
For wells; then banned it on religious lines:
"This is black magic, an affront to God."
Yet ancient, modern, everything that lives
Enjoys the benison abundant water gives.

The tensed stick moved again, bee-straight from painted barn
To willow bluff. The diviner prodded the dry earth
Centring a slight depression: "Here;
There will be plenty of pure, cold water to fill a pond."
Willingly the men seized shovels and picks, the powdered dust
Rising to smother their derisive snorts of: "Maybe a geyser!"
Down and down and down—nothing but feathery soil—"Ten feet,
She had said nine!" The farmer paced nervously away, returned,
And stooped to crumble loam in his hand—darker, more solid!
"Moist, it is moist," he whispered, and was dumb.

The farmer's wife taking faint cheers as assurance of success,
Charged from her stronghold: "No, not there, dig here,
In the angle of the house where anyone knows a well should be.
Men are always thinking of pasture and barn."
The diviner, tolerant of lay-mind quirks, explained:
"Deviate three feet, yes two, from the source to be tapped,
And failure is sure." The water gurgled suddenly in the hole!

The crowd moved forward sheepishly to shake her hand;
But the "water-witch" craved "Sleep!" To her no novelty
This triumph of the supersensory urge that had set in train
The gush of water from a thousand precious wells.

NATHANIEL A. BENSON [1903-]

Nathaniel Anketell Michael Benson, son of Thomas and Katherine (Sheehan) Benson, was born in Toronto and educated in Toronto schools and at University College and Ontario College of Education. He has had a varied experience as journalist in Toronto and Winnipeg, as teacher in Ontario, and in advertising in Toronto and New York. In the latter city he served as dramatic critic for Toronto *Saturday Night.* His literary interests are primarily in drama and poetry. He edited the anthology *Modern Canadian Poetry* (1930). His *Twenty and After* (1927) won the Jardine Poetry Prize in 1926. Other poetic works are *Poems* (1927), *The Wanderer* (1930), elegiac poems on the death of George VI and of Franklin Delano Roosevelt, and *The Glowing Years* (1937).

HOLY NIGHT

The loud, tumultuous and troubled world
Is laid away this night, and wrapped in sleep;
Silently stand doubt's banners dumbly furled,
And in the sky one Star her watch doth keep
With her eternal precious light of faith
Streaming all-soundlessly from heaven's portal;
Hushed are my questionings, and that poor wraith
Of unbelief reborn in faith immortal.

White is the moon, and diamonded the snow,
But whiter burns the truth in my poor hearth,
Rekindled with a strange tremendous glow—
For He has come again to bless His earth
As once He came, long centuries ago,
When man and star stood marvelling at His birth.

YEAR'S END

The year is dead, for Death slays even time,
  And was it not a proud and foolish thing
To cry "We love forever?"—'Twas sublime,
  For there's no heart that may forever sing;
One sweet, tremendous, transient hour of love
  Is worth a thousand unawakened years;
One perfect memory shall eternal prove,
  However deep the price we pay in tears.

Life is an envious miser, and he guards
  The wonder-stone of love with jealous pride,
And only the courageous pass his wards
  To wear the jewel for which great kings have died;
Thus, having known the best that life affords,
  We have done more than make the seas divide.

ALAN CREIGHTON [1903-]

Alan Creighton, son of Charles J. and Harriet (Hendry) Creighton, was born in Halifax, N.S. He attended Hantsport High School, Victoria School of Art and Design, and Halifax Conservatory of Music. For some years he was a professional musician. He now resides in Toronto. He has published two books of verse, *Earth Call* (1935) and *Cross-Country* (n.d., ca. 1940), and has contributed poetry and literary criticism to periodicals in Canada and abroad.

PASTORAL

The farmhouse skyline, draped with trees,
Is like a summer coast, green-boughed;
The cattle drift on rolling seas
Of luscious field against curled cloud.
They move as lazy ships, wave-borne;
Their bodies glisten sharply red,
With shaggy brow and curving horn,
Large waggling ear, grass-bending head.
With dainty hoof and solemn lurch
They munch along their quiet search.

RETURN OF A REAPER

The ache of wide millions
With brown fingers
Groping through dynasties
Has at last made swift factories.
The green gods of harvest
Have receded beyond church and school-house.
Yet, here are machine-shop temples,
Mahogany-desk altars
And the thunder of another god
Down hard aisles of street.

How grimed are these hurrying votaries—
They for whose freedom
Whole nations grew old
In the dust of the fields!

SPRING WORKMAN

The world is a gift again,
As he goes home through little grooves
Noisy with stores pushing commodities.
In burnt-grass air his wife hangs clothes
Which flap like regimented shapes,
Man-empty and crucified,
While his children play under the soft sky
Between a tartar-shouting sign
And steel traffic flashing like swords
Along the highway.

EARLE BIRNEY [1904-]

Alfred Earle Birney, son of William George and Martha Stout (Robertson) Birney, was born in Calgary, Alberta, and educated at the University of British Columbia, the University of Toronto, the University of California, and, on a Royal Society of Canada Fellowship, at the University of London. In 1952 he was awarded a Federal Government Fellowship for a year's work abroad and in 1953 the Lorne Pierce Medal of the Royal Society of Canada. He served in the Second World War. He has taught English literature at the University of California, the University of Utah, the

University of Toronto, and the University of British Columbia, where he has been a professor since 1946. He has edited *Canadian Poetry Magazine*, the literary section of the *Canadian Forum*, and an anthology, *Twentieth Century Canadian Verse*. He has supervised Foreign Language Broadcasts of the CBC International Service, written articles and reviews for magazines, published a picaresque novel of the Second World War, and enriched Canadian poetry by four volumes, *David and Other Poems* (1942), *Now is Time* (1945), *The Strait of Anian* (1948), and *Trial of a City and Other Verse* (1952). Each of the first two won a Governor-General's Medal, and he has been awarded two prizes for individual poems. (Cf. Brown and Percival, as above.)

SLUG IN WOODS

For eyes he waves greentipped
taut horns of slime. They dipped,
hours back, across a reef,
a salmonberry leaf.
Then strained to grope past fin
of spruce. Now eyes suck in
as through the hemlock butts
of his day's ledge there cuts
a vixen chipmunk. Stilled
is he—green mucus chilled,
or blotched and soapy stone,
pinguid in moss, alone.
Hours on, he will resume
His silver scrawl, illume
his palimpsest, emboss
his diver's line across
that waving green illim-
itable seafloor. Slim
young jay his sudden shark;
the wrecks he skirts are dark
and fungussed firlogs, whom
spirea sprays emplume,
encoral. Dew his shell,
while mounting boles foretell
of isles in dappled air
fathoms above his care.
Azygous muted life,
himself his viscid wife,
foodward he noses cold beneath his sea.
So spends a summer's jasper century.

DAVID

I

David and I that summer cut trails on the Survey,
All week in the valley for wages, in air that was steeped
In the wail of mosquitoes, but over the sunalive weekends
We climbed, to get from the ruck of the camp, the surly

Poker, the wrangling, the snoring under the fetid
Tents, and because we had joy in our lengthening coltish
Muscles, and mountains for David were made to see over,
Stairs from the valleys and steps to the sun's retreats.

II

Our first was Mount Gleam. We hiked in the long afternoon
To a curling lake and lost the lure of the faceted
Cone in the swell of its sprawling shoulders. Past
The inlet we grilled our bacon, the strips festooned

On a poplar prong, in the hurrying slant of the sunset.
Then the two of us rolled in the blanket while round us the cold
Pines thrust at the stars. The dawn was a floating
Of mists till we reached to the slopes above timber, and won

To snow like fire in the sunlight. The peak was upthrust
Like a fist in a frozen ocean of rock that swirled
Into valleys the moon could be rolled in. Remotely unfurling
Eastward the alien prairie glittered. Down through the dusty

Skree on the west we descended, and David showed me
How to use the give of shale for giant incredible
Strides. I remember, before the larches' edge,
That I jumped a long green surf of juniper flowing

Away from the wind, and landed in gentian and saxifrage
Spilled on the moss. Then the darkening firs
And the sudden whirring of water that knifed down a fern-hidden
Cliff and splashed unseen into mist in the shadows.

III

One Sunday on Rampart's arête a rainsquall caught us,
And passed, and we clung by our blueing fingers and bootnails
An endless hour in the sun, not daring to move
Till the ice had steamed from the slate. And David taught me

How time on a knife-edge can pass with the guessing of fragments
Remembered from poets, the naming of strata beside one,
And matching of stories from schooldays. . . . We crawled astride
The peak to feast on the marching ranges flagged

By the fading shreds of the shattered stormcloud. Lingering
There it was David who spied to the south, remote,
And unmapped, a sunlit spire on Sawback, an overhang
Crooked like a talon. David named it the Finger.

That day we chanced on the skull and the splayed white ribs
Of a mountain goat underneath a cliff, caught tight
On a rock. Around were the silken feathers of kites.
And that was the first I knew that a goat could slip.

IV

And then Inglismaldie. Now I remember only
The long ascent of the lonely valley, the live
Pine spirally scarred by lightning, the slicing pipe
Of invisible pika, and great prints, by the lowest

Snow, of a grizzly. There it was too that David
Taught me to read the scroll of coral in limestone
And the beetle-seal in the shale of ghostly trilobites,
Letters delivered to man from the Cambrian waves.

V

On Sundance we tried from the col and the going was hard.
The air howled from our feet to the smudged rocks
And the papery lake below. At an outthrust we balked
Till David clung with his left to a dint in the scarp,

Lobbed the iceaxe over the rocky lip,
Slipped from his holds and hung by the quivering pick,
Twisted his long legs up into space and kicked
To the crest. Then grinning, he reached with his freckled wrist

And drew me up after. We set a new time for that climb.
That day returning we found a robin gyrating
In grass, wing-broken. I caught it to tame but David
Took and killed it, and said, "Could you teach it to fly?"

VI

In August, the second attempt, we ascended The Fortress.
By the forks of the Spray we caught five trout and fried them
Over a balsam fire. The woods were alive
With the vaulting of mule-deer and drenched with clouds all the
  morning,

Till we burst at noon to the flashing and floating round
Of the peaks. Coming down we picked in our hats the bright
And sunhot raspberries, eating them under a mighty
Spruce, while a marten moving like quicksilver scouted us.

VII

But always we talked of the Finger on Sawback, unknown
And hooked, till the first afternoon in September we slogged
Through the musky woods, past a swamp that quivered with frog-
  song,
And camped by a bottle-green lake. But under the cold

Breath of the glacier sleep would not come, the moonlight
Etching the Finger. We rose and trod past the feathery
Larch, while the stars went out, and the quiet heather
Flushed, and the skyline pulsed with the surging bloom

Of incredible dawn in the Rockies. David spotted
Bighorns across the moraine and sent them leaping
With yodels the ramparts redoubled and rolled to the peaks,
And the peaks to the sun. The ice in the morning thaw

Was a gurgling world of crystal and cold blue chasms,
And seracs that shone like frozen saltgreen waves.
At the base of the Finger we tried once and failed. Then David
Edged to the west and discovered the chimney; the last

Hundred feet we fought the rock and shouldered and kneed
Our way for an hour and made it. Unroping we formed
A cairn on the rotting tip. Then I turned to look north
At the glistening wedge of giant Assiniboine, heedless

Of handhold. And one foot gave. I swayed and shouted.
David turned sharp and reached out his arm and steadied me
Turning again with a grin and his lips ready
To jest. But the strain crumbled his foothold. Without

A gasp he was gone. I froze to the sound of grating
Edge-nails and fingers, the slither of stones, the lone
Second of silence, the nightmare thud. Then only
The wind and the muted beat of unknowing cascades.

VIII

Somehow I worked down the fifty impossible feet
To the ledge, calling and getting no answer but echoes
Released in the cirque, and trying not to reflect
What an answer would mean. He lay still, with his lean

Young face upturned and strangely unmarred, but his legs
Splayed beneath him, beside the final drop,
Six hundred feet sheer to the ice. My throat stopped
When I reached him, for he was alive. He opened his grey

Straight eyes and brokenly murmured "over . . . over."
And I, feeling beneath him a cruel fang
Of the ledge thrust in his back, but not understanding,
Mumbled stupidly, "Best not to move," and spoke

Of his pain. But he said, "I can't move . . . If only I felt
Some pain." Then my shame stung the tears to my eyes
As I crouched, and I cursed myself, but he cried,
Louder, "No, Bobbie! Don't ever blame yourself.

I didn't test my foothold." He shut the lids
Of his eyes to the stare of the sky, while I moistened his lips
From our water flask and tearing my shirt into strips
I swabbed the shredded hands. But the blood slid

From his side and stained the stone and the thirsting lichens,
And yet I dared not lift him up from the gore
Of the rock. Then he whispered, "Bob, I want to go over!"
This time I knew what he meant and I grasped for a lie

And said, "I'll be back here by midnight with ropes
And men from the camp and we'll cradle you out." But I knew
That the day and the night must pass and the cold dews
Of another morning before such men unknowing

The ways of mountains could win to the chimney's top.
And then, how long? And he knew . . . and the hell of hours
After that, if he lived till we came, roping him out.
But I curled beside him and whispered, "The bleeding will stop.

You can last." He said only, "Perhaps . . . For what? A wheel-chair,
Bob?" His eyes brightening with fever upbraided me.
I could not look at him more and said, "Then I'll stay
With you." But he did not speak, for the clouding fever.

I lay dazed and stared at the long valley,
The glistening hair of a creek on the rug stretched
By the firs, while the sun leaned round and flooded the ledge,
The moss, and David still as a broken doll.

I hunched to my knees to leave, but he called and his voice
Now was sharpened with fear. "For Christ's sake push me over!
If I could move. . . . Or die. . . ." The sweat ran from his forehead,
But only his head moved. A kite was buoying

Blackly its wings over the wrinkled ice.
The purr of a waterfall rose and sank with the wind.
Above us climbed the last joint of the Finger
Beckoning bleakly the wide indifferent sky.

Even then in the sun it grew cold lying there. . . . And I knew
He had tested his holds. It was I who had not. . . . I looked
At the blood on the ledge, and the far valley. I looked
At last in his eyes. He breathed, "I'd do it for you, Bob."

IX

I will not remember how nor why I could twist
Up the wind-devilled peak, and down through the chimney's empty
Horror, and over the traverse alone. I remember
Only the pounding fear I would stumble on It

When I came to the grave-cold maw of the bergschrund . . . reeling
Over the sun-cankered snowbridge, shying the caves
In the névé . . . the fear, and the need to make sure It was there
On the ice, the running and falling and running, leaping

Of gaping greenthroated crevasses, alone and pursued
By the Finger's lengthening shadow. At last through the fanged
And blinding seracs I slid to the milky wrangling
Falls at the glacier's snout, through the rocks piled huge

On the humped moraine, and into the spectral larches,
Alone. By the glooming lake I sank and chilled
My mouth but I could not rest and stumbled still
To the valley, losing my way in the ragged marsh.

I was glad of the mire that covered the stains, on my ripped
Boots, of his blood, but panic was on me, the reek
Of the bog, the purple glimmer of toadstools obscene
In the twilight. I staggered clear to a firewaste, tripped

And fell with a shriek on my shoulder. It somehow eased
My heart to know I was hurt, but I did not faint
And I could not stop while over me hung the range
Of the Sawback. In blackness I searched for the trail by the creek

And found it. . . . My feet squelched a slug and horror
Rose again in my nostrils. I hurled myself
Down the path. In the woods behind some animal yelped.
Then I saw the glimmer of tents and babbled my story.

I said that he fell straight to the ice where they found him,
And none but the sun and incurious clouds have lingered
Around the marks of that day on the ledge of the Finger,
That day, the last of my youth, on the last of our mountains.

MONODY ON A CENTURY

The promise of our years was caught
As petals by the rose;
The loosening fingers of the sun
Were daybrief to unclose.

Yet bloom was whorled with coral tongues
And tremulously veined
And heart was cupped with velvet palms
Archaically stained.

Now bud is rot and fragrance rust
Around the martialled bees,
And men with boots will put an end
To making similes.

VANCOUVER LIGHTS

About me the night, moonless, wimples the mountains,
wraps ocean, land, air, and mounting
sucks at the stars. The city, away and below,
webs the sable peninsula. Streaming, the golden
strands leap the seajet, by bridge and by buoy,
vault the shears of the inlet, climb the woods
toward me, falter and halt. Across to the firefly
haze of ship on the gulf's erased horizon
roll the lambent spokes of a restless lighthouse.

Now through the feckless years we have come to the time
when to look on this quilt of lamps is a troubling delight.
Welling from Europe's bog, through Africa flowing
and Asia, drowning the lonely lumes on the oceans,
tiding up over Halifax, and now to this winking
outpost, comes flooding the primal ink.

On this mountain's brutish forehead, with terror of space
I stir, of the changeless night and the stark ranges
of nothing, pulsing down from beyond and between
the fragile planets. We are a spark beleaguered
by darkness; this twinkle we make in a corner of emptiness,
how shall we utter our fear lest the black Experimentress
never in the range of her microscope find it? Our Phoebus
himself is a bubble that dries on Her slide, while the Nubian
wears for an evening's whim a necklace of nebulæ

Yet we must speak, we the unique glowworms.
Out of the waters and rocks of our little world
we cunningly conjured these flames, hooped these sparks
for our will. From blankness and cold we fashioned stars
to our size, rulered with manplot the velvet chaos
and signalled Aldebaran. This must we say,
whoever may be to hear us, if the murk devour,
and none weave again in gossamer:

These rays were ours,
we made and unmade them. Not the shudder of continents
doused us, the moon's passion, nor crash of comets.
In the fathomless heat of our dwarfdom, our dream's combustion,
we contrived the power, the blast that snuffed us.
No one slew Prometheus. Himself he chained
and consumed his own bright liver. O stranger,
Plutonian, descendant, or beast in the stretching night—
there was light.

VERNA LOVEDAY HARDEN

Verna Loveday Harden, Mrs. Verna Bentley, is a native of Toronto. She has written articles as well as verse for Canadian and American magazines. Her books of poems are *Postlude to an Era* (1940) and *When This Tide Ebbs* (1946), for the title poem of which she received the Macnab Historical Association poetry award for 1945.

WHEN THIS TIDE EBBS

When this tide ebbs, then will uncovered lie
A strange collection on the quiet shore
Of curious things not found on ocean's floor
Nor shouldered in by boisterous waves that ply
Their unobstructed way; nor mounded high
By swirling winds when spring was at the door;
Nor carried here on tireless wings that soar
In unconcern across the dappled sky.

There will be hearts-blood rubies burning here
And pearl-pale, wistful hours that never knew
Fruition; dark, unuttered, lonely fear;
The tangled weeds where small misgivings grew;
But in the amber of the sand will glow
The gold of dreams we fashioned long ago.

POST MORTEM

This is the shack where the old man died;
Not unhappy, not afraid,
But weary of the long, long day
And aching from the effort of living.

This is the table where his last meal lay
Long untouched, when they found him,
The thick-sliced bread shrinking into the crust,
The tea stone cold,
The sugar being carried laboriously away
By small black ants.

This mended chair creaked under him
Though he weighed less each year;
That sweater hanging on the back of the door
Was far too wide for his shoulders.

He had only one cup and saucer.
His dog died years ago.
He never had a wife.

Let us go outside now.
The old man was not used to visitors
And he might resent our curiosity.

AUDREY ALEXANDRA BROWN [1904-]

Audrey Alexandra Brown, daughter of Joseph Miller and Rosa Elizabeth (Rumming) Brown, was born at Nanaimo, British Columbia, was educated there at St. Anne's Convent School and the public school, and makes her home there. *The Log of a Lame Duck* (1937), autobiographical prose, shows the fine spirit with which she met the handicap of ill health. Her poetic gift is amply manifest in six volumes of poems: *A Dryad in Nanaimo* (1931); the same, with eleven new poems (1934); *The Tree of Resurrection and Other Poems* (1936); *Challenge to Time and Death* (1943); *V.E. Day* (1946); *All Fool's Day* (1948). (Cf. Percival, *Leading Canadian Poets.*)

REVEILLÉ

Soul, do you hear the trumpets down in the valley,
  Where the lost battle waits for your broken sword?
The ranks are forming again for the last rally,
  The spears are set in array beside the ford;
It's dark at the foot of the hill, or you'd see them lying—
The piteous wreck of the mingled dead and dying.

Soul, will you answer the silver horns' sounding?
  Will you fling your life with the spent lives, the cost
Of a wild night and a mad day of wounding?
  The quarrel was none of yours, and the battle's lost:
There's nothing to gain but the barren gain and splendid
Of a blow for the weaponless, struck ere the fight's ended.

It is dark in the valley; here on the hill is morning;
  It were good to die here in the light, since die you must,
Strip off your bloody mail and your gold adorning,
  Lie down and be mingled quietly dust with dust.
—Not so shall my life forego its long endeavour;
Not thus will I lay my falchion by forever.

Nay, though I bleed, and the gallant sword be broken,
  Soul, we will fare together into the strife;
We will answer the cry before the cry be spoken,
  And loss shall be gain to us, and death shall be life.
Though the plume be shorn, though the gilt shield be rifted,
We will pass with the sword in the hand and the hand lifted.

AMBER BEADS

Golden as your singing-note,
Golden as a jasmine-wreath,
The bright beads lie about your throat
And turn and glitter as you breathe—
Till round your neck there seems to run
The sudden glory of the sun.

Yellower than the light that lies
In a tilted flask of wine,
Yellower than a leopard's eyes
The fifty mimic planets shine,
Ice to touch but fire within,
Clasping the coolness of your skin.

Treacherous lovely things! what fire
From days before the world began
Burns in them with a hot desire
Old as the stars, older than man—
To burst their chill captivity
And eat the earth and drink the sea?

THE GOLDFISH

Lazily through the clear
Shallow and deep,
He oars his chartless way,
Half-asleep,
The little paradox—so bright—so cold
Although his flesh seem formed of fire and gold.

High emperor of his dim
Bubble-empearled
Jet-shadowed greenish-shallowed
Water-world—
Like a live torch, a brand of burning gold,
He sets the wave afire and still is cold.

MUSEUM-PIECE

The unwinking frog of malachite
Stares from his sharply-golden eyes,
No piping swells his stony throat—
He is mute and he is wise.

Twenty centuries ago
Some craftsman in a merry mood
Carved him coldy-citadelled
In his eternal solitude.

He was the creature of a jest,
Man was the serious work of art;
But he has watched great kingdoms fall
And empires rend themselves apart.

He saw us sow the steely crop;
He sees it sprouting, breath by breath;
He watches as with eager hands
We whet the dulling scythe of Death.

Secure upon his shelf he smiles,
Knowing his ancient wrong redressed—
Himself become the work of art
And all humanity a jest.

NIGHT BOAT

Throb, throb, throb . . . the tall ship,
The white ship never launched upon the ocean
Moves beneath us with a steady motion,
A never-ending give-and-take-and-give,
Gentle, rhythmic and contemplative.
The cup is not jarred against the lip,
The foot is not shaken on the floor—
The ship times the heartbeat and no more.

Softly across a sea as dark as jet
And smooth as glass it goes with no wind sighing,
The glimmer of its wake behind it lying
Like a white peacock's train upon the night;
Its corridors are dim with veiled light—
And everywhere in arch and alcove set,
Sprawled at large or huddled in a heap
Men groan in heavy and hypnotic sleep.

There is a harbour for the ship; and they
Its breathing cargo shall awake tomorrow
Each to his separate world of hope and sorrow;
Only tonight, dazed with the watch I keep,
I look on them and think—"The night for sleep:
What if there never dawn another day,
And the ship slide forever by no shore,
And these its living-dead arise no more?"

THE DARK CAT

The dark cat, Death,
Caught me in youth and claimed me;
His bright teeth bit through
Sinew and bone and maimed me,
Then let me go, to run
My staggering course, and feel
The glory of the sun
That warmed but could not heal:
Ah, well; he had his sport, he never tamed me.

All the quicksilver, wild,
Unweighed unstinted rapture of the child,
Filling the veins with wine,
Still, still is mine:
I loved to run, I love it yet; but now
My heart, whole and complete,
Outruns my feet
To dance where danced the shadow of the bough.
Here where the vines are laced with vivid green—
Here where are seen
The spiderwebs all glittering-strung with dew—
Wheel-within-wheel of diamonds—here anew
I stand to look and feast my soul and still
I have not looked my fill.
If ever earth ran down, if any day
Was like another day,
And God forgot to make the fruit trees gay
With petalled pearl-and-rose
Why then, who knows?
I might forget to feel my spirit whole,
Who have immortal April in my soul.

O Death, your mouse
Is given the freedom of so fair a house—
A house so high,
Pillared with pines, roofed with the changing sky!
Though through green leaves I see
The glimmer of your green eyes watching me,
And feel your following breath,
I cannot fear you, Death.

You should have closed my ears and shut my sight
Before I looked on light,
Before I had begun:
You should have taken me away too soon
To count the silvery changes of the moon,
To coin the golden sun:
Then, then you might have had a victory
That now belongs to me.

More lovely is the light
To one that knew the darkness and that knows
The dark to which he goes—
A little dark, dissolved in clearer sight.
Too confident by half,
You'll snatch brief triumph from your last endeavour—
For when you pounce, I'll laugh
—The last laugh's mine!—and so escape forever.

FLORIS CLARKE McLAREN [1904-]

Floris Clarke McLaren, Mrs. J. A. McLaren, of Victoria, British Columbia, was born in Skagway, Alaska. In 1941 she became business manager of the recently discontinued *Contemporary Verse*, edited by Alan Crawley. She has won a prize for a short story and published a book of poems, *Frozen Fire* (1937), which vividly records various aspects of the Arctic scene.

FROZEN FIRE

I

The air is full of diamond dust tonight,
Cold glittering sparks between us and the snow;
The hills are ragged etchings, black and white, pointed with stars;
The crowning spruces go,
A still black army, down to the curving shore.
The frost lights glitter on every twig and brier
Till we set intruding feet on the jewelled floor
And shatter the cranberry bushes' frozen fire.

II

The still cold sharpens as the sun goes down;
The frost-fog thickens;
Plumes of white smoke stand
Straight up from every chimney.
Near at hand
A husky lifts a wailing quivering cry;
The low hills hold the sound
Answered, repeated, till from all around
The husky chorus swells to the winter sky.

III

Against the blue of spruces, and the grey
Of bare-boughed poplar, suddenly
As though a snowdrift burst in scattering fragments,
Ptarmigan rise with heavy whir of wings,
Show for a moment clear among the branches,
Then disappear,
White lost on white again.

IV

The northern sky
Is pale transparent green
Where one lost star
Has climbed the snowy peak, to see
The world.

V

No whisper stirs the valley
Where blue dusk already lies;
But where that sunset-reddened tusk
Stabs the cold skies,
The air is lashed and torn,
As great winds blow
Across the peak, to lift the frozen snow
In gleaming haze,
Till streaming snow plumes fly
Above the valley in the sunset sky.

VI

The hills are changed today,
The white mist shows
Ravines unseen before.

The bare peaks stand
Separate; as though last night
They moved apart, and pausing now
Exchange slow stare for stare,
Like grey old men
With ragged shawls tight-drawn.

VII

The pines stand dark against the sky,
Northern lights are streaming high,
Far along the snowy trail
Sounds the prowling wolf-pack's wail;
Cold and swift the night comes down:
How bitter black that trail to town!

LAURENCE DAKIN [1904-]

Laurence B. Dakin, son of Blair E. and Jeanette (Morris) Dakin, was born at Sandy Cove, Nova Scotia. He studied medicine at Columbia University but turned to literature, devoting himself to that subject at the Sorbonne and at Ca Foscari, Venice. He mastered several languages and the masterpieces of world literature. He has lived in Europe, South America, Asia, and the islands of the South Pacific. His poetic themes are of the world as he has been a citizen of the world. *The Tower of Life* (1946) is an allegorical narrative of blended poetry and poetic prose. Non-dramatic books of poetry are *Poems* (1932), *Sorrows of the Hopeful*, and *The Dream of Abaris* (1933). Exquisitely wrought closet dramas in verse are: *Ireneo—a Tragedy* (1936); *Prometheus, the Fire Giver* (1938); *Pyramus and Thisbe* (1939); *Marco Polo* (1946); *Tancred, Prince of Salerno* (1948), which has been set to music. *The House of Orseoli* (1952) is a narrative poem the symmetrical structure of which challenges comparison with that of the *Divine Comedy*.

From PYRAMUS AND THISBE

[*Act III, Sc. iii*]

PYRAMUS [*waiting for* THISBE *at the tomb of Ninus*]:
. . . How sweetly sings this stream
And fills my soul with longing for my love.
O come my spirit and be patient here,
Yet will your Thisbe, out of breath,
Come tumbling o'er excuses rich as love,
Where none is needed but her own sweet self.
Be quiet, O my soul! O yet be quiet!
The hand that marks the face of time is still,
And all the ages sleep.

From TANCRED

[*Act I, Sc. i*]

SONG

The peasant sun went crushing grapes,
Purple and gold along the road,
Where sylvan gods and antique shapes
Bear up the vine the clusters load.

Rock-hewn and grey the mountain towns
Throbbed into gold as he drew near;
Glowed with the fruit the vine-leaf crowns,
Over the doorways hanging clear.

His rustic face was lit with fire,
This lover of the Latin vine,
His Southern eyes burned with desire,
Before the wine-jars waiting wine.

Over old walls the clusters hung,
As he went crushing grapes content;
I felt the song he should have sung,
And thrilled with leafy merriment.

[*Act II, Sc. i*]

GUISCARDO:
All night I raced the moon,
Where the ruined castles lie,
Entwined with lazy June,
And her roses bobbing by.

I saw her peep and swoon;
Heard her in the treetops sigh;
All night I raced the moon,
Where the ruined castles lie.

She held me in her zone,
As a vision holds the eye;
A silver floating tune,
In the mirror of the sky;
All night I raced the moon,
Where the ruined castles lie.

[*Act III, Sc. i*]

GUISCARDO:

How gently sings my soul and whets its wings
For love's impatient flight; and like the lark
That floats above the clouds, to her white arms
I fly upsoaring, singing unaware
Of starry-gateways as my spirit climbs
Into the heaven of my love. O love,
My brown-eyed rapture of the siren coast,
Enfold with tender hands the Rose of Life,
And from the red depths of its petaled Cup,
Pour love's elixir in my thirsting soul,
And I will grow immortal loving you.
The stars will fade away, the sun grow cold
And sink forever in the wasting sea.
But we will live in this eternal love,
And drinking at the fountain of your lips,
Renew ourselves, and be forever young.

ALFRED GOLDSWORTHY BAILEY [1905-]

Alfred Goldsworthy Bailey, son of Loring Woart, Baron d'Avray, and Ernestine Valiant (Gale) Bailey, was born in Quebec and educated at the University of New Brunswick, the University of Toronto, and, on a Royal Society of Canada Fellowship, at the School of Economics and Political Science, University of London. He has had journalistic experience as city editor of the Fredericton *Daily Mail* and on the editorial staff of the Toronto *Mail and Empire.* He is Head of the Department of History at the University of New Brunswick. He has published one volume of history on a Canadian theme and three books of poetry: *Songs of the Saguenay and Other Poems* (1927), *Tâo* (1930), and *Border River* (1952). He has not yet wholly eliminated the tendency to obscurity characteristic of his poetry written under the influence of foreign models.

BORDER RIVER

Look up this river in the book of rivers.
Its reaches chatter with the tongues of centuries,
its searched for titles staked with imperial names.
Its never being fully found was all the reasons
written in the tides of chance that swept its borders.
For both its countries, bleeding from the same heart,
singing a song of waters tossed by history,
found their own flag, strung from the beating halyard,
unfurled in a neighbour's eye by the hand of faith,
bound by the wonder of wind, with love for signal.

For beneath the stratum of Benjamin Church's corpulent boast,
blowing the islands over with the gaff of Falstaff,
(with cutlass arabesqued in empty Acadian air)
lies the body of Champlain embalmed in a casque of praise,
proclaimed as the ghost of a stone museum of spectral affections,
trapped in centennial fever by federal continents,
and heaped with the blessings of millions of priestly fingers,
thumbed in the books and learned by rote forever.

Yet if a cairn were put upon his bosom's sward
it could teach the mummers something for a day of international
    mourning,
marking the count of time, to point a finger
at the sign-manual of the common dream,
lost by men whose counsels failed, who wrecked
the common structure of their Father's house.
Here in the horn of Passamaquoddy the waters
come brimming about the chronicled shores of the island
with living oceans of uncreated joy
that hands could seize and quicken together and hold forever.

TÂO

The river god cries far,
And through the ringing deep, strange voices drone;
Then high above Lâotse's voice sounds alone,
"Worship the golden star."

The tall pagodas gleam,
Bathed in the falling lights of dark'ning day;
And reeling vapours dim and fold away
The gurgling of the stream.

The golden days of Han
Saw junk-sails catch the winds of Kiang-si,
Sail through the past, nor heed the strife to be,
Scrolled on the Teacher's fan.

EVAN V. SHUTE [1905-]

Evan Vere Shute, "Vere Jameson," son of Richard James and Elizabeth Jane (Treadgold) Shute, was born near Lion's Head, Ontario, and educated at the University of Toronto, where he took degrees in Arts and Medicine, followed by graduate work in Detroit, Montreal, and Chicago. He has been a practising specialist since 1933. His literary output includes many stories for children, three volumes of prose, and four books of verse: *Moths after Midnight* (1945), *The Sultan of Jobat* (1947), *Omar from Nishapur* (1948), and *Hy-Brasil* (1952), characterized by reflection, sympathy, and humour.

LUCK

If I had won my Wendy
I'd have kept a jade,
If Caroline had "yessed" me, a
Perpetual old maid,
And what my Minnie would have been
Makes me still afraid.

Had dear Prunella been my lot
I'd have died in debt.
Then Laura and her parents came
With winsome bait, and net,
Too bad the folks went with the girl.
—It has me shivering yet!

When first I laid my eyes on Anne
I hoped she'd be my wife,
Till I met Mary at a dance,
Which promptly changed my life.
That lasted a delirious month
Of kisses and of strife.

If I were fiend or hard to please
Or were a fickle man
You'd understand why I fell out
With Alice, Joan, and Nan.
But every epic has an end
And I found Marian.

Amazingly, she spoke like Anne,
Had Mary's lilt and grace,
Prunella's dimple, Wendy's nose,
And Laura's happy face.
But she is so much more she seems
Their dear ghosts to erase.

Now she has never met the rest,
Nor scarcely heard one name.
She values me for constancy
Whose loving, steady flame
Lights up a gallery of old loves
—Each in an empty frame!

TWENTY YEARS AFTER

It seems so strange that I once loved you so,
And dreamt of you, and held your face to mine,
Touched with amazement your least furbelow,
Thought you had overflowed even God's design.
I dare not say it, though no doubt it's true,
That the same eyes I loved are those I see
And that they comprehend my thought of you
And wince at it no more than repartee.
For both of us are fat and I am bald.
Your skin is dry, and powdered not too well.
Your talk is trifling, and that son who called!
—I'm glad I fathered no such cockerel.
The years have soaked up much more than they gave.
Dig in your heels against the slippery grave!

NIGHT COMES APACE

Night comes apace lest there be too much day.
Beauty possessed, our surfeit turns away.
The book well-mastered is the text forgot.
The mind adores where it is held at bay.

A pretty theorem, a little sum
Were tax infertile on man's premium.
We are not tantalized by rule of four—
The problem's worthy our sensorium.

Had it been easier t'were scarcely God,
But it's magnificent, and I applaud.
Spin universes on *your* finger-tip?
—Beware such silly vanity and fraud.

POOR FOOL

He took the quaint cup in unpractised hands
And held it up against the day's new light.
The crystal was so fragile every flaw
Stood naked as a swimmer in the night.

He held it but a moment e'er it broke
And split its sacred distillate on dust.
Strange such a fool should come on such a wine!
Stranger to drop it—as each mortal must!

NEIL TRACY [1905-   ]

Neil Tracy was born in Sherbrooke, Quebec, and educated at Bishop's College, Lennoxville. In his booklet of poems, *The Rain It Raineth* (1938), this blind poet appealingly speaks from the heart to the heart.

I DOUBT A LOVELY THING IS DEAD

I doubt a lovely thing is dead,
  An inward thing, so clear and sweet;
I come at night and lay my head
  Against its breast, and hear no beat;
  I touch its hands, and feel no heat.

Lo! I have slain a lovely thing,
  For I am blind in soul and sight;
If it would live, it needs must sing,
  It could not prosper in the night;
  It waned, and waited for the light.

With loneliness and empty rooms,
  With dust and ashes of the past,
I sat and heard the busy looms
  Work out the warp of First and Last;
  Where night and day the shuttle cast.

A gentle thing, that blooms in love,
  That lies with Beauty in her bed;
How slow for me the counters move
  Through senseless fingers, on their thread;
  Alas for me, that it is dead!

VERNAL HOUSE [1905-   ]

Vernal House, son of Arthur Edwin and Marguerite (Armitage) House, was born in Brantford, Ontario, and educated there and at Hamilton Central Collegiate Institute. He came to Toronto in 1926 and, while employed as a telegrapher and writer of market letters in a brokerage office, tried to work his way through the University of Toronto, but the double load was too much for his health, and he had to drop the college work. From 1929 to 1931 he lived at Greenwich Village. During the Second World War he served as a radio technician in the Royal Canadian Air Force. Since 1945 he has been a C.P.R. telegrapher stationed in the news room of the Toronto *Globe and Mail.* "In Tribute" shows the sane attitude to tradition in general that, when specifically applied in his judgments of poetry, accounts for the particular excellence of his criticism in that field.

IN TRIBUTE

When I in wild defiance fled
From cane and pedagogue,
Sharp arrowtips of hate
Besieged my unrepentant mind,
Not yet exposed to wilful fate
But hatching stern revenge
Upon the gray-faced arbiters
Of my impatient youth.

Infighting all the way,
The sworn enemy of all
Who battered at the holy gates
That guard the citadel of self,
I met head-on the age-old wall
That patiently awaits through time
The rebel and unheeding young
Who seek elusive truth.

Time had not then disclosed
The discipline of years,
Nor had my dream been caught
Within the dragonteeth of fears.
Ardor fades and anger dies
And questions snare the mind
With bitter and recurring doubts
The ancient young had fought.

I had expected much,
I had foreseen too little,
The fragile and rebellious self
Has crumbled like a brittle
Plant that struggles on its own
In bare unnourished stone—
Come back, old graying guides,
That I, in tribute, may atone.

GORDON LeCLAIRE [1905-]

Gordon LeClaire, son of Napoleon and Catherine Anne (Sproule) LeClaire, was born at Ormstown, Quebec, and educated at Macdonald College, Irvine Studio for the Theatre, New York, McGill University, and the University of California. He has had a distinguished career as a teacher in

Montreal schools, has travelled in Canada and United States as poetry recitalist and lecturer in metaphysics, has served as Canadian Editor of American literary magazines, and has directed and acted in plays. His books of poems are: *Intimate Moments* (1936); *Sonnets to the Stars and Other Poems* (1936); *Star Haunted* (1937); *Though Quick Souls Bleed* (1939); *Dust Into Flame* (1943); and *More Life in Living* (1947).

MISER

The house lies vacant now, forbear to knock—
Five doors that might greet Beauty as a guest
Are barred forever—(fools alone protest
Against the iron will of chain and lock).
Within, a wrinkled heart ticks like a clock
Tattooing broken rhythm to attest
A tenant soul once dwelt there that possessed
The power to drink from living's honeyed rock.

Only the hulk remains—the dry-veined stone
Now crumbles under carrion vines of hate
And venomed greed. Through windows glazed with gloom
One views the cobwebbed mind, and, creeping prone,
The batlike years that blindly lie in wait
To stalk their prey from room to haunted room.

OLD SEAWOMAN

Door closed against the splinters
Of light from the sunset prow,
Spindrift of eighty winters
Lies frostwhite on her brow.

Each manchild now a rover
From sea to engulfing sea,
Her long travail is over;
And, like Penelope,

She weaves nets of dream in her arbor
Unravelled by each new dawn,
Her soul—an abandoned harbour,
The ships forever gone.

LOVE

One word beyond all rules
Of syntax none can parse:
One syllable that holds
All tragedy, all farce—

Whose beauty haunts each line
Of this brief role we live.
No dangling participle,
Nor split infinitive

Defines the noun's lithe wings
Nor limits the verb's dart
That, like a skewer of flame,
Impales the heart.

VIOLET ANDERSON [1906-]

Violet Anderson was born in Dundas, Ontario, and educated at the University of Toronto. She lives in Toronto, is married, and has two children. She has edited a number of volumes for the Canadian Institute on Public Affairs (Couchiching Conference), and has published verse in the *Canadian Forum*, the *Canadian Poetry Magazine*, *Saturday Night*, *Northern Review*, and *Poetry* (Chicago).

THE CLOAK

A young girl of thirteen
will try on guilt for size,
find it hangs heavy on her shoulders
and discard it, easily,
turning at will to lipstick,
daffodils, and the intricate
designs of telephone calls.

Her bedroom defies weight,
slippered with the clutter of her things—
perfumes, glass cats, and pearls—
by which she lightly moves towards her love.
But the old old cloak
lies black across the chair
as if some sad dark ancestor
had come and gone, leaving behind
his cross-shaped human self
that she might dance it away.

The outcome is inevitable.
She who walks in housewife shoes
heavily towards her household stairs
bearing the daffodils she bought
with such extravagance a week ago
leaves, in her room, the morning
newspaper with its daily burden,
and a tidy empty chair.

THROUGH THE BARBER SHOP WINDOW

The barber shop is blank,
the chairs cold with emptiness,
waiting, as ambulances wait, or
operating tables
(in hospital corridors the night nurses arrive
rustling
crisp with charts and starch
to whisk about old ills)
So one is kept alive, with one's hair cut,
regularly.
Breathing, as in an iron-lung.
At the back of the shop, a coloured man
comes up the steps from the cellar.
The small light catches his
old hat, his bent shoulders,
while the chairs stand, darkly,
sullenly useless and sadistic.
He places his hand on the newel post
lifting his body slowly
reaching with hunched effort the tired level
of the day's
work
done.

CHARLES BRUCE [1906-]

Charles Tory Bruce, son of William H. and Sarah J. (Tory) Bruce, was born at Port Shoreham, Nova Scotia, and educated there, at Guysborough Academy, and at Mount Allison University, where he edited the *Argosy*, the student weekly. After graduation he joined the staff of the Halifax *Chronicle*. Since 1928 he has been with the Canadian Press, in New York, Halifax, Toronto, New York again as Superintendent, and then once more Toronto, where he has been since 1940, except for a period (1944-1945) as Superintendent in London, England, and in Toronto he has been General Superintendent since 1945. One of his excellent short stories has won an award, and he has written a novel. His books of poems are *Wild Apples* (1927), *Tomorrow's Tide* (1932), *Grey Ship Moving* (1945), *The Flowing Summer* (1947), and *The Mulgrave Road* (1951), for the last of which he won the Governor-General's Medal. Mount Allison conferred upon him the Litt.D. *honoris causa.*

From THE FLOWING SUMMER

The Hayfield

The herring-run was over. The long days
Burned with the singing heat of late July—
A time of indolence and drifting life
Before the haying. With the boy next door
Lee tramped the beaches and explored the woods
And hunted berries on the pasture slope
That dipped toward the river. By the barn
They raised a tent of blankets, rough and hot,
And loafed serenely in its woven dark.
Young Eric Mitchell had encountered Lee
With faint suspicion, watching for a sign
Of noisy talk or city-bred conceit,
And found only a shyness like his own.

"We'll soon be at the haying," Eric said.
"My father does the mowing for Old Jack;
Your granddad helps him cut the winter's wood;
That keeps it even." On this friendly coast
The work was shared in half a hundred ways
Without too much accounting of time spent
Or reckoning of hours. The work was done—
With little probing of its economics
When Sandy Mitchell ran his horse-drawn mower
For Old Jack Graham's labour with an axe.

The old man grumbled now: "It's late enough;
And Sandy waiting for a set of blades
To get his mower going. It's time we got
The browntop started in the upper field.
This afternoon we'll grind a scythe and mow."
The Woman counselled: "Take it easy, now;
Wait till the mower's fixed." But nothing said
Could hold him idly patient. In the barn
They sharpened to an edge a rusty scythe,
Lee at the grindstone's crank and the old man
Holding the blade against the turning stone.

Grey timothy and shining browntop grew
In sloping fields around the Graham place. . . .
The old man shed his coat; the whetstone rang;
With shuffling feet wide-set and swinging arms
Timed to the rhythm of the marching blade
He walked with shoulders bending to the task
Into the long slow labour of the scythe.

Before the deft inexorable stroke
The browntop tumbled in a gathered swath . . .
The stubbled channel in the standing hay,
Cleared of its colour and its leaning height,
Was flat as water, and like water flicked
By rippling wind, the shaven ground was lined
With little ridges, curved and regular—
The pencilled record of the sharpened steel.

Lee's work was easy-going—shaking out
The green and heavy hay on the mown ground
Under the drying sun. But Jack at last
Offered the idle scythe. His grasping hands
Closed on the handles of the curving snath;
The bare and shining tip of the swung blade
Scraped on the earth, and strands of rooted hay
Snarled in the angle of the bolted heel.

But Jack was patient. "Take it easy, boy;
Don't hurry and don't press it; use your hands
To keep the scythe in balance; let the swing
Come natural and easy." And the knack
Came to him quickly; but the falling dark
Found him a tired youngster, on the grass
Beside the doorstep. On the second day,
After the morning's effort and the brief
Leisure at noon, they borrowed Mitchell's horse
And raked the first day's mowing, piled and pitched
The dried hay on the hayrack, hauled it home,
And stowed and tramped it in the dusty mows.

Day followed day, and in the slanting fields
No lurch of rolling swell came up to break
The stubborn grip of labour; and no flash
Of moving silver in a dripping net
Lightened the continuity of work.

The only object now was: get it done;
And with each rack unloaded in the barn
Lee felt the impulse of a sighted end.

The Attic

Sunlight and summer wind are never sure;
With a week's labour done and half the hay
Already in the barn, the morning sky
Turned low and grey and threatening. "Get the rakes";
The old man hustled now. "We've got to put
This stuff in cocks." With hurried rake and fork
They piled the hay in hummocks, heaped it up
And packed it close in little shining stacks
Against the wet thrust of the coming rain.

When the last rounded cock was built and trimmed
The first drops pelted on the dotted field.
Kitchen and parlour darkened in the grey
Dusk of the rain. "Look here," The Woman said,
"You haven't tried the attic. That was where
Roy had his hide-out. Maybe you can find
Something amusing in the stuff he left.
I haven't bothered with the place in years."

Hooked to a beam across the dingy loft
He found a battered sack, a punching bag
Stuffed hard with rags; behind an ancient trunk
A fielder's glove devised of padded felt
Was anchored in a rusty muskrat trap.
Piled in the corners, and below the slant
Of the steep ceiling, books and wornout boots,
And bundled papers, and a spinning-wheel,
Recorded here the drift of simple time.

And when at length The Woman climbed the steps
Half-wondering, herself, what hoarded thing
Could hold his interest thus, she found him deep
In the rough pages of a pasted book
Bulky with clippings; half-tone prints of Cobb
Hook-sliding into third; Carpentier
On the ring floor in Jersey; records made
In fifty years of track and field; the text
Of an old poem of Kipling's, pasted there
For some lost reason none could fathom now:

"When d'you think that he'll come back?"
Not with this wind blowing and this tide.

Lee closed the scrapbook with a question: "Dad's?"
"Yes. He was always saving odds and ends.
It's queer to think about him, living here,
And now a man grown up, and gone away
And his son getting to the size he was. . . .
And this stuff in the attic. . . . Well, come down
Out of the dark, and get your supper, now;
The rainstorm's over, and it's getting late."

Long after, Lee was bothered by the sense
Of knowing someone, on the edge of time,
Whose name he could not say, whose boyish face
Blurred in a dream of papers and old books
And rusty iron in a dusty room.

The Dreaming Trout

"I found the place last winter." Eric's voice
Was low and careful with the studied ease
That veils achievement with a still reserve.
But slow excitement gathered in them both,
Here at the woodroad's end, among the spruce
On sloping land above the crooked stream
The boy had followed in the winter woods.

The brook was little but a string of pools
Linked by a trickle. Up its tangled banks
And through its twisting bends and past a flat
Low bed of gravel, where the water lay
In the brown shallows of its placid course,
They scrambled through the bush to Eric's dam.

Dead tree-trunks, rocks and earth contained the flow
Of this forgotten brook a mile beyond
The river highway, in a shaded pool
Knee-deep and quiet, ringed with spruce and birch.

Lee followed Eric in a grave content,
Half-conscious of a new possession shared,
Only half-listening to the running talk:

"The brook was frozen over, but this spring
I dammed it up and made the little lake . . .
The brook's too small for trout; there's nothing here;
I'll have to get my hands on two or three
Up in the river, when I get the chance,
And bring 'em down to try it in the pond."

Yes. That was all it wanted. On the bank
The boys relaxed and lay with little said,
Eric reflecting on the narrow dam
With larger plans in mind, and Lee alone
Beyond the corridors of measured thought.

His eyes were on the water. The faint wind,
Timed with the distant sweep of moving clouds,
Drifted the lake with changing light and shade—
Now clear with stillness and reflected light,
Now dark with rippling shadow.

And his mind
Lived in the moment, till the city street,
The school, the playgrounds, and the Graham place,
Even this water in the sunny woods,
Moved in a world of clarity and dream,
Now sharper than his inner sense could bear,
Now vague as shadows in a waking night,
Half-seen or half-remembered.

But his eyes
Were fixed, unknowing, on a silver gleam
That lived and vanished in his vacant sight,
To gleam and vanish, gleam and die again;
Till the quick waking of his startled brain
Took in the message, read the coloured word,
Believed the shining truth.

His warning hand
Beckoned to Eric softly. Neither spoke:
In the clear amber of the pool a trout
Was still as death between the surface drift
And the brown stones and broken roots below;
The tawny back, the speckled flank and side,
A slick unmoving curvature of form
Beyond the caught leaves at the water's edge.

Only a flickering of lazy fins
Betrayed the living grace of the still fish.
Again the light wind and the sweeping cloud
Assailed the birches with a rippling shade.
The travelling shadow passed. And when the stream
Was lucent with its inner light again
The dreaming trout was gone.

With staring eyes
They saw the water and the pebbles there,
The stirring tendrils and the polished roots,
And looking at nothing. All there was to see
Had lived a moment in the water's light
And fled between the sunlight and the wind.

The sun was dropping in the darkened spruce
When Eric sighed and clambered to his feet.
"Come on, then, Lee. We'd better beat it home.
It's almost time to get the cows and milk."

FISHERMAN'S SON

I

Now I am thankful this unbroken flesh
Has known hard rowing, and the trenchant bite
Of cold salt water, as reluctant mesh
Came up at sunrise from the tidal night.
Wisdom was in the brief recurrent shock
Of bodies braced against a plunging line;
Familiar meaning in the liquid knock
Of building swell concerned with buoyant pine.

Only in some dark hour of stress we learn
How strength and wit lie dreaming in the brain. . .
Now at its need the wakened mind shall turn
An oilskin to the dictatorial rain:
What shall a little wind of words avail
Against a heart close-hauled, with shortened sail?

II

This ghost is much embarrassed that his son,
Learned in a gentler way of thought and speech,
Should still consider where the mackerel run
And three grey fish huts on a windy beach.
Embarrassed but unsurprised. He long has known
That kinship tempered in an offshore blow,
More eloquent than blood to mark its own,
Pulsed always in us. And he knows I know.

Lord, I address myself to you: be kind;
Mindful of how the cosmic current sets.
Though immortality be a state of mind,
Let there be clean firm bottom for the nets.
When it is time for this quick flesh to die
Let herring school through heaven's hot July.

WORDS ARE NEVER ENOUGH

These are the fellows who smell of salt to the prairie,
Keep the back country informed of crumbling swell
That buckles the international course off Halifax
After a night of wind:

Angus Walters and Ben Pine, carrying on for Tommy Himmelman
and Marty Welch;
Heading up the tough men who get into the news,
Heading up the hard men of Lunenburg and Gloucester,
Keeping the cities bordered with grass and grain
Forever mindful that something wet and salt
Creeps and loafs and marches round the continent,
Careless of time, careless of change, obeying the moon.

Listen to little Angus, squinting at the *Bluenose:*
"The timber that'll beat her still grows in the woods."
Yes, these are the fellows who remind you again of the sea.

But one town, or two,
Are never enough to keep the salt in the blood.

I haven't seen Queensport Light over the loom of Ragged Head
in years,
And never a smell of rollers coming up the bay from Canso.
No one ever heard of Queensport outside of a bait report;
No one ever saw the name of Ragged Head anywhere.

Off that obscure beach Will Bruce and George McMaster
Set their herring nets, and went farther out for mackerel.
The mackerel never ran, but in July
Fat herring tangled in wet twine were silver-thick,
And the flat low in the water as we hauled around
To head back for the huts;
In full daylight now,
After the grey dusk of a windless morning;
After the bay, gently stirring in half darkness,
Tipped down again to blush at the sun's rim.

Cleaning fish is a job you would balk at;
But nothing is mean with gulls hovering down,
Sun brighter than life on glistening eelgrass,
The bay crawling again in a quickening southwest wind.

There was always time, after the wash-barrels were empty,
After hand-barrows were lugged up the beach to the hut,
And herring lay behind hand-wrought staves, clean with salt.

Time to lie on warm stone and listen,
While the sting went out of crooked fingers and thighs ceased to
ache;
Time to hear men's voices, coming quietly through a coloured
cloth of sound
Woven in the slap of water on fluent gravel.

Their talk was slow and quiet, of fish and men
And fields back on the hill with fences down,
Hay to be made through long hot days with never a splash on the
oilskins,
Or the lift of water awake under half-inch pine.

The mackerel never ran; and if the herring
Had been only a story, a legend for midnight telling,
These would have launched their flats and tended the empty nets.

I know it now, remembering now the calm;
Remembering now the lowering care that lifted
From a face turned to the wind off Ragged Head.

These are the fellows who keep the salt in the blood.
Knowing it fresh in themselves, needful as hope,
They give to the cities bordered with woods and grass
A few homesick men, walking an alien street;
A few women, remembering misty stars
And the long grumbling sigh of the bay at night.

Words are never enough; these are aware
Somewhere deep in the soundless well of knowing,
That sea, in the flesh and nerves and the puzzling mind
Of children born to the long grip of its tide,
Must always wash the land's remotest heart.
These are the fellows who keep the salt in the blood.

BACK ROAD FARM

This house is built within a sheltering
Sweep of the hills. You will not find the sea
From attic windows; and the seasons bring
No lift and change of tide, here in the lee
Of the land's high windbreak, where the buffeting
Onshore wind is tripped on the mountain's knee.
No mist of blowing salt is flung to sting
The trusting flesh. You will not find the sea.

This property is private. Drifting rain
Beats on its shingles and its native stone;
The wind of August on its leaning grain
Is dark with shadow, and the leaves are blown
To a soft thunder. But the hills remain;
Their strength is certain and their purpose known.
Only at night, in the stillness, low and plain
You can hear the far deep rumour of sea on stone.

BIOGRAPHY

His speckled pastures dipped to meet the beach
Where the old fish huts stood. At his front door
A man could stand and see the whole wide reach
Of blue Atlantic. But he stayed ashore.

He stayed ashore and plowed, and drilled his rows,
And planned his hours and finished what he planned.
And made his profits: colts and calves and ewes
And buildings and piled stone and harrowed land.

He was a careful man, a trifle cold
To meet and talk to. There were some who thought
His hand was a bit grasping, when he sold;
A little slow to open when he bought.

But no one said it that way. When you heard
His habits mentioned, there would be a pause.
And then the soft explanatory word.
They said he was dry-footed. And he was.

LEO KENNEDY [1907-]

Leo Kennedy was born in Liverpool, England, of Irish parentage. He was brought to Canada at the age of five and was educated in Montreal, where he came in contact with the McGill poetry group. He went to the United States, and followed journalism as a career in Chicago and New York. His book of poems is *The Shrouding* (1934). (Cf. Collin, as above.)

RITE OF SPRING

[*A fragment*]

Interment of the Living.

April is no month for burials.
Blood root and trillium break out of cover,
And crocuses stir blindly in their cells,
Hawthorns bloom whitely, laburnums shudder
Profusion from dim boughs—slight daffodils
Defy the pale predominance of colour.
April is rather a month for subtle spells

And incantations chanted from old poets
By tremulous girls who are sick with the April weather
And boys whose glances are craven and bold together.
April is no month for burials.

And yet we must take the old loves and bury them under,
Empty the heart of ghosts that grieve and stumble
Down corridors sealed up to air and light:
We must gather last year's laurels before they crumble
And bury them out of sight.

For we must hurry them into the earth, and spread
A coverlet to hide each sheeted head
And stamp the mound out flat without misgiving—
Then gather flowered offerings for the living!

Lay them austerely in grave cloths scented with lilac.

Do not weep for the dead, Remorseful Lovers.
Do not regret the hawthorn spray that mattered
And is now crumbled and piteously scattered
With heat and frost between you and its flowering.
Do not recall the fragrance overpowering!
Do not remember the folded hands nor the eyes
Under the violet lids, nor the April bosom
Caressed to a breathless tumult of delight—
Make no dolorous plaint for the spilled bright
Hair, or for the brow too dearly cherished—
All these have perished
With the bent throat, and the lips that wooed and flattered—
And the words best understood when left unspoken—

All these things endured their time and are broken.

New loves await you with every burst of lilac,
Do not remember the dead in their lilac shrouds;
Do not recall their lilac-scented dust!
Strange mouths await your mouth, and other fingers
Prepare to touch you with a touch that lingers. . . .

Where sapling boys and girls are sweetly aching
For sudden April gusts, perfumed and heady—
For willow sprouts, and the smell of fresh earth breaking.

Set them into the earth to sprout and blossom.

DICK DIESPECKER [1907-]

Richard Alan Diespecker, son of Rudolph Louis and Anne Elizabeth (Bradley) Diespecker, was born at Adstock, England, and attended schools in Pretoria and Capetown, South Africa, and in Victoria, British Columbia. He continued his education at Victoria College and the University of British Columbia. He has worked at advertising, accounting, journalism, and directing of radio programmes (for which he has won three notable awards). In 1949 he was made Radio Director of the Vancouver *Daily Province.* He has written one novel and one book of poems, *Between Two Furious Oceans* (1944).

From BETWEEN TWO FURIOUS OCEANS

All these are your essence, you are their flesh and their force.
But you are more than these vital, uncountable things;
You are more than the rock and the tree and the root,
More than the yellowing grain, the whip of the bitter wind,
The sweat and the strain, the sinuous fish, the beaver pelt . . .
You are all these things and more, much more.

. . .

You are the Sunday morning mellow bells of God;
The tall cathedral and the wooden country church;
Parsons and monks and garment-heavy nuns; the cross
That burns by night upon the summit of Mount Royal;
Confession, the fingered beads, the lonely parish priest;
Beloved hymns that shake the good Protestant rafters;
The thundered sermon from the Presbyterian pulpit,
And the Anglican's polite responses; business as usual
At the Four Square Gospel, and the honest informality
That cheers the congregation at every United Church;
The cantor's solemn chant; the sour cornet notes
And the auto horns, drowning the anxious singer
At the Salvation Army meeting at the busy intersection.

You are the summer Saturday afternoon at home,
Stretched out full length upon the sun-bright backyard lawn;
The sounds that break the quiet, a kitchen screen-door's slam,
A far-off street car, children playing in the street,
Droning bees, a radio playing in a neighbour's home.
You are the hollyhocks that hide the pinewood fence,
The pampered rose bush and the bumptious dandelion.
You are the early morning and the milk truck's tinny shout,
Barking dogs, sparrows, bicycle bells and pans
Clattering in the kitchens up and down the street.
You are the calm contentment of the winter's night,
Reading and knitting in a circle round the fire,
Thick cream, hot-buttered toast and strawberry jam and tea.
You are the night shift in the pulp and paper mill;
Farmers lighting their lanterns in the greying dawn;
Bell-hops and stenographers and shoe-store clerks;
The clanging ambulance and the necroscopic hearse;
The baby's new-born wail and Death's sedentary stare.

You are the discord of the tuning orchestra
Before the majestic symphony;
The wild unbroken stallion of the plains;
You are the child growing to manhood,
Torn with the passions of his new maturity,
Quick with rage and hasty in decision,
Heady with strength and heedless of advice.
You are field and farm, mountain and lake and stream,
Steel and fire and human flesh;
Industry and sloth, love and hate.
You are a new nation, the raw nugget;
The untempered blade, the uncontrolled flame . . .
You are the white-hot steel, taking your shape
Under the hammer blows of Time. . . .

MONA GOULD [1908-]

Mona Helen (McTavish) Gould, Mrs. John Graham Gould, daughter of Alfred John and Ellen Jane (Howard) McTavish, was born in Prince Albert, Saskatchewan, and educated in the public and collegiate schools of London, Ontario. She has had wide experience in journalism, advertising, and publicity work, and has written film scripts and magazine articles. In 1952 she was made editor of the Woman's Page of *New Liberty*. Her two books of terse, pointed poems are *Tasting the Earth* (1943) and *I Run with the Fox* (1946).

THIS WAS MY BROTHER

This was my brother
At Dieppe,
Quietly a hero
Who gave his life
Like a gift,
Withholding nothing.

His youth . . . his love . . .
His enjoyment of being alive . . .
His future, like a book
With half the pages still uncut—

This was my brother
At Dieppe . . .
The one who built me a doll house
When I was seven,
Complete to the last small picture frame,
Nothing forgotten.

He was awfully good at fixing things,
At stepping into the breach when he was needed.

That's what he did at Dieppe;
He was needed.
And even death must have been a little ashamed
At his eagerness!

CAROL COATES

Alice Carol (Coates) Cassidy, Mrs. Haanel Cassidy, is the daughter of the late Dr. H. H. Coates, noted authority on Buddhism in Japan, where she spent her early life. Since graduating with distinction from the University of British Columbia in 1930, she has been engaged in educational work successively in Toronto, New York, Michael Hall (England), and Edinburgh. Her poetic output includes *Fancy Free* (1939), *Poems* (1942), and *Invitation to Mood* (1949).

LIGHT

Fresh light from a morning sky blocked through clouds,
blazing the tight tea bushes to a brittle green—
hot light of noon on bare rock, baking the summer heat
into the cracked parchness of earth—
serene light, filtering through bamboo plumes,
waving the afternoon away in graceful quietude—
frail light, falling from the shrinking sun
dreaming across illimitable distances of sea—
half moonlight, shimmering on rice fields
filled with harvest,
lying in the highway of the wind—
full moonlight,
feeling the freedom of your face,
against the pattern of the pillow,
sleeping.

COUNTRY REVERIE

Here is dominion for peace—
escape from the corporate world,
to air, unladen with the soot of cities,
to sky, uncluttered with commercial spires.

Here is the privilege, the power, the glory,
to satisfy the eye with soothing green,
to feel beneath the feet the patina of stones,
to sense against the flesh the shock of sunburned water.

Here upon the spirit the burden of loveliness is laid—
a satiety of air, of sun, that drugs the blood to dreamless sleep.
Here can the soul lazily expand,
stretch,
stand tiptoe to touch the stars.

CHORAL SYMPHONY CONDUCTOR

Darkness encloses the concert hall,
and from the white cuffs of the conductor,
hands, subtle as a ballet dancer's,
hold sound in awe.

Quietly they relent to unfold the promise of a note,
beckon the basses, rouse the sopranos, implore the tenors,
and hush the cellos to a whispering echo.

A lull falls, pulses, swells,
while hands seek rhythm in the subterranean depths of a drum,
draw melody from the ripple of a flute,
and with a final magic surge,
raise a shining fountain of song to shower the stars.

Now the violins scale perilous heights,
look down on trumpet, horn, bassoon, boisterous in battle,
on stalwart voices, steady, on the march,
till the hands, like a mighty sword,
cut concord, sever rhapsody, surround chorus with silence.

In benediction they pause,
secure from each his measured obedience,
summon momentum,
till, by the fervour of a heavenward finger,
urge sound to rise majestic,
ride valiant through the celestial arch of his arms.

THE CIRCLE

O seeker of the Greater Light,
draw with the compass of compassion
the circle of thy life.
With centre fixed in Cosmic Will,
and radius wide,
circumscribe the symbol of the Infinite.

Then shall all they who move in its confines,
sense, though with slow awareness,
the significance of centre,
and feel, in the swing of dedicated will,
the infinity of its embrace.

THOMAS SAUNDERS [1909-]

Thomas Saunders was born in Scotland and came to Canada at the age of eleven. During the Second World War he served in the Chaplaincy of the Army in Canada, Great Britain, and Northwest Europe. He later became minister of Chalmers United Church, Winnipeg. His two books of poetry are *Scrub Oak* (1949) and *Horizontal World* (1951). He conducts a causerie in the Winnipeg *Tribune*.

HORIZONTAL WORLD

Some people, now, like mountains, where the shafts
Of rock, untimbered, thrust, in jagged lines,
Against the sky. I get a crick behind
My neck in land like that. Skyscraper-worlds—
Man-made or nature's—keep me looking up.
It's all right for a time, to get the view;
But I don't want to live in land like that.
I like a horizontal world, where I
Can live and breathe without the heavens falling
In on me.

I don't mind hills so much—
They seem more friendly. You can get on terms
Of living with a hill, neighbourly-like.
But why do people want to spoil the hills,
Cutting them up in patches they call fields?
Three strides, and you go barging in a fence,
Or topple in a ditch. I don't like men
Making a pattern of unpatterned hills.

Not that there's easy beauty on the plains—
You catch it only from the earth and sky;
And then by living there, not for a day,
Or months, but years. In time, even the snow
In winter takes its hold on you, till there
Is no place else a man can live and feel
On terms with living. Horizontal worlds,
Somehow, catch all the height and breadth of sky.

END OF STEEL

The old man had been listless, but he perked
Up at my question. "Yup," he said, "this was
The end of steel when I come here. Some folks
Went further west, but I stayed put. Because?
—Well, here was land, and why look further?"
He jerked
A hand out vaguely. "It was quite a hoax,"
He said, "them critters headin' west when all
I done was squat."

I eyed his buildings, bare,
Untended, and swept the niggard fields he'd claimed
As his.

A few miles west I'd seen the rare
Assiniboine valley, where the farmlands sprawl
Across the flats—rich, heavy land, enflamed
With June's wild roses and the green of crops.

"Some folks went further west, but I stayed put."
He seemed to find his mirth hard to conceal.
Others had ventured further in pursuit
Of land, and here and there had made their stops.
But he had squatted at the end of steel.

JEAN PERCIVAL WADDELL

Mrs. Jean Percival Waddell wrote three books of inspirational verse, *Down Aisles of Calm* (1934), *A Harp in the Wind* (1938), and *Candled by Stars* (1944), the last with an Introduction by Rev. Norman Stewart Dowd, Executive Secretary of the Canadian Congress of Labour, Ottawa.

HALF-LIGHT

Dark is the sapphire night
  Candled alone by stars.
Dream-lit are eyes when sleep
  Lowers shutters and bars.

Truth, wide-windowed to light,
  By the unknown is veiled.
May not the groping mind
  Know unblinded, unpaled?

Dusks and darks of the soul
  Dimming death's dawn of day,
Fold dun garments of night,
  Trembling, shudder away.

RHYTHM

Rhythm in the pulse of Time;
  Rhythm in the under-sea;
Rhythm in season and clime;
  Rhythm in the heart of me;

Rhythm in the scent of the flower;
  Rhythm in the note of a bird;
Dynamic urgence of Power;
  Vital force of a word;

Universe steady in sweep,
Weighted and starred above,
Swing wide and high and deep
Ordered and rhythmed of love.

Love! Living rhythm of all,
Vibrant in human life,
Shatter hate's deadly thrall,
Cut the currents of strife.

GRETA LEORA ROSE [1909-]

Greta Leora Rose, daughter of Rev. I. Adams and Leora Ernestine (Fuller) Rose, was born at Keswick Ridge, New Brunswick. She graduated from Acadia University in 1931, spent the next six years in Halifax, three teaching at the School for the Blind and three engaged in secretarial work, studied Library Science at Simmonds (1937-1938), and has since held different positions as librarian in New England, from 1946 to the present in Lynn, Massachusetts. Besides articles and poems in periodicals, she has published two books of verse, *Wings Over Walls* (1949) and *Cables and Cobwebs* (1952).

SPRING IS AT WORK WITH BEGINNINGS OF THINGS

Spring is at work with beginnings of things—
Things that lie close to the earth,
That sleep and grow in their sleeping,
Then awake with the miracle, birth.
Green folded fingers press through the soil,
Guarding their secrets of bloom.
Grasses that carpet each meadow and hill
Are lifted once more from the loom.
Steaming brown furrows the plough has upturned,
Making a cradle for seeds.
Sowing and reaping, the seasons revolve,
Meeting the depth of man's needs.
Out of earth's mystery, into the light,
Gifts are now placed in our hand.
Over and over the drama unfolds—
Life through the heart of the land.
With perfect creation each kingdom is formed,
In wisdom each given its worth,
When spring is at work with beginnings of things—
Things that lie close to the earth.

DOROTHY ROBERTS

Mrs. Dorothy Mary Gostwick (Roberts) Leisner is the daughter of George Edward Theodore Goodridge and Frances Seymour (Allen) Roberts. She has had some journalistic experience and has published *Songs for Swift Feet* (1927).

THE GOOSE GIRL

In kirtle of myrtle the goose girl goes
From hill to hill on her flyaway toes,
With geese so gabbly and gobbly and grey.
Oh, the braids of her ripe corn hair are gay
With brown-eyed Susan and cinnamon rose,
While kingcup and clover tangle her toes.

Shepherds skip after her, piping away.
For her flighty heart they would play all day.
There's a winding of horns when cowherds spy
Her pass where the hillside is humpy and high.
Many and many the merry swains
That kiss her in apple and hawthorn lanes.

Oh, her skin smells sweet as the cinnamon rose,
And little and little the shepherd knows,
As he follows her far and pipes and blows
To her flighty heart and flyaway toes,
That it matters no whit what yokels sing—
For some day the goose girl will marry a king!

SISTERS

My sister and I when we were close together
Clear to each other
Used to slide down beneath the river surface
And in a twist of current see the race
Of water break us from our sunny grace.

Wavering, shattered, glimmering, each saw
No happy girl she knew
But underwater strangeness, shift and flaw,
Until the bubbles of our laughter drew
Us bursting up to the air.

Then we lay bare
And sure and shapely in each other's eyes—
We who no more to certainty can rise

But caught submerged in current of the years
See, wavering, each a shape that never clears.

A. M. KLEIN [1909-]

Abraham Moses Klein, son of Colman and Yetta (Morantz) Klein, was born in Montreal and educated in Arts at McGill University and in law at the University of Montreal. In addition to his legal practice, he has found time to lecture on poetry at McGill. His thorough mastery of the history and culture of his race is shown in his novel, *The Flying Scroll* (1951), and in much of his poetry. *Hath not a Jew* (1940), *The Hitleriad* (1942), and *Poems* (1944), were followed by *The Rocking Chair and Other Poems* (1948), which won the Governor-General's Medal and tied for second place in the annual writing contest of the Quebec government for Canadian literature in English, and the contents of which poetically interpret French-Canadian life in the Province of Quebec. (Cf. W. E. Collin and E. K. Brown, as above.)

DESIGN FOR MEDIÆVAL TAPESTRY

Somewhere a hungry muzzle rooted.
The frogs among the sedges croaked.
Into the night a screech-owl hooted.

A clawed mouse squeaked and struggled, choked.
The wind pushed antlers through the bushes.
Terror stalked through the forest, cloaked.

Was it a robber broke the bushes?
Was it a knight in armoured thews,
Walking in mud, and bending rushes?

Was it a provost seeking Jews?
The Hebrews shivered; their teeth rattled;
Their beards glittered with gelid dews.

Gulped they their groans, for silence tattled;
They crushed their sighs, for quiet heard;
They had had their thoughts on Israel battled

By pagan and by Christian horde.
They moved their lips in pious anguish.
They made no sound. They never stirred.

Reb Zadoc has memories.

Reb Zadoc's brain is a German town:
Hermits come from lonely grottos
Preaching the right for Jews to drown;

Soldiers who vaunt their holy mottos
Stroking the cross that is a sword;
Barons plotting in cabal sottos;

A lady spitting on the abhorred.
The market-place and faggot-fire—
A hangman burning God's true word;

A clean-shaved traitor-Jew; a friar
Dropping his beads upon his paunch;
The heavens speared by a Gothic spire;

The Judengasse and its stench
Rising from dark and guarded alleys
Where Jew is neighboured to harlot-wench

Perforce ecclesiastic malice;
The exile-booths of Jacob where
Fat burghers come to pawn a chalice

While whistling a Jew-hating air;
Peasants regarding Jews and seeking
The hooves, the tail, the horn-crowned hair;

And target for a muddy streaking,
The yellow badge upon the breast,
The vengeance of a papal wreaking;

The imposts paid for this fine crest;
Gay bailiffs serving writs of seizure;
Even the town fool and his jest—

Stroking his beard with slowly leisure,
A beard that was but merely down,
Rubbing his palms with gloating pleasure,

Counting fictitious crown after crown.
Reb Zadoc's brain is a torture-dungeon;
Reb Zadoc's brain is a German town.

Reb Daniel Shochet reflects.

The toad seeks out its mud; the mouse discovers
The nibbled hole; the sparrow owns its nest;
About the blind mole earthy shelter hovers.

The louse avows the head where it is guest;
Even the roach calls some dark fent his dwelling.
But Israel owns a sepulchre, at best.

Nahum-this-also-is-for-the-good ponders.

The wrath of God is just. His punishment
Is most desirable. The flesh of Jacob
Implores the scourge. For this was Israel meant.

Below we have no life. But we will wake up
Beyond, where popes will lave our feet, where princes
Will heed our insignificantest hiccup.

The sins of Israel only blood-shed rinses.
We teach endurance. Lo, we are not spent.
We die, we live; at once we are three tenses.

Our skeletons are bibles; flesh is rent
Only to prove a thesis, stamp a moral.
The rack prepared: for this was Israel meant.

Isaiah Epicure avers.

Seek reasons; rifle your theology;
Philosophize; expend your dialectic;
Decipher and translate God's diary;

Discover causes, primal and eclectic;
I cannot; all I know is this:
The pain doth render flesh most sore and hectic:

That lance-points prick; that scorched bones hiss;
That thumbscrews agonize, and that a martyr
Is mad if he considers these things bliss.

Job reviles.

God is grown ancient. He no longer hears.
He has been deafened by his perfect thunders.
With clouds for cotton he has stopped his ears.

The Lord is purblind; and his heaven sunders
Him from the peccadillos of this earth.
He meditates his youth; he dreams; he wonders.

His cherubs have acquired beards and girth.
They cannot move to do his bidding. Even
The angels yawn. Satan preserves his mirth.

How long, O Lord, will Israel's heart be riven?
How long will we cry to a dotard God
To let us keep the breath that He has given?

How long will you sit on your throne, and nod?

Judith makes comparisons.

Judith had heard a troubadour
Singing beneath a castle-turret
Of truth, chivalry, and honour,
Of virtue, and of gallant merit,—
Judith had heard a troubadour
Lauding the parfait knightly spirit,
Singing beneath the ivied wall.
The cross-marked varlet Judith wrestled
Was not like these at all, at all. . .

Ezekiel the Simple opines.

If we will fast for forty days; if we
Will read the psalms thrice over; if we offer
To God some blossom-bursting litany,

And to the poor a portion of the coffer;
If we don sack-cloth, and let ashes rain
Upon our heads, despite the boor and scoffer,

Certes, these things will never be again.

Solomon Talmudi considers his life.

Rather that these blood-thirsty pious vandals,
Bearing sable in heart, and gules on arm,
Had made me ready for the cerement-candles,

Than that they should have taken my one charm
Against mortality, my exegesis:
The script that gave the maggot the alarm.

Jews would have crumpled Rashi's simple thesis
On reading this, and Ibn Ezra's version;
Maimonides they would have torn to pieces.

For here, in black and white, by God's conversion,
I had plucked secrets from the pentateuch,
And gathered strange arcana from dispersion,

The essence and quintessence of the book!
Green immortality smiled out its promise—
I hung my gaberdine on heaven's hook.

Refuting Duns, and aquinatic Thomas,
Confounding Moslems, proving the one creed
A simple sentence broken by no commas,

I thought to win myself eternal meed,
I thought to move the soul with sacred lever
And lift the heart to God in very deed.

Ah, woe is me, and to my own endeavour,
That on that day they burned my manuscript,
And lost my name, for certain, and for ever!

Simeon takes hints from his environs.

Heaven is God's grimace at us on high.
This land is a cathedral; speech, its sermon.
The moon is a rude gargoyle in the sky.

The leaves rustle. Come, who will now determine
Whether this be the wind, or priestly robes.
The frogs croak out ecclesiastic German,

Whereby our slavish ears have punctured lobes.
The stars are mass-lamps on a lofty altar;
Even the angels are Judaeophobes.

There is one path; in it I shall not falter.
Let me rush to the bosom of the state
And church, grasp lawyer-code and monkish psalter,

And being Christianus Simeon, late
Of Jewry, have much comfort and salvation—
Salvation in this life, at any rate.

Esther hears echoes of his voice.

How sweetly did he sing grace after meals!
He now is silent. He has fed on sorrow.
He lies where he is spurned by faithless heels.

His voice was honey. Lovers well might borrow
Warmth from his words. His words were musical,
Making the night so sweet, so sweet the morrow!

Can I forget the tremors of his call?
Can kiddush benediction be forgotten?
His blood is spilled like wine. The earth is sharp with gall.

As soothing as the promises begotten
Of penitence and love; as lovely as
The turtle-dove; as soft as snow in cotton,

Whether he lulled a child or crooned the laws,
And sacred as the eighteen prayers, so even
His voice. His voice was so. His voice that was. . .

The burgher sleeps beside his wife, and dreams
Of human venery, and Hebrew quarry.
His sleep contrives him many little schemes.

There will be Jews, dead, moribund and gory;
There will be booty; there will be dark maids
And there will be a right good spicy story. . .

The moon has left her virgil. Lucifer fades.
Whither shall we betake ourselves, O Father?
Whither to flee? And where to find our aids?

The wrath of people is like foam and lather,
Risen against us. Wherefore, Lord, and why?
The winds assemble; the cold and hot winds gather

To scatter us. They do not heed our cry.
The sun rises and leaps the red horizon,
And like a bloodhound swoops across the sky.

BAAL SHEM TOV

Be his memory forever green and rich,
Like moss upon a stone at a brook's edge,
That rabbi of infants, man of children's love,
Greybeard and leader of tots, the Baal Shem Tov!
Who, hearing a child's song float on sunlit air
Heard far more piety than in a prayer
That issued from ten synagogal throats;
Who seeing an urchin bring a starved mare oats,
Beheld that godliness which can break bars
Of heaven padlocked with its studded stars;

The Baal Shem Tov, who better than liturgy
Loved speech with teamsters and with gypsies! Be
His memory every splendid like a jewel,
His, who bore children on his back to school
And, with a trick to silence their small grief,
Crossed many a stream upon a handkerchief.
Oh, be there ever pure minds and bright eyes,
Homage of children ever, eulogies
Of little folk so that the humble fame
Of the Baal Shem, the Master of the Name,
May be forever green and fresh and rich,
Like moss upon a stone at a brook's edge.

THE ROCKING CHAIR

It seconds the crickets of the province. Heard
in the clean lamplit farmhouses of Quebec,—
wooden,—it is no less a national bird;
and rivals, in its cage, the mere stuttering clock.
To its time, the evenings are rolled away;
and in its peace the pensive mother knits
contentment to be worn by her family,
grown-up, but still cradled by the chair in which she sits.

It is also the old man's pet, pair to his pipe,
the two aids of his arithmetic and plans,
plans rocking and puffing into market-shape;
and it is the toddler's game and dangerous dance.
Moved to the verandah, on summer Sundays, it is,
among the hanging plants, the girls, the boy-friends,
sabbatical and clumsy, like the white haloes
dangling above the blue serge suits of the young men.

It has a personality of its own;
is a character (like that old drunk Lacoste,
exhaling amber, and toppling on his pins);
it is alive; individual; and no less
an identity than those about it. And
it is tradition. Centuries have been flicked
from its arcs, alternately flicked and pinned.
It rolls with the gait of St. Malo. It is act

and symbol, symbol of this static folk
which moves in segments, and returns to base,—
a sunken pendulum: *invoke, revoke;*
loosed yon, leashed hither, motion on no space.
O, like some Anjou ballad, all refrain,
which turns about its longing, and seems to move
to make a pleasure out of repeated pain,
its music moves, as if always back to a first love.

GRAIN ELEVATOR

Up from the low-roofed dockyard warehouses
it rises blind and babylonian
like something out of legend. Something seen
in a children's coloured book. Leviathan
swamped on our shore? The cliffs of some other river?
The blind ark lost and petrified? A cave
built to look innocent, by pirates? Or
some eastern tomb a travelled patron here makes local?

But even when known, it's more than what it is:
for here, as in a Josephdream, bow down
the sheaves, the grains, the scruples of the sun
garnered for darkness; and Saskatchewan
is rolled like a rug of a thick and golden thread.
O prison of prairies, ship in whose galleys roll
sunshines like so many shaven heads,
waiting the bushel-burst out of the beached bastille!

Sometimes, it makes me think Arabian,
the grain picked up, like tic-tacs out of time:
first one; an other; singly; one by one;—
to save life. Sometimes, some other races claim
the twinship of my thought,—as the river stirs
restless in a white Caucasian sleep,
or, as in the steerage of the elevators,
the grains, Mongolian and crowded, dream.

A box: cement, hugeness, and rightangles—
merely the sight of it leaning in my eyes
mixes up continents and makes a montage
of inconsequent time and uncontiguous space.
It's because it's bread. It's because
bread is its theme, an absolute. Because
always this great box flowers over us
with all the coloured faces of mankind. . .

THE SPINNING WHEEL

You can find it only in attics or in ads,
heirloom a grandmother explains, woodcut
to show them native, quaint, and to be had
at the fee feudal; but
as object it does not exist, is aftermath
of *autre temps* when at this circle sat
domesticity,
and girls wearing the black and high-necked blouse
at its spokes played house.

Now it is antique, like the *fleur de lys*,
a wooden fable out of the olden time,—
as if the epileptic loom and mad factory
that make a pantomime
out of this wheel do so for picturesqueness
only, and to achieve a fine excess,
not for the dividend
surely. No. Just to preserve romance,
the rites, the wage-rates of old France.

Symbol, it still exists; the seigneur still,
though now drab and incorporate, holds domain
pre-eminent; still, to his power-foaming mill
the farmer brings his grain
his golden daughters made banality;
and still, still do they pay the seigneury
the hourly corvée,
the stolen quotient of the unnatural yields
of their woven acres and their linen fields.

MONTREAL

I

O city metropole, isle riverain!
Your ancient pavages and sainted routs
Traverse my spirit's conjured avenues!
Splendour erablic of your promenades
Foliates there, and there your maisonry
Of pendent balcon and escalier'd march,
Unique midst English habitat,
Is vivid Normandy!

II

You populate the pupils of my eyes:
Thus, does the Indian, plumèd, furtivate
Still through your painted autumns, Ville-Marie!
Though palisades have passed, though calumet
With tabac of your peace enfumes the air,
Still do I spy the phantom, aquiline,
Genuflect, moccasin'd, behind
His statue in the square!

III

Thus, costumed images before me pass,
Haunting your archives architectural:
Coureur de bois, in posts where pelts were portaged;
Seigneur within his candled manoir; Scot
Ambulant through his bank, pillar'd and vast.
Within your chapels, voyaged mariners
Still pray, and personage departed,
All present from your past!

IV

Grand port of navigations, multiple
The lexicons uncargo'd at your quays,
Sonnant though strange to me; but chiefest, I,
Auditor of your music, cherish the
Joined double-melodied vocabulaire
Where English vocable and roll Ecossic,
Mollified by the parle of French
Bilinguefact your air!

V

Such your suaver voice, hushed Hochelaga!
But for me also sound your potencies,
Fortissimos of sirens fluvial,
Bruit of manufactory, and thunder
From foundry issuant, all puissant tone
Implenishing your hebdomad; and then
Sanct silence, and your argent belfries
Clamant in orison!

VI

You are a part of me, O all your quartiers—
And of dire pauvrete and of richesse—
To finished time my homage loyal claim;
You are locale of infancy, milieu
Vital of institutes that formed my fate;
And you above the city, scintillant,
Mount Royal, are my spirit's mother,
Almative, poitrinate!

VII

Never do I sojourn in alien place
But I do languish for your scenes and sounds,
City of reverie, nostalgic isle,
Pendant most brilliant on Laurentian cord!
The coigns of your boulevards—my signiory—
Your suburbs are my exile's verdure fresh,
Your parks, your fountain'd parks—
Pasture of memory!

VIII

City, O City, you are vision'd as
A parchemin roll of saecular exploit
Inked with the script of eterne souvenir!
You are in sound, chanson and instrument!
Mental, you rest forever edified
With tower and dome; and in these beating valves,
Here in these beating valves, you will
For all my mortal time reside!

RALPH GUSTAFSON [1909-]

Ralph Barker Gustafson, son of Carl Otto and Ella Gertrude (Barker) Gustafson, was born at Lime Ridge, Quebec, and educated at Bishop's College and Oxford University. He taught school, lived for a while in London, England, spent 1942 to 1946 with the British Information Service, and has since lived in New York. He has edited one anthology of Canadian prose, two of Canadian poetry, written a monograph on the composer Villa-Lobos, articles, short stories of distinction, and *Poetry and Canada* (1945), and five books of poems: *The Golden Chalice* (1935), for which he received the David Prize of the Quebec government; *Alfred the Great* (1937), a play in blank verse; *Epithalamium in Time of War* (1941), for his sister's wedding; *Lyrics Unromantic* (1942); *Flight into Darkness* (1944).

ON THE ROAD TO VICENZA

Lopsided with God
The village leans.
The heat burns down.
Orange and parched olive
Only, the landscape.
On its iron swivel
From Philadelphia
The coarse bell clanks
The Saints' sweet martyrdom.

In the shade
Of her doorsill
The mother sits
Picking the crust
Of a three-year sore
Interesting
On one foot

As who should swat a fly
On Titian's Virgin's nose

LEGEND

Whoever is washed ashore at that place—
Many come there but thrust by so fierce a sun
The vast cliffs cast no shadow, plunge a passage
Inland where foliage and whistling paradise-birds
Offer comfort—whoever has got up,
Standing, certainty under his adjusting heels
And height tugged by the tide, ocean rinsing
From flank and belly, ravelling loins with wet,
Whoever has stayed, solitary in those tropics,
The caverns of his chest asking acres,
he,
Doomed in that landscape but among magnificence,
By shell and seafoam tampered with, his senses
As though by her of Aeaea used, exquisite—
He, that salt upon his time's tongue,
Knows, standing the margin ocean and sand,
Ilium toppled thunder his ears, what's left
Of Helen naked drag between his toes.

DEDICATION

"They shall not die in vain," we said.
"Let us impose, since we forget
The hopeless giant alphabet,
Great stones above the general dead,"
The living said.

"They shall not be outdone in stones.
Generously, sculptured grief shall stand
In general over numbered bones
With book and index near at hand
For particular sons.

"And we the living left in peace
Will set aside such legal date
At such and suchlike time or state
Or place as meet and fitting is,
Respecting this."

O boy, locked in the grisly hollow,
You who once idly peeled a willow-
switch, whistling, wondering at the stick
Of willow's whiteness clean and slick,
Do not believe that we shall bury
You with words: aptly carry
Cloth flowers, proxy for love.
O we have done with granite grief
And silk denials: summing you
Within the minutes' silence—two!
More than you had need to target
Hate, against the pitiless bullet's
Calculated greed oppose
Heart's anger: falling, gave to us
What power to lance the pocket of
An easy past, what use of love
Teaching children's laughter loud
On shutters in an evil street,
What edge, O death, of days, delight?
What linch of love, spate of sun?
And shall we with a sedentary noun
Signature receipt, having had read
The catechism of the generous dead?

You who live, see! These,
These were his hills where laughter was
And counted years of longing, grain
And wintry apples scorched in sun,
Of corded hemlock deep in snow.
Here at his seven birches growing
Oblique by the boulder the fence has stopped—
Rusted wire, posts lopped
For staking. To circle love, he said.
And there are other fables made:
Of plough and intricate loom; the broken
Soldier on the sill; and latin
Parchment framed, conferring letters
On hooded death; the axe, the motto
Against the wall; abandoned hills.

Fables for stout reading. Tales
Listened to by twice-told death.
Our tongue how silent, muscles lithe
O land, hoist by the lag-end of little
Deeds? What lack of monstrous metal,
Monumental mouths; over
This land what love, wheel, lever
Of God, anchorage, pivot of days,
Remembering?

    Old and certain the sea,
The mountain-tilted sky, old,
Older than words, than you are old,
Boy, who never thought to point the hill
With dawn! Only as these, our telling:
As men labour: as harvest done:
At dusk a joyful walking home.
Of nearer things: how he was young,
And died, a silent writing down.

R. E. RASHLEY [1909-]

R. E. Rashley was born in Leicester, England, and came with his parents to Canada *via* Australia when two years old. Except for another two years in Australia, he has lived in Saskatchewan. He is Director of Correspondence Courses for the University of Saskatchewan. He has published *Voyageur and Other Poems* (1946) and *Portrait and Other Poems* (1953).

VOYAGEUR

Sing a little as the feet unwearied
Pattern a wreath for momentary flowers,
Stop where the flicker tail more wisely
Stores wheat,
Or even more wisely still,
Bores into the hard crust beneath the blowing,
Laugh while sun invigorates
And echo back the coyote cries,
Small rosebud mockery in mirth
Learning what later years will wish to unlearn.

Strike out with secure leather
Confidently,
Not seeing that all the other feet
Have only beaten the ground dry,
Stamped out the live roots, left the soil to drift;
Step out with fine live muscle
And green bone springing,
Eye on the distance, mind in the wide sky,
Journey the spring out and the summer
Muscle leaning, bone hardening,
But the coyote fear still over the horizon,
Closing a little in, crying a little in the night
And the dull weather.

Creep into a cold wind and a grey sky,
Snow drifting,
Toes no longer gripping, loose in the drift,
Looking about for a rock in a world of shift,
Seeing for the first time the waste travelled,
Feeling for the first time the emptiness,
Seeing only the vague snow,
Searching in vain for a star,
Hearing, insistent now, the lone companion,
The coyote crying in the night and the dusk.

And more and more as the ways weary
The coyote, trembling along the bush edge,
Slinking along between little hills,
At night slips out to the hill tops
And cries in many voices,
Fear calling fear by secret names,
Doubt in confusion
And mind divided, incoherent in the dark
Unanswering.

Feeling the panic of impermanence,
Slipping out of a shifting empty world,
Seek desperately for landmarks,
Take what you find about you in the dusk,
A buffalo skull, splinter through eyesocket
Fixed to a stump, O, so securely,
A thigh bone pointed on a rock,
Or here where a house stood, pile
Dead stones,
Plant weeds in arrows on the hillsides,
Make marks.

And in the end the wide wind rippled world
Always alien, now empty,
The voyageur quite vanished,
And from the hill the small ignoble clamour,
The coyote, lonely on the wind swept summit.

PORTRAIT OF AN INDIAN

Spring made little promise
And the summer burned.
Fall came meagrely;
Winter struck with a blade of ice.
The years, one after the other, were much in this wise.

And one spoke, in defeat, counselling his people:
"From nothing we come, into nothing we go.
A little shadow runs across the grass
Into the sunset."

One warrior was covered with wounds.
He delighted in saying
How he had broken the feathered ends
And thrust the bared rods out through his body.
Indeed, it was true;
It could have been done in no other way.

Only those survived
Who grew to unrelenting vigilance,
Who lit their counter-fires of patience
Down wind against the blaze
And thrust against the ice, as cold, as hard,
Pride.

A bitter clime!
But where else, out of only flesh and bone,
Could time carve out such perverse granite
Or wind and winter mate like this in line.

CATERPILLAR

This yellow velvet visitor
Is a mysterious stranger
To the little boy on the street
Who squats watching it ripple over concrete.

To me,
It is a deep cut bank
Grown rank with willows,
Pungent in the blazing noons,
Which flowered at the appropriate time
Into brilliant identical caterpillars.

The little urchin,
Taken to just such a place,
Would recall a heaven of cars on the street,
Rain in the gutters,
Fruit stores, and movies, and the debris
Of careless living, gathered behind garages, maybe.

It is the same longing for home that stirs us all.
But home is just where the child first played
As a child.
The real longing is for the irrecoverable,
Barely-forgotten, child's world.

DOROTHY LIVESAY [1909-]

Dorothy Livesay, in private life Mrs. Duncan Cameron Macnair, of Vancouver, British Columbia, is the daughter of John Frederick Bligh and Florence Hamilton (Randal) Livesay, both authors. She was born in Winnipeg, Manitoba, and educated at Glen Mawr and Trinity College, Toronto, at the Sorbonne, and again at the University of Toronto. She has been very active in radio work and has been awarded the Lorne Pierce Gold Medal of the Royal Society of Canada for her contribution to literature. Her poetic achievement is shown in *Signposts* (1932), *Day and Night* (1944), awarded the Governor-General's Medal, and ranked as the publisher's best in its field for 1944, *Poems for People* (1947), also awarded the Governor-General's Medal, and *Call My People Home* (1950). (Cf. W. E. Collin and E. K. Brown, as above.)

EPILOGUE TO THE OUTRIDER

We prayed for miracles: the prairie dry,
Our bread became a blister in the sun;
We watched the serene untouchable vault of sky
—In vain our bitter labour had been done.

We prayed to see the racing clouds at bay
Rumpled like sheets after a night of joy,
To stand quite still and let the deluged day
Of rain's releasing, surge up and destroy.

We prayed for miracles, and had no wands
Nor wits about us; strained in a pointed prayer
We were so many windmills without hands
To whirl and drag the water up to air.

A runner sent ahead, returned with news:
"There is no milk nor honey flowing there.
Others allay the thirst with their own blood
Cool with their sweat, and fertilize despair."

O new found land! Sudden release of lungs,
Our own breath blows the world! Our veins, unbound
Set free the fighting heart. We speak with tongues—
This struggle is our miracle new found.

CONTACT

He gave his card. How many times have I
Accepted without looking, smiled, and stuffed
It into pocket, said a short good-bye
Dismissed the person and the incident.
But on the night we met, the inner mind
Prayed for a sign: O name your name aloud
And let there be no printed card, designed
To hide in diary, pocketed until
The cleaner's man inserts it with his bill
(After the loss, the frantic search.) Be proud!

Proclaim yourself; and let my wakened eyes
Perceive the stranger. Be the one who came
As love long known, yet taking by surprise—
Stopping the breath with banner of a name.

IMPROVISATION ON AN OLD THEME

If I must go, let it be easy, slow
The curve complete, and a sure swerve
To the goal. Let it be slow and sweet
To know how leaf consumes its time,
How petal sucks to the sun's heat;
Or as old bones, settling into soil,
Eyes too remote for earth's light
Set on a solar circle whose bright
Business brims the universe.

Let me know well how the winds blow
Smoky in autumn with leaf reek;
And summer's sleek surrender,
Torching the maple; let my branches sigh
For snow, and in a muffled mantle, let me go.

Keep me for quiet. Save me ever from
Disastrous ending sounding without drum,
No decent exhalation of the breath—
The dazzling violence of atomic death.

THE INHERITORS

I

Where tom-tom drummed
Stunning its wings
Bold as the thunderbird
The cloud clapped sky;
Where the beach fires blazed
And totems camped
Holding the village
History high—

There came the dark ones
Home to their dancing
To the sun's pulsing
Rhythm vibrating
To bird wings drumming
Thunder creating.

There shrouding cedars
And pointing pines
Swayed in the circle
Of curving thighs
And sand's cool crescent
Burned with the feet
Of winged sun's leap
And the tom-tom beat.

II

Now it is vanished—
Wrested away
The tide washes up
Where children play
No carved bird watches
The waiting sky
No thunder snatches
The wind away.

But out on the smooth, the glistening curl
Where foam flecked-footprints stabbed and whirled
Far now the children, black as midgets
Dance in the crescent, plunge to the sun:

Leaping and diving, in silhouette motion
Circling and swaying, caught in creation
Caught in the echo of ancient music
Beating on treetop, throbbing on tom-tom—
Bound by the heart-beat pulse of a drum!

INTERVAL WITH FIRE

Before I began to burn
with new found fire
this wintry summer had blown,
had flown over.

Before I made the discovery
staked the claim
and stood at the rock's end
crying a name,

stood arrested
on the alpine meadow
in amber light
flowing like honey—

before realization
of the total wonder
winter spoke
clouds massed in thunder.

I lifted my pack
turned to rock's shadow
closing my eyes
from the amber meadow.

Where storm swung down
to chasms again
I weighed my way
in the chill rain.

. . .

Now in the valley
past fisted cedars
black bog, lecherous arms
of devil's club

safe over burnt-out ledges
knee deep in slash
(the whited sepulchres
of our devotion)

safe at the level of
hitch-hike settlements
overflow from
a city's coldness

where the old man broods
on his apple tree, bitten
brown with evil
by the moth's bulldozer

and the old woman gathers
sour blackberries
from a wet season,
a sodden September—

safe, but unsure
(back in the common place)
that there had ever been
an amazement

upon my eyes, a blast
of energy electrifying
my mind, a morning
when the heart blossomed.

(For the time of every day
is the time of misgiving:
in the habit of living
begins disbelief).

So safe, but unsure
in the wet glitter of blessing
showered from a cherry-tree
shaken in September—

the sky turned
and the rain shoved over:
I felt an arresting hand
held on the shoulder.

Sun called and controlled me
his shadow shared me
I rose to the mountains
where fire is no stranger.

His day is now mine,
an entering river
his blaze in my blood
flowing forever.

LAMENT

What moved me, was the way your hand
Lay in my hand, not withering,
But warm, like a hand cooled in a stream
And purling still; or a bird caught in a snare,
Wings folded stiff, eyes in a stare,
But still alive with the fear,
Heart hoarse with hope—
So your hand; your dead hand, my dear.

And the veins, still mounting as blue rivers, clear,
Mounting towards the tentative finger-tips,
The delta where four seas draw near—
Your fingers promontories into colourless air
Were rosy still—not chalk (like cliffs
You knew in boyhood, Isle of Wight);
But blushed with colour from the sun you sought
And muscular from garden toil;
Stained with the purple of an iris bloom,
Violas grown for a certain room;
Hands seeking faiënce, filagree,
Chinese lacquer and ivory,—
Brussels lace; and a walnut piece
Carved by a hand now phosphorus.

What moved me, was the way your hand
Held life, although the pulse was gone.
The hand that carpentered a children's chair,
Carved out a stair
Held leash upon a dog in strain,
Gripped wheel, swung sail,
Flicked horse's rein,
And then again
Moved kings and queens meticulous on a board,
Slashed out the cards, cut bread, and poured
A purring cup of tea;
The hand so neat and nimble
Could make a tennis partner tremble,
Write a resounding round
Of sonorous verbs and nouns—
Hand that would not strike a child, and yet
Could ring a bell and send a man to doom.
And now unmoving in this Spartan room
The hand still speaks;
After the brain was fogged
And the tight lips tighter shut,
After the shy appraising eyes
Relinquished fire for the sea's green gaze—
The hand still breathes, fastens its hold on life:
Demands the whole, establishes the strife.

What moved me was the way your hand
Lay cool in mine, not withering;
As bird still breathes, and stream runs clear—
So your hand; your dead hand, my dear.

GUY GLOVER [1909-]

Guy Glover was born in London, England, and came to Canada with his parents in 1913. Educated in Calgary and Vancouver, he graduated with honours from the University of British Columbia. An amateur actor and theatre director (1931-1936), he became a professional actor and theatre director in London, England (1936-1939). Mr. Glover joined the staff of the National Film Board of Canada in 1941, where he is now Executive Producer. He is also a Director of the Canadian Ballet Festival Association. Mr. Glover has written poetry, literary and ballet criticism which has appeared in *Poetry* (Chicago), *Northern Review, Canadian Art* and *Queen's Quarterly.*

THE LUCIFER

Cold as the thin Marquis who bit when kissing,
Bold as the arctic flyer with the dated plane,
He stood in the doorway daring our whispers.
He had many true-loves—but never one.

Freighted with wishes as dangerous as dynamite,
Glutted with hysteria as a sailor's dawn,
He wept in his anguish, each tear an eyeful.
He had many true-loves—but never one.

Wrung as the pale Princess who bruised so easily,
Strong as the Bull with the head of a man,
He passed through us swiftly, each of us feeling.
He had many true-loves—but never one.

Pierced as the Saint whose arrows were dozens,
Lost as the Angel with his knowledge of sin,
He packed up his troubles and went home to Mother,
He had many true-loves—but never one.

JOSEPH SCHULL [1910-]

John Joseph Schull, son of Charles Henry and Alice Aveline (Travers) Schull, was born at Watertown, South Dakota, and came to Canada in 1913. He attended two schools in Moose Jaw, Saskatchewan, and took extramural courses from the University of Saskatchewan and Queen's University. Between 1935 and 1941 he engaged in advertising and in writing in Montreal.

He then served in the Second World War till 1945. He has written radio plays, short stories, serials, successful stage drama, and two books of vivid narrative poetry, *The Legend of Ghost Lagoon* (1937) and *I, Jones, Soldier* (1945).

From THE LEGEND OF GHOST LAGOON

THE PIRATES' FIGHT

I

The breeze was crisp and the sea lay blue
When Solomon Sleavy roused his crew,
Kicked the sleepers and beat the drunk,
Swore so loud that the sp'rits'l shrunk,
Weighed up anchor, took on rum,
Cursed his first mate's visage glum,
Flung a glance across the sky,
Scanned the sea with squinted eye,
And lean, black *Kate* in the sunshine gay
Slid from Guadiana Bay.

Behind them glimmered the tree-clad hills,
Threads of the Guadianan rills,
Wandering silver, trickled down
To the rippling bay and the white-walled town
Retreating now as the open sea
Swung before them, the wind broke free,
The white spume rose from their purling way
And their tall sails filled in the sparkling day.

The gulls wheeled high and the sharks fled fast
Where grinning *Kate* and her gallants passed:
The sun shone hot on the long guns' necks
And the rogues that swarmed on the narrow decks,
Stripped and steaming, yellow, black, brown,
With gold arm rings from a looted town;
With bright scarves stained by Senoras' tears,
Pearls in their nostrils, pearls in their ears,
Silver anklet, heavy gold chain
And the fabulous gauds of the tearful Main.
For never a king, since time was time
And treasures heaped in the hands of crime,
Knew splendours such as the daily ken
Of Solomon Sleavy and Solomon's men.

But little care now in the knaves' regard
Had the gaudy trappings. From yard to yard
They swung and clambered; the great sheets boomed,
The singing cloud of the canvas loomed;
Sea-children all, through the straining ropes
They yelled and laughed with a new day's hopes.
For *Kate* was off to the open sea
Where wealth and battle and blood would be;
The goal was rich and the stake was high
(A gleam foretold in their chieftain's eye)
And what the seeking or where they went
They knew nor cared; they were well content.

II

Nearer, nearer the pirate glides;
Her rogues grin up at the mighty sides
Of the wounded Spaniard. Alongside now
Volleys roar from her stem and bow.
Soldiers lined at the rails looked down
On the dreadful visages, sweat-stained, brown,
The naked bodies, the knives a-flash,
The flaming kerchiefs; the blades they clash
With a hideous glee.

They touch. A shout
Breaks again as the hooks swing out,
Out and up to the lower ports.
With oaths and scuffles, with kicks and snorts
They swarm up ropes to the gilded sides
In a hideous wave. The black *Kate* rides
Empty now by the doomed ship's stern.
The decks high over her roar and churn
As the desperate ranks of the Spaniard's crew
Line the rails in the gun smoke blue.

Knives, swords, axes—they wield them well
And many a rascal spins to hell
Through the fair blue water with sudden splash—
A halberd's plunge or a cutlass slash
Letting the water into his heart.
But more swarm into his place, or dart
Up the rigging to drop on deck.

ANNE WILKINSON [1910-]

Anne Wilkinson, daughter of George and Mary (Osler) Gibbons, was born in Toronto, and now lives in that city. Her poetry has been included in several poetry magazines and anthologies. Her collection of poems, *Counterpoint to Sleep*, was published in 1951.

SUMMER ACRES

I

These acres breathe my family,
Holiday with seventy summers' history.
My blood lives here,
Sunned and veined three generations red
Before my bones were formed.

My eyes are wired to the willow
That wept for my father,
My heart is boughed by the cedar
That covers with green limbs the bones of my children,
My hands are white with a daisy, sired
By the selfsame flower my grandfather loved:

My ears are tied to the tattle of water
That echoes the vows of ancestral lovers,
My skin is washed by a lather of waves
That bathed the blond bodies of uncles and aunts
And curled on the long flaxen hair of my mother;

My feet step soft on descendants of grass
That was barely brushed
By the wary boots of a hummingbird woman,
The Great Great Grandmother
Of my mid-century children.

II

September born, reared in the sunset hour,
I was the child of old men heavy with honour;
I mourned the half-mast time of their death and sorrowed
A season for leaves, shaking their scarlet flags
From green virility of trees.

As ears spring cartilaged from skulls
So my ears spring from the sound of water
And the whine of autumn in the family tree.
How tired, how tall grow the trees
When the trees and the family are temples
Whose columns will tumble, leaf over root to their ruin.

Here, in my body's home my heart dyes red
The last hard maple in their acres.
Where birch and elm and willow turn,
Gently bred, to gold against the conifers
I hail my fathers, sing their blood to the leaf.

CLARA BERNHARDT [1911-]

Clara Bernhardt, daughter of Arthur R. and Ida M. (Theurer) Bernhardt, is a native of Preston, Ontario, and was educated in the schools there and by private tuition. She had some journalistic experience on the Kitchener *Record.* She has published two novels and three books of verse: *Silent Rhythm* (1939), *Far Horizon* (1941), and *Hidden Music* (1948).

A SAILOR'S WIFE

What matters all his love for me?
His eyes are longing for the sea.

To know again the pungent brine,
And hear a sullen typhoon whine;

To sight the sighing Java shore,
And stalk the streets of Singapore.

His eyes see jungles in Malay,
A limpid, phosphorescent bay,

Perhaps a stormy native girl,
A symphony in bronze and pearl.

He looks beyond our cottage wall,
And smiles to veil the incessant call,

While I . . . I suffer wordlessly,
Because he left the sea for me.

KAY SMITH [1911-]

Kay Smith teaches English and dramatics in the vocational high school of Saint John, New Brunswick. Her poems have appeared in magazines, in three anthologies, and in *Footnote to the Lord's Prayer* (1951).

WHAT THEN, DANCER?

What will you do
when the strings break,
with the sense of the bird flown over,
when you stop pirouetting on the gilded lawn,
what then, dancer?
What then of the week-end guests,
when the pattern of the stricken dance
eats the hands that fall in bleached lace,
the frosting sugar of the polite face,
what then, dancer?

What will you do
when the strings break,
under the mountain of all this music,
what then under frozen skies,
what will you do with the stranger,
with the image of the broken dancer
to break yet again in men's eyes,
stunned near the stone rim of the antique fountain?
What will you do
when the strings break,
when you stop pirouetting on the gilded lawn,
what then, dancer?

WHEN A GIRL LOOKS DOWN

When a girl looks down out of her cloud of hair
And gives her breast to the child she has borne,
All the suns and the stars that the heavens have worn
Since the first magical morning
Rain through her milk in each fibre and cell of her darling.

Hard baring the gift touches the hidden spring,
Source of all gifts, the womb of creation;
From the wide-open door streams the elation
Shaping all things, itself shapeless as air,

That models the nipple of girl, of bud, the angel
Forms unscrolling their voices over fields of winter,
That whittles the ray of a star to a heart's splinter
For one lost in his palace of breath on the frozen hill,
Flying the big-bellied moon for a sail,

And releases the flood of girl, of bud, of the horn
Whose music starts on a morning journey.
In mother, child and all, the One-in-the-many
Gathers me nearer to be born.

IRVING LAYTON [1912-]

Irving Layton, the Ishmael of Canadian poets, at least so far as his attitude that every man's hand is against him is concerned, has had a varied experience as waiter, supervisor of an orphan asylum, proofreader, and member of the Contact Press trio, Toronto, is the author of *Here and Now* (1945), *Now is the Place* (1948), prose and verse, *The Black Huntsmen* (1951), and some of the poems in *Cerberus* (1952).

JEWISH MAIN STREET

And first, the lamp-posts whose burning match-heads
Scatter the bog fires on the wet streets;
Then the lights from auto and store window
That flake cool and frothy in the mist
Like a beaten colloid.
In this ghetto's estuary
Women with offspring appraise
The solemn hypocrisies of fish
That gorp on trays of blue tin. . .
Then enter the shops
And haggle for a dead cow's rump.

Old Jews with memories of pogroms
Shuffle across menacing doorways;
They go fearfully, quietly;
They do not wish to disturb
The knapsack of their sorrows.

O here each anonymous Jew
Clutches his ration book
For the minimum items of survival
Which honoured today—who knows?—
Tomorrow some angry potentate
Shall declare null and void.

WORDS WITHOUT MUSIC

Their dufflebags sprawl like a murder
Between the seats: themselves are bored
Or boisterous. These are ignorant soldiers
Believing that when forever the violent die
The good receive their inexhaustible cow—
Grade seven and superman have arranged everything.
The other passengers are unimportant liars:
Salesmen, admen, the commercial trivia,
Blown between the lines of memoranda,
And across the aisle, disposed on thirty beds,
Two limp virgins eyes below the navel.
Slowly the train curves around rich
Suburban Westmount that squats upon a slum,
Then like a hypodermic plunges past
Uniform fenceposts into open country;
There's glazed sunlight upon the hard serrated
Fields. Air is thin slightly neurasthenic
Over the distant indiscriminate trees
That posture on hillsides gross and secretive
As women staling. Pins withdrawn suddenly
Barns collapse like real estate models. The senses
Run like swift hares along the fences.
These are the fire-lands and this a sealed train
Of cold excursionists, throats buttoned up
With yellow timetables.
On folded hands
The minutes drop like dandruff. The
Jetted column survives in a black foetus,
And the goats leap into their faces shrieking.

NEWSBOY

Neither tribal nor trivial he shouts
From the city's centre where tramcars move
Like stained bacilli across the eyeballs;
Where people spore in composite buildings
From their protective gelatine of doubts,
Old ills, and incapacity to love
While he, a Joshua before their walls,
Sells newspapers to the gods and geldings.

Intrusive as a collision, he is
The Zeitgeist's too public interpreter,
A voice multiplex and democratic,
The people's voice or the monopolists';
Who with last-edition omniscience
Plays Clotho to each gaping customer
With halcyon colt, sex crime in an attic,
The story of a twice-jailed bigamist.

For him the mitred cardinals sweat in
Conclaves domed; the spy is shot. Empiric;
And obstreperous confidant of kings,
Rude despiser of the anonymous,
Danubes of blood wash up his bulletins
While he domesticates disaster like
A wheat in pampas of prescriptive things
With cries animal and ambiguous.

His dialectics will assault the brain,
Contrive men to voyages or murder,
Dip the periscope of their public lives
To the green levels of acidic caves;
Fever their health, or heal them with ruin,
Or with lies dangerous as a letter;
Finally enfold the season's cloves,
Cover a somnolent face on Sundays.

ANNE MARRIOTT [1913-]

Joyce Anne (Marriott) McLellan, Mrs. Gerald Jerome McLellan since 1947, daughter of Edward Guy and Catherine Eleanor (Heley) Marriott, was born in Victoria, British Columbia, and educated there in day and night school. She then took a correspondence course from the London School of Journalism and a radio-script writing course from the University of British Columbia. She has written many radio scripts, reviews, and stories, and her awards for poetry culminated in the Governor-General's Medal. Her striking originality of diction combined with clarity of expression is exemplified in *The Wind Our Enemy* (1939), *Calling Adventurers* (1941), winner of the Governor-General's Medal, *Salt Marsh and Other Poems* (1942), and *Sandstone and Other Poems* (1945). (Cf. E. K. Brown, as above.)

SANDSTONE

In this buff-gray cliff
Ash-crumbling under rock-blow,
Gouged by the sea's claws,
See the prints of the old generations.
Slice the stone cleanly, see
Webbed beech-leaf signature,
Ribbed shell-mark where now no shell is,
Soft wood time-turned flinty,
Bone of the unknown, unvisioned creature
Once as your bone.

Wind sucks broken sand with a terrible breathing,
Stone that shattered bone by bone is shattered,
Sea snatches out taloned green fingers
To shatter all;
Outjut of sandstone falls and is crumb and is dust.

Take the path, upward in stone,
To where strong trees bind encouraged soil together.
On atrophied fallen, forgotten,
Stands steady the supple new growth
Beyond the strained stretch of the clutching tide.

From THE WIND OUR ENEMY

I

Wind
flattening its gaunt furious self against
the naked siding, knifing in the wounds
of time, pausing to tear aside the last
old scab of paint.

Wind
surging down the cocoa-coloured seams
of summer-fallow, darting in about
white hoofs and brown, snatching the sweaty cap
shielding red eyes.

Wind
filling the dry mouth with bitter dust
whipping the shoulders worry-bowed too soon,
soiling the water pail, and in grim prophecy
graying the hair.

III

The wheat was embroidering
All the spring morning,
Frail threads needled by sunshine like thin gold.
A man's heart could love his land,
Smoothly self-yielding,
Its broad spread promising all his granaries might hold.
A woman's eyes could kiss the soil
From her kitchen window,
Turning its black depths to unchipped cups—a silk crepe dress—
(Two-ninety-eight, Sale Catalogue)
Pray sun's touch be gentleness,
Not a hot hand scorching flesh it would caress.
But sky like a new tin pan
Hot from the oven
Seemed soldered to the earth by horizons of glare . . .

The third day he left the fields . . .

Heavy scraping footsteps
Spoke before his words, "Crops dried out—everywhere—"

IV

They said, "Sure, it'll rain next year!"
When that was dry, "Well, next year anyway."
Then, "Next—"
But still the metal hardness of the sky
Softened only in mockery.
When lightning slashed and twanged
And thunder made the hot head surge with pain
Never a drop fell;
Always hard yellow sun conquered the storm.
So the soon sickly-familiar saying grew,
(Watching the futile clouds sneak down the north)
"Just empties goin' back!"
(Cold laughter bending parched lips in a smile
Bleak eyes denied.)

VII

People grew bored
Well-fed in the east and west
By stale, drought-area tales,
Bored by relief whinings,
Preferred their own troubles.

So those who still had stayed
On the scorched prairie,
Found even sympathy
Seeming to fail them
Like their own rainfall.

"Well—let's forget politics,
Forget the wind, our enemy!
Let's forget farming, boys,
Let's put on a dance tonight!
Mrs. Smith'll bring a cake.
Mrs. Olsen's coffee's swell!"

The small uneven schoolhouse floor
Scraped under big work-boots
Cleaned for the evening's fun,
Gasoline lamps whistled.
One Hungarian boy
Snapped at a shrill guitar,
A Swede from out north of town
Squeezed an accordion dry,
And a Scotchwoman from Ontario
Made the piano dance
In time to "The Mocking-Bird"
And "When I grow too Old to Dream,"
Only taking time off
To swing in a square-dance,
Between ten and half-past three.

Yet in the morning
Air peppered thick with dust,
All the night's happiness
Seemed far away, unreal
Like a lying mirage,
Or the icy-white glare
Of the alkali slough.

IX

The sun goes down. Earth like a thick black coin
Leans its round rim against the yellowed sky.
The air cools. Kerosene lamps are filled and lit
In dusty windows. Tired bodies crave to lie
In bed forever. Chores are done at last.
A thin horse neighs drearily. The chickens drowse,
Replete with grasshoppers that have gnawed and scraped
Shrivelled garden-leaves. No sound from the gaunt cows.

Poverty, hand in hand with fear, two great
Shrill-jointed skeletons stride loudly out
Across the pitiful fields, none to oppose.
Courage is roped with hunger, chained with doubt.
Only against the yellow sky, a part
Of the jetty silhouette of barn and house
Two figures stand, heads close, arms locked,
And suddenly some spirit seems to rouse
And gleam, like a thin sword, tarnished, bent,
But still shining in the spared beauty of moon,
As his strained voice says to her, "We're not licked yet!
It must rain again—it *will!* Maybe—soon—"

X

Wind
in a lonely laughterless shrill game
with broken wash-boiler, bucket without
a handle, Russian thistle, throwing up
sections of soil.

God, will it never rain again? What about
those clouds out west? No, that's just dust, as thick
and stifling now as winter underwear.
No rain, no crop, no feed, no faith, only
wind.

PRAIRIE GRAVEYARD

Wind mutters thinly on the sagging wire
binding the graveyard from the gouged dirt road,
bends thick-bristled Russian thistle,
sifts listless dust
into cracks in hard gray ground.
Empty prairie slides away
on all sides, rushes toward a wide
expressionless horizon, joined
to a vast blank sky.

Lots near the road are the most expensive
where heavy tombstones lurch a fraction
tipped by splitting soil.
Farther, a row of aimless heaps
names weatherworn from tumbled sticks
remember now the six thin children
of a thin, shiftless home.

Hawk, wind-scouring, cuts
a pointed shadow on the drab scant grass.

Two graves apart by the far fence
are suicides, one with a grand
defiant tombstone, bruising at the heart
"Death is swallowed up in victory."
(And may be, God's kindness being more large
than man's, to this, who after seven years
of drought, burned down his barn,
himself hanged in it.)
The second, nameless, set around
with even care-sought stones
(no stones on this section)
topped with two plants, hard-dried,
in rust-thick jam-tins set in the caked pile.

A gopher jumps from a round cave,
sprints furtively, spurts under fence, is gone.
Wind raises dead curls of dust, and whines
under its harsh breath on the limp dragged wires,
then leaves the graveyard stiff with silence, lone
in the centre of the huge lone land and sky.

WOODYARDS IN THE RAIN

The smell of woodyards in the rain is strong
like six-foot lumberjacks with hairy chests
and thick axe-leathered hands.
The scent is raw, it slices through
pale drizzle and thin mist
biting the sense.
I like to watch piled wetness dripping off
the yellow-brown stacked shingles, while behind
the smoke churns up in black revolving towers
from lean mill chimneys.
Now the broad-hipped tugs
sniff through the squall and swing the oblong booms
by tar-stained wharves,
as with a last fierce gesture rain
smallpocks the oil-green water with a hurled
ten million wire nails.

DOUGLAS LE PAN [1914-]

Douglas V. Le Pan, son of Lieut.-Col. Arthur D'Orr and Dorothy L. (Edge) Le Pan, was born in Toronto and educated at the University of Toronto and Oxford University. After holding a position as lecturer, first at the University of Toronto and then at Harvard, and serving in various capacities during the Second World War, he joined the Canadian Department of

External Affairs, spent three years in London on the staff of the High Commissioner, studied for a year on a Guggenheim Fellowship, and returned to Canada in 1949. The next year he was appointed special assistant to the Hon. L. B. Pearson, succeeding the late R. G. Riddell (1908-1951), who had been appointed head of Canada's permanent delegation to the United Nations. While in London he published *The Wounded Prince and Other Poems* (1948), with an Introduction by Cecil Day Lewis. His second book, *The Net and the Sword*, appeared in 1954.

ONE OF THE REGIMENT

In this air
Breathed once by artist and *condottier*,
Where every gesture of proud men was nourished,
Where the sun described heroic virtue and flourished
Round it trumpet-like, where the face of nature
Was chiselled by bright centuries hard as sculpture;
His face on this clear air and arrogant scene,
Decisive and impenetrable, if Florentine.

Where every hill
Is castled, he stands like a brooding tower; his will
An angry shadow on this cloudless sky,
Gold with the dust of many a panoply
And blazonings burnt up like glittering leaves;
His only cognizance his red-patched sleeves;
Fair hair his helmet; his glancing eye, the swagger
Of his stride are gallant's sword and dagger.

And in his mind
The sifting, timeless sunlight would not find
Memories of stylish Florence or sacked Rome,
Rather the boyhood that he left at home;
Skating at Scarborough, summers at the Island,
These are the dreams that float beyond his hand,
Green, but estranged across a moat of flame;
And now all bridges blown the way he came.

No past, no future
That he can imagine. The fiery fracture
Has snapped that armour off and left his bare
Inflexible, dark frown to pluck and stare
For some suspected rumour that the brightness sheds
Above the fruit-trees and the peasants' heads
In this serene, consuming lustrousness
Where trumpet-tongues have died, and all success.

Do not enquire
What he has seen engrained in stillest fire
Or what he purposes. It will be well.
We who have shared his exile can trumpet-tell
That underneath his wild and frowning style
Such eagerness has burned as could not smile
From coats of lilies or emblazoned roses.
No greater excellence the sun encloses.

COUREURS DE BOIS

Thinking of you, I think of the *coureurs de bois*,
Swarthy men grown almost to savage size
Who put their brown wrists through the arras of the woods
And were lost—sometimes for months. Word would come back:
One had been seen at Crêve-coeur, deserted and starving,
One at Sault Sainte Marie shouldering the rapids.
Giant-like, their labours stalked in the streets of Quebec
Though they themselves had dwindled in distance: names only;
Rumours; quicksilvery spies into nature's secrets;
Rivers that seldom ran in the sun. Their resource
Would sparkle and then flow back under clouds of hemlock.

So you should have travelled with them. Or with La Salle.
He could feed his heart with the heart of a continent,
Insatiate, how noble a wounded animal,
Who sought for his wounds the balsam of adventure,
The sap from some deep, secret tree. But now
That the forests are cut down, the rivers charted,
Where can you turn, where can you travel? Unless
Through the desperate wilderness behind your eyes,
So full of falls and glooms and desolations,
Disasters I have glimpsed but few would dream of,
You seek new Easts. The coats of difficult honour,
Bright with brocaded birds and curious flowers,
Stowed so long with vile packs of pemmican,
Futile, weighing you down on slippery portages,
Would flutter at last in the courts of a clement country,
Where the air is silken, the manners easy,
Under a guiltless and reconciling sun.

You hesitate. The trees are entangled with menace.
The voyage is perilous into the dark interior.
But then your hands go to the thwarts. You smile. And so
I watch you vanish in a wood of heroes,
Wild Hamlet with the features of Horatio.

CANOE-TRIP

What of this fabulous country
Now that we have it reduced to a few hot hours
And sun-burn on our backs?
On this south side the countless archipelagoes,
The slipway where titans sent splashing the last great glaciers;
And then up to the foot of the blue pole star
A wilderness,
The pinelands whose limits seem distant as Thule,
The millions of lakes once cached and forgotten,
The clearings enamelled with blueberries, rank silence about them;
And skies that roll all day with cloud-chimeras
To baffle the eye with portents and unwritten myths,
The flames of sunset, the lions of gold and gules.
Into this reservoir we dipped and pulled out lakes and rivers,
We strung them together and made our circuit.
Now what shall be our word as we return,
What word of this curious country?

It is good,
It is a good stock to own though it seldom pays dividends.
There are holes here and there for a gold-mine or a hydro-plant.
But the tartan of river and rock spreads undisturbed,
The plaid of a land with little desire to buy or sell.
The dawning light skirls out its independence;
At noon the brazen trumpets slash the air;
Night falls, the gulls scream sharp defiance;
Let whoever comes to tame this land, beware!
Can you put a bit to the lunging wind?
Can you hold wild horses by the hair?
Then have no hope to harness the energy here,
It gallops along the wind away.
But here are crooked nerves made straight,
The fracture cured no doctor could correct.
The hand and mind, reknit, stand whole for work;
The fable proves no cul-de-sac.
Now from the maze we circle back;
The map suggested a wealth of cloudy escapes;
That was a dream, we have converted the dream to act.
And what we now expect is not simplicity,
No steady breeze, or any surprise,
Orchids along the portage, white water, crimson leaves,
Content, we face again the complex task.

And yet the marvels we have seen remain.
We think of the eagles, of the fawns at the river bend,
The storms, the sudden sun, the clouds sheered downwards.
O so to move! With such immaculate decision!
O proudly as waterfalls curling like cumulus!

GEORGE WHALLEY [1915-]

George Whalley was born in Kingston, Ontario, and educated at Bishop's College, Lennoxville, Quebec, at Oxford University as Rhodes Scholar from Quebec (1936-1939), and King's College, London. Throughout the Second World War he served in the Royal Canadian Navy and on loan in the Royal Navy. Since being demobilized he has taught English, first at Bishop's College and then at Queen's University. He has written numerous critical articles for literary magazines and has published a book of criticism, *Poetic Process* (1953), and two books of poetry, *Poems: 1939-44* (1946) and *No Man an Island* (1948).

WE WHO ARE LEFT

Perhaps it is well now
with the men the war has killed,
now that they are free
and nothing can touch them.

No more for them
the madness of sandstorm,
the misery at sea
or flight's monotony:

no more the listless
waiting for old letters
or the sudden brilliance
of brief ecstasy.

Perhaps it is well for them
no more to be troubled
by agony of starlight
or dawn or a new Spring.

Old, old and grey
the pattern of suffering:
the men waiting, the women
waiting and the time passing.

But death still crushes,
and time makes no less bitter
the long incredible anguish
of questioning childless arms.

NIGHT FLIGHT

What hand trimmed these strident feathers for flight
And rigged such flimsy gear—a matter of ear-shot,
A catch of the breath—to freeze the crawling traffic
So that we heard in an instant of threatening rain
A random arrow of geese transfix the night?
What fingers hooked the string and held it humming
Fiddle-taut to the ear while surge of shoulder
Flexed the bow to a thought's prophetic will?
What cosmic archer with crow's-foot eyes disposed
Uncompassed wings to tread the darkness southward?

The beaks cry defiance to solitude
And the trackless sky, where no star flashes
"Come"; only the tidal pitiless sun
Impels them, beyond memory, towards
An unforeknowable target of repose.
Across the creaking burden of the chorus
The leader striding the silence invokes their care,
Cries out to this pitiful grace of bones
And ragged feathers linked by hook and barb
To a crazy Icarus-venture. Hooded eyes
Peer unamazed at a highly improbable course
Great-circled in octopus juice on the black air.
For the leader's unworded words strike on their ear-holes
Familiar magic. These Atlas necks
Are long-bows strained to a planet's compulsion:
These birds are archer and arrow, artists
Annihilating will to discover purpose.

These wingbones are structured against the gales
Of Tierra del Fuego; these singing feathers
Are tough enough for that sorrowful region where
The Horn fractures his beak in the South Ice.
But they will come to rest short of that passion
For no divined reason, dropping down
Weary some dawn by a lake where wild rice
Whispers to water.

NEUFVILLE SHAW [1915-]

Neufville Shaw, son of John William and Ruth (Badgley) Shaw, was born in Westmount, P.Q., and graduated from McGill University. He is Science Master in the Town of Mount Royal High School. His verse has appeared in *Northern Review*, *Preview*, *First Statement*, and *Other Canadians*.

DROWNED SAILOR

He couldn't hear their roar
Nor see their belly shake
Sea green.
Brown was the sea weed
That ringed his frigid ear
And distant the rasp
Of the claw upon his cold snow bone.

Carving the thin horizon
Was the torn sea shudder,
That day,
When time still moved,
When the ships were full
And knived the sea dance—

Gulls hung whistling in the empty air.
New green was the colour
And far below was near
At hand.
The fish were intimate
And the casual shadow passed
His disrobing flesh,
And the careful trace turned fluid.

BRUDE RUDDICK [1915-]

Bruce Ruddick, son of Dr. W. W. and Ernestine (Saucier) Ruddick, was born in Montreal and educated at McGill University (B.Sc., M.D.C.M.) and New York Psychoanalytic Institute. He is at present a practising psychoanalyst in Montreal. He has contributed prose and poetry to *Preview, Northern Review,* and *Voices.* He has also prepared scripts for four National Film Board films on "Mental Mechanisms."

PLAQUE

Under the viaduct, by the hot canal
While horse and cop clomped overhead and the barges
Were lifted in Lock 6, he was conceived
Oh no more wondrously than any bulb or grub.
Fed while the 8.04 speckled the breast,
And commuters' shadows streaked across the oilcloth
He flourished like corn or crow.
Where cats scamper and horse cavorts
He learned to stand and spit at the passing cars—
Triumph of the cortex over the natural response.

Spent four years learning to hate.
At ten was adopted by a fine big firm.
At fifteen was a pin-boy at Mike's.
At twenty fronted for a bookie's.
Was drafted and prepared to make the world safe
For Belmont and Narraganset and the boys at Mike's.
Staggered and hit the curb.
Was sent back via Postal Telegraph.
The lady who answered couldn't read
And the dark words finally
Sputtered under a frying pan.

Oh lament your strong and white winged heroes
Here no bronze nor crepe marks.
The passing freight flutters the laundry hung out like cliches.

FREIGHTER

In concord then they set up hasty ways
on city's edge swept by the inland waves.
Built her to formula like a hundred more
as low and ugly as their stunted love.
Men from the bread-line and from rodeo
poured out the metal down in dark Lachine,
rivet and rib were knit on wooden ghosts,
death in her beams and in her hurried plates.
Not built to pick her languorous ways among
the Isles of Peace that now are armed or burned,
no spice or jewel rests cosy in her gut,
but snubbed to wealthy harbour she receives
her streamlined properties for scenes of waste,
and no boy ever whistles to see her sail.
Guttural here and silent in the gulf
she'll plough her secret track among the waves
and pound uneasy waters on the heads
of rotting heroes and of rolling whales.
Built while the day is eager she will sail
till profits or a million sailors die,
or, lost some night in heaving tons of space,
she'll swell a warning in a Cabinet Voice.
Or, when the thing is done and heroes go
back to the early east or windy west,
rusting she'll lie tilting in the bay
while boys and tides maraud about her bows.

R. A. D. FORD [1915-]

Mr. Ford was born in Ottawa, in 1915, and graduated from the University of Western Ontario, of which his father, Mr. Arthur Ford, editor-in-chief of the London *Free Press,* was afterward Chancellor. He took his Master's degree at Cornell University, became Assistant in History at Cornell, 1938-1940, and then joined the Department of External Affairs. Mr. Ford has served at various times in the Canadian Diplomatic Missions in Rio de Janeiro, Moscow, and London, and has been Chargé d'Affaires of the Canadian Embassy in Moscow, 1951-1954. He has published poems and articles in Canada and abroad.

TWENTY BELOW

The woman watches her husband rubbing his nose,
frozen while chopping a hole in the river's ice,
now thawing slowly between his hands and snow—
sitting by the stove with his peasant eyes nowhere
and his feet in their ribbed grey homespun stockings placed
in the oven, the fire roaring with the top grate raised,
the pipes and flues across the room near white
with heat. The mongrel restless at his side
creeps closer to the fire. The children doze,
half living only through the frozen days.

The woman goes to the window and presses her hand
against the glacial pane, and leans her head
against the frame. Her breath has made a hole
in the frost. She can see outside the northern cold
smothering the world; and an impossible sleep
and silence falling from a sky of slate,
even the pines grey and rigid and still,
the mighty hills mere shadows on the pale
immeasurable horizon.

Without reason,
feeling only her heart oppressive within her
and her life stopped dead and motionless in the hoar
and drifted week, she weeps, and the tears become
cold rivulets that cut across her cheeks.

The cold presses into the room
from every side through the logs and stones and chinks
between the logs, so the circle of people sinks
into sopor, and the woman takes her sadness
and thaws it before the flames.

LYNX

Consignee of silent storms and unseen lightning,
soft violence, oppressor of new fallen snow,
moving like the winter solstice through
the beautiful woods, none so
lovely even in eyes yellow in white
fur the betrayer; the leap without
muscle swelling, small cloud blotting
out the bright day—Will not languish
in the cruel trap, the cruel eyes
and cruel claws wounded, the hunters shouting
in victory, gloating at the anguish
in the mighty legs broken—
Will not linger broken but pass
suddenly with great pain into the Indian night.

BACK TO DUBLIN

From Drogheda all along the coast, the Irish sea,
Followed by the ghost of the Marquis of I don't
Remember, but his car overwhelmed us with dust
Near Rush and his castle, a constant grey
Landmark all over Meath, appeared to say
Continually to us, second immigrants: what
Is the use of coming back to stare? While others, the poor
Relations, either jeered or seemed to think
We were there to gloat, had never heard
Of Joyce or Yeats, and glorified Thomas Moore,
Pointed out the shell marks in the Dublin streets,
And deferred the debate on the price of hogs
To show us where the Liffey meets with God.

No glory to come back, none to be there,
And none but the seer to tender why the pilgrimage
To the rain-washed isle; never got to the grave
Under Ben Bulben, nor Tara's Halls, nor Innisfree
In the heat of the year—but just to stand
Near the stained walls of the ancient town
And dream of sailing to Byzantium—
An old man and a damaged harp,
Weaving the sweetest pattern on the warp
Of a broken continent—that was the fee,
That was my ticket to come in.

JAMES WREFORD WATSON [1915-]

James Wreford Watson, son of Rev. James and Evelyn M. (Russell) Watson, was born at Sanyuan, Shensi, China, and educated at the British School, Kuling, China, at Watson's Boys' College, Edinburgh, at Edinburgh University, and at the University of Toronto. After teaching geography at Sheffield University for two years and at McMaster for twelve, he was appointed chief of the federal Geographical Bureau in 1949, and since 1950 he has been Director of the Geographical Branch of the Department of Mines and Technical Surveys. He has written extensively on geography, both singly and jointly, especially on Canadian geography. Some of his poems appeared in *Unit of Five* (1944), but he has so progressively eliminated any tendency to the obscurity of the neometaphysicals as to be worthy, in his *Of Time and the Lover* (1950), of the Governor-General's Medal for poetry.

THE GATINEAUS

O tide-enwreathed and time-tormented Man,
the hills abide under the quiet stars;
the firm root sucks the rock and branches in
a cloud of song; the rivers are
a braid of twisted gold across the breast
of the all-mothering plain. Look out and see,
above the heave and wrack of all that frets
the temporary heart, the changeless scene.
And in this huge and venerable land—
the dark begetter of the continent,
strike down your days, and let your hours be veined
with the original granite of content.

So have men done before, and so have been
one with the steadfast rock and timeless plain.

For these have faced the long vicissitude
of the invading and relentless tide,
withstood the shock and gouge of ice, and stood,
bared of all grace but still unbowed, to ride
the everlasting circumpolar sweep
of the rain-bursting and wind-battering storm:
and shall outride, O Man, however deep
your swell of swollen tears and sea of harms,
the flux and turmoil of the human day.
Then count not your affairs too high. The sky
falls not for you. For all your grief the grey
great granite of existence shall not lie,
but stands unmoved above the glimmering plain
beneath the stars, as it has ever been.

So make this place your stand. And you shall stand
above the shock of change, firm and secure.
Here in the virtue of this ancient ground
put on the strength to set against despair.
Though the heart fail, sing of the iron will
the steady mind and the enduring hope.
This is a land of fire-born, ice-bred hill,
of the abiding crest and tempered slope,
of the eternal in man's ways, the stark
passion that thrusts into the shaking skies
and pride that lasts beyond the encircling dark.
This is your North, your fixed point in the stress
of time and circumstance. Swing to its strength,
and let it be the hill in you at length.

OUR LOVE SHALL BE THE BRIGHTNESS

Our love shall be the brightness
the impossible, sweet day
shall break at last, shall break, love,
however dark the way.

O dark may be the worldwoe
all over the winter world,
and dark may be the winter
in which our loving's furled.

But, love, the day will break, yet.
The brightness from on high
will cover the earth with beauty, and
inhabit the human sky.

STAY, TIME

Stay, Time, for but this
moment of love.
All else, whatever,
I'll let you have:

the moon on the roses,
the sun on the sea,
the little rain running
across the spring day,

the green corn appearing,
the apple of joy,
the high heat of summer
and cloud-purple sky.

All these I'll give you—
Whatever I have;
if you will but stay for
this moment of love.

SIC TRANSIT GLORIA MUNDI

Come, break your heart, then, with the world's beauty
that so eludes you, though you be so close,
your breast upon the soil, where through the grasses
the long line of the little hillock grows,
and elms enormous hold the heavy sky up
and immemorial lark song scatters down
the pomp of summer morning, and swells more loud.

But when the long lanes of the evening light
lead through the willowy arrowed wood
to the perfection of sensory night
ah! the heart hungers, that this might forever
linger, the sudden stillness after sparrows
until the cricket sings, and your frail cry
be true that beauty will not fail
and all this glory will not die.

WE SHALL HAVE FAR TO GO

We shall have far to go
to climb the breathless heights
with time removing as we move
one after one the lights.

The search beams on the cloud
grope like a blind man's hand,
and through the night the sirens spell
the new tongue of the land.

This worse than fear, than death,
loss of the steady eye,
with headlamps dipped to the moment and
no knowledge of the sky,

this eyeblink of a view
and momentary man
that cannot piece the puzzle up
nor yet unroll the plan;

How shall he hold the heights
and prove his ancient power
whose very map and compass are
the mortal hour?

PATRICK ANDERSON [1915-]

Patrick Anderson was born in England and educated at Oxford and Columbia universities. For several years he taught in a private school in Montreal, manifested a strong interest in experimental magazines, and wrote plays for a left-wing puppet theatre. From Montreal he went to the University of Malaya, thence to England, and recently back to Canada. His work shows the strong influence of Eliot and the neometaphysicals. He published *A Tent for April* (1945), *The White Centre* (1946) and *The Colour As Naked* (1953).

From POEM ON CANADA

II. The Coming of the white man

Wide was the land.
  And North.
    My Aunt bought lakes—
Aunt Hildegarde, living on Lincoln Terrace,
one of the genteel poor, unmarried,
playing at patience, stroked those cards
whose red is scarlet as the tongues of lovers
or as the autumn maples, with their dogs' tongues—
remembered the years in Ottawa, a Brockville childhood,
and sometimes opened the close cedar drawer
under the knicknacks between the aspidistras
and showed me the deed. Crumpled it was and dusty—
deed to five thousand acres no one had ever seen
and three lakes, all unnamed. Aunt Hildegarde
had bought this stake in natural Canada
for a thousand dollars, timber and all.

I thought, as a child would, of her trees, her birds,
her streams, her little glaciers and her thaws
and of the beavers of Aunt Hildegarde.
When, as sometimes happened, she grew severe
I dreamt how seriously across her boundaries
a moose had stepped, and stood there gentle and grim.
In Spring she smiled as all her birds returned.
In Summer dozed, consulting butterflies—
an old lady, with a muskeg all her own.
When she sleeps, I thought, beside her medicine bottles,
It does not sleep. Maybe the Indians cross it
as shadows slur her features when she nods
by the parlour fire, reading the *Globe and Mail.*

When I grew older, I thought of those lakes as mirrors
in which Aunt Hildegarde had never seen herself—
brisk pits to show her soul and Canada's.
And, as a matter of fact, she often declared
she'd visit them one day. But she never did.
A cancer engrossed her, she grew thin and died.
Her lawyers, they say, had a hell of a time
trying to sell that marvelous empty
neck of the woods that no one had ever seen.

And the land was. And the people did not take it.

V. Cold Colloquy

What are you . . .? they ask, in wonder.
And she replies in the worst silence of all her woods:
I am Candida with the cane wind.

What are you . . .? they ask again, their mouths full of gum,
their eyes full of the worst silence of the worst winter in a hundred years
and the frames of their faces chipped round the skaters' picture—

What are you . . .? they ask.
And she replies: I am the wind that wants a flag.
I am the mirror of your picture
until you make me the marvel of your life.
Yes, I am one and none, pin and pine, snow and slow,
America's attic, an empty room,
a something possible, a chance, a dance
that is not danced. A cold kingdom.

Are you a dominion of them? they ask, scurrying
home on streetcars, skiing the hill's shoulder
and hurrying where the snow is heaping colder and colder.
Are you a dominion of them? they ask.
Most loyal and empirical, she says, in ice ironic,
and subject of the king's most gratuitous modesty, she says.
What do you do then?
Lumbering is what I do and whitening is what I wheat,
but I am full of hills and sadness;
snow is where I drift and wave my winds
and as silence my doom, distance is my dream.
Mine are the violet tones of the logs in rivers,
my tallness is the tallness of the pines and the grain elevators
tubular by the scarps of coal, at Quebec.
My caves are the caves of ice but also the holes of Cartier
where the poor squat, numb with winter,
and my poverty is their rags and the prairies' drought.

What is the matter then . . .? they ask, and some are indifferent,
What is the matter then . . .? they ask.

The matter is the sections and the railways, she replies,
and the shouting lost by the way and the train's whistle
like wild-life in the night.
The matter is the promise that was never taken, she replies,
above your heads the cool and giant air
and the future aching round you like an aura—
land of the last town and the distant point,
land of the lumber track losing itself
petering out in the birches, the half-wish
turning back in the wastes of winter or slums
and the skiers lovely and lonely upon the hills
rising in domes of silence. The matter is
the skiers, she replies, athletically lonely,
drowsed in their delight, who hunt and haunt
the centres of their silence and excitement:
finding the cirrus on the high sierras
sluice down the dangers of their dear content—
the matter is being lost in a dream of motion
as larks are in their lights, or bees and flies
glued on the humpbacked honey of summertime.

What should we do then, what should we do . . .? they ask,
out of the factories rattling a new war,
on all the Sundays time has rocked to motion.
What should we do then . . .? they ask, English and French,
Ukrainians, Poles, Finns, at drugstore corners
of streets extended to the ultimate seas
of their defended but ambiguous city.

—Suffer no more the vowels of Canada
to speak of miraculous things with a cleft palate—
let the Canadian,
with glaciers in his hair, straddle the continent,
in full possession of his earth and north
dip down his foot and touch the New York lights
or stir the vegetable matter of the Bahamas
within the Carib gutter. Let
the skiers go with slogans of their eyes
to crowd a country whose near neighbourhood's
the iron kindness of the Russian coasts—
through deserts of snow or dreary wastes of city,
the empty or the emptily crowded North.

And see, she says, the salmon pointing home
from the vast sea, the petalled plethora
and unplumbed darkness of the sea, she says:
gliding along their silvery intuitions
like current on its cables, volt upon volt,
to flash at last, sparking the mountain falls
of Restigouche—spawning a silver million.

SLEIGHRIDE

In front the horse's rump bright as a lantern
goes its gauche way—the runners squeak
on the cobbled ice. With hands plunged in the hair
of my muffled rug and a clown's red nose, I leave.

I kick my feet on the boards to keep them warm,
and pull my headband over the rims of my ears
while the driver trails his whip in the banks of snow
a-glow at the sides like waves of wonderful summers.

And my eyes cry, I smile an archaic smile
and my cheeks are rouged with aliveness and mad love
while around in a settled circle the dull hills
control the valley whose applegreen ice I leave.

Goodbye Goodbye I say and the sleigh keeps on
like shuttle in slot but crazily all the same,
working its roughouse wood, retching its iron—
I am not anywhere now but an Adam in Time.

I wrinkle my face for the cold and cuff my flesh
and watch the fringe of the rug flap over the sides
and the shadow that slides on the drift, the quick compelled
shape of the two in blue with velvet heads.

Is anyone ever so new as upon a journey,
so full of physical news or so flashy with nerves
as one who is moved, and nakedly, freely
watches his body reel in the straight and the curves?

So I submit to this lane, to this alteration,
I cough with faith and my breath is a bulging prayer,
and I drowse in the pleasure as well as the terror of Time
with a hallelujah hello from a nest of fur.

FREDERICK E. LAIGHT [1915-]

Frederick E. Laight, the son of English parents, was born in Regina, Saskatchewan. His mother died in 1915, and he lived for eight years with his grandmother in England and for one year in Australia. On his father's re-marriage, the son returned to Canada, continuing his education at the Scott Collegiate, Regina. He spent 1937 to 1943 in the civil service. He had begun radio work in 1942 and by 1943 was able to give up his civil service position. In less than a year he was production manager. He has won several prizes for poems and his verse has appeared in periodicals and in three anthologies.

SOLILOQUY

I have seen tall chimneys without smoke,
  And I have seen blank windows without blinds,
  And great dead wheels, and motors without minds,
And vacant doorways grinning at the joke.

I have seen loaded wagons creak and sway
  Along the roads into the North and East,
  Each dragged by some great-eyed and starving beast
To God knows where, but just away—away.

And I have heard the wind awake at nights
  Like some poor mother left with empty hands,
  Go whimpering in the silent stubble lands
And creeping through bare houses without lights.

These comforts only have I for my pain—
The frantic laws of statesmen bowed with cares
To feed me, and the slow, pathetic prayers
Of godly men that somehow it shall rain.

MICHAEL HARRINGTON [1916-]

Michael Harrington was born in St. John's, Newfoundland, and was educated at the schools and the university there. He founded and was the first editor of *Memorial Times.* After graduation he was employed in the Newfoundland civil service and then at the United States Army Base at Fort Pepperrell. Next he took over the "Barrelman" radio programme, devoted to Newfoundland history, arts and letters, folk music, and contemporary achievements of Newfoundlanders. He won first prize for a poem in open competition at the age of sixteen. His books of poems are *Newfoundland Tapestry* (1943) and *The Sea is Our Doorway* (1947).

THE SECOND IRON AGE (1939-1945)

Under enormous and cemented cliffs,
Vast organisms, wheels and levers sleep,
Potent and doomful, lithographic, splayed.

High above windswept, lonely, arid land,
Swoop and devour, pulsing birds of prey,
Their beaks are iron-bound, and their craws inflamed.

Over gaunt ribs of prairie, tundra, steppe,
Steel-gutted pachyderms, laminate, abrase,
Crunching the bone to bone and flimsy bone.

Beneath the salty undulations, where
Blinded with ooze, the protozoa crawl,
Man-made cetacea, diabolic, slink.

And between, under, and above the earth,
The caterpillar with its thousand legs,
Defies Man's pitiless, insensate rage.

Sleeping uncurled in leaves, between sun-blasts,
It sudden sheds its weird, uncleanly robes,
Dazzling the sun, a brilliant butterfly!

Thus from the vortex and the maelstrom's swirl,
Man will arise and spit his brackish soul
Out of himself and be a god again.

GAZETEER OF NEWFOUNDLAND

I have travelled sometime up and down our coast,
And looked into pretty and bleak places, where the most
To be seen was water; inland, over a marsh, and out
Where the "gut" writhed in the dusk, with saltwater trout
Splitting the oily surface with a razor fin;
Or the kelp trailing like tawdry hair; and the tide coming in
At Admiral's Beach, Seldom Come By, Harbour Deep and Burin.

I have been in harbours where only the mailboats go
Ashore, and the hills look as if they were meant only for snow;
Entering through bizarre channels, where the iron rock
Falls down, helpless and sheer; and sixty fathoms mock
The shoals inside, where idle anchors hold
The steamer, and the northeaster is always cold,
(Battle Harbour, Gaultois, Englee and Cuckhold)

Cold as an icicle, cold as a sheep's back
After the shearing. I have seen the low clouds make a track
Of shadow over the sunless reefs where the salmon
Shoot like swift, sinister arrows, and the shore looks like a famine;
Looked on the fabulous mountains of our western lands,
The dark ravines, the motley shale, the shining sands
Of Codroy and the Gravels, Blow-me-down and Highlands.

I think, too, that long before me our people
Were poets; because they named their coves by a steeple
Of rock; a black gulch, the soft or hard way the weather
Was when they landed; or after the place, the leather
Came from in their boots, or the dark colour
Of a river under a wooden bank like green velour—
Port Royal, River of Ponds, Blue Pinion and Safe Harbour.

They did not sit up nights thinking out fancy titles,
They were too happy to have arrived. Their church recitals
Gave thanks to God for a smooth crossing, a snug anchorage,
A "good run of fish" in June, plenty of salt in storage. . . .
They left us a legacy of names brilliant in history's gloom,
Heart's Delight, Cloud Mountain, Piper's Hole, Badger's Quay and
  Broom—
Field, Lawn and Cape Onion, Juniper Stump, Turk's Gut, and
  Spanish Room.

P. K. PAGE [1916-]

Patricia Kathleen (Page) Irwin, Mrs. William Arthur Irwin, daughter of Major-General Lionel Frank and Rose Laura (Whitehouse) Page, was born in England and came to Canada in 1919. She was educated at St. Hilda's School for Girls, Calgary, Alberta, and took a position with the Film Board, to which her future husband was also appointed late in 1949. Early in 1953 he was made Canadian High Commissioner to Australia. She has written short stories for magazines, contributed poems to *Unit of Five* (1944), and published one book of poetry, *As Ten, as Twenty* (1946). Her imagery is sometimes daring beyond the point of clarity.

LANDLADY

Through sepia air the boarders come and go,
impersonal as trains. Pass silently
the craving silence swallowing her speech;
click doors like shutters on her camera eye.

Because of her their lives become exact:
their entrances and exits are designed;
phone calls are cryptic. Oh, her ticklish ears
advance and fall back stunned.

Nothing is unprepared. They hold the walls
about them when they weep or laugh. Each face
is dialled to zero publicly. She peers
stippled with curious flesh;

pads on the patient landing like a pulse,
unlocks their keyholes with the wire of sight,
searches their rooms for clues when they are out,
pricks when they come home late.

Wonders when they are quiet, jumps when they move,
dreams that they dope or drink, trembles to know
the traffic of their brains, jaywalks their street
in clumsy shoes.

Yet knows them better than their closest friends:
their cupboards and the secrets of their drawers,
their books, their private mail, their photographs
are theirs and hers.

Knows when they wash, how frequently their clothes
go to the cleaners, what they like to eat,
their curvature of health, but even so
is not content.

For, like a lover, must know all, all, all.
Prays she may catch them unprepared at last
and palm the dreadful riddle of their skulls—
hoping the worst.

ADOLESCENCE

In love they wore themselves in a green embrace.
A silken rain fell through the spring upon them.
In the park she fed the swans and he
whittled nervously with his strange hands.
And white was mixed with all their colours
as if they drew it from the flowering trees.

At night his two-finger whistle brought her down
the waterfall stairs to his shy smile
which, like an eddy, turned her round and round
lazily and slowly so her will
was nowhere—as in dreams things are and aren't.

Walking along the avenues in the dark
street lamps sang like sopranos in their heads
with a violence they never understood
and all their movements when they were together
had no conclusion.

Only leaning into the question had they motion:
after they parted were savage and swift as gulls.
Asking and asking the hostile emptiness
they were as sharp as partly sculptured stone
and all who watched, forgetting, were amazed
to see them form and fade before their eyes.

CULLEN

Cullen renounced his cradle at fifteen.
Set the thing rocking with his vanishing foot,
hoping the artifice would lessen the shock.
His feet were tender as puffballs on the stones.

He first explored the schools and didn't understand
the factory made goods they stuffed in his mind,
or why the gramophone voice always ran down
before it reached the chorus of its song.
Corridors led "from" but never "to,"
stairs were merely an optical delusion,
in the damp basement where they hung their coats
he cried with anger and was called a coward.
He didn't understand why they were taught
that life was good by faces that said it was not.
He discovered early that "the writing on the wall"
was dirty words scrawled on a shadowed part of the hall.
Cullen wrote a note on his plate with the yolk of his egg
saying he hardly expected to come back,
and then, closing his textbooks quietly
he took his personal legs into the city.
Toured stores and saw the rats behind the counters
(he visited the smartest shopping centres)
Saw the worm's bald head rise in the clerks' eyes
and metal lips spew out fantasies;
saw pink enamel of salesgirls chip and harden
beneath the outer folds of respectable darkness
as they sold garments they could only touch—
lovely as wind blowing imagined hair,
these webs for the flesh that they would never wear.
He heard the time clock's tune and the wage's pardon,
saw dust in the storerooms swimming towards the light
in the enormous empty store at night;
young heads fingering figures and floating freights
from hell to hell with no margin for mistakes.
Cullen pricked his eye and paid a price
to sit on the mountain of seats like edelweiss—
watched the play pivot; discovered his escape
and with the final curtain went backstage;
found age and sorrow were an application,
beauty a mirage, fragrance fictionary,
the ball dress crumpled, sticky with grease and sweat.
He forgot to close the stage door as he went.
He ploughed the city, caught on a neon sign,
heard the noise of machines talking to pulp,
found the press treacherous as a mountain climb.
Capitols required an alpenstock
And the five vowels twisted beneath his shoes.
A's and g's were his largest stumbling blocks.

He struggled with the foothills of the Times
until he learned to walk between the lines
Tried out the seasons then, found April cruel—
(there had been no Eliot in his books at school)
discovered that stitch of knowledge on his own
remembering all the springs he had never known.
Summer grew foliage to hide the scar,
bore leaves that looked as light as tissue paper
but actually were heavy as a plate.
Fall played a flute and stuck it in his ear,
Christmas short-circuited and fired a tree
with lights and bubbles; stood like a Christ; unseen,
counted its presents on an adding machine.
Cullen renounced the city, nor did he bother
to leave his door ajar for his return,
found his feet willing and, strangely, slipping like adders
away from the dreadful town.
Decided country, which he had never seen,
was carillon greenness lying behind the eyes
and ringing the soft warm flesh behind the knees.
Decided that country people were big and free;
found himself lodgings with fishermen on a cliff,
slung his hammock from these beliefs and slept.
Morning caught at his throat when he saw the men
return at dawn like silver armored Vikings;
the women were malleable as rising bread—
in fact the environment was to his liking.
Sea was his mirror and he saw himself
twisted as rope and fretted with the ripples—
concluded quietness would comb him out:
for once, the future managed to be simple.
He floated a day in stillness, felt the grass
grow in his arable body, felt the gulls
trace the tributaries of his heart and pass
over his river beds from feet to skull.
He settled with evening like a softening land,
withdrew his chair from the sun the oil lamp made,
content to rest within his personal shade.
The women, gathering, tatted with their tongues,
shrouds for their absent neighbours and the men
fired with lemon extract and bootlegged rum
suddenly grew immense.

No room could hold them—he was overrun,
trampled by giants, his grass was beaten down.
Nor could his hammock hold him for it hung
limp from a single nail, salty as kelp.

Cullen evacuated overnight,
he knew no other region to explore;
discovered it was 1939
and volunteered at once and went to war
wondering what on earth he was fighting for.
He knew there was reason, but couldn't find it
and marched to battle half an inch behind it.

SUMMER RESORT

They lie on beaches and are proud to tan—
climb banks in search of flowers for their hair,
change colours like chameleons and seem
indolent and somehow flat and sad.

Search out the trees for love, the beach umbrellas,
the bar, the dining-room; flash as they walk,
are pretty-mouthed and careful as they talk;
send picture post-cards to their offices
brittle with ink and soft with daily phrases.

Find Sunday empty without churches—loll
not yet unwound in deck chair and by pool,
cannot do nothing neatly, while in lap,
periscope ready, scan the scene for love.

Under the near leaves or the sailing water
eyes hoist flags and handkerchiefs between the breasts, alive,
flutter like pallid bats at the least eddy.

Dread the return which magnifies the want—
wind in high places soaring round the heart
and carried like a star-fish in a pail
through dunes and fields and lonely mountain paths.
But memory, which is thinner than the senses,
is only a wave in grass that the kiss erases.
And love once found their metabolism changes
the kiss is worn like a badge upon the mouth—
pinned there in darkness, emphasized in daylight.

Now all the scene is flying. Before the face
people and trees are swift; the enormous pool
brims like a crying eye. The immediate flesh
is real and night no curtain.

There, together, the swift exchange of badges
accelerates to a personal prize giving
while pulse and leaf rustle and grow climatic.

THE STENOGRAPHERS

After the brief bivouac of Sunday,
their eyes, in the forced march of Monday to Saturday,
hoist the white flag, flutter in the snow storm of paper,
haul it down and crack in the midsun of temper.

In the pause between the first draft and the carbon
they glimpse the smooth hours when they were children—
the ride in the ice-cart, the ice-man's name,
the end of the route and the long walk home;

remember the sea where floats at high tide
were sea marrows growing on the scatter-green vine
or spools of grey toffee, or wasps' nests on water;
remember the sand and the leaves of the country.

Bell rings and they go and the voice draws their pencil
like a sled across snow; when its runners are frozen
rope snaps and the voice then is pulling no burden
but runs like a dog on the winter of paper.

Their climates are winter and summer—no wind
for the kites of their hearts—no wind for a flight;
a breeze at the most, to tumble them over
and leave them like rubbish—the boy-friends of blood.

In the inch of the noon as they move they are stagnant.
The terrible calm of the noon is their anguish;
the lip of the counter, the shapes of the straws
like icicles breaking their tongues are invaders.

Their beds are their oceans—salt water of weeping
the waves that they know—the tide before sleep;
and fighting to drown they assemble their sheep
in columns and watch them leap desks for their fences
and stare at them with their own mirror-worn faces.

In the felt of the morning the calico minded,
sufficiently starched, insert papers, hit keys,
efficient and sure as their adding machines;
yet they weep in the vault, they are taut as net curtains
stretched upon frames. In their eyes I have seen
the pin men of madness in marathon trim
race round the track of the stadium pupil.

MIRIAM WADDINGTON [1917-]

Mrs. Miriam Waddington was born in Winnipeg and educated there and at the University of Toronto, where she did graduate work in sociology, continued at the Pennsylvania School, Philadelphia. She is engaged in social work in Montreal. Her literary work includes magazine articles and poetry, a collection of the latter of which is *Green World* (1945).

INVESTIGATOR

I who am street-known am also street knowing:
Just ask me—
I know the tangle of hot streets behind the poorhouse
Pouring from the city like coiled intestines,
The smell of the brewery as it splays long fumes in the alleys,
And the streets pushed against the zoo
With litter of peanut shells and empty candy boxes.
Also the streets climbing crazily up the river bank
Between bridge and jail.

My hand knows the familiar gesture
Of measuring a child's height in passing.
Even if I were blind I would see the grey figure,
Hear the thin high call of the city's authorized salvage collector.
I could tell you and no exaggeration
Of the in and out of houses twenty times a day,
Of the lace antimacassars, the pictures of kings and queens,
The pious mottoes, the printed blessings, the dust piling up on
bureaus,
The velour interiors, the Niagara souvenirs,
The faded needlepoint, the hair pulled tight
And the blinds drawn against the day and the feel of sun.

Then down between lake and railway tracks
The old houses running to seed, the grass grown tall,
The once mansion made into quaint apartments
Where a foul granny with warts all over her face
Sits counting last year's newspapers lost in a timeless litter
While her hunchback son runs nimble messages to covetous eyes.

Out on the street again into the fainting heat
Where bloom the rank garbage cans to the jazz of trolleys,
Past the garden where the old man drooling senile decay
Lets the sun slip ceaselessly through his fingers,
And for humour
A long lean lap-eared dog sitting on a roof
Blinks wet eyes at me.

CADENZA

Trees shake gentle skaters out
On the arena of my sleep,
Silent colours turn and grow
On the surface of the night
Where red by red is multiplied
And blue divides its blue with ice,
And flying music lifts the edge
From tightly nailed memory.

Skaters turn and dancers whirl
In flashing curves, and voices lift
The heavy rafters of my sleep
With spiralled shouts that coalesce
And rocket skywards, close on stars—
Their sharp points cut a jagged line
Into the careful shape of peace;
Then colour captures spring
And I wake prisoner
In morning's branches.

RESTRICTED

They live in their country
We in ours,
We share a road, the lake, the sun,
All the attributes of place.

We walk in twos,
They go in fours,
For we are few, and they
With all the bravery of birth
Take pride in numbers;
And this reads
Innocently in each fair and
Blue-eyed face.

We are outside and they are in.
Uneasily we breathe the air
Which they so cleverly divide
And wear as careless as a cape
Which them reveals but us must hide.

Lonely with indefinite sin
We take the air, go for a stroll,
Share all the attributes of place
Though we are broken, they are whole.

LULLABY

hush dove the summer
thrush lies dead deep
under withered leaves
and yellow sickled smooth.

hush and the blue edges
of your folded wings
quiver in my hands, stain
the white apron of morning.

at dark the fluted moon
floats in the window
and the curtains weep
their white arms

cradle your sigh and hush—
night will put a kiss
on the tired brow
of your imperilled love

and with his ribbled touch
promise you a prince
almonds and raisins
at your feet,

rose petals and honey
against your mouth
and on your thighs a spell
of silver needles bring.

if he never comes?
you will lie asleep
for a hundred years
on your pillared hope.

hush uneasy grief
that curves the beetled woods,
kerchiefs folded white
between the birches blow

and night's sweet gypsy now
fiddles you to sleep
far from snows of winnipeg
and seven sister lakes.

BERTRAM WARR [1917-1943]

Bertram Warr was born in Toronto, where he attended different schools. After a period of office work in Toronto, he spent some time in unconventional travel, with necessary brief stays at various places, Muskoka, Halifax, and, after working his way across the Atlantic, Liverpool and London. There he enrolled at Birkbeck College, University of London. Drafted into the Royal Air Force in 1941, though he would have preferred to enlist in the Red Cross service, he was eventually killed in action. A broadsheet of his poems published in England is entitled *Yet a Little Onwards* (1941). Of Canadian publication is *In Quest of Beauty: Selected Poems* (1950). (Cf. *Contemporary Verse*, October, 1945, and *The Poetry Review* [English], November-December, 1950.)

POETS IN TIME OF WAR

(In Memory of Wilfred Owen)

Poets, who in time of war
Divide in visionary horror
Soul's dream from body's mission;
Knowing a holier connection
Than the will to destruction
Compelling the boy in arms to kill his brother:

All who tell the grave story
Of love, the sad essentiality
Of pain, whom no bitterness
Bars from life's true loveliness
Whose words are a tenderness
Of hands, caressing wards of maimed humanity:

Spirits who dream and move onward,
Leaving to us your dreams gathered
And resounding forever in the air
O, believe us, this bodily despair
Stuns not our spirits, for there,
Serenely, our visionary heritage has flowered.

TREES, WHO ARE DISTANT

Trees, who are distant as another's reality,
Anguish or joy, invade our famished city.
Armed with your foreign beauty, move through our streets,
Bringing to taut and shattered structures the sweet
And placid harmonies of artlessly complaining leaves.
Entice with you a million exiled flowers
And singing birds. Perhaps the grievous hours
Will finish then. Men will sit unclothed in the grass wonderingly
Listening to the strange melody of poised lilies.

RONALD HAMBLETON [1917-]

Ronald Hambleton was born in Preston, England, and came to Canada in 1924. He was educated in Vancouver. After a period of varied work on the Pacific Coast, he settled in Toronto. Travel in England brought him into contact with some of the neometaphysical poets, and in 1944 he edited an anthology, *Unit of Five*, containing the work of four other experimentalists and his own. From 1951 to 1953 he was again abroad. In his new book of poems, *Object and Event* (1953), he has partly outgrown the influence of the metaphysical school.

COMRADES AS WE REST WITHIN

Comrades, as we rest within
Our glittering homes,
Around us roam
Canada's three syllables,
Cold, like a madman's grin,
Wanting to be affable.

Over in London, the scene is
Different: there the fourth
Wall is down by force
Of an artificial rage;
There where acts are heinous
All the world's a stage.

There everyone is returning
To a grinning room,
And the afternoon
Grins back from the street.
Far off, something is burning,
But nothing concrete.

Only the concrete stands, the
Skeleton, the basic grimace;
Only the flesh burns, the lace,
The weak, the terror-frozen,
With no choice but a
Grave to stick toes in.

After, the apologists
Will rationalize to death
Acts that the rising breath
Thickens to think of, and
The eyes will receive the mists
From city and land.

But here, at present, we
Walk naturally in homes,
Thinking, if at all, of domes
Shattered, medals struck,
Of nights immediately
Remote as Habbakuk.

And here we neglect to change
The set immobile grin—
(but how should I begin?)
Here Love has no capital,
And finds it a little strange
Beginning with a miniature hell.

SOCKEYE SALMON

Caught in the glib catcher's net
With the fly that wanders, is the wonder fish;
Threshes a moment in the windowed lace
Till the eye is opaque and supremely glazed.
Not projects outward no tangent beam,
Not gets the increase of scenery
Passing afflict the retina.
Being unfit to negotiate
The invisible livelihood of lungs,
It flails in a harder-to-swim-in sea.
Outward in material lies its wherewithal,
And the gills adjust, discriminate,
But is caught by the introspective air
That moves captor's brain and viscera.

Hung like a murderer with stretched-out neck,
Prepared for dissection, absorption, use,
Subject to putrefactive air,
In gaunt symmetry lies the wonder fish;
The trip from the egg to the waterfall,
The leaping lively or lying sunned,
The spawning, the schooling, the quick increase,
Are value and profit and capital.
No natural course is dissatisfied,
No function corrupted, there is no waste.
Use has been served up with vinegar,
The matter discussed with great dispatch.

In the ribbed lucent shallows is the window clear;
And the eyes' connection established there
All harmony, because all enmity
Has logically come to stay;
Cements by its close attractive gaze;
For man and fish find purest pleasure
In their prostituting mutual sight.

THAT STRAIN AGAIN

Come live with me and be my love,
And we will newer pleasures prove
In concrete landscape, split with air,
Where we, like pieces, shuttle there.

There from the shapeless countryside
With frightening limits we can hide,
And watch the sun in shadow mark
His straight-edge course from dawn to dark.

In this rectangular morass
Between the boxes we shall pass
And let our leaping loving race
Obstructive crowds, in check and chase.

Around you, from the tower keep,
Two agile guards at angles leap;
For they, by nature celibate,
Must force, or must prevent, a mate.

The nightly tours enjoyed by us
Are even more miraculous,
For city's thousands busily
Ignore what so entrances me.

In file and rank, on square and street,
The people intersect, not meet;
Developing a seventh sense:
The radar of indifference.

These silent waves around you flow,
Yet you without impedance go;
And I, a single-stepping king,
Outstripped by queenly sauntering.

LOUIS DUDEK [1918-]

Louis Dudek, the son of Polish-Canadian parents, was born in Montreal, where he came under the influence of the editorial group of the modernist magazine *First Statement.* He was educated at McGill University and, after five years' work in advertising, at Columbia University. Since then he has taught English at McGill University. Recently he became interested in Contact Press, Toronto. He contributed poems to *Unit of Five* (1944), and has published *East of the City* (1946) and *The Searching Image* (1952). He has poems also in the anthology *Cerberus* (1952).

A STORE-HOUSE

There is a small store-house of knowledge in which I sit sometimes
 on hard wooden cases
leaning against stacks of material kept there for use;
the door is ajar, and I can see a lawn,
some buildings, a segment of street
where people pass. But no one looks in through my door.

I sit, leaning and looking at the samplings I get
of the world; I meditate about it:
of the numbers of girls in colleges compared with men, and of the
 future of society;
of the muscles of coloured coal-heavers opening a manhole;
of labour, power, and ignorance;
of the idiocy of avarice, of fear, and of the danger of ideals;

of the pity of people, that plod like dray-horses or senseless nuns
set on a narrow plank of purpose, with their beautiful wandering eyes
shielded by habit, the death and anodyne of life.

And sometimes I want to cry, and sometimes to call out,
to raise a banner before my shack, make up a congregation.
But I know that no one will look into my door—
the people pass by too busy.

God knows, I will go out
and walk in the streets.
Perhaps I will meet other men sitting in doorways, sad as I am;
if I find them, we will sit aside somewhere
and talk this over.

THE MOUNTAINS

In streets, among the rocks of time and weather,
with the crisp noises around, and the surrounding voices,
hearing the steel of wheels repeatedly, like bayonets,
and the sound of guns from buildings, where the windows
icily shut suddenly like visors, and men are marching;

past the trucks stooped in rows like horses
with sacks thrown tenderly over their shoulders,
the hooded and silent heroes in garages—
I walk, though the frost-fire plays in my fingers
and my eyes are crying in this freezing weather.

And amazed, I hear a few anxious voices
rise extemporizing in the hoar-frost air,
singing, on this plateau, our latest position
high in the mountains, near the dividing line
where it is coldest, and the rocks are a parapet.

Yes, soon, the hills scaled, we shall look down
into bright greenery, valleys, and rivers
thinning into wheat-fields! And the cold air like water
will flow from us, while we gaze and gaze
at the low valleys, and the meandering rivers.

NARRATIVE

Through your eyes' round and perfect pupils
Set like green jade, reticular inside a glass,
Looking down, and trying to reach and know,
I have seen disintegrate the light appearances
Around the edge of each slight, sensitive orbit,
And past the primitive palings of your pupils
As into sleep, the leap from this white world
Into a realer dream, I shot my sky spearheads;
Your perfect pupils opened to me, my warrior,
And panting bravely then, I entered there
Through your eyes, to look one still moment
Into an actual future, a summer's playtime,
Boys in a green field, their change and motion,
Trees in a warming wind, and hectic light,
Voices and shouts in horizontal sunlight—
And in green field, the spry boys playing.
Their figures there were forward, bright and springy
(The ache to make them real is real, love!)
And now we cannot leave them, loving or waiting.
For we must go now, we must follow their way
To where the air's electric, sunlight prosperous.
And we must run, love, run crying, yet singing
Even though we know, even though we both know
That here we cannot live or love the same again.

I HAVE SEEN THE ROBINS FALL

I have seen the robins fall
One by one, from the trees, their throats dry;
And I have heard their music cease,
Stalked to silence in the high stark trees.

The fingers of grass I have seen bent
In the dry air, and split to sharp forks;
The sea dashing on a dandelion
Crusted, and turned to rusted iron.

I have seen a white salt spread on your stones,
With the crushed powder of pure, white bones,
And all the poems that sang in my heart
Turned to the same white, bitter salt.

MARGARET AVISON [1918-]

Margaret Avison was born in Galt, Ontario, and graduated from the University of Toronto. She is librarian and research worker at the University of Toronto Library. Miss Avison has contributed verse to leading periodicals in Canada and abroad, and is represented in anthologies.

RIGOR VIRIS

One bland elipse in cornflower blue
Fans out beyond the gunneysack,
The profiles of Egyptian smiles
Confuse the clues these chimneystacks
Suggest of smoking miles,
    Wed sun to smoke instead,
    And blazon that parade
    Of all intolerables, in flowing frieze
Against a pink brick wall in a dun autumn.

  Can this sere serried dance revive him now
    Whose imminent demise
    Stales the blown sky, and air
    Embattled, and lends glare
    To dying light in a lost season? (How
      Ragged among the slag he sprawls,
      Deployed within a static plan!
      Along the trillion prism walls
      Of diamond creeps the prisoned man.)

  Evening is come too close now
  For breath to come between.
  Leaves blacken on a silver bough.
  The ocean's sullen green
  Sprouts in the cruel white of foam-flowers, whittled
      For vanishing.

Now, Child Pandora, lift the lid again
And let the clamoring mysteries be dumb.
In this clear twilight contour must contain
Its source, and distances with contours come
Opening peacock vistas that can no man entomb.

NATHAN RALPH [1919-]

Nathan Ralph Goldberg, son of Strul and Gertie (Lazarovitch) Goldberg, was born in Montreal and educated at Stanstead Academy, Strathcona Academy, Sir George Williams College, and the University of Toronto. He served in the Royal Canadian Air Force during the Second World War and wrote a history of the City of Edmonton Squadron. His literary work includes one play and two books of verse, *Twelve Poems* (1941) and *Coffee and Bitters* (1947).

WHEN THEY GROW OLD

When they grow old
And sit fondly
Together,
Silently, midst
The tired hours
That blink and nod—
At last to fall asleep . . .
When they grow old,
Wary of words.
Stare
From rich embroidered gowns
And upright starched collars. . . .
Such cheap attention
To the trivial
Daily news,
And the sorely
Pampered costumed Pekingese;
With a measured trifle
For two human souls. . . .
When they grow old
And cling to decorum—
They are teased
By fear
And snickering death.

ANTHONY FRISCH [1921-]

Anthony Frisch, though a Canadian citizen, was born in Naples, Italy, of Austrian parents. He was educated at Emmanuel College, Cambridge, and McGill University, Montreal. During the war he served with the R.C.A.F., and later was on the staff of the Montreal *Gazette* and for a time with the Department of National Health and Welfare. His home is now in Toronto.

At McGill University he was awarded the Chester MacNaghten Prize for creative writing, and later he won the E. J. Pratt Prize and Award at the University of Toronto. Among his published works are: *Though I Speak, Poems* (1949); *The House, Poems* (1950); *Third Poems* (1951); *Steine aus Kanada, German Poems* (Vienna, 1953); and *Poems* (1954).

JOAN OF ARC TO THE TRIBUNAL

My Lords, my Lord of Warwick,
Bishops, Almighty Lord!
Patres of St. Dominic!
Yes! I took up the sword!

Yes! I have battled for France,
This sweetest, this my land,
My people, in Orleans,
In Flanders and Brabant.

I, Joan the Maid, who tended
Fields and flocks in Lorraine:
I fought, and I defended
My King, and I have slain.

Put on your caps, and shoulder
Your rags of bastard black:
Old men, I shall grow older
Than you, when men look back!

THE CONVICT

As convicts go, when it is time, to cells,
To be locked up, each one for his own deed,
Go we to offices each day, though our bells,
Perhaps, seem more respectable. Indeed

We shall add notches to expansive belts
And slowly comb more carefully less hair;
Inform the boss at nine(ish) that the snow melts
And, at five, that spring seems in the air,

While in St. Vincent, one-legged, twenty-three
And carving leather-patterns with a knife,
Shall sit a man, and near him there shall be
Typed on a blue card: LEVESQUE, A. And: LIFE.

RAYMOND SOUSTER [1921-]

Raymond Souster, son of A. H. and N. R. Souster, was born and educated in Toronto. Two years of work in a bank preceded his four years (1941-1945) in the Royal Canadian Air Force, after which he returned to banking. Though his poetry is free from all the faults of the metaphysicals, he was represented in *Unit of Five* (1944) and in *Other Canadians: An Anthology of Poetry, 1940-1946* (1947). All his own are the volumes *When We Are Young* (1946), *Go to Sleep, World* (1947), and *City Hall Street* (1951). In *Cerberus* (1952) he is one of three, the other two being Dudek and Layton. His true worth will have a better chance of adequate recognition when he obeys the scriptural injunction, "come out from among them, and be ye separate."

SUNDAY NIGHT WALK

Sunday night we go to church,
And after the benediction when the doors swing open
Into the world of human joy and weakness

We walk slowly along St. Clair going east
Feeling ourselves among crowds
Careless and gay tonight though there is nothing
For them to do but walk and rewalk these streets
Or crowd the corner hamburgers and restaurants,

And then we are suddenly away again
From the noise of the street-cars, from the half-light
Dim of the street-lights, suddenly aware of stars
Over us and the delicate traceries of trees,

This is real grass, it is green, and the pond at the bottom
Of the road is a real pond and the real moon in it,
Even the two ducks floating upon it are real,

And we are real, our love is real,
The world is real, is very real,

But then the world is tired, very tired of reality.

THE FALLING OF THE SNOW

Like the idle fingers of wind caressing the forehead of God
Is the falling of the snow,
White rice
Of a marriage of joy
Thrown softly and silently from the churchsteps of heaven.

Look up and taste its whiteness
See and breathe its stainless purity

Falling all without favour
On the head of the rich magnate
And the bum with his head in the garbage,
Falling on the graves of our young, late, foolish dead,
And the cold silent killer's lips of the guns.

"THIS POEM WILL NEVER BE FINISHED"

This poem will never be finished,
It will be written over and over
This year and all the years

This poem is you
This poem is your face
Your hair your hands O all of you

And I am your poet
Who will always be singing
More beautiful songs as you climb
In splendour above the eternal rose.

NEED OF AN ANGEL

The bushes lean in the wind
And find it soft now, feeling the hand
Of spring over their breasts, shaking their limbs
With fire and ice. And the buds
Stir and throw their green murmurous
World above the dirt.

In me spring wakens, winds
Catch my hair, in the sun my eyes ache
With the diamond-cut brilliance.

But who will come to touch me into fire,
Who push the hesitant saplings into light,
Who start an eddy through this stagnant heart,
Who lead through forests of darkness to the dawn?

SPEAKERS, COLUMBUS CIRCLE

Unknown in history or in time they stand
On their small raised platforms beside the Flag,
And drown us in their theories, irritations—
We who have gathered simply for the sport
Or to kill time before a date or show—

In their faces we read an enormous patience
And an almost childish joy at mouthing words
Some smooth, some sharp, like pebbles on a beach.

But their voices are shreds of agony lost
In the traffic's merciless bedlam, their arms' waving
So puny beside the cold granite strength of buildings
Shooting at the sky. And we turn quickly from them,
Knowing too well that here is mirrored for us
The farcical, tragic impotence of our world.

WHEN I SEE OLD MEN

When I see old men
With noses in books
Every night in dead corners
Of lonely rooms;

When I watch the look
They give young girls
Passing in the street
That ends in a sigh;

When I hear the petty boasting
A glass of beer lights in them,
The inevitable memories
Of their once greatness;

Then I pray that my old age
Shall be brief as the fluke matador's
One golden season,
The year unmarked by horns
And heavy with contracts
And the cries echoing around the hoarse arena.

REALITY

The glow of the restaurant is faked, the dream
Of the movie is blown like an unsubstantial cloud
In the street again, and what is real is the traffic's not loud
But more a muffled insinuating scream,
The raw wind that whips and clutches at papers and bites
The old grey flanks of buildings, and a man who stands
Mind blank to perfumed amours, cabarets, weekends, all our
    carefully-planned civilized delights,
Holding a box of shoe-laces in unendingly shaking hands.

ELIZABETH BREWSTER [1922-]

Elizabeth Brewster was born at Chipman, New Brunswick, and educated at the University of New Brunswick, Radcliffe College, and the University of London, winning two important scholarships in the process. She later entered upon a course in library school leading to a degree in the summer of 1953. In that year she was one of the two winners of the E. J. Pratt prizes and medals for poetry. Her poetry chap-book is *East Coast* (1951).

EAST COAST—CANADA

Lying at night poised between sleep and waking
Here on the continent's edge, I feel the wind shaking
The house and passing on:
Blowing from far across fabulous mountain ranges,
Far over the long sweep of the prairies,
Blowing from England over swelling seas,
Blowing up from the populous south.

The wind travels where we cannot travel,
Touches those we cannot touch;
For few and lonely are the sentinel cities of the North
And rivers and woods lie between.
Far, few, and lonely. . . .

Space surrounds us, flows around us, drowns us.
Even when we meet each other, space flows between.
Our eyes glaze with distance.
Vast tracts of Arctic ice enclose our adjectives.
Cold space.
Our spirits are sheer columns of ice like frozen fountains
Dashed against by the wind.

Drown it out. Drown out the wind.
Turn on the radio.
Listen to the news.
Listen to boogie-woogie or a baseball game.
Pretend we belong to a civilization, even a dying one.
Pretend. Pretend.
But there are the woods and the rivers and the wind blowing.
There is the sea. Space. The wind blowing.

RIVER SONG

Where are the lumberjacks who came from the woods for Christmas,
Drinking, fighting, singing their endless ballads,
Eating pork and pancakes for breakfast, gravy dripping over?
Where are their wives, milking the cows in winter,
Slopping out to the barn in rubber boots,
Shoveling out the snow drifts?
Churning, baking the crisp-scented bread in huge loaves?
Bearing their ten children?
Where is the shrill scream of the mill whistle,
The smell of a town built on sawdust and pine shavings?
Where are the logs afloat on the wide river?
Oh sad river,
Sing a song of pain for your children gone,
Oh glory gone.

THE EGOIST DEAD

In the cool, impersonal room
Bathed by darkness now he lies.
Silence, settling grain by grain,
Presses downward on his eyes.

Never will the untiring clock
Tick him back to prayer or lust;
Hate and benevolence lie dead,
And even the unfailing "I" is dust.

Eternity, that seemed to stretch
Elastic-like at his command,
Finds a neat and compact space
In the hollow of his hand.

EVICTION

I should have cut my life
Down to the essential bone,
Paring all falsenesses;
I should have sought the sun

To burn away
The excesses of my pride;
In order to have lived,
I should have died.

But, lingering in shade
And softnesses,
I rented vacancy
Thinking I purchased ease·

And would be tenant still
Paying my life as fee,
If the sheriff pain
Had not evicted me.

GENEVIEVE BARTOLE

Genevieve Bartole is a native of Saskatchewan and lived on a farm till she was fifteen. After some time as a hospital laboratory and research worker, she went in 1940 on a scholarship to the School of Library Science, Columbia University. She was later appointed librarian for the Saskatchewan Department of Public Health. Her poetic gift is well manifested in *Figure In the Rain* (1948).

CANADIAN FARMER

His heart was light, and all the living day
Was good, for summer brought the sun and rain,
And in their wake bright fields of shining grain.
The drowsy noon-days nodding on their way
Made valiant perfume in his mound of hay.
He knew content; whate'er he knew of pain
Was furrowed back into the soil again,
Or blown to nought by slow winds of decay.

Then came the drought, and as the lean years passed,
Among the gasping fields he learned to pray.
He lived in hope, and toiling empty-handed,
Not dreaming hope might cheat him of his last,
He only thought: "The wind is south today,
And on the wrinkled earth a snipe has landed."

NORMAN LEVINE [1924-]

Albert Norman Levine was educated at Carleton College, Ottawa, and at McGill University, where he won the Peterson Memorial Prize in Literature and the Chester McNaughton Prize for creative writing and served as poetry editor and editor-in-chief of *Forge*, literary magazine of McGill. From 1942 to 1945 he served in the R.C.A.F. Later he was awarded a Beaver Club Scholarship for study in Great Britain. He is the author of a novel and of two books of poetry, *Myssium* (1948) and *The Tight Rope Walker* (1950).

CRABBING

Timbers heaving to heaven we sailed at seven
With bait aboard, wet, so sliced for smell,
Gurnards stinking, guts, cut and skewered;
And our faces still fresh from the bundled bed.
We sailed alone and silent in the light of morning,
From harbour shelter and a three sided bell.
Saw the wind yawn to stretch skin over water,
Cough the white gossip, clot, into silence.
Sun over water. Sea sick with colour.

And hungry the gull with her "turrow turrow"
Gathered an escort of gliding white hulls.
Cherry splashed beaks plunged heads into water,
Slitbeak smiles spread morning's laughter.
They, and the rudder, looked for our market
And by all the braille signs we found the stall.
There we circled, staring at landscape, waiting
For the tide to be well and truly in. Now sea domestic
Broke skin for marker, and there, the flagstick, rose.

We stood by the wheelhouse where spray was spitting
And lifted the black sheath on to the mizzen
Cupped up to heaven, steady for direction,
We cut our engine and steered with sail.
Soon the blue fullness laid out its carpet
In continual cadence of floor, wall, floor.
Silently we came forward, now weaving, now sliding
Slow as a boxer with hands cautious in rhythm,
Pulling a rope's strength and wetness aboard.

And while we were heaving, now to horizon,
The winch kept turning as a potter's wheel;
Rope swung dripping, ourselves waiting. What lodger
Within prison-wire, turned chimney, inside?
The first cage broke angry out of its grievance.
Craw, Craw, was shouted in simple alphabet.
(a Craw for a Crayfish: a Blue for a Lobster)
Words of children, all sound and colour
Formed a sweated sentence with a hardworked verb.

After the first, the others filled spaces:
Of Craw empty, Blue empty, and sometimes Crab.
Nervous jewels of colour, now covered, now hidden
As cage changed to parlour and prepared to receive
The new bait, now hanging, so silent by chimney.
While still in that rhythm the pots went over
Side, to foam pulling, depth, under bubbles
Stretching ropes, straightened, behind us, dove.
And there we left them, for tomorrow's tide.

Returning we let rudder find fast its direction,
And running as a hurdler, we rose, up and over,
Oak ribs to water keeled back those tons.
Shuddering we shot on, sometimes to heaven.

And land goes with us walking
In shapes the shadows formed. Where stone pierced bone
The earth made windows. Who watched our homecoming.

JAMES REANEY [1926-]

James Crerar Reaney, son of James Nesbitt and Elizabeth (Crerar) Reaney, was born at Stratford, Ontario, and educated at the University of Toronto (University College). He has taught creative writing at the University of Manitoba. His publications include startlingly cynical short stories and the powerfully imaginative but decidedly cynical book of poems entitled *The Red Heart* (1949), for which he was awarded the Governor-General's Medal. (Cf. E. K. Brown, *Letters in Canada* (1949).)

THE PLUM TREE

The plums are like blue pendulums
That thrum the gold-wired winds of summer.
In the opium-still noon they hang or fall,
The plump, ripe plums.
I suppose my little sister died
Dreaming of looking up at them,
Of lying beneath that crooked plum tree,
That green heaven with blue stars pied.
In this lonely haunted farmhouse
All things are voiceless save the sound
Of some plums falling through the summer air
Straight to the ground.

And there is no listener, no hearer
For the small thunders of their falling
(Falling as dead stars rush to a winter sea)
Save a child who, lolling
Among the trunks and old featherticks
That fill the room where he was born,
Hears them in his silent dreaming
On a dark engraving to a fairy-tale forlorn.
Only he hears their intermittent soft tattoo
Upon the dry, brown summer ground
At the edge of the old orchard.
Only he hears, and farther away,
Some happy animal's slow, listless moo.

THE RED HEART

The only leaf upon its tree of blood,
My red heart leaps heavily
And will never fall loose,
But grow so heavy
After only a certain number of seasons
(Sixty winters, and fifty-nine falls,
Fifty-eight summers, and fifty-seven springs)
That it will bring bough
Tree and the fences of my bones
Down to a grave in the forest
Of my still upright fellows.

So does the sun hang now
From a branch of Time
In this wild fall sunset.
Who shall pick the sun
From the tree of Eternity?
Who shall thresh the ripe sun?
What midwife shall deliver
The Sun's great heir?
It seems that no one can,
And so the sun shall drag
Gods, goddesses and parliament buildings,
Time, Fate, gramophones and Man
To a gray grave
Where all shall be trampled
Beneath the dancing feet of crowds
Of other still-living suns and stars.

THE GRAMOPHONE

Upon the lake
At Gramophone
A beastly bird
Sits on the bank
And dips its beak
Of sharpened bone
Into a haunted
Tank
That ripples with an eternal stone.

When the ladies descend the stairs,
Some eat their fans
And others comb their hair.
But Miss Mumblecrust
Picks up that beastly bird
And dips its beak
Into that round lake
That ripples with eternal stone
And dips its beak of sharpened bone
Into a pool of a young man singing
"I'm all alone
By the telephone!"

ALFRED W. PURDY [1918-]

Alfred W. Purdy was born near Wooler, Ont., of Scottish, Irish, English and French extraction. He attended Trenton Collegiate and Albert College, Belleville, and then spent six years in the R.C.A.F. His poetry has appeared in leading periodicals both in Canada and the United States.

LANDSCAPE

The snow fell slowly over the long sweep
Of mountain, without aim,
Direction or purpose; at the wind's whim,
The snow came.
Presently over the cool cotton blanket
There was a sound,
A movement on the upper mountain:
A woman's hair unbound,
And falling over white shoulders;
Swerving swift and slow,
The men with winged feet etching intricate
Patterns in the snow.

And presently the light went out, the sun
Dwindled behind a peak and died.
Inside the trees, a wolf or the ghost of a child
Stirred briefly and cried.
Moon-shine turned over shadows and formed
Other shadows, mannikins moved
When a tree moved; and the wind
Carefully erased the grooved
Trail the skiers made. And again,
The rustle of wings in the night.
And again the smooth white
Cup of brightness on the mountain; and man
Far in his outpost cities slept. The moon
Peered between the trees in a slow
Deliberate dance; and paused dramatically
At the barricades, and turned to go
With a soft flow of silver on the planet's edge:
Snow and the threat of snow. . . .

ACKNOWLEDGMENTS

For permission to use copyrighted material, grateful acknowledgment is made to the following authors and authors' estates:

William Talbot Allison for "O Amber Day, amid the Autumn Gloom"; Violet Anderson for "The Cloak" published in *Canadian Forum* and "Through the Barber Shop Window" published in *Poetry* (Chicago); Margaret Avison for "Rigor Viris"; Clara Bernhardt for "A Sailor's Wife" from *Silent Rhythm;* Arthur S. Bourinot for "Dark Flows the River," "Johnny Appleseed," "Nicolas Gatineau," "Only Silence," "Sonnets to My Mother," "Tom Thomson," "What Far Kingdom" and "Winter Sketch"; Charles Bruce for "Back Road Farm," "Fisherman's Son" and "Words Are Never Enough" from *Grey Ship Moving;* Mrs. Janey G. Cann for poems by Charles Mair; Alan Creighton for "Spring Workman" from *Cross Country,* "Pastoral" and "Return of a Reaper" from *Earth Call;* Laurence Dakin for selections from *Pyramis and Thisbe* and *Tancred;* Dick Diespecker for "Between Two Furious Oceans"; Rev. James B. Dollard for "The Fairy Harpers"; Louis Dudek for "I Have Seen the Robins Fall" first published in *Northern Review* and "Narrative"; Arthur Wentworth Hamilton Eaton for "The Phantom Light of the Baie des Chaleurs"; Helen Merrill Egerton for "Sandpipers"; Ernest Fewster for "The Cliff Rose" and "The Pearly Everlasting"; R. A. D. Ford for "Back to Dublin," "Lynx" and "Twenty Below"; Ralph Gustafson for "Dedication" from *Flight into Darkness* (Pantheon Books Inc., N.Y.), "On the Road to Vicenza" and "Legend" first published in *The Fiddlehead;* Mrs. Norman Gregor Guthrie for "A Bed of Campanula" by "John Creighton"; Katherine Hale for "Eternal Moment," "Giant's Tomb in Georgian Bay," "Lost Garden" and "Portrait of a Cree"; Ronald Hambleton for "Comrades as We Rest Within"; Vernal House for "In Tribute" published in *Saturday Night;* Watson Kirkconnell for "The Crow and the Nighthawk" and a selection from *The Tide of Life;* Frederick E. Laight for "Soliloquy"; Wilmot B. Lane for "Owning"; Irving Layton for "Jewish Main Street," "Newsboy" and "Words without Music" originally published by First Statement Press; Gordon LeClaire for "Love," "Miser" and "Old Seawoman"; Norman Levine for "Crabbing" published in *Contemporary Verse;* William Douw Lighthall for "The Caughnawaga Beadwork Seller"; Dorothy Livesay for "Lament" published in *The Fiddlehead;* Cecil Francis Lloyd for "March Winds" and "Truth" from *Landfall;* the executors of J. D. Logan for "Heliodore"; T. G. Marquis for a poem by Agnes Maule Machar; the daughter of William E. Marshall for "To a Mayflower" and a selection from *Brookfield;* Andrew Merkel for a selection from Tallahassee; Mrs. Peter McArthur for poems by Peter McArthur; Anges Foley MacDonald for "Eternal" from *Once and Again;* Wilson MacDonald for eight poems; Edgar McInnis for "Fire Burial" first published in *Saturday Night;* Claire Harris MacIntosh for "The Spirit of the Bluenose" and "The Barn in Winter"; Arthur Phelps for "The Wall"; James Reaney for "The Gramophone," "The Plum Tree" and "The Red Heart" from *The Red Heart;* Dorothy Roberts for "The Goose Girl" and "Sisters" published in *The Fiddlehead;* Lloyd Roberts for "Deep Dark River," "The Fruit Rancher" and "One Morning when the Rain-Birds Call" ;Theodore Goodridge Roberts for "The Blue Heron," "Fiddler's Green" and "The Lost Shipmate" from *The Leather Bottle;* Greta Leora Rose for

"Spring Is at Work with Beginnings of Things"; W. W. E. Ross for "The Saws Were Shrieking" and "The Summons"; Bruce Ruddick for "Freighter" and "Plaque"; Laura Goodman Salverson for "Premonition"; F. R. Scott for "Recovery," "Saturday Sundae," "Someone Could Certainly be Found" and "Windfall" from *Overture*, "Conflict" and "Full Valleys"; the Estate of Frederick George Scott for "Dawn," "In the Woods" and "The Unnamed Lake"; Neufville Shaw for "Drowned Sailor"; Evan V. Shute for "Luck," "Night Comes Apace," "Poor Fool" and "Twenty Years After"; Kay Smith for "What Then, Dancer?" and "When a Girl Looks Down"; the Estate of Norma E. Smith for "Evangeline" from *The Hills and Far Away;* Alan Sullivan for "Suppliant" and "The White Canoe"; the Executors of Edward William Thomson for "The Canadian Rossignol"; Neil Tracy for "I Doubt a Lovely Thing Is Dead" from *The Rain It Raineth;* Miriam Waddington for "Cadenza," "Investigator" and "Restricted" from *Green World* and "Lullaby" from *Contemporary Poetry;* Mrs. B. H. Warr for "Poets in Time of War" and "Trees Who Are Distant" by Bertram Warr; George Whalley for "Night Flight" published in *Queen's Quarterly;* Anne Wilkinson for "Summer Acres"; O. T. G. Williamson for "At the Place of the Roman Baths" and "The Gipsies" by "Richard Scrace."

For permission to use copyrighted material, grateful acknowledgment is made to the following publishers:

Thomas Allen, Limited, for "In Flanders Now" by Edna Jaques.

Behrman House, Inc., 1261 Broadway, New York 1, N.Y., for "Design for Mediaeval Tapestry" and "Baal Shem Tov" reprinted from *Hath Not a Jew* by A. M. Klein, by permission of the publishers.

Chatto & Windus Ltd. for "Canoe-Trip" and "Coureurs de Bois" from *The Wounded Prince* by Douglas LePan.

Clarke, Irwin & Co. Ltd. for "One of the Regiment" from *The Net and the Sword* by Douglas LePan.

The Copp Clark Co. Ltd. and Charles G. D. Roberts for "The Summons" from *Dream Verses* by Elizabeth Roberts MacDonald.

Coward-McCann, Inc. and the author for "Song of Cradle-Making" and "Song of the Full Catch" from *Songs of the Coast Dwellers* by Constance Lindsay Skinner.

J. M. Dent & Sons (Canada Limited, for "Sea Song" from *When Half Gods Go* by Norah Holland, "Capilano" and "Bring Torches" by A. M. Stephen.

Little, Brown & Co. and the author for "Morning in the North-West," "Sappho's Tomb" and "The Sod-Breaker" from *Open Water* by Arthur Stringer.

McClelland and Stewart Limited for the following poems—"Border River" from *Border River* by Alfred Goldsworthy Bailey; "Smoking Flax" from *My Pocket Beryl* by Mary Josephine Benson; "At Quebec" from *Poems of Jean Blewett;* selections from *Bliss Carman's Poems;* "Buffalo" and "Summer Days" from *Deeper into the Forest* by Roy Daniells; selections from *The Poetical Works of William Henry Drummond;* "The Mountain," "The Network," "The Lost Tribe," "Alone" and "Time's Bright Sand" from *Strength of the Hills* by Robert Finch; "Off to the Fishing Ground" from *The Watchman and Other Poems* by L. M. Montgomery; "Fires of Driftwood" and "Helen—Old" from *Poems of Isabel Ecclestone Mackay;* selections from *The Complete Poems of Marjorie Pickthall;* "If a Maid Be Fair" from *Wayside Gleams* by Laura Goodman Salverson; "The Husbandman" and "A Wedgwood Bowl" from *White Winds at Dawn* by Frances Beatrice Taylor; "The Poplars" from *A Canadian Twilight* by Bernard Freeman Trotter; "The Gatineaus," "Our Love Shall Be the Brightness," "Sic Transit Gloria Mundi" and "Stay, Time" from *Of Time and the Lover* by James Wreford Watson.

The Macmillan Company of Canada Limited for the following poems—"Sea Lavender" and "She Plans Her Funeral" by Louise Morey Bowman; "Reveillé" from *The Tree of Resurrection* by Audrey Alexandra Brown; "Biography" from *The Mulgrave Road* by Charles Bruce; poems from *Halt and Parley* by George Herbert Clarke; "This Was My Brother" from *Tasting the Earth* by Mona Gould; "Tim, the Fairy" and "The Violin Calls" from *The Shepherd's Purse* by Florence Randal Livesay; "All Night I Heard" by Gertrude MacGregor Moffat from *A Book of Verses;* "Canoe Song at Twilight" from *Mary Magdalene* by Laura E. McCully; "Frozen Fire" from *Frozen Fire* by Floris Clarke McLaren; "The Ground-Swell," "The Ice-Floes," "The Sea Cathedral," "Burial at Sea," "Erosion," "Invisible Trumpets Blowing" and a portion of "The Cachalot" from *The Collected Poems of E. J. Pratt;* lines from *The Legend of Ghost Lagoon* by Joseph Schull; "Old Man Pot" from *Sea Wall* by Lyon Sharman; and "Anastasis" from *Garden of the Sun* by Albert E. S. Smythe.

The Musson Book Company for "The Corn Husker," "Shadow River," "The Song My Paddle Sings" and "The Trail to Lillooet" from *Flint and Feather* by Pauline Johnson.

The Editor of *The Nation* for "Indian Dance" by Frederick Niven.

Thomas Nelson and Sons (Canada) Ltd. for "Holy Night" from *The Glowing Years* and "Year's End" from *The Wanderer* by Nathaniel Benson, "In April," "The House of the Trees" and "Woodland Worship" from *Lyrics and Sonnets* by Ethelwyn Wetherald.

Northern Review for "I Have Seen the Robins Fall" by Louis Dudek and "The Lucifer" by Guy Glover.

The Proprietors of *Punch* for "In Flanders Fields" by John McCrae.

G. P. Putnam's Sons and the author for "Jesous Ahatonhia" from *Sea Dogs and Men at Arms* by Jesse Edgar Middleton.

The Ryerson Press and the authors for selections from—*The Prayer of the Good Trouper* by Harry Amoss; *The White Centre* by Patrick Anderson; *Tâo* by Alfred Goldsworthy Bailey; *Figure in the Rain* by Genevieve Bartole; *David and Other Poems* by Earle Birney; *East Coast* and *Lillooet* by Elizabeth Brewster; *All Fool's Day* by Audrey Alexandra Brown; *The Flowing Summer* by Charles Bruce; *Blue Homespun* by Frank Oliver Call; *Merry-Go-Round* and *High on a Hill* by Marjorie Freeman Campbell; *Collected Poems of Wilfred Campbell; The Artisan* by Sara Carsley; *The Victorian House* by Philip Child; *The Saint John* by George Frederick Clarke; *Invitation to Mood* by Carol Coates; *Songs* by Helena Coleman; *Quinte Songs and Sonnets* by Herbert T. J. Coleman; *Monserrat* by William Edwin Collin; *For This Freedom Too* by Mary Elizabeth Colman; *Seedtime and Harvest* by Barbara Villy Cormack; *The Blossoming Thorn* by John Coulter; *Sheepfold, The Wind in the Field* and *River without End* by Leo Cox; *The Neighing North* by Annie Charlotte Dalton; *East of the City* by Louis Dudek; *Last Mathematician* by Hyman Edelstein; *Ebb Tide* by Doris Ferne; *By Cobequid Bay* by Alexander Louis Fraser; *Songs of the Western Islands* by Hermia Harris Fraser; *Poems* by Anthony Frisch; *Object and Event* by Ronald Hambleton; *When This Tide Ebbs* by Verna Loveday Harden; *The Sea Is Our Doorway* by Michael Harrington; *The Flower in the Dust* and *Crisis* by Doris Hedges; *Marshlands* by John Frederick Herbin; *The Rocking Chair* by A. M. Klein; *Collected Poems of Raymond Knister; Rearguard and Other Poems* by Elsie Laurence; *By Stubborn Stars* by Kenneth Leslie; *The Blossom Trail* by Lilian Leveridge; *Poems for People, Call My People Home* and *Day and Night* by Dorothy Livesay; *The Cry of Insurgent Youth* by Guy Mason; *Sandstone and Other Poems* by Anne Marriott; *I Seek My Way* by Mary Matheson; *Rhyme and Rhythm* by Sister Maura; *Other Songs* by John Hanlon Mitchell; *The Dying General* by Goodridge MacDonald; *East by West* by J. E. H. MacDonald; *Complete Poems of Tom MacInnes; Viper's*

Bugloss by L. A. MacKay; *Not Without Beauty* by John A. B. McLeish; *The Man of Kerioth* by Robert Norwood; *Frosty Morn* by Margot Osborn; *As Ten As Twenty* and *Unit of Five* by P. K. Page; *Song in the Silence* by Martha Eugenie Perry; *Midwinter Thaw* by Lenore Pratt; *Twelve Poems* by Nathan Ralph; *Voyageur* and *Portrait* by R. E. Rashley; *Selected Poems of Sir Charles G. D. Roberts; Horizontal World* by Thomas Saunders; *Selected Poems of Duncan Campbell Scott; Complete Poems of Robert W. Service; Leaves in the Wind* by Verna Sheard; *The Complete Poems of Francis Sherman; News of the Phoenix* by A. J. M. Smith; *Go to Sleep World, City Hall Street* and *Unit of Five* by Raymond Souster; *The Rose of the Sea* by Lionel Stevenson, *Forfeit and Other Poems* by Kathryn Munro Tupper; *Candled by Stars* by Jean Percival Waddell; *The Poetical Works of Albert Durant Watson; Unit of Five* by James Wreford Watson; *The Vagrant* by Frederick B. Watt; *Poems 1939-44* by George Whalley; *The Captive Gypsy* by Constance Davies Woodrow.

Charles Scribner's Sons for "The World in Making" from *The Works of Gilbert Parker*.

Every reasonable care has been taken to trace ownership of copyrighted material. Information will be welcome which will enable the publishers to rectify any reference or credit in subsequent editions.

INDEX OF AUTHORS